C000175781

MEDICINE, MYSTICISM AND MYTHOLOGY: *Garth Wilkinson, Swedenborg and Nineteenth-Century Esoteric Culture* is the ninth volume in a series of publications exploring Swedenborg's place and influence within the history of ideas. Other titles in the series include: *Discovering Swedenborg* by Gary Lachman (2009); *Swedenborg: Introducing the Mystic* by R W Emerson, ed. Stephen McNeilly (2010); *Gardens of Heaven and Earth* by Kristin King (2011); *The Grand Theme and Other Essays* by Anders Hallengren (2013); *Philosophy Literature Mysticism: an anthology of essays on the thought and influence of Emanuel Swedenborg*, ed. Stephen McNeilly (2013); *Imaginal Landscapes: reflections on the mystical visions of Jorge Luis Borges and Emanuel Swedenborg* by William Rowlandson (2015); *New Jerusalem: the good city and the good society* by Ken Worpole (2015); and *Distant Voices: Sketches of a Swedenborgian World View* by John S Haller (2017). In *Medicine, Mysticism and Mythology*, Malcolm Peet explores the life and cultural milieu of the nineteenth-century Swedenborgian James John Garth Wilkinson, whose largely forgotten influence touched a diverse range of intellectual fields and social reform movements. In the early chapters, Peet offers a brief biographical sketch of Wilkinson and a concise history of Swedenborg's reception in England, touching on the involvement of such figures as John Clowes, Robert Hindmarsh, Manoah Sibly, Ebenezer Sibly and Charles Augustus Tulk. Subsequent chapters go on to explore Wilkinson's early role in publishing the poetry of William Blake; his dealings with Thomas Carlyle and Ralph Waldo Emerson; his lifelong friendship with Henry James, Sr; his association with Daniel Dunglas Home, Thomas Lake Harris and Andrew Jackson Davis; his homoeopathic practice and its influence on James Tyler Kent; and his engagement with such causes as utopian socialism, environmentalism, women's suffrage, antivivisectionism and the deregulation of medicine. The book concludes with a broader study of Wilkinson's interest in mythology, psychology and Christian spiritualism.

MALCOLM PEET is a retired Consultant Psychiatrist and an Honorary Professor in the School of Health and Related Research at the University of Sheffield. Internationally recognized for his research on the relationship between nutrition and mental well-being, Malcolm also holds a Master's Degree in Western Esotericism. Since his retirement from clinical practice, Malcolm's intellectual focus has been on spirituality, particularly that of Emanuel Swedenborg and his followers.

medicine
mysticism and
mythology

Frontispiece: J J Garth Wilkinson in 1879, aged 67.
Swedenborg Society Archive, section M.

medicine mysticism and mythology

Garth Wilkinson, Swedenborg and Nineteenth-Century Esoteric Culture

Malcolm Peet

The Swedenborg Society
20-21 Bloomsbury Way
London WC1A 2TH

2018

Typeset at Swedenborg House.
Printed at T J International, Padstow
Book design and artwork © Stephen McNeilly

Published by:
The Swedenborg Society
Swedenborg House
20-21 Bloomsbury Way
London
WC1A 2TH

ISBN 978-0-85448-205-4
British Library Cataloguing-in-Publication Data.
A catalogue record for this book is available from the British Library.

FOREWORD

In 1912, Frederick H Evans made the following observation in his study
James John Garth Wilkinson. An Introduction: 'I am perversely proposing
to arouse an interest in the writings of James John Garth Wilkinson, born
1812, died in 1899, author of some twenty-five works, all of which are completely
neglected by the ordinary reading world, and known to but few among the
super-intelligent'.[1] Since Evans wrote at the beginning of the twentieth century,
the situation has fortunately improved. Wilkinson's name can now be found in a
number of critical texts, and articles have even trained the lens on selected themes
in his work. But although he no longer suffers the neglect that he once did, it is
fair to say that critical accounts have emphasized a partial portrait of Wilkinson or
merely attempted to sketch selected aspects of his work. What a pleasure, therefore,
to read Malcolm Peet's well-researched study of Wilkinson, encompassing the
totality of his publications and activities. For newcomers, it will be an indispensible
introduction. For those readers who are already familiar with Wilkinson, the present
book brings to light previously unexamined archival material. In particular, the
examination of letter correspondences allows us to see more clearly Wilkinson's
ardent interest in spirit seances. This information was actively suppressed by

---

[1]   Frederick H Evans, *James John Garth Wilkinson: An Introduction* (Reprinted
    privately: Mrs Frank Claughton Mathews, 1936), pp. 7-8.

Wilkinson's family. It was thus left out of Wilkinson's biography in an attempt to transmit to posterity a portrait that correlated with Wilkinson's own rejection of such practices in later years.

The benefit of examining the whole of Wilkinson's *oeuvre* is that it allows us to see his career as a prism for a number of significant nineteenth-century developments: the advocacy of modern mysticism; the embrace of mesmerism; the propagation of alternative medicine; the debates over vaccination; the interest in spiritualism; and the discussions of mythography that became so important for the understanding of history and culture. Wilkinson may inevitably stand in the shadow of the several more famous people he befriended or acquainted—a list that includes Thomas Carlyle, Ralph Waldo Emerson, John Ruskin, and Henry James, Sr—but the extent to which he may have inspired these people should not be neglected, as the present study points out.

An abiding point of reference throughout Wilkinson's life and the contacts he made was Swedenborgianism. Emanuel Swedenborg's work was evidently the guiding light in many of his projects, even if Wilkinson sometimes found himself at loggerheads with the sectarian Swedenborgian New Church. Swedenborgian influences are discernible in a host of different ways—directly in his work as a translator of Swedenborg's Latin texts and more indirectly as an axiom in his work as a medical practitioner. Furthermore, Wilkinson's pursuits within mythography and poetic composition were also openly carried out within a Swedenborgian framework of understanding. For non-Swedenborgians, Emanuel Swedenborg's works are of significant historical interest because they formed the main substance of what has variously been called the Mystical, Occult or Theosophical Enlightenment. Swedenborg espoused a structure of correspondences between the physical and spiritual worlds, which has had considerable impact on intellectual life from the late eighteenth century to the present. Wilkinson deserves attention because he shows the extent to which Swedenborgianism proved to be a protean form which believers could use to both explain a number of different phenomena and, at the same time, yoke them together within a unified frame of reference. For Wilkinson and others, Swedenborgianism constituted a set of elementary ideas that undergirded new investigations into both therapeutic and spiritual spheres of exploration. To fully appreciate the influence Swedenborgianism had on Wilkinson and the milieux in which he moved, Peet has usefully included a reception history of Swedenborgianism (and its motley offshoots) between 1770 and 1830.

When assessing the representation of Wilkinson in critical works up until now, the picture that emerges is that of an intriguing, if somewhat unobtrusive, presence in the nineteenth century. But, as Peet's new study helps to illuminate, Wilkinson's endeavours were often frontier explorations. In my own work, I was first made aware of Wilkinson's pioneering spirit many years ago in connection with my PhD thesis on William Blake. In 1839, Wilkinson was the first to publish William Blake's collection *Songs of Innocence and of Experience* in conventional letterpress. Thus, he has the honour of being one of the first to aid the dissemination of Blake's poetry. Had it not been for Wilkinson and other early admirers who were to follow, Blake may have been resigned to the cabinet of curiosities. In Wilkinson's rather personal and evaluative 'Preface' to the edition, Wilkinson pours praise on the *Songs* (although he also has misgivings about Blake's later works). It is clear that he perceives Blake as writing in alliance with Swedenborg. After all, it was probably the Swedenborgian Charles Augustus Tulk who introduced him to Blake's work. Wilkinson speaks of Blake's *Songs* as giving 'one impulse to the New Spiritualism which is now dawning on the world'. This was clearly an 'impulse' Wilkinson interpreted as having Swedenborgian affinities, as is clear in his claims that Blake's poetry goes beyond the 'Self' to embrace the 'universal man' (cf. Swedenborg's *Maximus Homo*) and that the poet's focus is on 'Spirits' rather than 'bodies'.

Wilkinson's admiration for Blake evidently stayed with him and influenced his own foray into poetic composition, the result of which was the collection *Improvisations of the Spirit* (1857). The poems included in this work were allegedly channelled to him through spiritual agency and taken down through automatic writing (i.e. by relinquishing the control the author usually exerts over writing and allowing a free flow of inspiration). Some of the poems bear an unmistakable resemblance to Blake, as several critics from the poet John Gray to the Blake-biographer Alexander Gilchrist have pointed out. The collection also prompted the Scottish poet James Thomson to write an extensive review and analysis of Wilkinson's book, which ran over three issues of *The Liberal* in 1873.

Critical studies within the past twenty years are increasingly drawing attention to Wilkinson as a figure at the forefront of nineteenth-century developments. Therefore, it seems no longer 'perverse' (as Frederick H Evans believed it to be) to assess Wilkinson's comprehensive philosophy. Peet's book stands as a testament to the usefulness of mapping Wilkinson's pursuits against a backdrop of important intellectual and social strands in the nineteenth century. It will be the authoritative study of Wilkinson for years to come.

Robert W Rix

ACKNOWLEDGEMENTS

I was introduced to the works of Emanuel Swedenborg by the late Professor Nicholas Goodrick-Clarke, who led the Masters degree in Western Esotericism at the Exeter Centre for the Study of Esotericism at the University of Exeter, UK and to whom this book is dedicated. The work began as a Ph.D. project and continued as a book after the sad death of Nicholas Goodrick-Clarke. Although I had achieved senior academic status within my own discipline of psychiatry, I found that there were considerable differences in approach and style between the sciences (within which today's psychiatry falls) and the humanities. For their help in making this transition, and for their expert knowledge, I am indebted to my initial academic supervisors, including Nicholas and Clare Goodrick-Clarke, Richard Noakes and Paul Bembridge. It goes without saying, though, that any errors or omissions are entirely my own responsibility.

I cannot express too highly my gratitude to the staff of the Swedenborg Society in London, who have been unfailingly helpful and supportive throughout this work. My particular thanks go to James Wilson, librarian, Richard Lines, former secretary, Alex Murray, assistant librarian, and more recently Stephen McNeilly, executive director at the Society. I would also like to thank the Swedenborg Society's publishing assistants Maia Gaffney-Hyde and Oliver Hancock. Staff at my home University of Sheffield and at the British Library have, as always, been efficient and helpful, and I am grateful also to staff at the Library of Harvard University for providing me with electronic copies of material that otherwise would not have been available to me.

CONTENTS

G arth Wilkinson (1812-99) was lionized by some of the leading intellectuals of his day on both sides of the Atlantic, including Ralph Waldo
Emerson, Henry James, Sr and Dante Gabriel Rossetti. Despite this, he
is virtually unknown today, except within the small circle of those who read the
works of Swedish scientist and mystic Emanuel Swedenborg (1688-1772), which
Wilkinson translated.

Wilkinson personifies the new middle class of liberally minded professionals and
intellectuals that emerged during the nineteenth century. He was a qualified medical practitioner, and yet he rejected orthodox medicine in favour of homoeopathy,
which was popular with the general public but abhorred by the orthodox medical
hierarchy. Together with other prominent English intellectuals, including William
Howitt and William Francis Cowper-Temple, he was an early adopter of several esoteric movements that swept across England during the nineteenth century, including
spiritualism and mesmerism. He campaigned for a variety of liberal social causes,
including the deregulation of medicine, the abolition of compulsory vaccination for
smallpox and the prohibition of vivisection. Wilkinson was not simply a participant
in these movements, but made active and original contributions—in his practice of
homoeopathy, for example, and in the development of the concept of the unconscious
mind, in which he collaborated with James Braid and William Benjamin Carpenter.
All of these activities were informed by Wilkinson's Swedenborgian beliefs, and a

closer examination reveals a considerable penetration of Swedenborgian thought into Victorian culture.

Wilkinson has attracted little previous scholarship. A biography written by his nephew Clement Wilkinson was published in 1911.[1] This work was partial and at times downright misleading. It claimed, for instance, that Wilkinson never participated actively in spiritualism, despite clear contrary evidence that was available to the author. The manuscript was seen in 1909 by Henry James, Jr, who described it as 'done so drearily & artlessly & impossibly...that I had no hesitation in saying that publication is wholly hopeless & unprocurable'.[2] Despite these serious flaws, the book is of value in pointing to useful factual information. Another short biography that relates mainly to theology was first published in *Homoeopathic World* in 1912 and reprinted privately in 1936 by Wilkinson's daughter Mary Claughton Mathews.[3] Elsewhere, two authors have published essays that focus on different aspects of Wilkinson's interests. Logie Barrow has discussed Wilkinson's liberally minded social activism, and Francis Treuherz has pointed to the similarity between Wilkinson's homoeopathy and the 'classical homoeopathy' developed later by James Tyler Kent.[4] Otherwise, Wilkinson has been mentioned only in passing or as footnotes in works with a different focus, particularly those relating to the James family (Henry James, Sr, and his famous sons psychologist William James and writer Henry James, Jr). Primary sources for the present work include Wilkinson's published works, many of which are now available electronically or as facsimile reprints, and his letters and papers, which are housed mainly in the Archive of the Swedenborg Society in London, with more in the Houghton Library at Harvard University. Extracts from some of Wilkinson's correspondence, particularly that with Henry James, Sr, have been published in various settings, including the biography written by Clement Wilkinson, and works relating to the James family.

I have not sought to provide every factual detail of Wilkinson's life, but have focused rather on the development of his thought and his practical application of Swedenborg's philosophy. To that end, I have gone into some detail about the reception of Swedenborg's philosophy before Wilkinson's time, as well as the major influences on Wilkinson's thought as a young man. These include Charles Augustus

Tulk, a follower of Swedenborg who was a friend of Samuel Taylor Coleridge and a patron of William Blake, and Henry James, Sr. Wilkinson himself was extremely well connected socially, becoming a personal friend of many prominent intellectuals in the UK, Europe and the USA.

Although a follower of Swedenborg, Wilkinson found himself in conflict as a young man with sectarian Swedenborgians because of his adoption of practices that were considered occult and his frustration with their conservative outlook. His own outlook became more conservative as he grew older. As a young radical he had travelled to Paris to support the uprising of 1848, and he adopted the utopian socialism of Charles Fourier. But in his old age he lost his revolutionary zeal and became a more orthodox follower of Swedenborg's philosophy. He spent his final years immersed in the Swedenborgian interpretation of ancient mythology.

This book seeks to highlight the major contributions that Garth Wilkinson made to the intellectual life and contemporary issues of his day. These contributions are conveniently divided into chapters that follow roughly the phases of his life, from his early encounter with the works of Emanuel Swedenborg, through his involvement with spiritualism and mesmerism, his homoeopathic medical practice, his involvement with the social and political movements of the nineteenth century and finally, in his later years, his absorbing interest in ancient mythology.

Chapter 1 offers a biographical overview of Wilkinson's life, as a framework on which the succeeding chapters can be hung. Although the primary focus is on biographical facts, the intention also is to highlight other areas relating to Wilkinson's personality and circumstances, particularly those that may give some insight as to the origins of his later interests. In this regard, his childhood and early experiences are particularly pertinent, and we are fortunate in having the first part of an autobiography to draw upon—although it was never finished, it gives a significant insight into his difficult childhood.[5]

Garth Wilkinson was influenced overwhelmingly by the philosophy of Emanuel Swedenborg, so Chapter 2 therefore considers in some detail the reception of Swedenborg's philosophy in England between 1770 when Swedenborg's writings began to be more readily available in English translation, through to 1833 when

Wilkinson first encountered Swedenborg's philosophy. There were significant differences in the reception of Swedenborg in England relative to mainland Europe. The most important of these was the early move by English Swedenborgians towards instituting a sectarian 'New Church' with its own dogmas and rituals. This has coloured the received history of Swedenborgianism in England, particularly as the sectarian Swedenborgians strove to downplay the esoteric interests of Swedenborg's early followers. One aim of this chapter is to redress that balance.

Richard Lines, a former secretary of the Swedenborg Society in London, takes the view that the three most important people in disseminating Swedenborg's ideas in England were John Clowes, Charles Augustus Tulk and James John Garth Wilkinson.[6] All three of these men were non-sectarians, and I shall show that all of them had esoteric interests that went well beyond the simple acceptance of Swedenborg's teaching. All three had contacts with the broader esoteric community within their social networks. The first two of these individuals form the backbone of the content of Chapter 2, and discussion of their social networks makes up the rest of the chapter. The last individual, Garth Wilkinson, is the primary focus of the rest of this book. He starts to be mentioned towards the end of this chapter, but the major focus here is on his antecedent influences, particularly through John Clowes and his friend Charles Augustus Tulk, who became an important early mentor of the young Garth Wilkinson.

Chapter 3 outlines the way in which Garth Wilkinson moved from an early interpretation of Swedenborg that was based on the subjective idealism of George Berkeley, to a position that emphasized the empirical and pragmatic aspects of Swedenborgianism, particularly those that he saw as consistent with contemporary developments within Victorian culture. The main focus of succeeding chapters is on the way in which Wilkinson went on to interpret Swedenborgian philosophy in relation to some of the popular interests of the nineteenth century, including mesmerism, spiritualism, homoeopathy, utopian socialism and the interpretation of mythology.

Mesmerism, which is discussed in Chapter 4, was popularized during the nineteenth century, when it became a philosophical focus for intellectuals as well as a subject of wonder for the general public. Wilkinson learned of mesmerism from Jules Du Potet de Sennevoy, who claimed himself to be a magician. Like some other radical followers of Swedenborg, Wilkinson thought that the phenomena of mesmerism were entirely compatible with Swedenborg's philosophy. He was one of the earliest physicians to use mesmerism in his medical practice, and he went on to collaborate with James Braid, the father of hypnosis, and physiologist William Carpenter, in the development of psychological theories of the unconscious mind, an idea that was regarded as absurd by many of his contemporaries. This work was a direct precursor of the ideas of Sigmund Freud and other psychodynamic theorists.

Another nineteenth-century movement that gained mass popularity amongst both intellectuals and the general public was spiritualism, which is discussed in Chapter 5. Again, the young Wilkinson was an enthusiastic early adopter of spiritualism, as were many other followers of Swedenborg at that time. He was centrally involved with the leading intellectuals in spiritualist circles and was a personal friend of some notable mediums, including Daniel Dunglas Home, who was perhaps the most famous of all. Later in life Wilkinson rejected spiritualism; he continued to believe in its manifestations, but regarded it as banal and spiritually dangerous.

Chapters 6 and 7 are devoted to Wilkinson's medical practice. This was based on the principles of vitalism, which holds that there is a life force which transcends mere physics and chemistry. Disturbances of the life force give rise to illness, and treatment aims to correct this primary cause rather than depending on chemical medicines and surgery, which are regarded as being directed at the secondary effects of illness on the bodily organs. Vitalist approaches to medical treatment were popular with nineteenth-century Swedenborgians, who regarded such treatments as being essentially spiritual in nature. Wilkinson's understanding of this paradigm in relation to Swedenborg's philosophy is discussed in detail in these chapters. Chapter 6 gives an historical and theoretical overview of vitalism as it was understood by Wilkinson, and Chapter 7 focuses more on Wilkinson's actual medical practice, which depended primarily on an unorthodox understanding of homoeopathy that incorporated mesmerism, herbalism and spiritualism. Wilkinson's approach to homoeopathy emphasized the primacy of mental symptoms, an approach that later became standard after being popularized by Swedenborgian follower James Tyler Kent.

The nineteenth century was a time of great social and political change, and this spawned new radical movements. Wilkinson's political activism is discussed in Chapter 8. The young Wilkinson held very radical political views, for example travelling to Paris in support of the uprising of 1848. He became an enthusiastic follower of the utopian socialism of Charles Fourier that was adopted by other radical Swedenborgians of his time. Wilkinson's flirtation with revolutionary politics as a younger man shifted in middle life to social activism within liberal protest movements against government interference. He campaigned against any form of social coercion, including compulsory vaccination, the requirement for medical practitioners to be licensed, and the compulsory internal examination of prostitutes. These activities, particularly the last, brought him into collaboration with prominent figures in the emerging women's rights movement. He also campaigned vigorously against vivisection.

Later in life, without losing his broadly liberal outlook, Wilkinson became a more conservative follower of Swedenborg's philosophy. At that time there was a strong intellectual interest in mythology, which had been fuelled by archaeological discoveries and related bestselling publications on archaeology and ancient mythologies. The predominant view of mythology at that time was that it represented an ancient, primitive attempt to explain the world and that this outlook had been made redundant by the progress of science. Wilkinson took a different view, based on Swedenborg's account of an initial Golden Age of man followed by a process of degeneration into various eras (called 'Churches' by Swedenborg) leading up to the Last Judgment in 1757, which had preceded the current era of the 'New Church' and would lead to a return of the Golden Age. Wilkinson was a scholar of ancient Icelandic and wrote a Swedenborgian commentary on the Icelandic *Voluspa*, an ancient poem from the poetic *Edda*, as well as books on Babylonian and Egyptian mythology. He continued writing on mythology until his death in 1899.

– 1 –

GARTH WILKINSON: A BRIEF BIOGRAPHY

We are no followers of Swedenborg…The truth, we believe, is not arrested or contained by any man.
Garth Wilkinson, writing in 1849[1]

I confess myself a Swedenborgian, a name which, a quarter of a century ago, I should have repugned.
Garth Wilkinson, writing to Ralph Waldo Emerson in 1874[2]

Fig. 1: Portrait in watercolours of J J G Wilkinson as a boy.
Swedenborg Society Archive, section M.

J ames John Garth Wilkinson was born in Acton Street, Gray's Inn Lane, London on 3 June 1812, the son of James John Wilkinson, a barrister who worked as a special pleader and who had also been appointed judge of the Court of the County Palatine in his native Durham.[3] His mother Harriet, née Robinson, hailed originally from Sunderland. He had six surviving younger siblings: William Martin (1814-97), Harriet Eleanor (b. 1815), Mary Ridley (b. 1817), George Blakeston (b. 1818), Elizabeth Rawling (b. 1822) and Harry Hugh (b. 1825). Another brother died soon after birth in 1820.[4]

From his own account, Wilkinson was an anxious, shy and sickly child who found little or no happiness in his home life. All his memories of early childhood at home relate to events that made him feel fearful or distressed. One prominent theme was a preoccupation with fears of death and the afterlife; as Wilkinson himself put it: 'From his earliest recollection the thought of death pursued him'.[5] He related this partly to his own nature, but it was reinforced by 'horrible tales' told to him by the household servants.[6] He suffered a morbid fear that he might come across a dead body in the street, and he described his horror at finding a dead rat, an experience which caused him to collapse amongst some nettles. During the time of his early schooling, he experienced unsettling dreams mainly relating to the theme of death. In another recurring nightmare that would waken him, he dreamed that his brain was being taken over by 'some subtle overwhelming influence' which 'seemed as if it must destroy him'.[7] He came to believe that he had committed an unforgivable sin against the Holy Ghost, and recalled writing prayers to the Devil which were 'full of bad words'.[8] His use at home of 'bad words', which he said he had picked up innocently from other children, resulted in severe punishment that involved being banished to the front parlour with the maid for days on end, with the family not speaking to him.

His first experience of real happiness came when he was sent away for a year to live with his aunt and grandmother in Sunderland at the age of about seven. He did not describe the circumstances that led to this exile, but it coincides with his mother losing a baby son. He transferred to a local school, where, being 'an exceedingly timid and shamefaced boy', he was bullied by the other boys.[9] He could not bear to be the focus of attention because of his 'unbounded shame about his own person', and he recalled a feeling of complete degradation when he was once obliged to dance in public.[10] Despite these disabling neurotic traits, the young Garth also had some pleasurable boyish experiences during his time in Sunderland. He felt a sense of community during rowdy excursions into town with other boys from his school. He particularly enjoyed the wildness of the surrounding countryside, and found his greatest happiness when staying with his grandmother during school holidays. He found friendship with country boys and servants. Strangely, for one who was so fearful of death, he took to shooting wild birds in the company of the son of his grandmother's tenants, and he recalled admiring the birds as much in death as in life. By the end of his time at Sunderland, he said, tellingly, that although his mother gave him a warm reception when he arrived home, 'his aunt and granny had become his mother'.[11] Of his father there is no mention in his autobiography, and of his siblings only his brother William is mentioned; he had also been sent away to the country, and Garth was taken on a visit to see him in what was apparently an emotional reunion.[12]

After his return to London, Garth was again sent away, this time to a boarding school in Mill Hill, London, which has been credited with being the first preparatory school in England.[13] It was established in 1816 by two teachers from Mill Hill School, Mr Thorowgood and Mr Wood, as a 'feeder' to the senior school, which was a Nonconformist grammar school for boys. Contrary to the original intention, the prep school developed independently of Mill Hill School, continuing to provide education

2

for the boys as they grew older, and the school moved to Totteridge in 1825, during Garth's time there.[14] In 1825 Garth's mother died shortly after the birth of Harry Hugh. According to his nephew, that was the end of Garth's home life until he married and had his own household. Harry Hugh himself died at the age of 5 in 1830.

At the time of the move to Totteridge, Garth's school had fifty-three pupils, but this increased rapidly to over one hundred.[15] There is little record of life at the school, though it is evident that discipline was severe.[16] The timorous young Wilkinson would certainly not have wished to incur the wrath of his teachers and it seems that he was a conscientious pupil. He had an interest in poetry and wrote home for books of Milton's poems as well as those of the Orientalist William Jones and other authors, and he used his own money to buy copies of Byron's poems as they were successively published. In 1826 he won a prize for his own poem entitled 'Babylon'. When he left school at the age of sixteen, Mr Thorowgood recommended presciently that he should keep up his Latin because 'you'll want it'.[17] Wilkinson remained in contact with Mr Thorowgood until his old teacher died in 1860.

Wilkinson had decided on a career in law, but his father pre-empted that decision by signing an indenture of apprenticeship for him with Thomas Leighton, a senior surgeon at Newcastle-upon-Tyne Infirmary.[18] Garth Wilkinson, whether he liked it or not, was to become a doctor.

In the early nineteenth century the hierarchy of medical men was, in descending order, physician, surgeon, apothecary. Physicians were educated at university in Oxford, Cambridge or Edinburgh, and generally had family connections in medicine. The more usual path into medical practice was the one taken by Garth Wilkinson, who learned surgery by apprenticeship and then spent some years as a hospital doctor, eventually becoming a Member of the Royal College of Surgeons and a Licentiate of the Society of Apothecaries.[19]

At the time when Garth Wilkinson started working for Thomas Leighton, the Newcastle Infirmary was a gaunt, ugly building, originally stone built but with a brick extension, housing around 130 beds with an annual throughput of some 1,000 patients.[20] There were five physicians and five surgeons in attendance, none of them particularly distinguished outside of their home town, as well as a resident medical officer.[21] In 1830 the number of beds was increased to accommodate patients previously housed at the lock hospital, where patients with venereal diseases were treated. Garth Wilkinson later became a prominent campaigner against legislation that mandated the compulsory examination of prostitutes operating near military bases, and their removal to lock hospitals if they were found to be infected.[22]

We do not know whether Wilkinson ventured into the poorer areas of the city. If he did so, then he would have found people living in appalling conditions consequent upon a rapid increase in the population following industrialization. In 1832, the year in which Wilkinson left Tyneside, there was an outbreak of cholera in Sunderland and Newcastle. In a report on the outbreak, the houses of the poor were noted to be filthy, damp and overcrowded. One area that was particularly ravaged by cholera was described as 'a dirty narrow lane, filled with mud and filth, which rise in accumulated heaps above the thresholds of the houses. . . Dung-hills are permitted to accumulate on the outside, and on entering the dwellings you are assailed with an offensive, stithy odour'.[23] It was noted that death ensued in half of the patients admitted to hospital, but only one-third of those treated at home, and it was suggested that this was caused by the stress of being moved to hospital. Wilkinson later took up the argument against transporting sick patients to hospital, not only citing the stress of the move, but also adding a uniquely Swedenborgian element to his argument by suggesting that sick people have 'spheres' of illness around them, and that collecting people together in hospitals enlarges the size of their collective sphere so that contagion spreads outside the hospital.[24] After his later conversion to homoeopathy, Wilkinson became much concerned with the treatment of cholera, which he believed had a better survival rate when managed homoeopathically.[25]

Wilkinson stayed with Thomas Leighton in Newcastle until spring 1832, studying pharmacy, chemistry and anatomy before moving on to surgery.[26] He observed many surgical procedures and post-mortem examinations, and a sense of his life as a young trainee doctor can be gleaned from similar contemporary accounts. The eminent surgeon James Syme (1799-1870), for example, described his own experiences when he was a surgical trainee in Edinburgh during the same period that Wilkinson was apprenticed in Newcastle. One of Syme's regular jobs was to bleed patients twice daily, a procedure that frequently led to their demise. He remembered the 'shrieks of unfortunate patients' who had been treated for syphilis with mercury, only to develop mercury toxicity with skin sores that were then cauterized with caustic potash or, if deeper, were scraped down to the bone.[27] Diseased eyes were 'roughly scooped out along with the contents of the orbit'.[28] No distinction was made between benign and malignant breast lumps, so that the whole breast was removed in all cases. Much time was spent dressing wounds, which were bandaged elaborately in a manner that promoted putrefaction. The stench on the wards can only be imagined.

Whilst in Newcastle, Wilkinson showed an early interest in the work of the Mechanics' Institutes where he would eventually lecture, pleading with his father to pay the subscription so that he could attend talks and meetings there. After leaving Leighton he spent about a year in Leeds attached to a local doctor named Bulmer, in whose house he stayed and from whom he learned the art of cupping. Wilkinson was disappointed to find that Bulmer's library contained more religious than medical books, but it seems that he gained much experience of medical practice whilst there as he was left for long hours in sole charge of the surgery. In what spare time he had, Wilkinson was entertained by friends of his father and also explored the surrounding Yorkshire countryside.

After returning to London, Wilkinson 'walked the wards' in Guy's Hospital until he qualified as a Member of the Royal College of Surgeons and as a Licentiate of the Society of Apothecaries in June 1834.[29] During the final part of his training, there were two events that would have a major impact on the rest of his life: he was introduced to the works of Swedenborg and he met his future wife. Both of these events took place at the home of his maternal uncle, George Robinson, who lived at Woodford in Essex. Robinson was a devout follower of Swedenborg, and Wilkinson's future wife, Emma Anne Marsh, was governess in his home. After a short period working as locum tenens in Aylesbury, Wilkinson set up in medical practice in Store Street, Bedford Square, London, in November 1835, but he found no satisfaction in practising orthodox medicine which he had come to loathe.

Wilkinson did not have a particularly religious upbringing. He recalled attending an Anglican Sunday school as a child with his brother William, and no doubt he attended acts of worship at school, but he admitted that in his early manhood he was sceptical about religion.[30] His spiritual awakening came when he began reading the works of Swedenborg. He appears to have had an early aversion to Anglicanism, writing to Emma in 1839 that he would 'as soon be married in a mosque as in one of the edifices of the Church of England', although they did eventually marry in an Anglican church.[31] He became reconciled to the Church of England and, like others before and after him, came to believe that this institution supported a broad enough spectrum of beliefs to accommodate Swedenborg's philosophy.[32] In 1847 he affirmed that:

> I am anxious to belong to no party as a Community but the Church of
> England, and, by my presence there, to contribute an individual mite
> toward making that name latitudinarian enough for the millions of diverse
> spirits who are comprehended under it already.[33]

He remained a member of the Church of England for the rest of his life and never joined the sectarian 'New Church' (a common umbrella term for the Christian churches that formally incorporate Swedenborg's teachings into their worship). Although opposed to the New Church as an institution, he was committed to the 'new church' in the sense that Swedenborg had intended it: as a new era of human spiritual history. His theology was Swedenborgian. Early in his life he accepted it as a general philosophy to be adapted freely to the social and political movements of his day, but later in life he adopted it as a concrete theology that varied little from that of his master. This change occurred gradually. As early as 1853 he observed that 'I have year by year seen more cause to take Swedenborg just as he writes, and not to want any gloss or accommodation'.[34] Even towards the end of his life, Wilkinson did not regard Swedenborg as infallible, pointing out the factual mistakes in his works such as his outdated anatomical knowledge, but he accepted Swedenborg's underlying theology, although even that was not, in Wilkinson's view, a full revelation.[35]

In his early years, before he had settled into married life and found his medical vocation as a practitioner of homoeopathy, Wilkinson privately showed strong tendencies towards melancholy and self-doubt. In 1836 he wrote to Emma that he was 'sufficiently disposed to be gloomy' and 'but an unhappy being at the best'. He begged her forgiveness for being such a failure, saying that he had been 'leading such a dissipated and irreligious career' that he did not know how to 'get rid of the awfully vile state of mind which these habits have produced'.[36] He had serious early pangs of doubt about his abilities as a writer, telling Emma 'I am quite convinced of my general incapacity to do any good as an original writer or thinker'.[37] In this context he developed an addiction to opiates, a habit which he broke with great difficulty in 1839.[38] Despite these melancholic tendencies, Wilkinson in his bachelor years had a very active social life, which included dinner parties and theatre-going.

Wilkinson's early life was characterized by his radical opinions in opposition to the forces of conservatism, his forthright manner of expressing those opinions, and his impatience for change. He had a fundamentally liberal outlook that stayed with him throughout his life, but as he grew older his impetuous radicalism was gradually replaced by a conviction that spiritual, social and political change, desirable as it was, should and would take place gradually.

The youthful Wilkinson's intolerance of inertia is well illustrated by his relationship with the Society for Printing and Publishing the Writings of Emanuel Swedenborg (known as the London Printing Society, and then as the Swedenborg Society from 1855), which he had joined by 1837.[39] His proficiency in Latin led him to offer his services to the Society in translating some of Swedenborg's works, but in October 1838 he wrote to Emma that his offer had been rejected by the Committee whom Wilkinson characterized as 'in general, a most incompetent set of men, with an unaccountable apathy, and do-nothing manner about them'.[40] Wilkinson did not keep these views private, but wrote an impassioned letter to the Committee in which he said that the New Church was distinguished by 'a dearth of literary ability'.[41] Despite this setback, Wilkinson continued with his translation work, writing to his fiancée at the end of May 1839 that his translation of Swedenborg's *Last Judgment*, which he printed privately, was with the binders.[42] In the same year he was elected to the Committee of the Printing Society.

The young Wilkinson regarded the hierarchy of the sectarian New Church as conservative and obstructive. He had repeated disagreements with them, particularly regarding the publication of those works of Swedenborg that were considered too

7

sensitive to be presented to the public. Consistent with his generally liberal outlook, he took the view that all of Swedenborg's works should be available to anybody who chose to read them. In his letter to the Publishing Committee in 1838, Wilkinson particularly resented the fact that the Committee not only did 'nothing positive' but had actively suppressed publication of Swedenborg's work *Conjugial Love*, which Wilkinson told them was a 'lamentable instance' of their apathy.[43] Wilkinson's antipathy towards the attitude of members of the New Church hierarchy, whom he described as the 'fossil Swedenborgians', led to significant bad feeling: in 1847 he told Henry James, Sr that 'Their feelings towards me are as bitter as gall, and probably before I write you I shall have ceased all connexion with their Societies'.[44] After he published his biography of Swedenborg in 1849 in both England and America, his English publisher William Newbery told him that 'the New Church people are very decided in their vituperation of the book, and that they patronize it not at all... However, it is eagerly read by many of those persons whose ear I have desired'.[45] The book fared no better across the Atlantic: his American publisher, Otis Clapp, told Wilkinson that he had been asked 'to cancel certain parts deemed offensive by the pious'.[46] At that time Wilkinson admired Swedenborg but did not regard him as prophetic, an attitude that showed in his writing.[47] Before he published his translation of Swedenborg's work *The Generative Organs* in 1852, Wilkinson wrote to Henry James, Sr that it was 'a book of singular suggestiveness, though not very compatible with the smugness and straitlacedness of many of the followers of Swedenborg'.[48] In 1860 he translated into English Swedenborg's *Dream Diary*, but publication of this work was opposed by many in the New Church because of its sexually explicit passages. Wilkinson's translation was not published in full until 1974; earlier published translations either omitted the sexual passages altogether or translated them into Latin so that they remained inaccessible to the general reader.[49] Some New Church members also opposed publication of Swedenborg's *Spiritual Diary*. This manuscript, which had been borrowed from the Royal Academy of Sciences of Stockholm and not returned, was seen by Garth Wilkinson in 1839 at the home of New Church minister Manoah Sibly, who would not release it for publication. Sibly died in 1840 ('in the nick of time', according to Wilkinson), allowing the Swedenborg Society to access the manuscript and for Wilkinson to be able to personally send it to Professor Immanuel Tafel in Tübingen for editing and publication. An English translation by J H Smithson was then made from Tafel's edition in 1846.[50] Wilkinson reflected later that the *Diary* would not have been published without his own 'persistent and insistent action', and recalled that a New Church minister had expressed the view that publication of the *Diary* would 'disband the Church'.[51]

Frustrated by the Swedenborg Society's exclusive focus on publishing those works of Swedenborg that were of interest to the sectarian New Church, Wilkinson was the main driving force in establishing a separate Swedenborg Association in 1844, with himself as its secretary. The Association had the aim of publishing Swedenborg's philosophical and scientific works as well as fulfilling a social and educational function.[52] Anglican clergyman Augustus Clissold, a follower of Swedenborg, donated his translations of Swedenborg's *Principia* and *The Economy of the Animal Kingdom* to the Association, together with substantial financial backing.[53] The Association held public meetings with speakers including Augustus Clissold, artist and historian Ralph Nicholson Wornum, and Swedenborgian physician John Spurgin. These meetings attracted large audiences of more than 300 people, including prominent literary men such as John Daniel Morell, author of the well-received book *Historical and Critical View of the Speculative Philosophy of Europe in the Nineteenth Century* (1846); poet John Abraham Heraud; and playwright John Westland Marston.[54] It might be expected that such a popular organization would have flourished, but unfortunately the Association gave away so many books (mainly through the energies of Wilkinson) that it ran out of funds in 1847 and was eventually unable to continue as an independent group.[55]

John Spurgin, a member of this group, was an enthusiast for Swedenborg's scientific works, particularly his physiological works *Regnum Animale* (usually translated as *The Animal Kingdom*, but more properly *The Kingdom of the Soul*) and *Oeconomia Regni Animalis* (*The Economy of the Animal Kingdom*), and it was Spurgin who urged their translation.[56] Swedenborg had written these works in the course of trying to understand the nature of the soul, and the study of human anatomy and physiology was an important step on his path to spiritual enlightenment. These works were regarded as absurd and outdated by conventional physicians, but naturally excited the interest of those doctors who followed Swedenborg's philosophy; they accepted that some of the factual anatomy was out of date but believed that this did not impair the underlying conceptual framework.[57] Wilkinson was enthused by Swedenborg's physiological works and began to translate *Regnum Animale*, which he regarded as 'the greatest and noblest work on Human Physiology', in 1839.[58] He did this on his own initiative, without any commission from the Swedenborg Society, and expected no payment.[59] His motives for undertaking this work were complex and included a sense of spiritual mission, the belief that it would improve his medical practice, and a hope that it would give him 'a certain standing among the men of letters in the land'.[60] His translation was published by William Newbery in 1843. In 1845-6 Clissold's translation of *The Economy of the Animal Kingdom*, reworked with a preface by Garth Wilkinson, was also published. Wilkinson continued to hold these works in high regard throughout his life, saying that they were the source of 'All the physiological knowledge that I have which transcends the text books'.[61]

Wilkinson went on to publish translations of Swedenborg's *Posthumous Tracts* (1847), *Hieroglyphic Key* (1847), *Outlines of a Philosophical Argument on the Infinite...and on the Intercourse Between the Soul and the Body* (1847), *The Generative Organs* (1852) and *Divine Love and Wisdom* (1883), the last of which Wilkinson regarded as his most important piece of work.[62] He also edited four of Swedenborg's works in their original Latin: three books of posthumously published works (which he co-edited with Manoah Sibly in 1840) and *Oeconomia Regni Animalis* (1847).[63] Furthermore, he published many of his own original books and papers, which are cited extensively throughout this study.

Wilkinson's literary activities brought him to the attention of leading thinkers in America. His friendship with Henry James, Sr was an intimate one, to the extent that James named one of his sons Garth Wilkinson James after his friend.[64] Garth Wilkinson and Henry James first met in 1844 during one of James's trips to England. The influential James was of considerable practical assistance to Wilkinson, promoting the publication of Wilkinson's essays and recommending Wilkinson to his friends. He also supported

Wilkinson financially during the difficult time when Wilkinson's medical practice was not flourishing and he was seeking to earn a living by writing and lecturing. James put him forward to write a weekly letter for the *New York Tribune* (although this proved to be a short-lived commission)[65] and arranged for him to contribute to the American Swedenborgian journal *The New Jerusalem Magazine*. Through James, Wilkinson was introduced to men visiting England who were prominent in the American literary world, including Henry Wadsworth Longfellow, Charles Anderson Dana, Nathaniel Hawthorne and Ralph Waldo Emerson.[66] James promoted Wilkinson's work amongst Swedenborgians in America, as well as to the American Transcendentalists with whom James was well connected. Emerson, the best known of the Transcendentalists, was an early admirer of Wilkinson. He praised Wilkinson's publication of *The Animal Kingdom* and *The Economy of the Animal Kingdom*, saying that:

> Swedenborg printed these scientific books in the ten years from 1734 to 1744, and they remained from that time neglected: and now, after their century is complete, he has at last found a pupil in Mr. Wilkinson, in London, a philosophic critic, with a coequal vigour of understanding and imagination comparable only to Lord Bacon's, who has produced his master's buried books to the day...This startling reappearance of Swedenborg, after a hundred years, in his pupil, is not the least remarkable fact in his history. Aided, it is said, by the munificence of Mr. Clissold, and also by his literary skill, this piece of poetic justice is done. The admirable preliminary discourses with which Mr. Wilkinson has enriched these volumes, throw all the contemporary philosophy of England into shade...[67]

Inspired by Swedenborg's anatomical works, Wilkinson began his own study of the human body and its spiritual connotations. In carrying out this work, Wilkinson had the advantage of access to Swedenborg's later theological concepts that were still embryonic when Swedenborg was carrying out his own anatomical studies. Wilkinson first presented his ideas as a series of lectures that were delivered to Mechanics' Institutes in London, Liverpool, Manchester, Derby and Leeds in 1849. Mechanics'

Institutes had been set up in the 1820s with the aim of teaching science to working-class mechanics.[68] There was a view that the Institutes were potentially subversive of the established order by encouraging independent thinking amongst the workers rather than government by the aristocracy, and this no doubt appealed to the liberally minded Wilkinson. Wilkinson's path into lecturing had been eased by his friendship with Emerson, who promoted Wilkinson's interests at that time. When Emerson made his own lecture tours around Mechanics' Institutes and similar venues in England after meeting Wilkinson in 1848, he recommended that they should invite Wilkinson to lecture to them. Wilkinson greatly appreciated this, writing to Emerson in 1849 that:

> I cannot tell you in the space of a letter how much your kind word has done for me in England...[In] a Lecture Tour, I found that you had everywhere been there also, dropping your charities from your unique urn.[69]

Wilkinson's motivation for presenting a series of lectures on anatomy to the public was twofold. Firstly, he felt passionately that people should be educated about their own bodies, so that they might be empowered to take care of their own health. Secondly, he used the lectures as an opportunity to introduce the Swedenborgian concept of correspondences, pointing out for example that the human body is not only derived physically from the world through the processes of digestion and assimilation, but also on a higher level *represents* the world as a microcosm of nature. Wilkinson subsequently put his lectures together as a book, *The Human Body and its Connexion with Man, Illustrated by the Principal Organs*, which was published in 1851 in England and America, with a dedication to his friend Henry James. The book was especially well received in America, particularly by the Transcendentalists. A review in the *New York Daily Tribune* described the book as 'probably the first attempt ever made, by a professional man, to connect the technical facts of anatomy and physiology with the truths of Revelation'.[70] Elizabeth Palmer Peabody said that Wilkinson's *The Human Body* 'splendidly illustrated' the principle that 'the human body is the metropolis of material nature, in which may be found in *vital order* all the elements of the material universe which are, outside of the human body, in a more or less chaotic state'.[71] Henry David Thoreau, when revising his well-known book *Walden,* said that Wilkinson's *The Human Body*:

> to some extent realizes what I have dreamed of,——a return to the primitive analogical and derivative sense of words...The faith he puts in old and current expressions as having sprung from an instinct wiser than science, and safely to be trusted if they can be interpreted...All perception of truth is the detection of an analogy; we reason from our hands to our heads.[72]

Henry James, Sr also wrote gushingly to Wilkinson about *The Human Body*, saying that:

> It would be a monstrous compliment to the world at large to say that you were ever going to be a popular writer...If you were well recognized, at your worth as a writer, you would so dwarf all our existing celebrities as to have the whole field of literature to yourself...You will have, you *must* have inevitably, a great fame; but it will be ratified only by the very best voices of the race.[73]

The American poet Walt Whitman is said to have followed Wilkinson in his concept of the efflux of the soul beyond the skin.[74] *The Human Body* was successful enough to go into a second edition in 1860.

In England, the influence of the *The Human Body* is more difficult to trace. A long review in the Scottish periodical *The North British Review* was sympathetic. Recognizing that the work reflects perennial truths, the reviewer says that the work is:

> Old yet new in its essence or pervading spirit, new and often startling in many of its developments, and big with a thousand suggestions, it is very difficult reading to the unaccustomed mind. It is thoughtful, far-reaching, profound, and occasionally difficult.

The reviewer thought that the work was difficult to review critically because 'the only good account of the book is itself', but that it 'may (with all respect for the striking originality of its author) be regarded as the Swedenborgian text-book on the subject, brought up to the present state of positive science'.[75]

Despite this positive review, the reaction of some prominent intellectuals was hostile: Thomas Carlyle described the work as 'a very cloudland indeed' with 'shadows and analogies being apparently all the same to it as facts, admeasurements and substances'.[76] Others, though, found inspiration in Wilkinson's work. These included Wilkinson's admirer, the Scottish poet James Thomson, as well as later intellectuals such as the New Age philosopher Dimitrije Mitrinović.[77]

At the same time that he began to translate Swedenborg's works, Wilkinson was also preparing for the publication of William Blake's *Songs of Innocence and Experience*, including a preface which was to be his first original published work.[78] This work, published in 1839, was the first commercially printed publication of Blake's *Songs*, which previously had been available only as a limited number of handmade prints produced by the author himself from his original engravings. It was Wilkinson's edition of the *Songs* that brought Blake out of obscurity to reach a wider audience. Wilkinson had become involved with this project because of the social contacts that he had developed as a result of his association with the Swedenborg Society. It is fair to suggest that, without his Swedenborgian connections, Wilkinson probably would have remained an obscure London general practitioner and would have left nothing to posterity. His first major social connections were made through the offices of Charles Augustus Tulk, a prominent Swedenborgian who was Member of Parliament for Poole at that time.[79] Tulk moved in literary circles and is best remembered as a friend of Samuel Taylor Coleridge, who had died before Wilkinson could have the opportunity to meet him. A follower of the idealist philosopher George Berkeley, Tulk's interpretation of Swedenborg's writings was so unorthodox that he came to be regarded within New Church circles as a heretic. The young Wilkinson at first adopted Tulk's ideas enthusiastically, but he soon rejected them in favour of a more orthodox interpretation of Swedenborg.

William Blake believed that his poetry was inspired by the spiritual and angelic worlds that he communed with, and when Garth Wilkinson later developed an interest in the popular movement of spiritualism which had been imported from America in the mid-nineteenth century, he too wrote poetry that he said was relayed through him from spiritual sources without the intervention of his own will or intellect. In 1857 he published a book of his poetry, *Improvisations from the Spirit*. This work, which is now unknown, was published anonymously and was written, according to Wilkinson, as a series of 'improvisations' produced by a process that he called 'Writing by Impression':

> A theme is chosen, and written down. So soon as this is done, the first impression upon the mind which succeeds the act of writing the title, is the beginning of the evolution of that theme; no matter how strange or alien the word or phrase may seem. That impression is written down: and then another, and another, until the piece is concluded.[80]

The book received some surprising praise from those who compared his poetry with that of William Blake. One of these was the poet James Thomson, whose 1879 review of Wilkinson's book in *The Liberal* was reprinted in an edited collection of his *Biographical and Critical Studies* in 1896. Thomson said that he could 'often fancy in reading [Wilkinson's poems] that I am verily reading Blake', and commented on 'how much that is pure and wise and beautiful is contained in this almost unknown book'.[81] However, his review was not without criticism of Wilkinson. For example, he believed that the poems suffered from a lack of editing that resulted from Wilkinson's conviction that the poems were divinely inspired and so should not be altered. Thomson also felt that Wilkinson was constrained too much by his Swedenborgian mode of thinking. The poems, thought Thomson, lacked the 'scope and depth and solid grandeur' that could be found in some of Wilkinson's other works, and which led to Thomson's overall assessment of Wilkinson as a man 'of massive and magnificent genius'.[82] The editor of this collection of Thomson's essays, renowned bookseller Bertram Dobell, remarked that 'henceforth any one who displays his ignorance of Wilkinson's writings will hardly be accepted as a competent critic of English literature'.[83] Another prominent intellectual of the time, the poet and painter Dante Gabriel Rossetti was similarly lavish in his praise of Wilkinson's book of poems, which he said:

contains, amid much that is disjointed or hopelessly obscure...many passages and indeed whole compositions...which are startlingly akin to Blake's writings, could pass, in fact, for no one's but his.[84]

As further evidence of the high regard in which Wilkinson's poetry was held by some intellectuals of his day, Ralph Waldo Emerson included two of Wilkinson's poems, 'Turner' and 'The Diamond', alongside works by Shakespeare, Chaucer, Wordsworth, Blake and other literary luminaries, in an anthology of poetry that he edited.[85]

As well as direct social contacts, Wilkinson made influential friends through his habit of sending copies of Swedenborg's works, including his own translations, to prominent people. These included Harriet Martineau, to whom he sent the first volume of Swedenborg's *Arcana Caelestia* in 1838, and Thomas Carlyle, to whom he sent copies of Blake's *Songs* and his translation of the *Last Judgment* in 1839.[86] He also formed an early friendship with William Alexander Dow, a neighbour who was well connected socially, and through him met Robert Browning in 1837.[87]

Wilkinson's social and political views reflected those prevalent in his day, seen through the prism of his Swedenborgian beliefs.[88] The young Wilkinson was an enthusiastic early adopter of two major social phenomena of the nineteenth century: mesmerism and spiritualism.[89] Like a number of other radical followers of Swedenborg, he believed that these movements were harbingers of the new age that was being ushered in as a result of the Last Judgment, which Swedenborg claimed had taken place in the spiritual world in 1757.

In January of 1840, Garth and Emma were married, and the couple made their home in Store Street. Wilkinson's wife Emma was a great strength to him, and she was undoubtedly influential with regard to both his religious convictions and his medical practice. However, her outspokenness did not commend her to all of Wilkinson's friends, particularly Henry James, Sr, who wrote that:

> Mrs. Wilkinson is a dear little goose of a thing, that fancies the Divine
> Providence in closer league with herself than most people, giving her intima-
> tions of events about to happen, and endowing her with peculiar perspicacity

in the intuition of remedies for disease, etc.; and Wilkinson, the great brawny fellow, sits by and says never a word in abatement of the enormous domestic inflation, though every visitor feels himself crowded by it into the most inconsiderable of corners. A sweet, loving, innocent woman like Mrs. Wilkinson ought not to grow egotistical in the company of a truly wise man . . . [90]

Henry's wife Mary developed a similarly disparaging view of Emma, finding her 'illiterate and déclassé'.[91]

When he married Emma, Wilkinson was struggling to earn a living from his medical practice, and his dissatisfaction with conventional medicine left him uncertain about his future career. The young couple struggled financially even after Henry James began paying Wilkinson a stipend for articles that he contributed to American periodicals. In 1846 Wilkinson wrote to Henry James that 'Medical in profession, and Literary in practice, I have fallen between two stools'.[92] He considered a change of career, casting his net wide. One possibility was to abandon medicine altogether: he wrote that 'circumstances at present threaten to float me quite out of the waters of medical practice, and to moor me far away in literature'. He considered a post as a Veterinary Surgeon in India and sought the help of his uncle William Sewell who was head of the Veterinary College in London, but his uncle declined to support him.[93] In 1847 he considered two appointments: a medical appointment under the prospective Health of Towns Bill, which mandated improvements in public health provision, such as better water supply and sewerage; and a full-time post as an Inspector of Schools, for which he applied but was unsuccessful.[94] Garth and Emma seriously considered the possibility of emigrating to America, and continued to toy with this idea until at least 1849; one of Wilkinson's reasons for not following this up was that his father was 'one of the most unadulterated Tories' and anti-republican, and would probably disinherit Wilkinson if they made the move.[95]

The Wilkinsons moved to Hampstead in 1847 in the hope of increasing his income from medical practice, but in that year he wrote to Henry James that 'My practice at Hampstead is at present—none'.[96] It was not until Wilkinson introduced homoeopathy into his practice that he could once again find satisfaction—and earn a comfortable living——from the practice of medicine.[97] His practice began to grow, but even so money was short, particularly when James ceased to finance his literary efforts. The Wilkinsons took in paying guests to make ends meet. They considered moving to 'Manchester, perhaps elsewhere, wherever an opening for a larger field of practice seems promised'.[98] Finally they moved to a smaller house in St John's Wood in 1850, because practice there promised to be more lucrative.[99] By 1852 his practice was flourishing and he hired a carriage for three or four days a week to make his rounds.[100] This brought with it other benefits, including a governess for his daughters and expensive schooling for his son.[101] His patients now included several prominent intellectuals and members of the higher social classes, and by 1856 he wrote to his father that he was seeing up to 40 patients a day.[102]

Wilkinson travelled widely in Europe, primarily as a tourist, particularly enjoying trips to Norway and Iceland.[103] Scandinavian mythology was one of his abiding interests and he began to study Norse literature and languages for relaxation as early as 1837.[104] Icelandic scholars were amongst his circle of friends and he published several works on Scandinavian and other mythologies.[105] Later in life, Wilkinson took his holidays mainly with his daughters, as well as at the home in Eastbourne of his great friend the Countess de Noailles, a political activist who, like Wilkinson, campaigned against vivisection and vaccination.

Despite his yearnings for America, Wilkinson made only one short trip there, in 1869. The poet Longfellow and his family were amongst his companions on the outward journey, and Wilkinson engaged him in conversation about spiritualism, saying that he found Longfellow 'more interested in it than Poets usually are'.[106] From his Travel Diary, it appears that his trip to America was largely one that might have been taken by any other tourist of his day, with an itinerary that included New York, Niagara, Montreal, Quebec, Lake Champlain, Lake George, Boston and Cambridge. He met up with several previous acquaintances and patients whom he knew from England, but visited Henry James for only a few hours, though Wilkinson said that he was 'received like a brother'.[107] They had 'a long philosophical talk' and James read to Wilkinson from his new book, *The Secret of Swedenborg*, which focuses on the Swedenborg-derived concept of the Divine Natural Humanity, a topic on which the two men disagreed fundamentally.[108]

Wilkinson met his namesake, Garth Wilkinson ('Wilkie') James, noting that he commanded a Negro Regiment.[109] On his return, Wilkinson wrote glowingly in his journal about his experience of America, saying that he now regretted having squandered previous holidays by spending them in Continental Europe. His view of the American attitude to money is of interest; he saw this as a positive characteristic. Impressed by the vitality and freedom that he found in America, he wrote in his journal that:

> I was impressed spiritually with the fact of a New Mission in Humanity,
> which America is carrying out. . .Making Money, & Getting on: not the
> Almighty Dollar, but the indefinitely plentiful Dollar as a Divine Need for
> men to execute their Mission. I was impressed with the Divine value of money
> as distinctively opposed to the Aristocratic and Avaricious value of it.[110]

At that time he thought that American values would 'educate, flow into and impress all countries. . .And that God is palpably with America all the time', although later in life he grew more circumspect about American materialism.[111]

The Wilkinsons had four surviving children, none of whom achieved any notable success. Their daughter Emma, Garth Wilkinson's favourite, was married in 1859 at the age of sixteen to Hermann Pertz, an engineer in the Prussian army, and they had two daughters and two sons.[112] Pertz served in the Franco-Prussian War of 1870-1. Britain maintained a neutral position over this war, but public opinion was on the side of the French. Wilkinson naturally sided with the Prussians and noted that they had a great cause to fight for, which was the quest for 'unity of a Great German Fatherland'. Wilkinson was in Berlin in 1870 with his daughter Emma, where they were involved in the provision of supplies for injured soldiers from both sides.[113]

Wilkinson's other two daughters both married well by the standards of the day. Florence married the wealthy Benjamin St John Attwood-Mathews, who was co-founder of the Alpine Club, in 1857. They lived at Llanvihangel Court, an extensive estate in Monmouthshire with views over the Black Mountains.[114] Wilkinson dedicated his book *Epidemic Man and His Visitations* (1892) to Attwood-Mathews, 'in memory of happy days in his home and of its gardens and groves of kindness and learning'.[115]

Wilkinson's third daughter Mary married Francis Claughton Mathews in 1871, and Garth Wilkinson developed a close friendship with his son-in-law, to whom he dedicated his book *The Affections of Armed Powers: A Plea for a School of Little Nations* in 1897.[116] Wilkinson's son James became a railway engineer, and was involved in the construction of the Lynn and Fakenham railway in Norfolk, and the Luleå line in the north of Sweden. In 1867 James married Eliza Hackett Ford at Stafford.[117] In one of his last trips to Norway in 1871, Garth Wilkinson was collecting information to assist his son's plan to build a railway between Sundsvall and Trondheim.[118]

Wilkinson's granddaughter Emma, daughter of Emma Pertz, was to become the mother of Cecilia Payne-Gaposchkin, a pioneering astrophysicist in America at a time when this profession was a male preserve. Cecilia had great respect for her great-grandfather Garth, saying that 'he produced...an amazing volume of poetry executed by automatic writing, *Improvisations of the Spirit*, which cast a strong influence over my early years...he [also] had a profound interest in ancient Icelandic literature, which has stimulated me in my turn to a study of the Edda'.[119] She also remembered Wilkinson's other two daughters, but much less fondly. Her remarks about them are worth quoting at some length:

> The two other sisters made rich marriages: Florence to St John Attwood-Mathews and Mary to Francis Claughton Mathews. Neither had children, and their preoccupation with material wealth gave me an abiding horror of money, and a feeling that there is something cruel and indecent about being rich. For they used their wealth in an attempt to reduce the descendants of their less-fortunate sister to subservience.
>
> I can see them now: horribly stout, clad in black satin, enthroned like Far Eastern idols, and fondling obese little pug dogs. They reigned over their estates, Aunt Florence in Monmouthshire, Aunt Mary in Hampshire, tyranizing [*sic*] over unhappy, obsequious 'companions'. I paid (by 'Royal Command'), one brief terrified visit to Great-aunt Florence. Her domain, Llanvihangel Court, was the grander of the two, complete with the Bed in which Queen Elizabeth Slept and the Bloody Footprint left on the stairs after

a duel. From her awful eminence she recommended that I should marry an
elderly bishop, a distant cousin of her late husband. I had, of course, never
met the bishop. I told her stoutly that I was perfectly capable of earning my
own living; I was 17. This was the last time I saw or heard of Aunt Florence
Mathews. She and her sister lived to great ages, and died unlamented.[120]

It is evident that Garth Wilkinson's liberal ideas had not permeated the world
of these two daughters, and that a substantial family feud developed later between
them and the children of Emma Pertz. Fortunately Wilkinson did not live to see the
rift, and his relationship with all his daughters appears to have remained cordial
during his lifetime.

Later in his life, Garth Wilkinson took a keen interest in ancient mythologies, which
he believed contained vestiges of the perennial truth, and which could be interpreted
along Swedenborgian lines.[121] His particular passion was for Scandinavian mythology
as portrayed in the *Edda*, a collection of traditional poems recorded in the 1270s in
a manuscript known as the Codex Regius. In order to pursue this interest, Wilkinson
learned Old Icelandic and was in contact with the leading Icelandic scholars of his
day. This led to him publishing a Swedenborgian exegesis of the *Voluspa*, a poem
that describes the history of the cosmos from its creation to the destruction of the
present order at Ragnarok, which is followed by the regeneration of a paradisaical
world. Wilkinson's interest extended also into Sumerian and Egyptian mythology.

As Wilkinson entered late old age, he suffered the inevitable losses of those close
to him. After his son-in-law Hermann Pertz, by then a Major, retired in 1879, he and
his family came to live in Norfolk, where he worked on one of James Wilkinson's
railway projects and the family lived in a house that Wilkinson bought for them.[122]
Wilkinson's dear wife Emma died in 1886, following which he largely retired from
medical practice.[123] After the death of Hermann Pertz, the widowed Emma Pertz and
her daughters came to live with the elderly Wilkinson, who was severely shaken when
Emma herself died in 1893. His granddaughters, Emma Leonora Helena Pertz and
Florence Harriet Louisa Pertz stayed with him until he died. He dedicated his book
on the *Voluspa* to them, describing them as 'my free comrades in life and work'.[124]

Towards the end of his life, Wilkinson became frail physically but retained his intellectual prowess, continuing to write until his death in 1899 at the age of 87. In his last
illness he was attended by his friend, the prominent homoeopath Robert Ellis Dudgeon.[125]
His nephew and biographer Clement Wilkinson recalled the elderly Wilkinson:

> At this time he was good to see. Above six feet in height and but little bowed
> by time; inclined to stoutness but far from unwieldiness; bearded almost to
> the waist, the hair grizzled but still showing some of its original brown; but
> slightly bald over a high-domed forehead; thick and rough of eyebrow over
> keen blue eyes which flashed under his gold-rimmed spectacles; handsome
> and tidy in his dress, he was a fine specimen of a cultured and kindly
> gentlemen. His voice was charming, strong, vigorous and deep as the thought
> behind it; prone to hearty laughter...Sitting by his dwarf revolving bookcase,
> on which rested his snuff box and a pile of books in many languages and
> on many subjects, he made a picture which never rises in the memory of his
> friends without bringing pleasure and thankfulness with it.[126]

Wilkinson's interests at the end of his life are well illustrated by his address book
from 1892.[127] This is focused less on literati of the kind that dazzled him as a young
man, and more on people who shared his political and moral beliefs. Aside from
family members, clergy (both New Church and others) and tradesmen, his correspondents included several of the most prominent homoeopaths of his day, some of
whom, including Dr Robert Ellis Dudgeon in London and Drs William Boericke and
William H Holcombe in America, had been long-term friends. There were echoes of
other friendships, including for example William and Henry James, Jr. Wilkinson
admired both these sons of Henry James, Sr; he described William as 'a remarkable writer...a new power in the world of thought' and said that he was William's
pupil.[128] His continuing interest in the arts is reflected by the inclusion of several
actors, artists, poets, singers and musicians.[129] Others were contacts from within the
Swedenborgian community, including Henry Septimus Sutton, a poet and friend
of Emerson, who had learned of Swedenborg through Wilkinson's writings.[130] He

was in contact with the leading campaigners against vivisection, including George R Jesse, Honorary Secretary of the Society for the Abolition of Vivisection; Sidney G Trist, editor of *The Animal's Friend* magazine; and Frances Power Cobbe, an Irish suffragette who had founded the British Union for the Abolition of Vivisection. Other friends and associates, such as the Countess de Noailles and Lady Mount Temple, were prominent supporters and patrons of a variety of liberal causes. Several of Wilkinson's later correspondents had close associations with Helena Blavatsky's Theosophical Society, including Herbert A W Coryn, one of Blavatsky's 'Inner Group', and homoeopath George Wyld, who was President of the Society from 1880 until 1882, when he became disenchanted with Blavatsky.[131] Wilkinson showed a keen interest in Africa, stimulated no doubt by Swedenborg's belief that African peoples were particularly enlightened spiritually.[132] His correspondents included Edward Wilmot Blyden, a lifelong champion for Africa and its people; Prince Momolu Massaquoi, the first indigenous African diplomat to Germany, who represented African Christianity at the Parliament of Religions in Chicago in 1893; Henry Hayman, the Liberian Consul General; and several missionaries on the continent of Africa.[133] He was in contact with experts in ancient mythology such as Sir Edwin Arnold, Archibald Henry Sayce and the Egyptologist Alfred Wiedemann, as well as some of the leading Icelandic scholars of his day, including Viktor Rydberg, a prominent Swedish intellectual, philosopher, expert on Norse mythology and Indo-European studies; Jón Hjaltalin, an Icelandic academic, Parliamentarian and Swedenborgian; Valtýr Guðmundsson, politician and historian of Icelandic culture; and the American scholar Willard Fiske. As well as these contacts that reflected Wilkinson's known interests, there were several intriguing entries, including senior staff at hospitals for the insane in America and Australia.[134]

When younger, Garth Wilkinson gained accolades from some of the most prominent intellectuals of his day. This fame faded as he grew older. In one of Wilkinson's obituaries it was observed that in his old age he had 'outlived his generation and his fame, which at one time was considerable'.[135]

Wilkinson's reputation, both during his own lifetime and in the hundred or so years since his death, has been inextricably tied to that of Emanuel Swedenborg.

In order to explore the underlying concepts in Wilkinson's thought and works and to place them in the appropriate nineteenth-century social and political contexts, it is first necessary to understand how Swedenborg's ideas had been received and spread in the years before Wilkinson first became acquainted with them.

– 2 –

The reception of Swedenborg in England, 1770-1830

All the Theosophical Illuminees *of this age in England, France, Sweden,*
or Germany, have drawn their principles from the Baron Emmanuel
Swedenborg. . . *they daily expect that great revolution which is to sweep from*
the earth every
prince and every king.
Abbé Barruel, writing in 1799[1]

It was to guard against the introduction of sentiments of this [revolution-
ary] description, and to convince the world that the Writings of Swedenborg
gave no countenance whatever to them, that a Protest was entered in the
Minutes of this Conference against all such principles of infidelity and
democracy as were then circulating in the country. For it is well known,
that the members of the New Church, actuated by the religious principles
which they profess, always have been, and still are, among the most loyal
and peaceable subjects of His Majesty. . .
Robert Hindmarsh, on the General Conference of the New Church in 1792[2]

Fig. 2: Print made from a steel engraving of Emanuel Swedenborg by Alfred Roffe, commissioned by Wilkinson and made from his own copy of a copper-plate engraving by J Spack. Wilkinson presented the plate to the Swedenborg Society in 1878 and prints were included in many of the Society's publications.
Swedenborg Society Archive, section M.

E manuel Swedenborg made many visits to England, first to pursue his
scientific studies as a young man in 1710, returning next in 1744-5 at
the time of his spiritual crisis. After that he was frequently in England,
eventually dying in London in 1772.[3]

There is little unequivocal evidence that Swedenborg was involved more than
peripherally with esoteric groups in England during his lifetime. Marsha Keith
Schuchard has been the most active researcher in this area. She has provided cir-
cumstantial evidence that Swedenborg was a Mason.[4] This possibility had been raised
periodically since his death, usually with the same conclusion as that reached by A
Kahl, a Swedish historian of the New Church, that the suggestion 'lacks all historical
foundation'.[5] Schuchard also emphasized the esoteric aspects (particularly relating to
sexual Kabbalistic practices) of Swedenborg's possible association with the Moravians
in London.[6] We do know that Swedenborg attended the Moravian church in Fetter
Lane, but he subsequently denounced them by declaring that, in the next life, they
had been 'driven forth into desert places, where they live wretchedly' because of their
false doctrines.[7] Schuchard also suggests that Swedenborg was involved with Dr
Samuel Jacob Falk, a Kabbalist and Freemason who was known internationally for
his magical and healing powers and for his invocation of spirits. He was Polish-born,
but he travelled widely in mainland Europe and c.1739-40 moved to London where
he was recognized as a Baal Shem (master of the divine names).[8]

During his last years in England, Swedenborg received a number of visitors who would prove to be important in the subsequent transmission of his doctrines. The most frequent visitors were Thomas Hartley and Dr Husband Messiter, who acted as Swedenborg's physician during his last illness.[9] Hartley was an Anglican clergyman, and a neighbour and friend of the Behmenist theosopher William Law.[10] He was greatly impressed by Swedenborg's theosophy, and in 1770 published the first English translation of Swedenborg's *Intercourse between the Soul and the Body* under the title *A Theosophic Lucubration on the Nature of Influx*. In the preface, Hartley expressed his view that Swedenborg's theosophy 'far excel[s] whatever has come down to us of Hermes, Pythagoras and Plato'.[11] This translation proved to be pivotal in introducing several key figures, including Richard Houghton and Benedict Chastanier, to the work of Swedenborg.[12] Hartley also published an account of his correspondence with Swedenborg under the title of *Nine Queries Concerning the Trinity, etc., Proposed to the Hon. Emanuel Swedenborg, by the Rev. Thomas Hartley*, which was published in London by Robert Hindmarsh in 1785. Dr Husband Messiter, Swedenborg's other frequent visitor, was a Swedish-born Mason with Moravian connections.[13] Together with other Masons, he founded in 1776 the London Universal Society, a quasi-Masonic group with the aim of promoting Swedenborg's teaching.[14] On one of his visits to Swedenborg in 1771, Hartley brought with him the leading Quaker William Cookworthy, who went on to translate several of Swedenborg's works including *The Doctrine of Life for the New Jerusalem* (1772) and *Heaven and Hell* (1778).[15]

Despite the activity of these individuals in promoting Swedenborg's teaching in England, readership of Swedenborg remained confined to a relatively small group of individuals.[16] It was not until John Clowes became active that Swedenborg's work started to become widely known.

John Clowes (1743-1831)

After Swedenborg himself, John Clowes ranks as the first major figure in English Swedenborgian history. He was committed to the propagation of Swedenborg's teaching, both by translating his works from their original Latin and by teaching groups of adherents, in his own county of Lancashire and throughout the country.

He vehemently opposed the sectarian tendencies of the London Swedenborgians, and remained an Anglican Church minister throughout his adult life.[17] According to an early follower of Swedenborg, Clowes had:

> a talent for bringing down the interior truths which [the works of Swedenborg] contain to the comprehension of the most simple and common understanding . . . It is owing. . . to our having had a CLOWES, that the doctrines of the New Church have made greater progress in England, and in the United States of America. . . than in any other country upon earth.[18]

Born in Manchester in 1743, he was the son of barrister Joseph Clowes, who was a devoutly religious man and a strict disciplinarian. One man who had a pivotal influence on the life of the young Clowes was John Byrom, a cousin and close friend of his father. Byrom—Jacobite, poet, Fellow of the Royal Society and a friend and ardent follower of William Law—took a keen interest in John Clowes's education. This patronage continued after Byrom's death, when his son Edward Byrom, also a follower of William Law, endowed St John's Church in Manchester and arranged for John Clowes to be installed as the first incumbent there in 1769, with the aim that he would promote William Law's theosophy.[19]

John Byrom was a significant figure not only in the life of John Clowes, but also in the intellectual life of England at that time.[20] It is therefore appropriate to consider him in greater detail. He was born in Manchester in 1692 into a family of linen merchants. He was educated at Trinity College, Cambridge, where he later became a Fellow. From 1717 he studied medicine at Montpellier, though he left during the following year without gaining any qualification.[21] He earned a living teaching a system of shorthand that he had developed.[22] He had many wealthy clients, particularly in London, so that the work took him away from his home in Manchester for much of the year.[23] In 1724 he was elected Fellow of the Royal Society at the time when Isaac Newton was president. As a young man in London he was something of a bon viveur, but he developed an increasingly spiritual outlook. He was eclectic in his worship, attending a Moravian gathering in 1739 to hear the preaching of

Count Nikolaus Ludwig von Zinzendorf, and also sampling Methodist and Quaker meetings.[24] In 1729 he sought out William Law, after reading his *A Serious Call to a Devout and Holy Life* (1728).[25] Byrom became a follower of Law, whom he referred to as the 'Master', and they remained close friends into old age. Byrom's conversations with Law are recorded in his extensive journals, which were published by the Chetham Society in Manchester in the mid-nineteenth century. They discussed a wide variety of topics, including other mystics such as Antoinette Bourignon and Jean-Marie Bouvier de la Motte-Guyon (Madame Guyon), whom Law dismissed. He admired the medieval German mystics John Tauler and Heinrich Suso, who were followers of Meister Eckhart, and he reserved particular praise for Jacob Boehme.[26] Byrom accumulated an extensive library which mostly held works of theology and Christian mysticism, but also included the Hermetic *Poimandres* and works by many esoteric writers, including John Dee, Paracelsus, Cornelius Agrippa von Nettesheim, Johannes Trithemius, Johannes Valentinus Andreae, Jacob Boehme and Marsilio Ficino.[27] Byrom had an interest in the Kabbalah, remarking that 'if thou consultest the Rosicrucians and the Freemasons, thou wilt find in them certain remains of the ancient Cabbala, of which they have retained the secret without the understanding'.[28] From 1723 to 1730 he attended meetings of the 'Cabala Club', which met to discuss occult topics including magic and miracles.[29] Byrom also had in his possession more than 500 drawings containing geometric forms which modern-day alchemist Adam McLean has described as the 'geometric deconstructions of well known alchemical and hermetic emblems', with the source of the original drawings marked cryptically on the back of them.[30]

Through attending meetings of the Royal Society, John Byrom came to know William Stukeley, famous for his studies of the ancient monuments of Avebury and Stonehenge.[31] Although Stukeley is not known to have been a friend of Joseph or John Clowes, it is relevant to consider Stukeley briefly at this point because he illustrates an esoteric theme that was evident within the intellectual life of England at that time. Stukeley practised as a physician until he was ordained into the Church of England later in life, but he is best known as an antiquarian.[32] After extensive fieldwork which he had started decades earlier, before he knew Byrom, Stukeley published his two most famous works, *Stonehenge, a Temple Restor'd to the British Druids* (1740) and *Abury, a Temple of the British Druids* (1743).[33] The titles of these works immediately indicate Stukeley's preoccupation with ancient British religion. This reflected a more general fascination in eighteenth-century England with a supposed universal ancient religion that had been sparked by discoveries in Egypt, a phenomenon that has become known as Egyptomania.[34] It was widely believed that there were close similarities between the beliefs and practices of the ancient Egyptians and those of the Celtic Druids.[35] Stukeley interpreted the monuments of Stonehenge and Avebury as Druid temples. Inspired by Athanasius Kircher, who regarded Egyptian hieroglyphs as symbols of hidden mysteries, Stukeley interpreted the Avebury complex as a hieroglyph of a serpent, symbolic of the deity.[36] He defined himself as a Druid and combined this with his Christian faith by 'reconciling Plato & Moses, & the Druid & Christian Religion'.[37] This was facilitated by the claim of the Cambridge Platonist Ralph Cudworth that belief in the Trinity was universal in the pagan world.[38]

Stukeley used to discuss these issues frequently with his friend Isaac Newton, who had a close interest in such matters. Amongst the topics they discussed were the plans of Solomon's Temple that Newton had made, and the religion of ancient Egypt.[39] Newton believed that Stonehenge and other standing stones were derived from ancient Egyptian religious practices, the circles with a central fire representing the heliocentric universe.[40] When we recall the association between William Stukeley and John Byrom, it is clear that esoteric issues were respectable topics for discussion amongst members of the Royal Society at the time of Isaac Newton's presidency.

John Byrom's interests and associations formed the intellectual climate in the home of the young Clowes. Although this no doubt set the scene for the interests that Clowes himself would later develop, it seems that it had little discernable influence on him at the time when he went up to Trinity College, Cambridge in 1761. After gaining his BA in 1766 he was elected a Fellow of the College, was ordained by the Bishop of London, and worked as a private tutor to undergraduates for three years. However, a decisive turning point came *c.* 1769 when he developed a serious and life-threatening illness, following which he made a radical reappraisal of his direction in life. He felt that 'the veil of separation between him and the eternal world' had been rent, and he developed 'a full conviction of the comparative vanity of all earthly gain and glory, and at the same time of the substantial reality of those invisible and eternal goods announced in the Gospel'.[41] Before this religious experience Clowes had been offered the incumbency of St John's Church in Manchester by Edward Byrom. At that time he had declined the appointment, but following his experience the offer was renewed and he accepted.

It was around this time that Clowes first read the works of William Law in his father's library.[42] He went on to read the works of other Christian mystics including Thomas à Kempis, Jacob Boehme and Jane Leade. Clowes was introduced to the works of Swedenborg in spring 1773 (shortly after Swedenborg's death) by Richard Houghton of Liverpool, who had been a friend of John Byrom.[43] Houghton had a large library and Clowes was impressed to find that his theology 'was not that dry and barren science of mere speculation, which reaches no further than the intellect: it was the theology of the heart'.[44] Houghton had been introduced to Swedenborg's writings through reading *A Theosophic Lucubration on the Nature of Influx* (1770), translated by Thomas Hartley, whom we have already noted as a regular visitor to Swedenborg during his final years in London.[45] Houghton recommended to Clowes that he should read Swedenborg's *Vera Christiana Religio* (1771), which he obtained but did not immediately read, feeling that he knew enough from his own spiritual experiences without troubling himself with what he saw as abstract philosophy. Later in the year, the evening before a trip to see an old friend, whilst idly browsing the volume, the term *Divinum Humanum* caught Clowes's attention.[46] After travelling across the Pennine Hills to his friend's house, he had an intense spiritual experience. He described a feeling of '*divine glory*, surpassing all description, and exciting the most profound adoration', which he knew came from the *Divinum Humanum*, though there was no associated vision.[47] 'The *glory* continued during a full hour', he wrote, and this happened again the next morning, 'but, if possible, with increased splendour'. He hurried back home and immersed himself in his copy of *Vera Christiana Religio*. This was a revelatory experience for him, which opened his understanding 'to the contemplation of the most sublime mysteries of wisdom, convincing it of the being of a God, of the existence of an eternal world...of the true nature of creation'.[48] Thereafter Clowes was an avid reader, translator and disseminator of Swedenborg's works. He began corresponding with Hartley, whom he later met in London.[49] Hartley wrote a long preface to Clowes's translation into English of *Vera Christiana Religio* (*The True Christian Religion*). Thus we can see the spiritual baton being passed from Emanuel Swedenborg to Thomas Hartley, and thence, with the mediation of Richard Houghton, to John Clowes.

Clowes's open adoption of Swedenborg's writings, together with his inspired teaching, led to a huge increase in his congregation of the 'simple-hearted poor', such that he had to hold additional meetings in his own home.[50] This aroused the jealousy of other local clergy, who complained to the Bishop of Chester, Beilby Porteus, who would become Bishop of London in 1787 and whose support for Clowes saw opposition subside. Clowes did consider leaving the Anglican ministry because of doctrinal differences and discussed this with Hartley, who encouraged him to remain.[51] Clowes also found himself under increasing pressure of time from the translation of Swedenborg's works in addition to his pastoral duties, and he saw this as another reason for resigning his position. However, in another striking spiritual experience, he 'was made sensible of the presence of an angelic society' which told him 'do not do it; we will help you'.[52] From then on, he felt that most of his sermons and other published works were 'dictated throughout by spirits'.[53] Clowes continued with his translations, and in 1782 the Manchester Printing Society, sponsored by wealthy gentlemen who were members of Clowes's congregation, was established to foster their publication. In the following year, they published the first volume of the first English translation of Swedenborg's *Arcana Caelestia*, and Clowes went on to translate and publish all the remaining volumes.[54]

At the time of Clowes's ministry, Manchester and the surrounding county of Lancashire were undergoing the massive social changes associated with the beginning of the Industrial Revolution. Prior to this, Lancashire had been an isolated and backward area where traditional beliefs had been well preserved.[55] There was a widespread belief in 'boggarts'—spirits, goblins and other supernatural beings, which appeared to people and often played pranks on them—in Lancashire through to the nineteenth century.[56] It was believed that people born during twilight have the ability to see the spirits of the dead and dying, and many more people believed that they could hear spirits through knocking and other strange noises.[57] Every town had its wise men and cunning women, who could earn a good living by telling fortunes using primitive astrology and scrying, and by dispensing herbal remedies. The more literate of these would own a few occult books, which were handed down within families.[58] Perhaps because of this cultural background, Nonconformist religious groups prospered in eighteenth-century Lancashire. One manifestation of this was the formation of local groups whose members studied the works of Jacob Boehme and William Law. In 1775, Ralph Mather, a Methodist who later became an ordained Swedenborgian minister, described groups of spiritual 'seekers', most of whom who were followers of Boehme and Law. Such groups could be found throughout Britain, but they were particularly prevalent in Lancashire, where they apparently flourished amongst relatively uneducated working people. In the Manchester area near the town of Leigh, 'Wm. Compton, farmer', and in Leigh 'R. Darwell and young Geo. Darwell, and J. Marsh' were described as 'poor people, [who] love J. Behmen and W. Law'. In Bolton, which is now part of Greater Manchester, there were 'M. Owen, greatly advanced; M. Winkbridge, fifteen years in purifications; several more coming on; these are I think in general but low in the world, but it is a school of female philosophers'. Several are listed elsewhere in England, such as Bristol, including one person who learned German in order to read Boehme, and a girl's school run by a group of young women, one of whom 'bids fair for a Teresa'.[59] Such was the popularity in the region of Boehme's ideas that in 1752 a Manchester newspaper serialized *The Way of Christ Discovered.*[60]

It is from these groups of mystical Christians that the new Swedenborgian societies emerged around England, and particularly in Lancashire.[61] A cynic said of the people in these groups that:

> They have had from their infancy a predilection to the marvelous and
> surprising, and are but old turncoats from those enthusiasts, Bourignon,
> Leese, and Behmen, and perhaps for no other reason, but because the
> Baron's system has more novelty, and more unintelligibleness in it than
> either of his mystical predecessors...[62]

Swedenborg's accounts of his spiritual experiences resonated readily with the traditional beliefs of Lancashire folklore and the meetings around Lancashire became extremely popular. Some of the leaders of the Swedenborgian groups were still immersed in traditional practices. An example is Samuel Dawson, leader of the Bolton group, who was a local wise man and herbalist.[63] Clowes visited each group every six weeks and held a Swedenborg study class with the members, making good use of his ability to translate complex teachings into an intelligible form. Some mill owners were very sympathetic to his cause, providing a room on mill premises for the workers to listen to him.[64] Spiritual experiences were common amongst members of these groups. One account tells of a young girl who had frequent visions of a group of angels, followed by a vision of a 'female dressed in white' who gave a correct prophecy concerning the demise of Clowes's curate, who opposed his teachings.[65] Another member of the landed gentry heard a voice repeatedly telling him to 'Go to Mr. Clowes', which eventually he did.[66]

As well as visiting these groups local to Manchester, Clowes also made annual visits to societies in other parts of England, including Bath, Bristol, Stroud, Birmingham, Liverpool, Hull and London.[67] In his autobiography, Clowes gave no special prominence to the London Society: to him, it was simply another group to visit annually. However, this group, which in 1784 was renamed the Theosophical Society, assumed a very prominent place in the early history of English Swedenborgianism.[68]

Towards the end of his life, Clowes befriended the young Thomas de Quincey who later said of him that:

> thirty years are passed since then . . . and I have yet seen few men approaching this venerable clergyman in paternal benignity——none certainly in childlike purity, apostolic holiness, or in perfect alienation of heart from the spirit of this fleshly world.[69]

Clowes remained resolutely against sectarian separation of the followers of Swedenborg, and in 1806 he instituted annual meetings for the non-sectarians at Hawkstone in Shropshire. These meetings continued for more than fifty years.[70]

Robert Hindmarsh (1759-1835) and the Theosophical Society

Robert Hindmarsh was a key figure in the history of Swedenborgianism. He was largely responsible for the schism between the sectarian New Church and the non-sectarian followers of Swedenborg, and he was implacably opposed to anything that smacked of esotericism.[71] His own account of his activities in relation to the New Church, *The Rise and Progress of the New Jerusalem Church* (1861), has been described, even by a relatively sympathetic commentator, as being 'pervasively flawed' by significant omissions.[72] These omissions relate to verifiable events that reflected badly on the author.

The son of a Methodist minister, Hindmarsh trained as a printer and set up his own business whilst still a young man.[73] In 1782 he was lent some of Swedenborg's works by a Quaker friend of his father. At that time, Swedenborgian groups were meeting regularly in Lancashire, but only a few isolated individuals were reading Swedenborg in London. He sought out other readers of Swedenborg and eventually met with two or three of them each week at his house. The first public meeting was held in the following year, though this comprised only five people, primarily the friends who had been meeting informally. They moved to a room in the Inner Temple in London, and by advertisement began to attract more members. After a few meetings they moved to larger premises at New Court in Middle Temple, and in 1784 they adopted the ponderous name of 'The Theosophical Society, instituted for the Purpose of promoting the Heavenly Doctrines of the New Jerusalem, by translating, printing, and publishing the Theological Writings of the Honourable Emanuel Swedenborg'.[74] At their meetings Swedenborg's works were read in their original Latin and then discussed. The meetings grew in popularity and increased in frequency to twice weekly. In 1787 it was proposed that there should be separation from the established church. This was defeated by vote, but the minority formed a new society, whilst still attending the general meetings. John Clowes travelled to London with the express purpose of dissuading the separatists, but his intervention was fruitless and the first formal meeting of the new society, which called itself The New Church, Signified by the New Jerusalem, in the Revelation, was held in July 1787. The original Theosophical Society continued to meet for a short time, with dwindling membership.[75] The first public worship of the new sect was performed in a rented chapel in Great Eastcheap, London, in 1788. In the same year, the first priests were ordained by other members of the church, including Hindmarsh's father who had 'converted' from Methodism, one Samuel Smith, and Robert Hindmarsh himself who became ordained by lottery when he drew from a hat a ticket on which he had allegedly, unknown to the others, inscribed the word 'ordain'.[76] In the following year, Hindmarsh and five others were excluded from the church because of their support for concubinage, based upon their interpretation of Swedenborg's *Conjugial Love*.[77] Some of these excluded members immediately formed a new society, The Universal Society for Promotion of the New Jerusalem Church, which produced its own constitution and had as one of its goals the publication of an accurate translation of *Conjugial Love*.[78] In 1790 the Society published a short-lived journal, *The New-Jerusalem Magazine*, which contained biographical information on Swedenborg, extracts from his works and letters, and articles proposing the establishment of a Swedenborgian colony on the coast of Africa where slaves would be emancipated. The magazine was discontinued after a year because of poor circulation.[79] Hindmarsh did not join this new society, but continued to attend meetings that were open to all. In 1792 he persuaded the landlord of the chapel at Eastcheap to make him the sole tenant, and then surprised his fellow Swedenborgians by announcing that they would be allowed to continue meeting there only if they followed his ideas. Most of them went elsewhere to meet, but Hindmarsh continued to hold small meetings in the Eastcheap Chapel, where he devised a grandiose scheme of government for the New Church. This was unsuccessful: Hindmarsh was said to be 'very willing to govern, but unfortunately there were very few disposed to be his subjects'.[80] He left the church and his printing business, and became a stockbroker, but did not prosper. In 1811, finding himself without occupation, Hindmarsh associated himself with an eccentric Swedenborgian minister in Manchester, William Cowherd, who aimed to set up a printing office.[81] When this venture failed, Hindmarsh, at the request of the Manchester Swedenborgians, became active again in the Swedenborgian priesthood, eventually becoming minister of a newly built church in Salford, Manchester. He published several books and soon regained his status within the New Church, being elected President of the General Conference from

1818-22.[82] William White, admittedly taking a partisan stance against the sectarian Swedenborgians, concluded that 'Of Swedenborg's higher philosophy, Hindmarsh had no appreciation—I might almost say, no knowledge'.[83]

Non-sectarian Swedenborgians were more willing than Hindmarsh to adopt Swedenborg's ideas within broader and more esoteric contexts. In this regard, the early members of the Theosophical Society are of particular interest. Whilst the early Swedenborgians in Lancashire came mainly from followers of William Law, in a subculture where spirit manifestations were still an active part of local folklore, those in London who developed an interest in Swedenborg were more likely to have had other interests within the broader framework of Western esotericism.

A popular esoteric pursuit amongst members of the Theosophical Society in London was animal magnetism, which had been introduced to them by John Benoit de Mainauduc. De Mainauduc was born in Ireland of French parents.[84] He was taught medicine by the renowned physicians William Hunter and John Hunter. These doctors had Swedenborgian and esoteric connections: William was a reader of Swedenborg, and John Hunter, a Fellow of the Royal Society, was a vitalist and an associate of Peter Woulfe, an alchemist whose extensive rooms 'were so filled with furnaces and apparatus that it was difficult to reach his fireside'.[85] De Mainauduc did not complete his medical training, but instead bought his medical degree.[86] He had learned mesmerism in Paris, though not from Mesmer, who in his view practised a debased form of the art because, in his drive to achieve scientific respectability, he had ignored its esoteric antecedents in Fludd, Kircher, Paracelsus and Swedenborg.[87] He regarded animal magnetism as a gift of nature that could be applied by everybody, without the need for professional training or social position.[88]

One of de Mainauduc's Theosophical Society pupils who achieved considerable prominence as a healer in his own right was Philippe-Jacques de Loutherbourg. Born in Strasbourg, he came to in England in 1771 at the age of 30, and eventually became a naturalized citizen. He was an artist who was a member of William Blake's circle, and he also produced stage sets, including those at Drury Lane.[89] He painted numerous watercolours illustrating the teaching of his friend, the Masonic magus Alessandro di Cagliostro, and in his work *The Ascent of Elijah* (1814-15) he described Cagliostro ascending to heaven in a chariot covered with Masonic symbols.[90] De Loutherbourg learned animal magnetism from de Mainauduc in the 1780s.[91] He developed his own system of spiritual healing based on mesmerism and in 1789 opened a clinic at his home in Hammersmith in London which became enormously popular. Large crowds gathered outside his house on 'healing days' and he was reputed to cure all manner of ills, including serious physical illnesses and insanity caused by spirit possession.[92] Before taking up mesmerism, de Loutherbourg had been involved with practical alchemy, until his wife grew tired of his activities, wrecked his crucibles, and ejected from the house his associate, described as 'a *Charlatan*, from the Lower Rhine'.[93]

Alchemy was practised more generally by Society members. There is evidence that John Augustus Tulk, a prominent member of the Society, was an alchemist. Tulk was a man of inherited wealth who owned property in prime parts of London. In 1806 he published anonymously a translation from the French of an alchemical work, *The Testament of Nicholas Flamel*.[94] Marsha Keith Schuchard has determined that the annotations made by Tulk in his author's copy of this book demonstrate that he was a practising alchemist.[95] Tulk was intrigued by the ancient Jewish religious work, the Book of Enoch, extracts from which had been published in the Swedenborgian journal *The Intellectual Repository* in 1812-13.[96] He believed that Enoch was Hermes Trismegistus.[97] Also involved with alchemy and mesmerism was General Charles R Rainsford. Rainsford was a soldier who later in life became a Member of Parliament. In the course of his travels in the military, he collected and copied many esoteric manuscripts and joined several Masonic lodges and other esoteric organizations. His surviving papers reveal a strong interest in alchemy, Kabbalah and magic.[98] Like other Theosophical Society members, Rainsford learned animal magnetism from de Mainauduc.[99]

Another Theosophical Society member known to have been taught mesmerism by de Mainauduc was Freemason Benedict Chastanier.[100] After serving as an assistant to de Mainauduc, Chastanier himself became a teacher of animal magnetism.[101] Like many other Swedenborgians, he believed that Swedenborg was the true discoverer of animal magnetism, which he thought offered the possibility of the transmutation of nature to its original purity. Chastanier was also described by a contemporary as being 'in the practice of alchemy'.[102] Trained as a physician in Paris, Chastanier finally settled in England in 1773, having made several previous unsuccessful attempts to set up a medical practice in England. On one of those earlier visits in 1765, Chastanier had a spiritual experience that had a major impact on him, when he dreamed of an encounter with Christ. He became interested in the Kabbalah and studied the works of Boehme and Law. Friends arranged for him to visit the elderly Swedenborg, but it seems that he was not able to go.[103] He read extracts of Swedenborg's *Arcana Caelestia* in 1768, without knowing that the author was Swedenborg because the publication was anonymous. He became aware of the true authorship in 1776 when Hartley's translation of Swedenborg's *Theosophic Lucubration on the Nature of Influx* was recommended to him by one of London's occult booksellers.[104] In the same year, eight years before the foundation of the Theosophical Society in London, Chastanier was instrumental together with other Masons in setting up the London Universal Society with the aim of promoting Swedenborg's works.[105] Schuchard asserts that the Theosophical Society was not a separate society, but rather the publishing arm of the Universal Society, which preferred to keep a low profile at that time.[106]

Chastanier's Universal Society has been described as 'a pervading influence on the reception of Swedenborg in London, during the 1780s'.[107] The London Swedenborgians attracted many visitors from mainland Europe during the 1780s, including the Italian Freemason and magus Alessandro di Cagliostro and French Freemason and Illuminist Louis-Claude de Saint-Martin.[108]

Although mesmerism and alchemy were pursued enthusiastically by the early members of the Theosophical Society, these interests waned as the group became increasingly sectarian in outlook. After joining the ranks of the New Church, Chastanier gave up mesmerism, denouncing it as 'the science of the abyss'.[109] However, he does not appear to have given up his belief in communication with spirits; in 1791 he published *Emanuel Swedenborg's New Year's Gift to his Readers* which he claimed was dictated by the spirit of Swedenborg.[110] A Society member who was initially interested in mesmerism, but then (like most sectarian Swedenborgians) rejected it, was Dr William Spence. In his *Essays in Divinity and Physic*, published by Robert Hindmarsh in 1792, Spence describes animal magnetism as 'animal magicism'. He said that people who carry out these 'magical tricks' do not realize that their phenomena are caused by malign spirits,[111] pointing out that the risks of spirit contact had been described by Swedenborg. Spence was also an advocate of the therapeutic merits of 'conjugial love'. He claimed to have advised the physicians attending King George III during his period of insanity, after their heroic attempts at treatment with blisters, which 'generally irritate and inflame the disease', had failed. He suggested that the King should return to conjugial love with his wife. 'I heard soon after, that Her Majesty was again admitted into her royal consort's company... the event is known to have proven my expectations'.[112] He also described the case of a nobleman who was cured of his insanity when 'during a lucid interval' a young lady 'had the courage to accept his hand honourably'.[113] It is plain that Spence encouraged only lawful and respectable 'conjugial love'; he was not amongst those excluded from the Theosophical Society because of their support for concubinage.

Many members of the Theosophical Society also attended meetings organized by Jacob Duché. Duché was an Anglican clergyman from Philadelphia who had studied theology in England at Cambridge. After writing to George Washington advising him to rescind the Declaration of Independence, he found himself to be no longer welcome in America, and he came to England in 1778.[114] In London, he contacted a group of mystical Christians who followed Jacob Boehme and William Law, led by John Payne.[115] He was appointed Chaplain to the Asylum for Female Orphans in 1782. Duché began following Swedenborg openly in 1785, but he remained an Anglican minister and so never joined the sectarian Swedenborgians.[116] He held well-attended services at the Orphan's Asylum, and on Sundays he held evening meetings in his apartment at the Orphan's Asylum, at which Swedenborg's works were read.[117]

In the London of the 1780s there were thus three groups that were promoting Swedenborg: the quasi-Masonic London Universal Society that had been formed in 1776; the Theosophical Society founded in 1784 which became sectarian in 1787; and Duché's group which formed around 1785 but was never a formal society. There was considerable overlap in both aims and membership between these groups. In view of the international connections of many of the members of these groups, and the growth of Swedenborgian groups in mainland Europe at that time, it is not surprising that there were significant cross-channel exchanges and collaborations.

Swedenborgians in Europe

The most important of the Swedenborgian groups in mainland Europe was the Illuminés d'Avignon. This group was originally established in Berlin in 1779 and led by Dom Antoine Pernety, who was joined by Count Tadeusz Grabianka.[118] Their initial focus was on alchemical experiments.[119] Pernety was a high-ranking Mason who had published alchemical interpretations of Greek and Ancient Egyptian mythology, and who had developed a strong enthusiasm for Swedenborg shortly before founding the society.[120] 'Count' Grabianka (a very wealthy nobleman, but not a count) was born in Poland in 1740. He had studied alchemy and other esoteric arts before joining Pernety's circle in 1778, and as a result of his influence the group developed the millennial belief that they would be the vanguard of 'the new reign of Jesus Christ on the earth'.[121] Pernety's group arrived in Avignon in 1785, having moved on the instruction of their oracle, 'La Sainte Parole' ('The Holy Word'). Grabianka first travelled through Western Europe in an attempt to gather support for an international network of like-minded societies.[122] Grabianka's travels included a long stay in London during 1785-6. On arriving in London he immediately contacted Chastanier and told him that La Sainte Parole had advised the Avignon group to follow Swedenborg, saying 'Have not I declared these things to my servant, Emanuel Swedenborg? follow ye him'.[123] Grabianka knew Chastanier because in the previous year they had both been delegates at the Congress du Philalèthes (an international congress of esoteric Masons) in Paris, together with General Rainsford, the Marquis de Thomé and William Bousie (an Englishman living in Paris).[124] Grabianka was accepted with enthusiasm into the Swedenborgian groups in London. Hindmarsh noted that Grabianka 'wonderfully succeeded in gaining the good opinion of those with whom he conversed' and that he 'seemed to speak the very language of the New Church'.[125] However, Hindmarsh became mistrustful of him, suspecting that his visit was a ploy to convert Theosophical Society members to the Catholic faith, a suspicion that he regarded as confirmed when Grabianka told Society members that there is a fourth member of the Trinity, the

Virgin Mary, with whom the Avignon group was in communication.[126] Towards the end of 1786, Grabianka returned to Avignon, 'after taking a most affectionate leave of the Society assembled at Mr. Duché's'.[127] Shortly afterwards Grabianka and five other members of the Avignon group wrote to the London Society to tell them that their group had been formed by Jesus Christ himself, and they had learned that 'the angel that stands before the face of the Lamb, is already sent to sound his trumpet on the Mountains of Babylon, and give notice to the nations that the God of heaven will soon come to the gates of the earth...and to manifest his power and glory'.[128] They sought to gather together into an international society all those who were 'elevated and directed by the love of truth'.[129] There was no corporate response from the London Society, but several individual members, including General Rainsford, maintained contact with the Avignon group, despite the fact that Chastanier (who by this time had become a member of the sectarian New Church) had warned Rainsford against it, saying that their beliefs were 'as far from the principles of Swedenborg as the Orient is from the Occident'.[130] Duché also had some ongoing connection with the Avignon group: his son Thomas, a talented artist, toured the continental occult societies in 1788, shortly before he died at a young age.[131]

The Avignon group attracted great interest amongst English mystics who were not followers of Swedenborg. Two of these individuals, artisans William Bryan and John Wright, published accounts of their experiences.[132] They heard of the Avignon Society from members of the Theosophical Society (though they were not themselves members of the Theosophical Society).[133] Bryan was a practitioner of animal magnetism who believed that he had occult powers that would enable him, if he so willed it, to demolish any obstacle in his path simply by blowing on it.[134] He was regarded as a healer 'with a sort of half-physical and half-miraculous power of curing diseases, and imparting the thoughts or sympathies of distant friends'.[135] The two men, leaving their families in distress, travelled to Avignon, where, after much hardship, they arrived and were initiated into the Society, with whom they stayed for seven months. Wright described some of his experiences within the group, including a climb to the top of a hill where he saw the angel Raphael, and spirit manifestations resulting in furniture shaking 'as though it was all coming to pieces'.[136]

Another European society that had close links with the Theosophical Society was the Exegetic and Philanthropic Society, which was formed in Stockholm in 1786 by Carl F Nordenskiöld and Carl B Wadström with the stated aim of translating Swedenborg's works into several languages.[137] Nordenskiöld and Wadström had both been early members of the Theosophical Society.[138] They developed a plan, never to be fulfilled, to establish a Swedenborgian colony for emancipated slaves on the west coast of Africa.[139] They became much involved with mesmerism as a means of communicating with the spirit world. This move towards esoteric practices was given further momentum by Theosophical Society members who were also involved with the Avignon group, including the Marquis de Thomé, General Rainsford and Abbé Pernety.[140] In June 1787 the Exegetic and Philanthropic Society in Stockholm sent a letter addressed to the Societé des Amis Réunis in Strasbourg, and other similar groups, in which they proposed that these groups should join together in promoting spirit contact through somnambulists after 'the power of Magnetism has produced a partial cessation of the functions of the soul'.[141] This could be used in the treatment of disease, in which the malevolent spirits causing the illness could be dislodged by means of the influx of good spirits encouraged by the magnetizer, who must first be in good moral condition himself. Somnambulism was seen as confirmation of Swedenborg's revelations and as a promise of a new age of enlightenment. This proposal was rejected by the Strasbourg group who had developed their own paradigm for magnetic cure which depended on psychological mechanisms rather than the intervention of spirits.

Even though the Theosophical Society was a hotbed of esoteric activity in its early days, these interests were increasingly discouraged. There are two major reasons for this. Firstly, the sectarians were deeply suspicious of the esoteric arts, believing that they were contrary to the writings of Swedenborg. Secondly, the events of the French Revolution led to a deep suspicion and suppression of all esoteric pursuits, and of the organizations that promoted them.[142] Swedenborgians were viewed with suspicion from the late 1780s, though they were generally considered to be harmless: in the words of one contemporary commentator, 'Let men enjoy their *influxes*: let them converse with their *angels*. . . If they suffer us to sleep in peace, let them dream on'.[143] Tim Fulford has emphasized the political dimension of mesmerism in the 1790s, when it was regarded by conservative thinkers as being radically subversive, attacking the established institutions such as medicine, social class and gender divisions, the church and government. The French Revolution was seen as having resulted from a Masonic conspiracy involving magnetizers and other practitioners of the esoteric arts, and it was believed that the same influences could promote revolution in England.[144] Such anti-esoteric ideas combined with conspiracy theories were promoted by three significant books: *History of Jacobinism* (1797) by Abbé Barruel, a French Jesuit priest who fled to England during the French Revolution; *Proofs of a Conspiracy* (1798) by John Robison, Professor of Natural Philosophy in Edinburgh; and *Proof of the Illuminati* (1802) by Seth Payson, a Congregational pastor from New Hampshire.[145] Barruel declared that 'All the *Theosophical Illuminees* of this age in England, France, Sweden, or Germany, have drawn their principles from the *Baron Emmanuel Swedenborg*'.[146] Furthermore, 'they daily expect that great revolution which is to sweep from the earth every prince and every king'.[147] Robison similarly claimed that German Masonry was 'much disturbed by the mystical whims of J. Behmen and Swedenborg—by the fanatical and knavish doctrines of the modern Rosycrucians—by Magicians—Magnetisers—Exorcists &c'.[148] The belief that the Masonic Illuminati were directly responsible for the French Revolution was reiterated by Seth Payson in America, with a grave warning that these groups, thought by many to be defunct, were still active at the start of the nineteenth century and had spread to America.[149] Some individual followers of Swedenborg, including Carl Nordenskiöld and Carl Wadström, openly supported the French Revolution; Nordenskiöld translated Thomas Paine's *Rights of Man* into Swedish.[150] Followers of Swedenborg at this time commonly saw a relationship between his writings and the revolutionary politics of Paine, who was a prominent supporter of the French Revolution, but the sectarian New Church affirmed its opposition to the Revolution.[151]

The Sibly brothers and the wider esoteric context in late eighteenth-century England
Although many followers of Swedenborg towards the end of the eighteenth century believed that his philosophical system provided a unifying framework within which occult pursuits such as mesmerism and spirit contact could be subsumed, this was

only one part of the spectrum of esoteric activity that thrived in London at that time. The overlap between Swedenborgian esotericism and the wider occult context is well illustrated by the example of the Sibly brothers, Manoah (1757-1840) and Ebenezer (1751-99).

Manoah Sibly first became aware of Swedenborg's doctrines in 1787. He joined the Theosophical Society and was ordained into the New Church in 1790.[152] A professional astrologer himself, in 1789 he published a translation of *Tabulae Primi Mobilis* (1657) by Placido de Titi, under the title of *Astronomy and Elementary Philosophy*.[153] In the introduction, Sibly says that this volume contains 'all that is useful and necessary to form an adept in the Sidereal Mysteries'.[154] Manoah's brother Ebenezer was a Swedenborgian sympathizer but never joined any of the associated societies. Like his brother he wrote on astrology, publishing *A New and Complete Illustration of the Celestial Science of Astrology* (1784-8). However, his esoteric interests were much wider than this. He was a vitalist physician and was deeply involved with Hermetic and Paracelsian approaches to medical practice. He was a student of alchemy and natural magic, a Freemason, and a member of the Harmonic Society of Paris that had been established in 1783 to study mesmerism. His *Key to Physic* was published together with a new edition of *Culpeper's English Physician; and Complete Herbal* that he had revised. Though his *Key to Physic* ran into five editions which spanned the late eighteenth and early nineteenth centuries, he has been largely ignored by historians of esoteric medicine.[155] Ebenezer Sibly also wrote on magic and it is here that his interest in Swedenborg becomes manifest. His work *A New and Complete Illustration of the Celestial Science of Astrology* is in four parts.[156] The first three parts relate to astrology, and the fourth to magic, with particular emphasis on the conjuration of spirits. He contrasts astrology, which he regards as an entirely natural way of making predictions based on influences from the stars, with magic that involves intercourse with spirits, which is diabolical. Part four begins with a long and detailed exposition of Swedenborgian doctrine relating to the spirit world. He then moves to the classification of the spirits that he says are used by the magi. These include: angels and demons; the souls of the dead; astral spirits that are temporal and live in nature; igneous spirits and metallic spirits that live in volcanoes and the earth; ghosts and apparitions; and the seven guardian spirits of humanity with their antithetical malign demons, all of which he names. Magicians, he says, can invoke only the malign and earthbound spirits, and never the angels or righteous spirits from heaven. They commonly delude themselves that they can protect themselves against any malign influences from the spirits that they conjure, and some, such as John Dee, believed wrongly that they could converse with angels. Whilst cautioning against such practices, he offers information, in some cases quite detailed, about procedures for the invocation of spirits. Sibly's account demonstrates well the tension between the practice of invoking spirits and the belief of many Swedenborgians that it is wrong and dangerous to do so.

Ebenezer Sibly had contact with at least one other prominent follower of Swedenborg, General Rainsford. They were members of the same Masonic lodge, and both men were in the circle of an alchemist, possibly Scandinavian, called Sigismund Bacstrom, whom Adam McLean describes as 'one of the most important scholars of alchemy in the last few centuries'.[157] Bacstrom was initiated into the Societas Roseae Crucis by comte Louis de Chazal on the island of Mauritius on 12 September 1794. He led an esoteric group in London who were carrying out alchemical work at the end of the eighteenth and beginning of the nineteenth centuries.[158]

Manoah Sibly was the proprietor of an occult bookshop of the type that proliferated in London towards the end of the eighteenth century.[159] One of the best known of these bookshops was that of John Denley. Denley appears as 'D——' in the introduction to *Zanoni* by Edward Bulwer-Lytton.[160] Bulwer-Lytton describes the bookshop as having 'the most notable collection, ever amassed by an enthusiast, of the works of Alchemist, Cabalist, and Astrologer'.[161] Bulwer-Lytton had esoteric interests and became involved in mesmerism and spiritualism in the mid-nineteenth century.[162] His book *Zanoni* purported to be based on a ciphered manuscript obtained from an elderly man in Denley's bookshop. Other patrons of Denley included astrologer Robert Cross Smith and Samuel Taylor Coleridge.[163]

One associate of Denley who was particularly important in the history of esotericism in England was Francis Barrett, who published *The Magus, or Celestial Intelligencer* in 1801. This book was based on material from the library of Ebenezer Sibly, part of which had been acquired by Denley after Sibly's death.[164] *The Magus* is known particularly for its colour plates of invoked demons. Barrett was one of the few people in England who continued to write openly about such topics, which were still viewed with suspicion in the early nineteenth century in the aftermath of the French Revolution.[165] It has been suggested that *The Magus* was based entirely on the works of Agrippa, but this view has been disputed.[166] *The Magus* was a significant influence on magicians later in the nineteenth century and it is still used as a sourcebook today.[167]

Having touched on the wider esoteric context in England of the late eighteenth and early nineteenth centuries, we can now return to the more specifically Swedenborgian aspects. Although esoteric pursuits amongst the English followers of Swedenborg did not become prominent again until the mid-nineteenth century, the era of Garth Wilkinson, there were important currents of Swedenborg-related esotericism even during this relatively fallow period. An important vehicle for this was Charles Augustus Tulk.

Charles Augustus Tulk (1786-1849)

Whilst esoteric pursuits such as alchemy and spirit invocation were regarded as highly suspect in the wake of the French Revolution, the esoteric tradition found expression in the arts, through such people as Samuel Taylor Coleridge and William Blake. A leading Swedenborgian who played an important role in this transmission through his support and sponsorship was Charles Augustus Tulk, the son of John Augustus Tulk.

Charles Augustus Tulk was born into a very wealthy family which had inherited valuable property in central London. His father had been a member of Hindmarsh's reading group and was a founder member of the New Church.[168] Clearly his father was a major influence on the young Charles Augustus, but we have little information about other formative influences. We know that John Clowes was a mentor to Tulk. Clowes and the young Charles Augustus Tulk first met at the Hawkstone meeting of non-separatist Swedenborgians in 1813, when Clowes invited Tulk to preside, an invitation that was taken up in the following year. Before that time Clowes knew John Augustus Tulk, the father of Charles Augustus, but it is evident that the younger Tulk was still a stranger when he was first invited to Hawkstone.[169]

It has been suggested that Benedict Chastanier was a family friend of the Tulks. [170]
In view of the idealist interpretation of Swedenborg that Charles Augustus Tulk would
later develop, it is of interest that Chastanier has also been credited with entertaining
such views, saying that:

> thought alone is the real, the truly living...The qualities we deem essential
> to matter...may really be non-existent, and matter may be quite other than
> we think it is...Matter is true only for matter; pure spirit needs it not...it
> is the corrupted spiritual which has sought after what is material and has
> vitiated it. [171]

Tulk met Coleridge in 1817, shortly after the publication of his *Biographia
Literaria*, when both men were staying at the seaside town of Littlehampton. [172] Tulk
introduced Coleridge to Swedenborg's works by 1819 and Coleridge went on to read
at least eleven of Swedenborg's volumes. [173]

The influence of Friedrich Wilhelm Joseph Schelling on Coleridge is well recognized, and Coleridge believed that Swedenborg's works foreshadowed 'much of
what is most valuable in the physiosophic works of Schelling'. [174] A detailed analysis
of Swedenborg's influence on Schelling has been developed by the German scholar
Friedemann Horn. [175] This influence is especially apparent in two works that were not
published until after Schelling's death: *Clara*, which was written in 1816-17; and the
Stuttgart Lectures, which were originally delivered in 1810. In *Clara*, Swedenborg is
mentioned directly several times, including a reference to 'the Swedish visionary', who
'must have had his inner being opened...so that he could look into that world'. [176] In
his *Stuttgart Lectures*, Schelling used the principle of correspondences to account for
the relationship between nature and the spirit world, remarking that 'as the world of
spirits overall is bound to nature by means of a necessary *consensus harmonicus*,
so too are the individual objects of the spiritual and the natural worlds'. [177]

Coleridge regarded Tulk's philosophy as compatible with his own:
If I mistake not, one formula would comprise your philosophical faith &

mine——namely, that the sensible World is but the evolution of the Truth,
Love, and Life, or their opposites, in Man . . . [178]

The two men maintained a close friendship, with frequent correspondence and visits.
Their interests extended beyond the philosophical; they campaigned together for improv-
ing working hours and conditions for children in cotton factories. [179] Despite Coleridge's
great interest in Swedenborg's philosophy, he maintained many reservations. Perhaps
fearing that he would become identified with the sectarian Swedenborgians, Coleridge
rarely mentioned Swedenborg positively except in his letters to Tulk. [180]

Mainstream Swedenborgians regarded Tulk as an idealist who was under the
influence of Coleridge, Berkeley and the German philosophers:

> Till after the year 1817, this gentleman [Tulk] held the doctrines of the New
> Church in the same manner as they are held by the readers of Swedenborg
> in general . . . [but then he made] the acquaintance of a celebrated writer
> [Coleridge], well known as the most popular advocate, in this country, of
> the German philosophy,——of the doctrines of Kant, Fichté, and Schelling . . .
> From this time he began to instance Malebranche and Berkeley . . . as writers
> who in some points were superior to Swedenborg. [181]

Given Coleridge's comment about the similarity of Tulk's philosophy to his own, it is
unfair to suggest that Tulk's ideas had originated from his meeting with Coleridge.
Tulk also denied any familiarity with German philosophy, saying that 'From the little
I know of the idealism of Fichte, it is very far from the spiritualism of Swedenborg.
Of Schelling and Hegel I know as little, and that not directly from their works'. [182] It
is easy, though, to understand why Tulk was regarded as an idealist, when we read
him saying that:

> So powerful is the domination of natural thought . . . that few persons
> will believe, what nevertheless is the truth, that all natural forms are
> conceived and brought forth into the plane of the sentient faculties by

spheres of thought and affection…Even the fixed laws of nature which so forcibly impress the natural mind with the absolute externeity of sensuous forms, are correspondential effects which represent our natural modes of thinking. [183]

Tulk's essential thesis was that the natural world is mediated through the mind of man, and therefore the state of nature depends upon the spiritual state of man. This relates not only to individuals, but to humanity in general, because the natural world is a compound of all human minds:

Though every sentient mind contributes its portion, it is not a separate portion. It is linked together and blended with the sensations of others, producing the appearance of a Place which we share in common with others. To the sphericity of the Earth, every human being, thinking in the same Natural Plane, contributes. [184]

Each level of the natural world, said Tulk, relates to a particular level of the human mind. For example, at the lowest level:

The mineral kingdom is created by an influx of the divine life into the sentient faculties, and is the representative image of the foundation on which all human consciousness rests. That foundation is the love of self. [185]

Human minds can be regarded as 'a multitude of mental spheres' that operate in different ways and on different levels but are linked by their affinities, and which in sum '[produce] to the senses a planetary body, on which such connected forms of thought and affection representatively live'. [186] Tulk saw this as analogous to the 'relation of the planets to their central sun, and to one another'. In this formulation, miracles do not offend the laws of nature because there are no such laws; nature behaves in a manner that corresponds to the minds of those who generate it. Apparent miracles simply reflect a mental paradigm shift.

This formulation became known as 'Tulkism', and it was rejected by mainstream Swedenborgians. However, to the end of his life Tulk insisted that he was misunderstood, and that he was not an idealist. In response to criticism in the Swedenborgian journal *The Intellectual Repository*, he wrote 'I am neither an *Idealist* on the one hand, nor a *Naturalist* or *Materialist* on the other; but that I am, what Swedenborg has taught me to be, a SPIRITUALIST'.[187]

It is plain that Tulk's concept of spiritualism here differs from that which is usually understood today. His position was that the sensual world is a reflection of the absolute reality that stems from God, mediated by spiritual influx from the Divine Human into the human psyche, the state of which determines the final outcome:

> there is not a single object in nature...that does not correspond as an effect with some condition of the human will and understanding, which mental condition is the mediatory cause of its production, and without which it could not be brought into existence.[188]

For Tulk, the only true reality is spiritual, which means that the natural world cannot be considered as real. He supports this position by citing Swedenborg:

> It has been said more than once in the works of this incomparable writer [Swedenborg], that the Spiritual World...is *real*, and that comparatively the natural world is *not real*. This is said of the natural world, notwithstanding its materiality, its fixed space, and the regular march of its seasons, its days and hours.[189]

In his later work, Tulk emphasizes that he uses the words *real* and *unreal* 'in a very different sense from that which is usually given to them in relation to this world'.[190] In Tulk's system, the only true reality is the ultimate cause which is spiritual, whereas the natural, material world is a reflection or image of that reality. He points out the contrast between this and natural modes of thinking, in which matter is believed to be the source of nature and of man, and the natural world, which is outside us objectively, is perceived by our external senses.

Followers of Swedenborg took exception to the idealist concept that the material world has no separate objective existence, a philosophy that is commonly attributed to Berkeley.[191] Tulk regarded Berkeley's philosophy as having been on the right lines, although 'a rude, unfinished truth'.[192]

Such was the antipathy between Tulk and the mainstream Swedenborgians that there were vitriolic exchanges between them in the pages of New Church publications. He was accused of heresy and duplicity. He in turn accused his detractors of taking a 'sensual and debased view of the subject', and to have gone no further in their understanding than 'a refined naturalism', without understanding 'even the elements of spiritual truth'.[193] Tulk took the view that Swedenborg, although divinely inspired, was still human and therefore fallible, and that greater spiritual understanding could be reached by reading the idealist philosophers in addition to Swedenborg. Still, he maintained that his ideas were entirely compatible with those of Swedenborg, and that apparent discrepancies were due to inadequate translations of Swedenborg from the original Latin. This stung his friend Clowes, who had done most of the previous translations, into writing to *The Intellectual Repository* to defend his work, declaring that 'the doctrine of the New Church, and the doctrine of Mr. T[ulk], are as opposite to each other as light and darkness'.[194] Tulk's case was not helped when it was discovered that he had written multiple articles in support of his position, using a variety of pseudonyms.[195] However, opposition to Tulk's views also had political undertones. Tulk's interpretation of Swedenborg was adopted enthusiastically in the mid-nineteenth century by American intellectuals including Ralph Waldo Emerson; a review of Tulk's *Spiritual Christianity* in *The Massachusetts Quarterly Review*, which at that time was co-edited by Emerson, declared that 'So far as we are aware none of the professed disciples of Swedenborg, with the exception of Mr. Charles Augustus Tulk, has attempted a rational reproduction of his theology'. This article, which was highlighted in the English Swedenborgian publication *The Intellectual Repository*, incensed mainstream English Swedenborgians and reinforced their rejection of Tulk's philosophy.[196]

Although it was widely condemned, Tulkism remained a significant force in Swedenborgian thought that surfaced at intervals throughout the nineteenth century in New Church periodicals. Certainly Tulk's philosophy influenced his protégé, the young Garth Wilkinson, although Wilkinson would later reject Tulk's formulation as he understood it, along with all other derivatives of idealism.

Tulk found his philosophy to be compatible with that of William Blake. Blake followed an idealist philosophy, saying for example that 'Mental Things alone are Real; what is call'd Corporeal, Nobody knows of its Dwelling Place: it is in Fallacy, & its Existence an Imposture. Where is the Existence Out of Mind or Thought? Where is it but in the Mind of a Fool?' [197] It has been observed that Blake's philosophy embraced a *prisca theologia* which held that 'the universe is an organic, vital, evolving whole, and that humans, having been made in God's image, are to use their imagination to help restore the post-lapsarian world to its original perfection, through the exercise of their intellect and imagination'. [198] Kathleen Raine, who has explored the spiritual meaning of Blake's enigmatic works, regards him as following in the tradition of the 'excluded knowledge' of the Western esoteric tradition. Blake named Swedenborg, Paracelsus and Jacob Boehme as his teachers, and he was much influenced by Berkeleyan philosophy. [199]

Tulk and William Blake

William Blake was born in London in 1757. He experienced visions of angels during childhood and, according to his friend Henry Crabb Robinson, was in 'constant intercourse with the world of spirits' during his adult life. [200] He received little formal education, being taught at home by his mother, after which he was apprenticed as an engraver before attending the Royal Academy, where he made an important and enduring friendship with his fellow-student John Flaxman, who became the first Professor of Sculpture at the Royal Academy, as well as a prominent Swedenborgian. [201]

Blake's engagement with Swedenborg's philosophy fluctuated considerably during his lifetime. [202] In the late 1780s he was an avid, though critical, student of Swedenborg. In 1789 he attended the First General Conference of the New Church, organized by the sectarian Swedenborgians, in the company of Tulk's parents, Charles Augustus being only two years old at the time. [203] Blake soon became disenchanted with the behaviour of the sectarian Swedenborgians, particularly when they sought to rid their organization of people whose interpretation of Swedenborg encouraged the practice of concubinage, as well as those who practised somnambulism and spirit contact.[204] Blake also supported the French Revolution, which would have put him in sympathy with some of the expelled Swedenborgians including Augustus Nordenskiöld and Carl Wadström.[205]

Blake's *The Marriage of Heaven and Hell*, which was critical of the notion that Swedenborg had been uniquely divinely ordained (a fundamental tenet of the sectarian Swedenborgians), was written following the rift between sectarian and non-sectarian Swedenborgians.[206] This is one of the best known of Blake's books, and it contributed much to the notion that he emphatically rejected Swedenborg's teachings. It is true that for the next decade he showed little interest in or even hostility towards Swedenborg's teachings, but from 1800, Swedenborgian concepts became pervasive in Blake's works.[207] According to Garth Wilkinson:

> Blake informed Tulk that he had two different states; one in which he liked
> Swedenborg's writings, and one in which he disliked them. The second
> was a state of pride in himself, and then they were distasteful to him, but
> afterwards he knew that he had not been wise and sane. The first was a state
> of humility, in which he received and accepted Swedenborg.[208]

This was a significant statement for Blake to make, if we consider his view (following that of Swedenborg) that the realm of the self is Satan, whereas heaven is the internal Divine Human of the imagination.[209]

Kathleen Raine has discussed the strong influence of Swedenborg on some of Blake's later works.[210] In *Milton*, Blake refers to Swedenborg as 'the strongest of men' but (no doubt with reference to the sectarian Swedenborgians) 'a Samson shorn by the Churches'.[211] Blake held Swedenborg's concept of the Divine Human as the template for the macrocosm of creation and in whose image every human microcosm is created. He equated the Divine Human and the human imagination, which contains all things, in the manner of Corbin's *mundus imaginalis*.[212] He said that:

> The world of Imagination is the world of Eternity... There Exist in that
> Eternal World the Permanent Realities of Every Thing which we see reflect-
> ed in this Vegetable Glass of Nature. All things are comprehended in their
> Eternal Forms in the divine body of the Saviour, the True Vine of Eternity,
> the Human Imagination... [213]

In Blake's system, the Divine Human is no longer the logical, scientific and rather concrete figure described by Swedenborg, but instead becomes a living, dynamic person that is the human imagination. Blake took a radical step beyond Tulk by saying that the human imagination *is* God, not just an intermediary between God and nature as proposed by Tulk. Nevertheless, there is a clear resonance between the ideas of Blake and Tulk. Both men believed that interpretation of the Scriptures could be achieved only from a spiritual perspective, and not from a natural mental set which was the state of humanity in general; as Blake put it, 'Both read the Bible day and night, But thou reads't black where I read white'.[214] Blake communicated through myth and symbol derived from the esoteric traditions.[215] Robert Rix points to Blake's use of references to animal magnetism, as well as anatomical symbolism after the style of Swedenborg.[216] Thus, Blake refers to 'Bowlahoola', which is 'the Stomach in every individual man' which extends also to the heart and the lungs, and 'Allemanda', which is the nervous system through which other realities can be contacted. 'Were it not for Bowlahoola & Allemanda... [there would be] no Human Form but only a Fibrous Vegetation'. 'In Bowlahoola Los's Anvils stand & his Furnaces rage... The Bellows are the Animal Lungs: the Hammers the Animal Heart/ The Furnaces the Stomach for digestion'.[217]

Charles Augustus Tulk met Blake through their mutual friend John Flaxman. Flaxman had been to meetings of the Theosophical Society and was for a short time a member of the sectarian New Church, but he left in 1799, dismayed by the internal squabbling in the sect, although he remained committed to Swedenborg's philosophy. In 1810 John and Charles Augustus Tulk and Flaxman were founder members of The Society for Printing and Publishing the Writings of the Hon. Emanuel Swedenborg, which in 1855 became the Swedenborg Society. Flaxman became a close family friend of the Tulks.[218] By 1816, Flaxman had introduced

Blake to Tulk, who first bought one of Blake's drawings in that year, though not without an argument between them about payment. Tulk's financial patronage then continued until Blake's death.[219] As Blake was virtually unknown outside of his own immediate circle during his lifetime, it was suggested later by Tulk's daughter that this patronage 'rescued [the Blakes] from destitution'.[220] In 1825 Tulk published two of Blake's poems—'The Divine Image' and 'On Another's Sorrow'—in *The Dawn of Light, and Theological Inspector*, a Swedenborgian journal that he edited, although he did not name Blake as the author.[221] Tulk also published the first article on Blake, 'The Inventions of William Blake, painter and Poet', in the *London University Magazine* of 1830. This included discussion of Blake's concept of Albion, quotes from Blake's poems, and an extract from Blake's *Book of Thiel*.[222]

In 1818 Tulk lent his copy of Blake's *Songs of Innocence and Experience* to Coleridge.[223] After reading this, Coleridge wrote to Reverend H F Cary, that 'He [Blake] is a man of Genius—and I apprehend, a Swedenborgian—certainly, a mystic *emphatically*. You perhaps smile at *my* calling another Poet, a *Mystic*; but verily I am in the very mire of common-place common-sense compared with Mr. Blake'.[224] Tulk introduced Coleridge to Blake in late 1825 or early 1826. The two men seem to have been kindred spirits: in his article in the 1830 *London University Magazine*, Tulk said that 'Blake and Coleridge, when in company, seemed like congenial beings of another sphere, breathing for a while on our earth; which may easily be perceived from the similarity of thought pervading their works'.[225] It was through Tulk that Garth Wilkinson was introduced to Blake's works, and it was Wilkinson who published the first typeset edition of the *Songs of Innocence and Experience*, with a Swedenborgian preface, in 1838.[226]

Blake provides an illustration of the close association between non-sectarian Swedenborgianism and other aspects of Western esotericism. He was a close friend of the artist John Varley. Varley was one of the foremost astrologers of his day. Between 1819 and 1820 the two men collaborated in a spiritual research project, in which Blake would draw portraits of spirits as they appeared to him, and Varley would construct a zodiacal interpretation based upon the moment when the apparition appeared to Blake.[227] These were mostly deceased historical or mythical figures such as 'The Man who Built the Pyramids' and 'Cassibelane the British Chief' who fought against Caesar. Varley had an interest in 'zodiacal physiognomy' by means of which, he believed, facial features can be related to the zodiacal ascendant at the time of birth. He published a book on this subject in 1828, entitled *A Treatise on Zodiacal Physiognomy, illustrated with engravings of heads and features, accompanied by tables of the time of the rising of the Twelve Signs of the Zodiac; and containing also new and astrological explanations of some remarkable portions of ancient mythological history.* [228] This enterprise illustrates not only an early application of what would now be called spiritualism, but also the two men's interest in ancient history and mythology which had been promoted by William Stukeley.

It is plain that it was quite acceptable for the early followers of Swedenborg in England, especially in northern England, to talk openly about their experiences of contact with spirits. Thomas Hartley, who knew Swedenborg personally, spoke with despair about the materialism of a world that had confined a woman whom he knew to a lunatic asylum because she claimed to converse with spirits. [229] The early Swedenborgians in London were involved in a variety of esoteric practices including alchemy and mesmerism, the latter used more for spiritual healing than for spirit contact. They were part of the network of practitioners of the esoteric arts within England as well as active participants in the international network of theosophical Illuminati. These activities were curtailed in the late 1780s, following the French Revolution and the formation of the Swedenborgian sectarian 'New Church' which became just another 'middle-class Protestant denomination' within which esoteric pursuits were outlawed. [230] Nevertheless, esoteric currents continued in Swedenborg's non-sectarian adherents, particularly Charles Augustus Tulk and his followers, as well as in those from the world of the arts, such as Samuel Taylor Coleridge and William Blake, whose esoteric belief systems were influenced by and concordant with those of Swedenborg as interpreted by Tulk. The scene was thus set for a resurgence of interest in mesmerism and spirit contact within the ranks of Swedenborg's followers when these movements became popular in Victorian England. The strong focus on healing amongst the early followers of Swedenborg also continued into the Victorian era, with interpretations of healing practices such as homoeopathy that took on a Swedenborgian flavour. The focus on democratization of institutions and support for revolutionary politics that characterized the early non-sectarian followers of Swedenborg also became manifest in the Victorian period. All of these trends are characterized in James John Garth Wilkinson, who was a translator of Swedenborg, publisher of Blake, spiritualist, mesmerist, homoeopath, and a supporter of the democratization of medicine and other anti-authoritarian social causes. Finally, an interest in ancient Egyptian and Greek legends as veiled esoteric revelations, a notion popular with the Illuminists and also forming a key part of the esoteric current in England through such figures as William Stukeley and William Blake, would resurface in Victorian England and was enthusiastically taken up by Wilkinson towards the end of his life. [231]

− 3 −

Early influences on Garth Wilkinson's thinking

*all the Choir of Heaven and Furniture of the Earth, in a word all those
Bodies which compose the mighty Frame of the World, have not any
Subsistence without [outside of] a Mind...*
George Berkeley, 1710[1]

*Thus metaphysics, after dreaming a while in Berkeleyism, became rambling
and delirious in Hume, and sank into confirmed idiocy or Cretinism in
Kant, who...endowed the monster with a power of propagating its kind, and
filling the world with a lineage of abominable inventions.*
Garth Wilkinson, 1847[2]

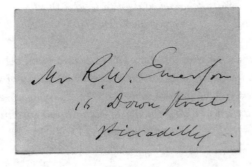

Fig. 3: Ralph Waldo Emerson's visiting card given to Wilkinson.
Swedenborg Society Archive, K/126.

W hat were the emotional and intellectual influences that led to Wilkinson being so well prepared to receive the doctrines of Swedenborg when he was introduced to them by George Robinson in 1833? In Swedenborg's works he could find a belief system that provided an answer to the neurotic fears about death and the afterlife which had troubled him when younger. Furthermore, Swedenborg was a scientist who declared that he had been catapulted into spiritual awareness immediately after making a close study of human anatomy and physiology. This must have deeply impressed the young Dr Wilkinson, fresh from his own medical studies. To cap it all, Swedenborg wrote his works in Latin, a language in which Wilkinson was adept.

Wilkinson's reading as a schoolboy would also have prepared him to understand and accept Swedenborg's philosophy. The youthful Wilkinson must have been moved by Milton's *Paradise Lost*; its sweeping portrayal of heaven, hell, Paradise and the Fall of Man presages his later interest in Swedenborgian theosophy.[3] The poetry of Sir William Jones carries a foretaste of Wilkinson's later involvement with idealist philosophy.[4] Jones is best known as a philologist who developed the concept of a primal Indo-European culture and language. He had a deep interest in ancient theologies and myths, particularly those from India.[5] His work, according to one scholar, 'stands in the hallowed tradition of *prisca theologia*'.[6] He regarded the idealist philosophy of George Berkeley as reflecting the philosophy expressed in ancient Sanskrit texts, and his poetry reflected this philosophy.[7] Finally, the influence of Wilkinson's future wife, Emma Anne Marsh, cannot be underestimated.[8] She was the governess at the house of his Swedenborgian uncle, and Wilkinson met her there in the same year that his uncle had introduced him to Swedenborg's works. They rapidly fell in love. The correspondence between Emma and Garth before they married shows an immediate common interest in Swedenborg. Such a strong emotional attachment to Emma could only have served to cement Wilkinson's interest in Swedenborg.

What was the philosophy that so inspired Garth Wilkinson for the rest of his life? Swedenborg wrote copiously, and there have been many attempts to summarize his works.

The philosophy of Emanuel Swedenborg (1688-1772)

Emanuel Swedenborg was born in Sweden in 1688, the son of a Lutheran priest in a well-to-do family.[9] After a university education, he travelled widely through England and Europe, in the manner usual for intellectually inclined young men from moneyed families. In England, he attended lectures by Isaac Newton and worked with John Flamsteed, the Astronomer Royal.[10] He then embarked on his own scientific career. In the first part of his life, Swedenborg became an internationally recognized scientist, publishing works on subjects including geology, mineralogy, astrology and engineering.[11]

In mid-life he turned to the study of the human body, with the specific goal of understanding the soul in whose image, he believed, the body is made. He was also concerned with the precise point of contact between the soul and the body. This question had occupied thinkers ever since Descartes conceptually separated the two and proposed that the pineal gland in the brain was the link between body and soul.[12] Swedenborg proposed instead that the intermediary between the material body and the soul is the *fluidum spirituosum* produced by the cells of the cerebral cortex of the brain.[13] At this stage of his thinking, Swedenborg clearly remained under the influence of Cartesian dualism, merely substituting the pineal gland with the *fluidum spirituosum* as the intermediary between the body and the soul.

At the age of 55, when completing his anatomical works, Swedenborg had visionary experiences following a period of vivid dreams which he recorded in a diary.[14]
After his visions, Swedenborg believed that he had access to the world of spirits and
angels, and that he was able to converse with them. He recorded discussions with
various philosophers, from Aristotle to Descartes, and was pleased to find either that
they had come round to his way of thinking, or that he could best them in debates.
This world was as real to him as the material one, and he regarded himself as living
simultaneously in two worlds. For Swedenborg, the truths that he learned after his
spiritual eye had been opened were as real as any other empirical observations. He
wrote many volumes of theological works based upon these revealed truths.

Swedenborg emphatically rejected the conventional Christian doctrine of a Trinity of
three persons, declaring that this was polytheism. Instead he proposed a unitary God in
whom the Father, the Son and the Holy Spirit are components.[15] Swedenborg's concept
of creation was that it begins with *Esse* (absolute Being) and *Existere* (coming into
existence). *Esse* is unknowable, and can only *be* when there is also *Existere*; therefore,
Esse and *Existere* are one, although 'distinctly', in that one necessarily follows the
other.[16] *Esse* and *Existere* constitute the Divine Human; here, they are represented as
divine love (*Esse*) and divine wisdom (*Existere*), which are the creative essences of the
whole cosmos. The cosmos is not created *ex nihilo*—nothing can be—and neither
was undifferentiated matter waiting somehow to be formed into the cosmos by God.
Rather, *Esse* is 'Substance in itself', and from this substance all things are originate.[17]

Within a Neoplatonic emanationist framework, Swedenborg developed a 'doctrine
of series and degrees' which is first described in detail in his *The Economy of the
Animal Kingdom* (1740-1).[18] According to this doctrine, the created world originates
in an undifferentiated formative substance from which everything else is formed in
a series of discrete degrees:

> There is a certain formative substance [*Substantia*] or force [*Vis
> formatrix*], that draws the thread from the first living point, and afterwards
> continues it to the last point of life. This is called by some the plastic force
> [*Vis plastica*], and the Archaeus; by others, simply nature in action.[19]

Here, Swedenborg is applying Aristotelian hylomorphism which proposes that ulti-mately form and matter do not exist independently except as mental constructs; the highest matter is only potentiality whereas form is its actuality: form *is* the substance of a thing.[20] Martin Lamm has suggested that Swedenborg's usage of terms such as *Archaeus* and *Vis plastica* indicates his familiarity with sources from the Western esoteric tradition, such as Paracelsus, Joan Baptista van Helmont, and the Cambridge Platonists Ralph Cudworth and Henry More. In contrast, Inge Jonsson has observed that Swedenborg could have obtained all the necessary concepts from contemporary sources that referred to both recent and older philosophy.[21]

Each degree in a series is distinct from, but dependent upon, the one above it. In his *Economy*, written prior to his theological period, Swedenborg gave an example of a series of degrees that relates to humans. He divided mental activity into four degrees, each of which he regarded as distinct from the others. The highest degree in Swedenborg's system is the *fluidum spirituosum* which is the agent of the soul. This represents the universe—it is 'the macrocosm in the microcosm'—and we are largely unable to apprehend it whilst we live in the material world. The next level is the intellectual mind, by means of which we understand, think and will. For Swedenborg, the fact that the intellectual mind can be insane whilst the governance of the body remains normal was proof that the soul and the intellectual mind are distinctly separate. Next comes the animus or animal mind, by means of which we are aware of sensory input and are able to imagine and desire on the basis of it. The final and lowest degree is subsumed by the organs of the five senses.[22]

Shortly after finishing his *The Economy of the Animal Kingdom*, Swedenborg developed his concept of correspondences, according to which the different degrees in a series, whilst remaining distinct, are linked by correspondence and thus form a unitary whole. As Lamm points out, this doctrine envisages nature as a giant organism in which the whole of nature is spiritualized because it emanates from a single source, which Swedenborg equated with the One of Plato.[23] His first attempt at systematizing the idea of correspondence was a manuscript that he wrote in 1742 and that was first published posthumously in 1784, *A Hieroglyphic Key to Natural and Spiritual Mysteries by Way of Representations and Correspondences*. This mainly comprised examples of correspondences, such as those between the world, man and human society; and the relationship between physical illumination from the sun and spiritual illumination from the spirit and angels of God.[24] This was written shortly before Swedenborg's own spiritual experiences, but there are clear indications here of Swedenborg's future theological concepts. Swedenborg's doctrine would become a detailed lexicon of correspondences between objects and events in the natural world (such as individual animals and plants, or earthquakes) and phenomena in the spiritual world.[25]

In his fully developed theology, Swedenborg regards the Divine Human as the archetypal form upon which all correspondences are based. This is the form of the Lord (i.e., Christ), who is 'the only real person'.[26] The whole of the created cosmos, and of heaven with its angelic communities, corresponds to the Divine Human. Human beings are thus microcosms of the natural world and of heaven:

> I have been taught. . .that it is not only elements of the human mind. . .
> that correspond to spiritual and heavenly realities, but that it is also in a
> general sense the whole person, and in a detailed sense everything within
> the person. . .there is not the smallest part or the smallest bit of a part that
> does not correspond. . .if it were not for this kind of correspondence of the
> human with heaven, and through heaven with the Lord. . .he would not last
> even a moment, but would dissolve into nothingness.[27]

Every bodily organ corresponds to some aspect of heaven. The most important organs in this respect are the heart, lungs and brain. The heart corresponds to the will—which determines the choices that we make—and those choices in turn are determined by what we love, so that in a spiritually enlightened person the heart corresponds to divine love. In a similar way, the lungs correspond to the understanding, and ultimately to divine wisdom, which is the Holy Spirit.[28] What we love is modulated by wisdom, and love is enlightened by wisdom just as blood from the heart is oxygenated by passing through the lungs. The convolutions of the brain correspond to the 'form of heaven's rotation'; only the human brain has this correspondence, so that only humans can mediate between the natural and spiritual worlds.[29]

In Swedenborg's theology, angels were not created by God, but are the spirits of the dead who have directed their love towards God. The evil spirits of hell are not fallen angels, as in the doctrine of mainstream Christianity, but they are the souls of people who have chosen material pleasure as their goal. After death, the souls of men enter the world of spirits, which is intermediate between heaven and hell. There, their internal characters become visible externally to other spirits, in a way that is not usual during life because we falsify our outer speech and behaviour in order to keep our innermost thoughts and impulses secret. Spirits then gravitate to either heaven or hell, depending on their inner proclivities.[30] The entire purpose or 'end' of creation is to produce 'an angelic heaven out of the human race'.[31] Each part of creation contributes to this end, through its uses to man. Thus, there are uses for sustaining the body such as food, clothing and shelter; uses for developing the mind through acquiring knowledge from teachers, books and so forth; and uses for spiritual development through religious and spiritual practices.[32] Man contributes to the process by his own actions, provided that these are in harmony with divine love and wisdom. Knowledge or wisdom without action is useless: 'knowledge... is a mere auxiliary cause intended to assist the discovery of matters that will affect behaviour'.[33] Just as man's body is a microcosm of creation, all of the uses of creation are reflected in man.[34] Evil actions, in contrast to good actions that are directed towards heavenly goals, arise from man's love of himself and the material world. Evil uses in the world relate to noxious things in the animal, vegetable and mineral kingdoms, such as poisonous snakes, locusts and other pests; poisonous plants and toxic minerals; and diseases. Such uses result from human sin, since the spirits of hell from which they come are deceased evil humans.[35]

There is a continual influx from the spiritual into the natural world. To explain influx, Swedenborg draws an analogy with the influx of warmth and light from the sun into the natural world. The spiritual equivalents are love and wisdom, which flow into humans from the Lord who is the 'Sun of heaven'.[36] He describes two kinds of influx: the general and the particular. General influx passes into creation in general and maintains it in a state of order, whereas particular influx passes only into the brains of humans so that they can develop spiritually and not remain in a base animal state of life. [37] There are three ascending levels of heaven—the natural, spiritual and celestial—and whereas nature in general receives influx only from the natural level, humans, because of the configuration of their brains, are potentially open to influx from higher spiritual levels. This influx into the human brain can be immediate or mediate. Immediate influx comes from the Lord, whereas mediate influx is effected through spirits, both good and bad, which attend all humans. [38] It is because man is open to these higher spiritual influences that he alone is able to mediate between the natural and heavenly worlds. [39]

It has been observed above that Swedenborg was plainly still under the influence of Cartesian dualism when he wrote his *The Economy of the Animal Kingdom*. After he entered his theological phase, Swedenborg discarded dualism. Swedenborg's visionary experience of Descartes is sometimes quoted mistakenly as confirming his continuing dualism. In a discussion of the interaction between the soul and the body, Swedenborg described an experience of the spiritual world in which he took part in a conversation on that topic between followers of Aristotle, Descartes and Leibniz. The conclusion, confirmed as correct by angels, was that the relationship of soul and body is the Cartesian one of 'spiritual influx' into the body. [40] However, it has been pointed out that this does not imply an acceptance of Cartesian philosophy; in particular, Swedenborg claimed that before he elucidated them, people were unaware of his doctrines of series, degrees and correspondences, which mean that soul and body are simply different degrees of one substance that originates in God. José Antonio Antón-Pacheco, Professor of the History of Philosophy at the University of Seville, in a recently published English translation of his overview of Swedenborg's philosophy, maintains that Swedenborg's project was nothing less than the refutation of Cartesian dualism:

The basis of Swedenborg's system is the verification of unity as a condition that makes all of reality possible...the necessity to postulate unity as a fundamental category stems from an effort to overcome Cartesian dualism...All of Swedenborg's philosophy, science, and technology is directed against this dual, schism-filled vision...The whole universe finds itself thus reunited and ontologically connected, and each of its parts are reflected in

all parts, and all parts are reflected in each one...thus resulting in a metaphysical solidarity of all beings.[41]

A unitary philosophy of this kind is plainly a variant of absolute idealism which is
akin to German *Naturphilosophie*.

Wilkinson's move from idealism to empiricism

Charles Augustus Tulk was Wilkinson's mentor during his initial involvement
with Swedenborg, and in Tulk's interests we can find the seeds of Wilkinson's
early enthusiasms.

It was noted in Chapter 2 that Tulk was regarded as an idealist in his philosophy,
and that he received opprobrium from mainstream Swedenborgians as a result. He
spurned the accusation that he was an idealist, insisting that he was a 'spiritualist',
by which he meant that the natural world is continuously created and maintained
by spiritual influx into the human mind, which mediates between God and nature.
Despite the rejection of Tulk's ideas by most Swedenborgians, he had followers
nevertheless. Copies of some of his letters to unnamed 'pupils' are preserved in the
Archive of the Swedenborg Society in London, and these give some insight into the
debates that were prevalent at the time when Wilkinson was under Tulk's influence:

> I was asked whether I admitted the existence of matter, and my reply
> was, that I admitted the existence of weight, color, size, form, sound and
> touch, and I suppose that comprehends pretty nearly what they called
> matter...Nature [is] altogether the scene of effects and causes [that have]
> their existence in the Intellect and Will...it was finally agreed by nearly
> the whole company that I was right, with the exception that the mind of
> man was not the spiritual world through which Nature was produced,
> but Spiritual Beings abstracted from Nature. My reply was, that these
> disconnected or rather disembodied spirits were admitted by E.S. to have an
> influence in determining the forms of Nature, but only to the amount in
> which their quality was received by man.[42]

After Wilkinson had started to read Swedenborg, he recognized that 'there was a certain parallelism between various books of metaphysics and the writings of Swedenborg', and he set about learning more of the subject in order to better understand Swedenborg.[43] He applied himself particularly to the study of Berkeley's philosophy and became an enthusiastic advocate of Berkeley's idealism. It was as a result of this interest that he was attracted to Tulk's writings and he asked Tulk to send him some of his books. Tulk visited Wilkinson in July 1836, and they 'proceeded at such a rate of eulogism on "the Bishop" [Berkeley] as would have made him blush'.[44] He sent copies of Berkeley's dialogues to his fiancée Emma.[45] He held study groups with two or three friends and scoured Swedenborg's works to find support for his new metaphysical insights.[46]

Initially, Garth Wilkinson accepted Tulkism enthusiastically, though not without some niggling doubts. These doubts eventually flowered into outright rejection of Tulk's views:

> Great as was my wonderment at Swedenborg, it seemed to me that Mr Tulk's views alone conducted me into the sweetest recesses of the New Church Writings, and I spent weeks, and months and years in lingering around these fancied spots. It is true that I sometimes had a hard battle with myself, to assure myself that they were truths, and not potent conjurations; but the will to be comfortable amid their pleasant imagery, was persistent enough to maintain me in this state for a long time. During this time I read through the *Arcana Coelestia*, and seized upon all the passages I could find, confirmatory of my then views: these however were few, far-between, and so far unsatisfactory, that even the best of them required induction and interpretation in order to make them give the desired evidence: without a great deal of lawyering skill, they would easily have been witnesses on the other side. On the other hand, the passages clean against Tulkism were tens of thousands; but this cloud of witnesses was modestly put out of court, under the pretext that their utterances were for the sensually-minded, while on the other hand, the former class of passages contained direct statements of principles, and were to govern all the rest. . . I

began...instinctively to loosen myself from these views, prompted thereto by the secret consciousness that they and Swedenborg were irreconcilable.[47]

Wilkinson's rejection of Tulk's Berkeleyan philosophy was complete when he realized that, if everything in the created world is mediated through man, then the incarnation of Christ was merely an image mediated through the human mind, and not an objective reality. At this time—about 1839—Wilkinson was studying Swedenborg's scientific and physiological works, and he found that through these works he was able to understand the development of Swedenborg's thought and so gain greater insight into his theological writings.[48] He claimed that Tulk had made 'a most daring violation of the Writings of Swedenborg' which was a result of his self-admitted inability to accept some of Swedenborg's doctrines such as the actual worldly temptations of the incarnate Lord, which 'all Swedenborg's followers but [Tulk] himself [believe] to be contained in E.S.'s writings'.[49]

Although Wilkinson offered intellectual reasons for his rejection of Tulkism, it is likely that peer pressure also played a role. In 1839 he was castigated in the columns of *The Intellectual Repository* for his acceptance of Tulk's ideas, which the journal editors thought had led him to mistranslate Swedenborg's Latin in order to introduce idealist concepts into his translation of Swedenborg's *Last Judgment*, which had been recently published privately by Wilkinson.[50]

Wilkinson's analysis of Tulk's idealism led him to dismiss all other forms of philosophy that he regarded as idealist. He made this explicit in his 1847 preface to his translation of Swedenborg's *Outlines of a Philosophical Argument on the Infinite, and the Final Cause of Creation; and on the Intercourse Between the Soul and the Body*. In a strident criticism of Transcendentalism, which he equated with idealism, Wilkinson thundered:

> Thus metaphysics, after dreaming a while in Berkeleyism, became rambling
> and delirious in Hume, and sank into confirmed idiocy or Cretinism in
> Kant, who...endowed the monster with a power of propagating its kind,
> and filling the world with a lineage of abominable inventions.[51]

He contrasted this with Swedenborg's philosophy, in which 'the objects of reason are treated as outwardly true, and the outward spiritual world itself, independent of our perceptions like the natural world, becomes a direct object of human knowledge'.[52]

Wilkinson believed that Swedenborg had followed a similar path when he rejected previous speculative philosophies of the soul. The turning point, thought Wilkinson, came when Swedenborg was writing his earlier works such as *Outlines of a Philosophical Argument on the Infinite* and the various manuscript fragments that Wilkinson had gathered together under the title of *Posthumous Tracts*.[53] According to Wilkinson, these 'immature' works of Swedenborg 'have done him...the inestimable service of freeing him from the dangerous and dark forests of philosophy'.[54] Referring to the publication of Swedenborg's early works by the Swedenborg Association, Wilkinson thought that 'If the only service which the publication of these treatises performed, were the negative one of making the cause of Idealism quite hopeless, as against the doctrines of the New Church, that service would be a sufficient claim for the support of all thinking New Churchmen'.[55] He called idealism a 'disease of the understanding'.[56] In his *Outlines of a Philosophical Argument on the Infinite*, Swedenborg rejected previous philosophical speculations that in his view failed to explain how the soul interacts with the body, beyond the vague concept of intermediate animal spirits. This concept, thought Swedenborg, leads readily to the conclusion that there is little difference between human and animal souls, and even to redundancy of the very concept of a soul.[57]

The influence of Ralph Waldo Emerson, Thomas Carlyle and Francis Bacon

Wilkinson's friendship with Emerson was discussed in Chapter 1, where it was noted that Emerson was effusive in his praise for Wilkinson and also gave him significant practical help for his lecture tour, for which Wilkinson was duly grateful. It is more difficult, however, to find the measure of any intellectual influence that Emerson might have had upon Wilkinson. Wilkinson wrote to Emerson that his lectures in England were 'potently instructive', saying that 'they are the promise of a new era in our perceptions of nature and society'.[58] Privately, Wilkinson was less complimentary, writing to Henry James, Sr that 'His second lecture was on Swedenborg...Entre nous I don't think our bright-minded friend imports very much beyond his own unavoidable brilliancy into his estimate of Swedenborg: he seems in fact to try him only by his own standard of beauty'.[59] After his own rejection of idealism, Wilkinson would have had little sympathy with Emerson's philosophy. In his best-known work, *Nature* (1836), Emerson wrote that 'Whether nature enjoy a substantial existence without, or is only in the apocalypse of the mind, it is alike useful and venerable to me'.[60] Six years later, in his lecture 'The Transcendentalist', he wrote more explicitly that 'What is popularly called Transcendentalism among us, is Idealism'. In blunt contrast to Wilkinson, he wrote of the 'extraordinary profoundness and precision of [Kant's] thinking'.[61] Later in life, Wilkinson judged everyone through the lens of his Swedenborgian beliefs, and he found Emerson seriously wanting. Emerson, in Wilkinson's view, was a 'breaker up of old things' rather than having a clear system of his own; furthermore, Emerson's views on Swedenborg displayed a 'great timidity and ghost fearing in shirking the whole problem of his [Swedenborg's] spiritual experience'.[62]

As a young man, Wilkinson also read the works of Thomas Carlyle. He was impressed by Carlyle's *Sartor Resartus* (1836) and *The French Revolution* (1837), and after reading them he wrote to Carlyle in 1838 enclosing a copy of Swedenborg's *Last Judgment*.[63] In the following year he sent Carlyle a copy of his own new translation of the same work and Carlyle replied saying that he was very impressed by Swedenborg, whom he called one of 'the most wondrous men'.[64] In 1844 Wilkinson commended Carlyle's 'doctrine of work' to the attention of his friend Henry James, Sr, whom he thought was not putting his spiritual wisdom to sufficient practical use.[65] In 1847 Carlyle described his first meeting with Wilkinson, 'whom to my surprise I found quite an agreeable accomplished secular young gentleman'.[66] They met frequently for the next few years, but then the relationship began to cool. Following his rejection of idealist philosophies, Wilkinson cannot have been impressed by the transcendental idealism that is inherent in Carlyle's works, and plainly Wilkinson's enthusiasm for Carlyle diminished when he realized that Carlyle's views conflicted with those of Swedenborg.[67] In 1850 he wrote to Henry James, Sr that he had been reading Carlyle's essay on Odin in his collection of lectures *On Heroes and Hero-Worship and the Heroic in History* (1841), and that he objected to Carlyle's characterization of early humans as primitive savages, which is in direct contrast to Swedenborg's concept of primal humans who had the spiritual purity of Adam and had degenerated gradually since then.[68] This relatively civilized intellectual criticism was put into the shade by Wilkinson's emotional response to Carlyle; following a dinner party, he wrote to Henry James, Sr that 'I can scarcely look at [Carlyle] without laughing. He is the greatest wind-bag of the day, the supreme quack, the chief sham, the most pastily constituted imposter'.[69] Carlyle also began to find Wilkinson tiresome. In 1851 Wilkinson sent him a copy of his newly published *The Human Body*, and Carlyle wrote to his friend Joseph Neuberg that he had found it 'a most surprising Book—shadows and analogies being apparently all the same to it as facts...a very cloudland indeed'.[70] Almost a year later, he wrote that he 'rapidly broke down' when reading Wilkinson's book, that he had not responded to him, and had not seen him since.[71] In March 1858 he wrote of a Swedenborgian friend who 'detests the *Dilettante* Swedenborg*m* of Wilkinson', and noted that 'Wilk*n* I believe is quite given up to *rapping*, to——in fact to quacking & being quacked, I believe, for Homeopathy &c &c accompany all that of the spirits'.[72] It was not until some fifteen years later that their acquaintance was renewed briefly.[73]

Amongst those whom Wilkinson blamed for propagating the falsehoods of Transcendentalism was Samuel Taylor Coleridge. He had never met Coleridge, who died two years before Wilkinson first met Tulk. However, he had access to Tulk's copy of the second volume of Swedenborg's *Oeconomia Regni Animalis* (1741), which had been annotated by Coleridge.[74]

Wilkinson took great exception to Coleridge's comments, and in 1841 he wrote a stinging criticism of them in *The Monthly Magazine*, a London-based periodical that was popular with intellectuals.[75] Amongst other things, Coleridge had criticized Swedenborg's use of the term *fluidum spirituosum*, saying that it lacked any specific meaning and might as well have been called 'xyz'. Wilkinson, after firing a broadside at 'synthetic philosophy', which according to his description is akin to idealism, characteristically emphasized the importance of inductive reasoning that starts from empirical observation. We live in the time and space of the natural world, using the natural brain; but Wilkinson emphasized that Swedenborg had not intended to advocate a materialistic philosophy, because the brain is also the recipient of divine life, which is possible because we are made in the image of God. Furthermore, the natural physiology of the natural mind corresponds with the spiritual physiology of the spiritual mind. Wilkinson agreed that the exact nature of the *fluidum spirituosum* is not precisely known, but regarded that as resulting from lack of study rather than because it was a redundant concept. As empirical starting points for developing further understanding of the *fluidum*, Wilkinson pointed to the fluid within nerve fibres, and the life-giving seminal fluid. The *fluidum*, he believed, is the highest of natural substances, with spiritual substance next in series above it. 'The doctrine, then, of a *fluidum spirituosum* is based on scientific grounds...no man can safely resolve the fluid into xyz without a danger of finally reducing his corporeal frame into the same algebraical subtilization'.[76]

Perhaps in response to his growing doubts about idealism, and no doubt influenced by Swedenborg's advocacy of inductive reasoning, Wilkinson decided in 1845 that he would study in more depth the philosophy of Francis Bacon 'with a view to measuring the moderns by him, and him by Swedenborg'.[77] Bacon is known best for his advocacy of inductive reasoning as the foundation of scientific method.[78] In his physiological works, Swedenborg championed the inductive method of inquiry, though he used it to ascend to general spiritual truths, rather than general laws of nature.[79] For Wilkinson, Bacon evidently measured up well; he cited him approvingly in his subsequent works, particularly noting Bacon's emphasis on the 'human uses' of science, without which it is pointless.[80] Wilkinson recognized that Bacon's works also possess an esoteric dimension. This is perhaps most evident in Bacon's *New Atlantis*, a fable about the Christian utopian island of Bensalem that is governed by the Fathers from a college called Salomon's House.[81] This fable has been interpreted both literally, as an account of collaborative scientific research for the social good; and esoterically, as a Rosicrucian allegory.[82] Wilkinson believed that the esoteric aspect of Bacon's work had not been appreciated, commenting that:

> there can be no doubt, that if Bacon himself were to publish his works now for the first time, he would be ranked amongst the mesmerists, the phrenologists,

and the other[s]...who are banished...[from]...the scientific world...
The inductive method would be far from fashionable if its larger tendencies
were seen...Would it not freeze a Royal Society to the very marrow, to be
identified in any way with a man who believed, as the great Lord Bacon did, in
witchcraft, and the medicinal virtues of precious stones?[83]

Wilkinson's encounter with German Naturphilosophie

In 1847, an English translation of Lorenz Oken's *Elements of Physiophilosophy* was
published. The translator was Alfred Tulk, who was the son of Charles Augustus Tulk
and a good friend of Garth Wilkinson, who had seen the manuscript before it was
published and had assisted Tulk in finding a publisher.[84] In the main, it was through
this book that German Romantic *Naturphilosophie* was disseminated in Britain.[85]

Naturphilosophie is essentially a theory of the unity of nature.[86] It was introduced
by the publication in 1798 of two works: *Von der Welt-seele* (On the Soul of the World)
by Friedrich Wilhelm Joseph von Schelling, and *Über das pythagoräiche Quadrat
in der nature* (About the Pythagorean Square in Nature) by Benedict Franz Xavier
von Baader.[87] Schelling developed his *Naturphilosophie* as a break from the system of
transcendental idealism (*Wissenschaftslehre*) developed by Johann Gottlieb Fichte.[88] In
Schelling's fully developed concept of *Naturphilosophie*, subjective human awareness
and objective nature are simply different degrees of organization within a single living
force.[89] Schelling described a hierarchical system, in which the whole of nature, from
the lowest form of organized matter up to the human mind, is a single living entity.[90]

Before Oken's book, Schelling's concepts were known in England, particularly by
physiologists, only 'by scattered fragments'.[91] Oken developed the *Naturphilosophie*
of Schelling and became its major propagator in Germany, as well as in England,
after Schelling moved on to new themes in the early decades of the nineteenth century.[92] Wilkinson admired Oken, describing him as 'an experimentalist of established
reputation as well as a philosopher of profound insight'.[93]

It is easy to see why Oken's philosophy would have appealed to Garth Wilkinson as
a follower of Swedenborg, when we read the basic premises of his *Naturphilosophie*
that Oken sets out in his opening pages. For example, Oken tells us that 'the laws

of spirit are not different from the laws of nature...the Spiritual is antecedent to nature', and 'the whole Animal Kingdom...is none other than the representation of the several activities or organs of Man; naught else than Man disintegrated'.[94] The book is sweeping in its extent, ranging from consideration of God, through cosmogenesis to detailed consideration of each kingdom of nature, including animal physiology. In keeping with other *Naturphilosophen*, Oken regarded the highest order, which subsumes both mind and nature, as mathematical.

At first sight it may appear incongruous that Wilkinson, the strident denier of idealism, should accept so wholeheartedly Oken's work, which plainly lies within the tradition of German idealism. The solution to this apparent inconsistency lies in understanding Wilkinson's concept of idealism. For Wilkinson, idealism meant immaterialist subjective idealism such as that of Berkeley. He did not recognize the absolute idealism of German *Naturphilosophie* as a member of the same genre, because it admits the existence of the material world within a unified whole. Indeed Wilkinson's own seminal work, *The Human Body*, can be regarded as following in the tradition of *Naturphilosophie*, and it was recognized as such by at least one contemporary thinker, Elizabeth Palmer Peabody, who said that Wilkinson's book 'splendidly illustrated' the 'grand intuition of Oken'.[95] In this context, it can be noted that Immanuel Kant recognized Swedenborg's thinking as a variant of idealism, much as Tulk concluded in the following century.[96]

Oken described his own idiosyncratic classification of nature.[97] This was so extreme that it was regarded by mainstream scientists as sullying the newly emerging discipline of transcendental anatomy, but despite this objection Oken's ideas gained substantial popular support; in 1856 the Scottish surgeon and anatomist Robert Knox wrote that 'the doctrines of this worthy and simple-minded enthusiast have been all the rage in England'.[98] Oken regarded the whole of nature as one organism whose taxonomic groups are organs that ultimately relate to the highest form, man, who subsumes all other life forms when considered teleologically.[99] Because of this, man becomes a godlike figure who beholds nature created in his image.[100] Rejecting simple classifications based on anatomical similarities, Oken proposed three broad divisions of living creatures (visceral animals, flesh animals and sense animals), with subdivisions below them based on a numerological system relating to the five senses, and with correspondences across categories. [101]

By the mid-nineteenth century, so-called 'transcendental anatomy' or 'philosophical anatomy' was widely accepted in England. [102] The concept underlying transcendental anatomy was that animal structures which vary between species, such as the vertebrae of mammals, are derived from a single common archetypal form. This belief was underpinned by the philosophy of Coleridge and bolstered by the publication of Oken's *Elements of Physiophilosophy*. [103] Robert Knox is credited with first introducing transcendental anatomy into Britain. [104] Knox was an Edinburgh graduate who had studied medicine in London at St Bartholomew's Hospital under John Abernethy, and had learned transcendental anatomy in Paris from Étienne Geoffroy Saint-Hilaire and Jean Léopold Nicolas Frédéric Cuvier. [105] Knox believed that 'A great plan or scheme of Nature exists, agreeably to which all organic forms are moulded'. [106] The best known of the transcendental anatomists was Richard Owen, who regarded the archetypal forms of nature as being akin to Platonic ideals. [107]

Politically radical transcendental anatomists embraced the pre-Darwinian evolutionary theory of Lamarck, which postulated that animals take on new characteristics as an adaption to their environment, and that these characteristics can be passed on to their offspring. This resonated with the political notion that individuals can better themselves and have the capacity to form their own organizations and ruling hierarchies through a democratic process. [108] Lamarckian evolution is consistent either with a materialistic viewpoint, according to which living organisms of themselves have the capacity to develop, or with a deistic or theistic outlook. A purely materialist outlook is difficult to reconcile with transcendental anatomy, which by definition requires the existence of archetypes that transcend the material world, and any form of evolutionary theory is of course entirely at odds with traditional biblical creationism, which postulates that species were created on earth in fully developed forms.

Wilkinson associated with advocates of a divinely ordained transcendental anatomy. Amongst these was Joseph Henry Green, an acolyte of Coleridge and Professor of Anatomy at the Royal College of Surgeons in London, whom Wilkinson introduced to Ralph Waldo Emerson. [109] Green denounced Lamarckism in favour of a theistic interpretation of philosophical anatomy.[110] He related this to the development of society, which he regarded as taking place under the 'pre-disposing power of a Divine providence'.[111] One of Wilkinson's collaborators and close friends, William Benjamin Carpenter, also regarded transcendental anatomy as reflecting the will of a divine mind: in 1838 he wrote that 'when our knowledge is sufficiently advanced to comprehend these things [the general laws of form], then shall we be led to a far higher and nobler conception of the Divine mind than we have at present the means of forming'.[112] Unlike Green, Carpenter was an advocate for social and medical reform.[113] Carpenter had been a student of transcendental anatomist Robert Edmond Grant, the first Professor of Comparative Anatomy at London University, where Wilkinson's early mentor Charles Augustus Tulk, who was a patron of the University, had also attended Grant's lectures.[114]

Although Wilkinson was in broad agreement with the concept of transcendental archetypes (though he would not have used that term), his detailed understanding of this idea was based on Swedenborg's philosophy and was very different from that of the philosophical anatomists. He believed that the whole of creation, including all material animal forms, had a primary reality in a corresponding spiritual form:

> *In primis*...all animals [descended] from Spiritual prototypes exactly like themselves in the upper spheres.[115]

> all primary creation is Incarnation; the spiritual world supplies the paternal spirit in seed, and the natural world the maternal flesh in matrix. When the creatures once arrive here, they breed in and through the conditions of nature...They may also be replenished by fresh descents and avatars of the spiritual world.[116]

Wilkinson found this reassuring as it meant that species cannot become permanently extinct; they will return if and when there is a spiritual use for them. For Wilkinson, the ultimate archetype for all of creation and for humanity was of course Swedenborg's Divine Human.

Possibly inspired by Oken's novel approach, Wilkinson soon proposed his own system of classification of animals, which was based on Swedenborg's concept of uses.[117] He believed that such a classification would enable an understanding of the inner, hidden laws of nature. Echoing Oken, and in accord with his Swedenborgian beliefs, Wilkinson proposed that man and nature are expressions of the same form; nature is a vast 'organization of living things', each of which has its own part to play and of which man is the universal representative: 'I hold that instead of being a *part*, he [man] is *the* animal kingdom *itself*, and contains all below him, as the universal includes the partial'.[118] Considering that nature is subservient to man, and giving due prominence to Swedenborg's doctrine of uses, Wilkinson believed that nature should be classified according to its usefulness to man. The idea that the ape is man's closest animal relative then becomes untenable.[119] Instead, Wilkinson proposed that domesticated animals should be at the top of the tree.[120] This early excursion into a transcendental view of the animal kingdom was only published in pamphlet form, and was to be eclipsed six years later in 1851 by the publication of Wilkinson's book on the Swedenborgian system of anatomy and physiology, *The Human Body and its Connection with Man*, which is considered in detail in Chapter 6.

William Blake and communication with Spirits
In 1830 Blake was virtually unknown[121] and many of those who *were* aware of him were likely to have been influenced by an account of him given by Allan Cunningham, which focused on Blake's alleged insanity.[122] An article by Tulk in the *London University Magazine* of 1830 refuted this view, and has been described as 'the most important criticism of Blake's poetry to appear before the 1860's'.[123] In 1838 Tulk lent Wilkinson his original copy of Blake's illustrated *Songs of Innocence and Experience* and Wilkinson wrote enthusiastically to his fiancée about it, saying that 'the poetry is as fine as anything of the day...The illustrations too are reckoned by my artistical friends very fine and profound'.[124] Wilkinson determined to publish a new edition of Blake's *Songs*, and after he had gathered subscribers including his brother William, the book was published in 1839. Wilkinson's edition of Blake's

Songs circulated amongst the literati of the day; for example, Wilkinson sent Thomas Carlyle a copy, and in America Elizabeth Palmer Peabody gave a copy to Ralph Waldo Emerson.[125] In 1838, Wilkinson saw for the first time some of Blake's illustrations from his other works. These filled him with a mixture of admiration and horror. He wrote to his fiancée:

> I must say the series of drawings, giving me an idea that Blake was inferior to no one who ever lived, in terrific tremendous power, also gave me the impression that his whole inner man must have been in a monstrous & deformed condition——for it teemed with monstrous and shocking productions. Those men who would see Hell before they die, may be quite satisfied that they veritably have seen it by looking at the drawings of Blake. At the same time all the conceptions are gigantic and appropriate, and there is an awful Egyptian death-life about all the figures.[126]

In the following year he saw more of Blake's drawings, which led him to doubt Blake's sanity:

> I almost wish I had not seen them. The designs...give me strongly the impression of being the work of a madman. Insanity seems stamped on every one of them; and their hideous forms, and lurid hellish colouring, exhale a very unpleasant sphere into my mind: so much so, I confess I should not like to have the things long in my house...I feel puzzled what to say of the man who was compounded of such heterogeneous materials, as to be able at one time to write the Songs of Innocence, and, at another, the Visions of the Daughters of Albion.[127]

Despite this unpleasant shock, Wilkinson remained an admirer of Blake. He acquired original illuminated copies of Blake's *Songs*, *America* and *The Book of Thel*, all of which he later gave to his daughters.[128] His friend Henry Crabb Robinson noted at their first meeting in April 1848 that Wilkinson was 'a great admirer of

Blake'.[129] Following this meeting Wilkinson sent Robinson a copy of the *Songs*, and Robinson recorded later that he had read Wilkinson's preface to the *Songs* in bed, and had found it 'most curious'.[130] In return, Robinson gave Wilkinson a copy of Blake's *Sketches*.[131] Wilkinson transcribed several of these poems, and sent them to Henry James, Sr at the end of April 1848.[132] James published nine of the poems in the *Harbinger* in the following June and July.[133]

What was the influence of Blake on Wilkinson? Wilkinson's early impressions of Blake are judged best by the content of his preface to the *Songs*. In this, Wilkinson lays particular emphasis on the spiritual inspiration of Blake's verse and etchings. He was critical of Allan Cunningham's account of Blake, saying that Cunningham is 'incapable. . .of dealing with the Spiritual phenomena, of which that extraordinary person was the subject and exhibiter'.[134] Wilkinson regarded genius, such as that of Blake, as the product of influences from the spirit world:

> it is, therefore, plain, that if the mind has unusual intuitions, which are
> not included by the common laws of nature and of body, and not palpable
> to the common eye, such intuitions must be regarded as Spiritual facts or
> phenomena; and their source looked for, in the ever-present influences. . .
> of our own human predecessors, all now spiritual beings, who have gone
> before us into the land of Life.[135]

Wilkinson thought that the spiritual influences that gave rise to Blake's *Songs* were benign, but that he later fell under the influence of spirits from hell which inflamed his base passions, so that he 'entered into, and inhabited, the Egyptian and Asiatic perversions of an ancient and true Religion'.[136] Ultimately, we are left:

> looking down into the hells of the ancient people, the Anakim, the
> Nephilim, and the Rephaim. Their human forms are gigantic petrifactions,
> from which the fires of lust and intense selfish passion, have long dissipated
> what was animal and vital.[137]

Wilkinson showed no evidence that he approved of, or even understood, Blake's underlying philosophy. Instead, he regarded Blake's work simply as further confirmation of the reality of the spirit world, and he hoped that others would be similarly impressed:

> If the Volume [Wilkinson's edition of Blake's poems] gives one impulse
> to the New Spiritualism which is now dawning on the world;——if it leads
> one reader to think, that all Reality for him, in the long run, lies out of the
> limits of Space and Time; and that Spirits, and not bodies, and still less
> garments, are men;——if it gives one blow, even the faintest, to those term-
> shifting juggleries, which usurp the name of 'Philosophical Systems'...it
> will have done its work in its little day... [138]

Wilkinson's friendship with Henry James, Sr (1811-82)

Henry James, Sr was a man of substantial inherited wealth. Although his sons Henry James, Jr and William James are better known, Henry, Sr was a well-known intellectual and author in his own right. He and Garth Wilkinson became friends as young men and their association was lifelong, though it changed in its nature. The initial closeness of their relationship is demonstrated by James naming his third son, born in 1845, Garth Wilkinson James.[139] Wilkinson in turn named his daughter Mary James Wilkinson, after James's wife.[140]

Raymond H Deck suggests that Wilkinson probably first met James at the home of Thomas Carlyle in 1843, before James travelled to Paris.[141] On his return to England in 1844, James experienced a mental breakdown. He developed an 'insane and abject terror, without ostensible cause, and only to be accounted for, to my perplexed imagination, by some damnèd shape squatting invisible to me within the precincts of the room, and raying out from his fetid personality influences fatal to life'. He felt 'reduced from a state of firm, vigorous, joyful manhood to one of almost helpless infancy'.[142] This state lasted in varying degrees for some two years. His physicians advised him to seek hydrotherapy for his distressed state of mind. He went to a new clinic near London that had been opened by Dr Joseph Weiss, a follower of Vincenz Priessnitz, an Austrian peasant who had originated this fashionable treatment.[143] Whilst there he met Sophia Chichester, who was familiar with the works of Swedenborg.[144] She suggested that James's problem was a Swedenborgian 'vastation' and she advised him to familiarize himself with Swedenborg's works.[145] He bought several of these works in 1844 at the shop of William Newbery, a leading Swedenborgian publisher. Perhaps through the agency of Newbery, James renewed his acquaintance with Garth Wilkinson. They became friends and began a frequent correspondence when James returned to America.

After reading Swedenborg 'with palpitating interest', James found a sense of salvation, specifically from his previous Calvinistic tendencies:

> I had...been in the habit of ascribing to the Creator, so far as my own life and actions were concerned, an outside discernment of the most jealous scrutiny, and had accordingly put the greatest possible alertness into his service and worship...[146]

Subsequently, James's philosophy was robustly idealistic, based upon his understanding of Swedenborg.[147] Frederic Harold Young, in his masterly account of James's philosophy, describes him as following Swedenborg's concept of 'trinal monism' in which the celestial, spiritual and natural worlds are one by virtue of the doctrine of degrees and the doctrine of correspondence.[148] James defended Berkeley on the grounds that he had been widely misunderstood, even by other philosophers, and said that: 'Idealism does nothing but assert the purely phenomenal nature of material things'.[149] Berkeley, says James, 'did not mean to say, that when men sleep or die...the earth becomes defunct *in se*, or goes into sensible annihilation. He merely meant to say that it became incognizable to any higher intelligence', and therefore 'utterly unknown'.[150] Young discerns a strong similarity between some of the concepts of James and those of Berkeley. James's position was that the common understanding of man's relationship to the world, which is that nature is an object that is appreciated by man subjectively, is precisely the reverse of the true relationship. He declared that the true object of man's activity is the 'inward or ideal sphere', and that the external world is simply the 'theatre' (or subject) 'of that activity'.[151] Object is prior to actions, in the same way that the idea of drinking a cup of tea precedes the physical act of doing so. [152] The natural world, being finite, can be understood only in terms of space and time; because man is a microcosm, such that nature exists only insofar as it is included in the existence of man, it is inevitable that the world can be known only by the finite intelligence of man, without which it is essentially unknown or unrealized. Using the sensory experience of a rose as his example, James declared that the senses 'clothe them [the phenomena of nature] with all their personality...Take away my sensuous organization...and you virtually take away the rose'. [153] True Being is supersensual, beyond space and time. [154] James followed Swedenborg in regarding the Divine Human as the ultimate causal template of the cosmos; even if no man was cognizant of nature, it would still be there, but completely unknown, unrealized, and lacking any quality. [155]

James was not precise about the ontology of nature, saying that it has an 'actuality' that is neither absolutely ideal nor absolutely material. Following Swedenborg and indeed all other philosophers in the Neoplatonic tradition, he preferred to regard nature simply as the outer limit of creative emanation from where reflection back to the Creator begins. He used the analogy of a mirror, saying that nature is 'but a *mirror* of the soul' and so, like a mirror, it provides only a reflected appearance of reality. [156] James saw creation as a two-way process, the return pathway being redemption, a notion that finds a parallel in the Neoplatonic concept of the descending emanation of God into the cosmos, and the return ascent back to God. [157] For James this can only take place through the agency of the conscious human mind, with the descent being 'a consciousness of separation from God' and the ascent a 'spiritual consciousness, a consciousness of union with God'. [158] Man's initial concept of nature as an external reality is necessary for the sense of individuality which allows that initial sense of separation from God, from which the reascent can begin. Garth Wilkinson developed the same idea physiologically, when he proposed that the brain and nervous system is the final conduit for this process.

Given the similarity between their philosophies, how much was James influenced by Tulk? His main biographers scarcely mention Tulk, and do not credit him as having had any influence on James. [159] We know that a letter from James was forwarded to Tulk by Wilkinson in 1845, after James's return to America following his first trip to England; Wilkinson, in his subsequent meetings with Tulk, 'noticed his [Tulk's] satisfaction at the correspondence thus begun'.[160] There are similarities of theme between the writings of the two men. For example, Tulk wrote in 1843 that 'Even the fixed laws of nature which so forcibly impress the natural mind with the absolute externeity of sensuous forms, are correspondential effects which represent our natural modes of thinking'.[161] James wrote in 1863 that 'what we call "the laws of nature" are the mind itself in its most general or bodily form'.[162] Of course, none of this proves that James was substantially influenced by Tulk, but there is sufficient evidence to justify a more in-depth study.

After they had grown to know each other following James's vastation, Wilkinson and James developed a close friendship, spending many hours together and continuing their correspondence after James returned to America.[163] James continued to show an active interest in Swedenborg after returning to America. He persuaded the editors of the American Swedenborgian periodical *The New Jerusalem Magazine* to publish articles by Wilkinson, who sent in an article on Swedenborg's scientific writings for the issue of April 1845.[164] From November 1846 Wilkinson began a monthly letter from London for the *Magazine* which continued for eighteen months.[165] Initially, Wilkinson reproached James for not lecturing and publishing about Swedenborg. Perhaps in response to this, James proposed to use his wealth to sponsor several periodicals that would be devoted to spiritual, and particularly Swedenborgian, topics. James proposed the publication of a new Swedenborgian monthly and encouraged Wilkinson to emigrate to America as its editor.[166] Wilkinson's letters show that he seriously considered this proposal. In his letters, he discussed the practicalities, such as the necessary salary and his preferred living and working arrangements. James began to pay Wilkinson a regular stipend in return for his articles, and this appears to have changed the character of their relationship. Whilst Wilkinson still chided James when he felt it appropriate, he would lapse into abject apologies if he sensed that he had offended his friend. When the proposal for a monthly periodical fell through, James decided to produce a daily newspaper, an idea which Wilkinson discouraged vigorously, suggesting instead a series to be entitled *Tracts for the New Times*. These did appear but ran to only three editions; the first was written by James, and the next two by Wilkinson. Later, James proposed to publish yet another radical monthly, *The New Times*, edited by himself but with Wilkinson as his London contributor and distributor. This venture also failed. The grand plan for emigration having completely evaporated, Wilkinson made only one short visit to America in 1869.[167]

James was disparaging about sectarian Swedenborgians, writing that their interpretation of his writings was a 'libellous misuse' which:

> comes altogether of a...superstitious belief in a fixed or finite spiritual
> world *existing somewhere in some outlandish limbo*, which is nevertheless intrinsically superior to and independent of this solid natural world.
> There is no ground in Swedenborg's books for this absurd spiritual world...
> His spiritual world is in fact a purely *subjective* world...[168]

Although disdain for sectarian Swedenborgians formed a common bond between James and Wilkinson, their underlying reasons for this were fundamentally different. Whilst the impatient and practically minded Wilkinson rebuked them for their indolence and conservatism, the philosophical James criticized them for their mundane and over-literal interpretation of Swedenborg's works, taking a metaphysical view that Wilkinson found to be lacking in usefulness. These differences soon led to tensions between the two men. James was dismissive of Wilkinson's 1849 biography of Swedenborg which he regarded as 'low information', and Wilkinson thought that James's *Moralism and Christianity* (1850) was too impractical, vacuous and lacking in social usefulness.[169] After James had written a 'tirade' against one of Wilkinson's lectures in 1849, Wilkinson described James as 'the most genial and unctuous of bullies' and asked him to 'Drop the attitude, my spiritual Falstaff, or you may kill me in a very different way to that you think', in that he might 'break a bloodvessel'.[170] James initially showed little interest in Wilkinson's forthcoming *opus magnum*, *The Human Body* (1851). Wilkinson was hurt, complaining that 'You are a little painful about my book & its forthcoming dedication. It is you, Sirrah, who have kept me working in Literature for these five years, & I have done nothing for you, if not this book'.[171] James praised the book after he had been prodded by Wilkinson, although adding that he did not see the point of Wilkinson's 'correspondential lore'.[172]

Referring to a visit to London planned by James, Wilkinson wrote in 1850 that 'Your philosophy & mine have become gradually so divergent, that I shall be obliged to wait until I can have about 20 long conversations with you in Sussex Lodge [Wilkinson's home]'.[173] In 1852 James wrote to Wilkinson to explain why his letters had decreased in frequency:

> I have thought it absurd to be boring you any longer with my
> transcendentalisms, when you persisted in despising them too much to
> admit them into the bare vestibule of your attention; and I, accordingly,
> have written very seldom of late.[174]

In 1853, when James was planning the trip to London, Wilkinson wrote that 'I do not think that you will find me altered to the extent that you have heard. It is true I am now in a new pursuit [homoeopathy] which excludes all old ones as active guests. . .Surely, my dear Henry James, you would not cramp me by insisting that I shall study, or without study swallow, your great batches of universals'.[175] In the same letter, Wilkinson expressed his enthusiasm for spiritualism, whilst denying that he had been personally 'near the spirits'. In 1855-6, the Jameses stayed near the Wilkinsons in London, and no doubt the proposed philosophical conversations took place during that visit. Following this visit, James was openly critical of his friend: in a letter to Emerson, he said that Wilkinson's wisdom did not match his imagination, that he was too much involved with spiritualism, and that, in scornful summary, Wilkinson was 'now finding his youth'.[176] James's *Christianity the Logic of Creation* (1857) appears to have been James's reaction to his philosophical conversations with Wilkinson.[177] It is framed as a series of letters to his friend 'W' in London, and sets out his theology. The preface to this book takes what appears to be a sideswipe at Wilkinson, saying that:

None of the sects exhibit so servile a temper as those who pretend to
the most authoritative information about spiritual things. Look at
Swedenborgians, for example. And *Mediumship*, as it is called, is growing
to be the aspiration and profession of thousands, who are not ashamed to
depose their proper human force and faculty, in order to become the unre-
sisting puppets of a remorseless spiritual jugglery.[178]

The book is centred mainly on James's Christology, particularly his belief that the real
Christ is outside space and time and can be understood only spiritually, which he saw as
being in contrast to the prevalent Christian focus on the worldly doings of the incarnate
Christ. This issue was a major point of contention between James and Wilkinson, and
Wilkinson rejected James's view just as he had rejected Tulk's idealistic concept of Christ.
Wilkinson was chided by Henry James in 1851 for his attitude towards Christ, which James
thought focused too much on the incarnate Jesus rather than a transcendent Christ whom
James, to Wilkinson's dismay, referred to as 'the Christ'. James pointed out Swedenborg's
view that 'The mischief of the old Church Christianity is . . . that they conceive of the Lord
only as a Person, or that they have no conception of the divine humanity'.[179] Whilst this
judgment is expressed harshly (Wilkinson certainly did hold the concept of the divine
humanity), it is not without some foundation, as the same tendency to focus primarily
on the incarnate person of Jesus can be discerned in Wilkinson's later work, *The Combats
and Victories of Jesus Christ* (1895). In 1869, Wilkinson made his one and only trip to
America, but saw James only briefly; his reception from James was cordial, but by then
the two men were poles apart in their philosophies, and James was very disillusioned
with Wilkinson. In 1879, after gap of some nine years in their correspondence, Wilkinson
replied to a letter from James about his book *Society the Redeemed Form of Man* which
had been published that year. He complained that James used the term 'Divine Natural
Humanity' in a general and diffused sense relating to the whole of humanity, rather
than to the incarnate Jesus, which was Wilkinson's concept:

The only term common to you & Swedenborg is the <u>Divine Natural
Humanity</u>. But is there any common idea between you here? I cannot find

one. Swedenborg's Divine Natural is Jehovah triumphant in Jesus Christ
over his infinite humanity, & over all the hells which had access to it: transforming his natural into the Divine Natural. Swedenborg goes to this end,
& to the consequences of a new & everlasting Church proceeding from this
Divine Natural. Your Divine Natural, unless I misunderstand you, is diffused
in all men, giving, or to give, them infinitude of some kind, & abolishing
Heavens & Hells as mere preparations for the Godhead of Humanity.

In the same letter, Wilkinson told James that he 'would be better, not as a man,
but as a Consistency, if you were detached from Swedenborg'[180] and he explicitly
bracketed James's philosophy with that of Tulk, which he had rejected long ago.

The breakdown in the relationship between the two men was confirmed by James's
son William, who wrote later that:

My dear Father thought J.J.G.W. highly remarkable as a young man (when
they both were, and my Father was in England—and indeed J.J. then *was*
remarkable); and afterwards, always afterwards, found him very tiresome.
But meanwhile he had named his third son for him, and the Wilkinsons
had named their third daughter (Mary James Atwood Mathews as she is
now, and most queer, and whom I saw about once in twenty years) for my
Mother; and the vain *geste* had taken place.[181]

The period during which James began to lose interest in Wilkinson, in the late 1840s
and early 1850s, is the time when Wilkinson started to give more practical support
to various nineteenth-century pursuits, including spiritualism, mesmerism, vitalist
medicine and radical politics.

– 4 –

The Mind-Body Connection: Garth Wilkinson's Contribution to Mesmerism and Hypnosis

I must make you understand me: I claim to be a sorcerer, *a* magician.
Jules Du Potet de Sennevoy, who introduced Garth Wilkinson to mesmerism[1]

*In Mesmerism, if we knew what wrinkle of the face and what play of
the fingers gave the shape correspondent to any drug, we might
produce its effects upon a susceptible patient by one look or one
pointing or one beckon.*
Garth Wilkinson, 1849, in a letter to Henry James, Sr[2]

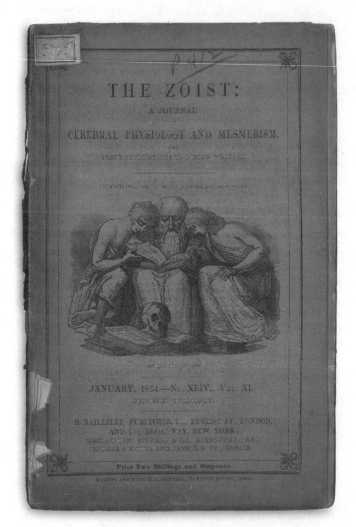

Fig. 4: Copy of *The Zoist*, January 1854.
Swedenborg Society Library, periodicals section.

T he nineteenth century was a time of major social upheaval related to the Industrial Revolution. The former agrarian economy had been dominated by the Tory-Anglican landowning aristocracy who ruled the plebeian workers, who themselves had little opportunity to rise above the social status into which they were born. The move from an agrarian to an industrial society that started in the eighteenth century spawned a new middle class of industrialists and merchants that did not fit readily into existing class structures, and who wished to have for themselves some of the privilege and status traditionally associated with the upper classes. The old social hierarchy, which had been regarded as a God-given natural order, was replaced by the liberal notion that individuals are born free and equal, and should have the opportunity to define their own social position according to their talent and effort. The new industrial working class also desired greater democratic involvement in society and more self-determination. These social changes also affected the medical profession. Increasing numbers of medical men came from middle-class backgrounds and had been educated by apprenticeship to surgeons or apothecaries, rather than by attending one of the prestigious medical schools that were dominated by the traditional Tory-Anglican elite. This new breed of doctors, like the industrialists, strove to gain social recognition. Whilst many attempted to emulate the established medical men, others developed a more radical liberal outlook that reflected the more general democratizing forces in society. These doctors were more likely to reject the treatment methods of the traditional doctors and turn instead to alternative therapeutic approaches such as herbalism, hydropathy, homoeopathy and mesmerism. In the context of a discussion of phrenology, a practice that was associated closely with mesmerism, historian Roger Cooter describes the adherents of these alternative approaches as younger doctors who had not yet established themselves professionally, who commonly needed to lecture or write in order to supplement their income, who tended not to be members of the established churches, and who were inclined to be politically liberal.[3] The young Garth Wilkinson fits this description exactly.

Similar divisions could be found within the ranks of the Swedenborgians. At one pole were the radical political reformers, such as those of the late eighteenth century who had been inspired by Swedenborg's writings to support the French Revolution and the abolition of slavery; whilst at the other pole were the sectarian New Churchmen who desired respectability within the social status quo. As discussed in Chapter 2, the radical Swedenborgians were early adopters of mesmerism and its offspring spiritualism, both of which were condemned by the leaders of the sectarian Swedenborgians for both spiritual and political reasons. This trend continued into the nineteenth century.

Mesmerism aroused enormous popular and intellectual interest in nineteenth-century Victorian Britain, and this interest became a part of the broader social and intellectual context of the times.[4] Mesmerism plainly had the power to influence and change people, which gave it an immediate political and spiritual significance quite beyond its initial use as a medical treatment. Furthermore, mesmerism could be utilized at all levels of society without the need for professional training. This made it a threat to the established social order and it was resisted by the orthodox medical profession. From a religious perspective, the mesmeric state opened up the possibility of individuals gaining spiritual revelations directly, without the need for an intermediate priestly class. This plainly challenged the authority of the established churches and it was duly rejected by them.

Although he became a radical political activist, Wilkinson's intellectual weapons came primarily from his Swedenborgian philosophy and from homoeopathy, which he regarded as a force for democratizing medical practice. The social and political implications of mesmerism were not his primary concern. Instead, he was interested in mesmerism primarily as a technique that could be applied therapeutically, as a method for gaining spiritual insights, and as a means of understanding the operation of the mind within an overall Swedenborgian philosophy.

Mesmerism: the background

Mesmerism has ancient roots which lie in healing and religious practices.[5] The advent of modern mesmerism was heralded by the healing activities of a German country priest, Johann Joseph Gassner, who used techniques related to mesmerism in order to cure illness by exorcism. Mesmerism proper was of course introduced by Franz Anton Mesmer (1734-1815).

Mesmer studied medicine in Vienna, where he wrote his doctoral thesis on the gravitational influence of the planets on human physiology.[6] His interest would later shift from animal gravitation to animal magnetism. He first investigated the curative effects of magnetism by applying magnets made in special shapes thought to correspond to different parts of the body. The magnets had been developed by his friend Maximilian Hell, who was professor of astronomy at Vienna. Mesmer subsequently came to believe that there is a universal magnetic fluid which could be channelled by a skilled operator such as himself without the need for magnets.[7] Mesmer thought that animal magnetism was an entirely natural phenomenon based on physical forces that had not yet been defined clearly. He developed various pieces of apparatus that were supposed to help channel the magnetic fluid, including his famous *baquet* which was used to treat several patients at once. This comprised a tub filled with water that had been 'magnetized' by Mesmer, from which protruded metal bars which patients could apply to themselves. However, magnetic phenomena soon developed a psychological and spiritual aspect. One of Mesmer's followers, Armand-Marie-Jacques de Chastenet, marquis de Puységur, is credited as the first person to describe the state of 'mesmeric somnambulism'.[8] In this state, the subject is not in a passive trance, but can speak and behave in a manner that superficially resembles sleepwalking. People also appear in this condition to develop supernatural powers,

97

including mind-reading, clairvoyance, precognition, and the ability to diagnose and propose treatment for medical diseases. Puységur recognized that this occurred through the agency of the will of the mesmerizer, which he believed acted upon the vital force of the subject, though he still held to the theory that the vehicle for this effect was the mesmeric fluid.

Puységur's work signalled a shift in the concept of mesmerism away from its use simply for healing and towards its use for magical and spiritual purposes. This was promoted through a plethora of esoteric societies that were established towards the end of the eighteenth century.[9]

Mesmerism attracted some interest in England in the latter part of the eighteenth century, but it was not until the Victorian era that it became widely popular.[10] This new surge of interest in mesmerism was stimulated by visiting French mesmerist Jules Du Potet de Sennevoy, who first came to England in 1837.

Baron Jules Du Potet de Sennevoy (1796-1881)

Baron Du Potet was taught mesmerism in France by the priest José Custodio de Faria and Joseph Philippe François Deleuze, who had written the first major history of animal magnetism in 1813.[11] Du Potet had demonstrated the phenomena of mesmerism to a committee of investigation convened by the Académie de Médecine in 1826, and the committee had concluded that the phenomena were genuine.[12] Du Potet arrived in England in 1837; he gradually became known, and eventually celebrated. He gave demonstrations of mesmerism in his rooms and at hospitals, where he used mesmerism therapeutically.

Du Potet believed that he practised a form of higher magnetism that had been known to the ancients and to more recent adepts such as Paracelsus (aka Theophrastus Bombast von Hohenheim), and which is the foundation of magic. According to Du Potet, this was achieved by the operator infusing his own soul into the magnetic fluid, resulting in powers far greater than could be achieved by those who merely directed the magnetism. By this means he could 'install himself' into the subject, who in effect would then be possessed by the operator and could be completely controlled.[13] This power could be used to alter other areas of the natural world by directing it according to the intention of the operator, though vigilance was required to ensure that it did not get out of control. By this means great harm or great good could be done.

The techniques used by Du Potet included magical figures drawn on the floor which he believed had occult influences on his subjects. He also used a magic 'mirror', a black circle of charcoal on the floor, in which his subjects saw visions. Du Potet declined to elaborate on whether these were dreams or true visions, saying 'it is my secret'.[14]

Du Potet emphasized that he was a magician, saying 'I must make you understand me: I claim to be a *sorcerer*, a *magician*'.[15] He explained that when he first used occult forces 'an occult power was conjoined to me, welding itself with my own strength, and I was allowed to behold *the light*. This was, of course, only my starting-point. . . This is the first degree of initiation, and here some time should be spent, before going further'.[16] He believed that everybody has the latent power to use occult forces, and that one who has the secret can 'unite his imaginative power' to the 'universal force' of nature.[17] This imaginative power, or 'image-making faculty of the soul', has a creative and life-giving power.[18]

It was Du Potet, a professed magician, who was responsible for starting the nineteenth-century revival of mesmerism in England, and who stimulated Garth Wilkinson, John Elliotson and many other prominent people to promote mesmerism actively.

Garth Wilkinson's introduction to mesmerism

It is likely that Wilkinson's interest in mesmerism was first aroused by his early mentor, Charles Augustus Tulk. We do not know the origin of Tulk's interest in mesmerism, but it is possible that his father, like others in the early Theosophical Society, was involved with this practice. The younger Tulk's mesmeric activities were described by Garth Wilkinson in a letter to Emma Marsh, then his fiancée, in 1837:

> He [Tulk] and I had a very long, and, to me, a most interesting conversation on 'animal magnetism', in which he is a professed believer, and of the effects of which he related some truly astonishing instances which had happened to himself—for he has been a practitioner of the art and mystery.[19]

Wilkinson did not become involved actively until he witnessed a demonstration of mesmerism by Du Potet in 1837.[20] He gave a first-hand account of this in a letter to his fiancée Emma:

> No doubt you have heard that Baron Dupotet has been for some time past in London performing Animal Magnetism. I have been frequently at his house to see his experiments and hear him lecture, which through the mouth of a gentleman who can read off his French into English he does. The Baron himself cannot speak English. Various opinions are entertained of his powers, though the majority of his audiences look upon his feats to be all humbug. Let me tell you the effects we have seen produced on some patients; promising that on the greater number no sensible results are produced and that females, exclusively or almost, are those who are affected. Now he has patients, who have been afflicted with fits, and between whom and himself I believe there is no collusion or agreement whatever. After a few motions of the hands you perceive a change of countenance of a remarkable kind, and in a period varying between ½ a minute and 3 or 4 minutes, they both fall into the most intense sleep. They are more like statues of sleepers than sleeping girls of the flesh and blood. This deep sleep continues, and will continue for hours (they say days and weeks) until the magnetizer addresses them; they immediately become conscious and give rational answers, but after a long conversation, and many actions, when finally awakened, they are quite unconscious of all that has happened during this state. Such is a brief description of what I have seen when I believe there was no juggling——time alone can show how much is true and how much false, but there is no doubt that Baron Dupotet does perform some extraordinary cures of nervous diseases.[21]

Within a few days, Wilkinson tested his own mesmerizing ability:

> Last night as Mr Hewitt & I were sitting together, I called Henry in. He had never heard of the strange effects and did not know what I was doing. After

an operation of about 5 minutes during the whole of which time he was laughing to himself at the absurd looking manipulations, his head suddenly declined, and he was quite asleep! I had difficulty in wakening him. Here there could be no fancy; and he is a remarkably wakeful boy. I shall try it again. When I asked him how he felt he said it was like a pleasant dream. [22]

His fiancée was evidently concerned that Wilkinson might mesmerize her; he reassured her by saying that he wished to keep her 'in subjection' only by the power of love, because 'love is more powerful than magic'. [23]

Wilkinson adopted mesmerism into his medical practice and by 1838 he was using it regularly. [24] Unfortunately we do not have details of this as there are few surviving primary records of his clinical activities. [25]

Wilkinson soon came to know John Elliotson, who was the first major English proponent of mesmerism in the nineteenth century.

John Elliotson (1791-1868)

John Elliotson, the son of a prosperous London apothecary, gained his medical education in Edinburgh where he graduated at the age of nineteen. [26] Before he became involved with mesmerism, Elliotson had developed a reputation as a nonconformist and eccentric with a volatile personality. He was critical of the mercenary motives of his medical colleagues and earned himself enemies as a result. Nevertheless, he established himself as a talented and popular teacher, as well as an able physician, and in 1832 he was appointed as the first Professor of the Principles and Practices of Medicine at the University of London.

Elliotson's first encounter with mesmerism was in 1829, when he witnessed a demonstration in London by an Irish chemist and Fellow of the Royal Society, Richard Chenevix. [27] Elliotson was impressed, but he had no further involvement with mesmerism until a friend invited him to a demonstration by Du Potet on 17 August 1837 at University College Hospital, London, where evidently Du Potet was already treating patients. [28] Elliotson was so impressed with Du Potet's demonstrations that he became an enthusiastic advocate for mesmerism. He held his own demonstrations at University

College Hospital in front of large audiences of medical men, Members of Parliament, clergy and other prominent members of society. These centred on two sisters, Elizabeth and Jane O'Key, who were patients of Elliotson at the hospital. Both girls were said to suffer from epilepsy as well as other 'very singular nervous diseases'.[29] His experiments and observations were reported in a series of articles in *The Lancet*, which was edited by his friend Thomas Wakley.[30] These reports described the phenomena induced by Elliotson in the O'Key girls, including states in which, for example, the girls appeared either delirious or stupefied, would mirror movements made by others apparently out of their sight, and would be insensitive to pain. Elliotson's observations were detailed and he believed that he was developing an understanding of the 'laws' that governed mesmerism.[31] He also experimented with magnetized water and metals, which he believed assumed the potency of the mesmerist.[32] He came to believe that a wide variety of illnesses, including epilepsy, insanity and even cancer, could be cured by mesmerism.[33] Eventually Thomas Wakley insisted that the O'Key girls should be examined at his home under conditions controlled by him. Wakley found that the phenomena shown by the girls occurred only when they believed that they were being mesmerized, whether or not that was actually the case. He concluded that the claims of the mesmerists were false and he published a strident condemnation of Elliotson's work.[34] As a result of this, Elliotson was instructed by the Hospital Committee to discharge Elizabeth O'Key from the hospital and to stop using mesmerism on the wards. His response was to resign both his academic and his clinical posts at University College and North London Hospital on 28 December 1838.[35]

Elliotson had held an interest in the esoteric even before he became actively involved with mesmerism. He had travelled in India, where he had observed snake charmers, and in Egypt, where he had met 'the necromancer of Grand Cairo so often described'.[36] He became familiar with the works of Joan Baptista van Helmont and Heinrich Cornelius Agrippa, and he referred to ancient and more recent reports of phenomena that relate to those of mesmerism.[37] With regard to these phenomena, Elliotson readily accepted what he had observed personally, but he remained sceptical regarding some of the more extreme phenomena attributed to the mesmeric state, such as clairvoyance, seeing with the fingers, and the visualization of internal organs.[38] With regard to the cause of mesmeric phenomena, Elliotson was essentially a fluidist, although he had some understanding of the psychological dimensions of mesmerism. Thus, Elliotson said that he was 'satisfied that an influence could be exerted by one person over another, independently of the senses or the imagination', and that the phenomena of mesmerism 'must be ascribed to a peculiar power; to a power acting...constantly in all living things, vegetable and animal'.[39] However, he also commented upon the power of the imagination, remarking, for example, that 'The power of mental impressions I know to be far greater than is generally apprehended: and in mesmeric states its power is greatly augmented'.[40]

Elliotson was aware of Swedenborg's works, initially no doubt as a result of his friendship with Tulk and later reinforced by Wilkinson. However, he concluded that 'any one conversant with Swedenborg's theological writings, and with the history of insanity, must know [that Swedenborg was]...a monomaniac for thirty years'.[41] In 1837 he publicly rejected the very idea of spirit apparitions, which he believed had been debunked.[42] However, in 1863, at the age of 72, he was converted to spiritualism after meeting the noted medium Daniel Dunglas Home in Dieppe. Home chastised Elliotson for dismissing him as a fraud without observing his abilities, and, after personal investigation of spiritualist mediums, Elliotson became convinced of the reality of the phenomena of spiritualism. The former atheist became a devout Christian.[43]

We do not know when Garth Wilkinson first became acquainted with Elliotson. Their mutual friendship with Charles Augustus Tulk may have led to an early meeting, or they may have met when they both attended Du Potet's demonstrations in 1837; certainly they already knew each other by March 1838, when Elliotson attended his 'friend' Garth Wilkinson to treat him for scarlet fever.[44] Wilkinson wrote to his fiancée after attending a demonstration of mesmerism that Elliotson gave in front of a large audience at his home in August 1839.[45] The two men were close friends; Wilkinson described riding with Elliotson in 1844, when he took the opportunity to show Elliotson an article about George Bush's views on mesmerism in relation to Swedenborg in *The New Jerusalem Magazine*, which Elliotson asked to borrow.[46] Towards the end of his life, and long after the death of Elliotson, Wilkinson referred to Elliotson as his 'revered teacher and friend'.[47]

Wilkinson's views on mesmerism

Wilkinson's considered attitude to mesmerism can be found in various documents and letters from the period 1840-51. It is clear that Wilkinson accepted the more extreme claims of mesmerism such as communication at a distance and clairvoyance. In 1847 he wrote to Elliotson's *The Zoist* magazine that he had 'a deep interest in the subject of mesmerism, and...a thorough knowledge of the truth of many of its least credible manifestations'. [48] When Edgar Allan Poe published a short story, 'Mesmerism in Articulo Mortis' (1845), about a man who had been mesmerized at the point of death, which delayed bodily decomposition and even enabled him to speak after death, Wilkinson wrote to Henry James, Sr asking him to confirm with friends of Poe whether or not the story was in fact true. [49]

One of the most widely read books on mesmerism in the mid-nineteenth century was *Facts in Mesmerism* (1840) by Reverend Chauncy Hare Townshend, who was a friend of Wilkinson. [50] Wilkinson reviewed this book in *The Monthly Magazine* of November 1840. [51] He took a very favourable view of Townshend's thesis, which he summarized by saying that:

> It [mesmerism] demonstrates a larger communion of man with nature,—
> a more universal presence of the soul in the body, than had hitherto been
> dreamt of in our philosophy. It shows all our human faculties in immedi-
> ate contact with God's creation...It reveals the mind as independent of
> the senses, and lays bare to reason the fundamental organism which is to
> constitute the spiritual body. [52]

For Wilkinson, the 'mesmeric medium' was the very stuff of the spiritual substance which, according to Swedenborg, constitutes the body of the soul after death. There was one point, however, on which he differed from Townshend: Wilkinson believed that the medium which connects the mesmerizer with his subject is different from the medium of mesmeric sensation that enables clairvoyance, whereas Townshend proposed that the two are one and the same. Wilkinson did not spell out his reasons for this dissent, other than that 'the two mediate between different things', but it is apparent that, if the two mediums were identical, then the soul in its body of 'soul substance' or 'mesmeric medium' after death would be able to perceive things in the material world, which is contrary to the teaching of Swedenborg, who emphasized that spirits are blind to the material world.[53]

In his review of Townshend's book, Wilkinson mentioned the therapeutic effects of mesmerism, commenting that it is 'one of the most potent, and yet the most gentle of remedial agents' which can be used to cure not only 'lighter ailments' but also those deemed incurable.[54] In his *The Human Body*, Wilkinson expands on this theme. After noting the antipathy of the medical profession to mesmerism, and comparing this to the reaction of the Church of Rome to the idea that the earth goes round the sun, he compares mesmeric treatment with herbal and other therapies based on sympathetic action:

> If herbs, waters, airs, fire and motion, which are such remote kindred to us, will cure our ills, surely man himself, who is comparatively own brother to every man, will go home to disease with a directer relationship of beneficence.[55]

According to Wilkinson:

> Mesmerism, in its simplest form, is a peculiar relation of two human be-ings, in which the one is voluntarily active, and the other, voluntarily, or naturally, passive, and certain attitudes either already exist, or are assumed, on both sides, corresponding to these two states; in which physical or mental changes are produced in the patient. . .[56]

Wilkinson proposed that the mesmerized subject permits the 'sphere' of the mesmerizer to occupy his or her body, thus displacing the subject's own will and volition.[57] In the mesmeric state, thought Wilkinson, the subjects voluntarily cede their own will to that of the mesmerizer, so that 'the radiance of the mesmerizer or active power rushes in to fill the space'.[58] By this means, every part of the subject receives the strength of 'the better man' and organs that have built disease according to 'the architecture of evil' are overwhelmed by the purer spirit of the mesmerizer, thus effecting cure.[59]

One of the most systematic and influential accounts of mesmerism in relation to the doctrines of Swedenborg was set out in *Mesmer and Swedenborg* (1847) by George Bush, an ordained Presbyterian minister and Professor of Hebrew at New York University. Bush proposed that the state of mesmerized subjects approximates to that of spirits, so that their abilities and their perception of the world are akin to those found in the spirit world as described by Swedenborg. He illustrated this by means of quotations from Swedenborg's works. Clairvoyance, for example, becomes possible because mesmerized subjects, like spirits, are not bound by time and space as are sensual people. Bush believed that everybody has an 'invisible aura' or 'sphere' surrounding them which 'emanates also from the interior spirit' and 'which is constantly exhaling from his person and spreading to some distance on every side...The first effect of the Magnetic condition is to produce a blending... of the respective spheres of the operator and the subject'.[60] Bush related this to Swedenborg's description of 'the sphere of affections and of thoughts therefrom which encompasses each angel, and by which his presence is evident to those near or far'.[61] The experiences of somnambulists, said Bush, are a providential means by which others could confirm the insights of Swedenborg through their own direct perception. Bush was at pains to point out that this should not be taken to imply that Swedenborg was merely in a mesmeric state when he was aware of the spiritual world; this would take away Swedenborg's claim to have a personal mission from the Lord. The difference, thought Bush, was that whereas mesmerized subjects are awake in the spiritual world but not in the sensual world, Swedenborg was fully and simultaneously participant in both worlds. In short, 'Swedenborg's extatic [*sic*] state was of a vastly higher order' than any that can be achieved through mesmerism.[62]

The concept of 'spheres' that was set out by Swedenborg and taken up by Bush was also a favourite theme of Garth Wilkinson, who regarded the 'Doctrine of Spheres' as central to an understanding of Swedenborg's philosophy. Wilkinson set this out most clearly in one of his later books, *The Greater Origins and Issues of Life and Death* (1885).[63] Here, Wilkinson explained that 'Everything is clothed in a garment of emanations from itself, the trains of which reach far and wide...A critical event, an ardent thought, can put its finger of love or desire upon a consciousness at the antipodes...Even coming things cast their spheres before them'.[64] For Wilkinson, the 'sphere-perceptions' and 'sphere-senses' reside in the brain, heart and lungs.[65] Those who lack this kind of perception 'are comparatively of mineral mind, and are incapable...of acquiring any knowledge of the world'.[66] Spheres blend into each other, creating societies and ultimately one man. Each person 'alters the world unconsciously by adding his sphere to it, as well as consciously by the work of his days'.[67] Human spheres, singly or in combination as whole nations, can spread evil influences and disease as well as good effects. Not only humans, but the whole mineral, plant and animal worlds have spheres, which blend together in 'a magnetism of sympathy, or antipathy, pervading all creation'.[68]

In *The Human Body*, Wilkinson explicitly related the effects of human spheres to those of mesmerism. Mesmerism, he thought, provides evidence that 'the skin, or the nervous system through it, pours forth a subtle radiation of tremendous efficacy on other organic creatures'.[69] Through this radiation, which Wilkinson characterizes as 'a manifold nervous fluid', man is 'constantly impressing a character upon external nature, literally magnetizing it'.[70] He says that 'philosophers' have suspected that 'the tigers, lions and snakes, and other ugly foes not seemingly of our household, were at first but the wind-cast seedlings of our passions, wicked words overheard and dramatized by nature'.[71] 'Spheral man' has sympathies and antipathies by means of which a person can 'recognize in the sympathetic friend some benign planet of our destiny; or in the repulsive presence of others, the malignant rays of an evil star'.[72] Wilkinson saw a ready explanation of clairvoyance and thought transmission in the 'Doctrine of Spheres'.[73] He also believed that the curative powers of mesmerism could be unlimited, although current knowledge suggested that diseases of the nervous system—particularly those that reflected abnormal function rather than abnormal structure—were the most susceptible to mesmeric cure.[74]

Wilkinson's thesis, outlined in his *The Human Body*, and amplified—though by then with no mention of mesmerism—in his later *Greater Origins*, emphasizes spheres of empathies and antipathies in which the whole of creation is united, and by means of which microcosmic affinities with the mineral and vegetable world as well as the greater macrocosm can be discerned by those with inner perception. Human spheres have a creative function by means of which a person's inner loves and desires create the world in their correspondential image. Furthermore, this faculty of spheral awareness can be put to use therapeutically. Wilkinson's interpretation of Swedenborg on these points is reminiscent of the philosophy of Paracelsus, who described a world of affinities and antagonisms, in which the whole natural world has correspondences with man that reach up to the stars and planets, and which can be discerned by a person who is able to see by the 'light of nature'.[75] Like Paracelsus, Wilkinson regarded epidemics as the result of collective human sinfulness.[76] We know that Wilkinson was aware of the work of Paracelsus and, like Paracelsus but in contrast to Swedenborg, he was concerned to put these insights to practical use in curing illness.[77]

Wilkinson was well aware of Swedenborg's own experiences of clairvoyance. He noted that Swedenborg, even before he entered into his visionary period, had acknowledged the reality of communication between people at great distances, which he said was made possible by 'the sympathy and magnetism of man'.[78] In his biography of Swedenborg, Wilkinson recounted the now well-known stories of Swedenborg's clairvoyance. These included his vision, before witnesses and accurate in every detail, of a fire in Stockholm; his vision of the location of a receipt for a substantial amount of money that a neighbour had asked him to retrieve for her; and a message for Louisa Ulrica, Queen of Sweden, that was given to him by her deceased brother and which contained information that according to the Queen was known only to herself and her brother.[79] Wilkinson concluded that:

The universe is telegraphically present to itself in every tittle, or it would be no universe. There are also slides of eyes in mankind as an Individual, adequate to converting into sensation all the quick correspondence that exists between things by magnetism and other kindred message bearers. It is however only fair to Swedenborg to say, that he laid no stress on these incidental marvels...[80]

It was Wilkinson's view that Swedenborg might have learned the technique of self-induced trance from the Laplanders. In 1847 he wrote to Elliotson's *The Zoist* journal suggesting that Swedenborg's early poems indicated that he had travelled in Lapland and thus gained first-hand experience of trance induction from the magicians there.[81] He quoted his translation of a paragraph from Swedenborg's *The Economy of the Animal Kingdom*, which he had recently published in the original Latin:

> Ecstacy [*sic*] or trance...is a state of separation between the body and the soul, while the life still continues; and at such times the soul is believed to have left the body, or, if it remains, the connexion between the two is supposed to be broken...In the northern latitudes there are certain reputed magicians who have the power of passing spontaneously into the state of trance, during which they are deprived of the external senses and of motion altogether, and are simply attentive or alive to the operations of the soul; and this to the end that, after they are wakened up again, they may disclose the particulars of thefts that have been committed, and in general gain a knowledge of any secrets desired to be ascertained.[82]

Wilkinson pointed out the obvious affinity between Swedenborg's clairvoyant experiences and the outcome of shamanic practices in northern latitudes.

Wilkinson's speculations about Swedenborg's association with the shamans of Lapland were unfounded, but there is evidence that Swedenborg did achieve meditative states which were associated with a marked diminution of respiration. In 1748, shortly before starting to write *Arcana Caelestia*, Swedenborg recorded in his *Spiritual Diary* that:

> I was first accustomed to breathe in this way in infancy when saying morning and evening prayers, and also at times afterward when explaining the concordance of the lungs and the heart, and especially when, for many years, I was writing from my mind the works that have been published [*Oeconomia Regni Animalis* and *De Regnum Animali*]. I then observed

frequently that the respiration was tacit, almost insensible...Thus I was
introduced to such respiration throughout many years from infancy,
and especially by intense speculation, in which the respiration became
quiescent; otherwise, an intense speculation of truth is not possible.
Sufficient air was drawn in to enable me to think. By this means it was
granted me to be with spirits and angels.[83]

Here, Swedenborg took a phenomenon that is now regarded as a normal physiological
accompaniment of meditative or hypnotic states, and elevated it to the status of a
divine gift.[84] In some other spiritual traditions, particularly those of the Hindu yogis
and the Hesychasts of Eastern Orthodoxy, breathing is used actively to deepen prayer.[85]

This discussion begs the question of whether Garth Wilkinson used trance techniques
for spiritual purposes. He does not directly refer to this, but it is clear that he practised
self-hypnosis, and there is evidence (discussed in Chapter 7) that he believed he could
induce in himself some of the more extreme phenomena claimed for hypnosis, including viewing the internal organs of his patients and receiving messages from the
deceased, such as Samuel Hahnemann, the originator of homoeopathy.

Alison Winter has discussed the different ways in which mesmerism was received
by the clergy.[86] There was debate around whether mesmerism was a purely natural
phenomenon, in which case it might be acceptable, or whether it had a supernatural
dimension. A purely natural explanation of mesmeric phenomena risked leading
people into atheism; Elliotson (before his conversion) was cited as an example of
this. On the other hand, if mesmerism was supernatural, then this raised the question of whether it was of divine or demonic origin. There were advocates for each
of these positions.[87] This led inevitably to controversy about the origin of miracles
described in the Bible, as well as the cause of visions, speaking in tongues and other
manifestations claimed particularly by Catholics and Dissenters. The notion that
mesmeric phenomena are of demonic origin was used to discredit sects that claimed
such phenomena amongst their members, and so it was inevitable that members of
the New Church, whose 'prophet' claimed to have gained his spiritual knowledge
through visions, would be keenly interested in mesmerism.

The controversy that mesmerism engendered amongst Swedenborgians in England is illustrated well by an exchange of correspondence in *The Intellectual Repository* of 1844. An initial letter from 'J. S.' (possibly John Spurgin) reported that New Church clergy were using mesmerism in their ministries and even making mesmeric passes from the pulpit.[88] He claimed that they had invoked visions of angels and spirits for their congregations by using mesmerism in this way. He denounced mesmerism in all its manifestations as a pernicious evil which played on the imagination of the vulnerable. This prompted a response from a correspondent more sympathetic to mesmerism, who agreed that mesmerism had no place in the pulpit, but proposed that its secular uses, particularly in surgical anaesthesia, were acceptable.[89] The letter was accompanied by a long editorial, in which it was asserted that 'we may, with some degree of certainty, affirm, that [mesmerism from the pulpit] will not occur again'.[90] After this stern disciplinary statement, the editor outlined the journal's view on mesmerism from the Swedenborgian standpoint. Readers were reminded of Swedenborg's theory of 'solar atmospheres' including an etheric sphere that carries global magnetic forces, and which corresponds to reasoning in the natural mind, which the editorial dubbed 'animo-magnetism'.[91] Having thus validated the concept to his satisfaction from a Swedenborgian perspective, the editor proposed that animo-magnetism can act on other less 'charged' minds in the same way that terrestrial magnetism can act on uncharged metallic objects. Although mesmerism was thus given a natural explanation, there were nevertheless spiritual consequences. Thus, it was pointed out that magnetized subjects undergo a cessation of bodily awareness to the point of surgical anaesthesia, and such states allow the internal senses—that is, the spirit—freedom to interact with other spirits in the same way as those in the spirit world do after death. This was given as an explanation of clairvoyance, the existence of which 'no individual, except he be actuated by a most determined and hostile prejudice, can deny'.[92] The editorial ended with the customary Swedenborgian warning about the dangers of attempting to make contact with spirits by any means, including mesmerism.

These dire warnings no doubt had their effect upon New Church ministers, but freethinking followers of Swedenborg continued to explore contact with the spirit world. As for Garth Wilkinson, he continued into old age to believe in the reality of mesmeric phenomena including clairvoyance, but after an initial enthusiasm for spiritualism he later abandoned this pursuit. He also turned from his exploration of mesmerism to the psychological understanding of hypnosis, and in doing so he played an important but hitherto unrecognized role in the development of psychology.

Garth Wilkinson was also a supporter of phrenology when he wrote *The Human Body*. The basic tenet of phrenology was that bumps on the surface of the skull reflect the brain morphology beneath them, and that each bump relates to a particular characteristic of the person. The shape of the skull thus represents the inherent characteristics of a person. Whilst this appears to reflect a conservative view of the unchangeability of individuals, phrenology developed a radical dimension with the publication in 1828 of *The Constitution of Man* by George Combe (1788-1858).[93] Combe focused on social and moral issues, and particularly on the potential for individuals to promote or suppress particular characteristics, leading to changes in their behaviour and hence in society more generally. He regarded the faculties of the brain as operating under the same 'natural law' as the rest of the body and of wider society. Just as the body in general requires input from the external environment to develop and function properly, so too do the faculties of the brain. Combe believed that even though mental faculties are inherited, they can be modified considerably by the social environment and particularly by education. In the early 1840s, the concept of 'phreno-magnetism' developed, in which the mesmerist manipulated cranial bumps to excite various psychological and physiological reactions based on the assumed correspondences of the undulations of the skull.[94] It was thought that this could be used to improve the moral and social character of individuals. Phrenology was adopted by some followers of Swedenborg, who were quick to point out that their master had described cerebral localization half a century earlier.[95] Furthermore, they claimed that Swedenborg had also described the correspondence between brain morphology and external skull protuberances.[96] Wilkinson regarded phrenology as an empirical science, 'a solid play-ground away from the abstractions of the old metaphysics'.[97] However, he did not accept that there is a simple relation-ship between skull protuberances and the morphology of the underlying brain. Instead, adopting Swedenborg's notion that brain areas are capable of motion, he proposed that very active brain areas might push others out of the way, so that they bulged; he used the analogy of invaders pushing an indigenous population up a mountain. Thus, there would be no simple correlation between brain morphology and the strength of activity of the different brain areas; more could be learned from empirical observation of the skull than from observation and dissection of the brain post-mortem, when movement had ceased. Characteristically, he extended this concept to suggest that above the whole human race is the 'skull of heaven' which 'has many shapes, and societies or brains fill them differently'.[98]

James Braid (1795-1860)

James Braid is best known for his development of hypnosis. Braid was the son of a landowner in Kinross, Scotland. After serving an apprenticeship to a surgeon in Leith, he trained at Edinburgh Medical School, graduating in 1820.[99] Whilst in Edinburgh, he was elected as a member of the prestigious Wernerian Natural History Society of Edinburgh.[100] Braid moved to Manchester in 1828 and spent the rest of his career there.

Braid's introduction to animal magnetism was in 1841 when, at the insistence of a friend, he attended a seance by visiting Swiss mesmerist Charles Lafontaine. Braid had been sceptical about animal magnetism before this demonstration and he found the first seance unimpressive. Nevertheless, he attended further seances and concluded that the phenomena that he witnessed—particularly fixed eye closure and analgesia—were real. He soon began experimenting with the technique and concluded that there was no need to postulate 'magnetic fluid' as the mechanism of trance induction.

In his first major published work on the subject, *Neurypnology* (1843), Braid was at pains to distance himself from mesmerism, which famously had been dismissed by the French Commission of Inquiry in 1784 as merely the effect of imagination. He made no mention of the importance of suggestion for his process of hypnosis and referred to imagination only so as to dismiss it as the basis of his hypnotic cures.[101] Instead, he put forward an entirely physiological explanation of his technique. He believed that his technique had physical effects on the brain. Braid postulated that staring fixedly at an object leads literally to paralysis of the eyelids, 'thus rendering it *physically* impossible. . .to open them'. [102] This, thought Braid, would in turn have the effect of 'destroying the equilibrium of the nervous system'. [103] Within a framework that was indebted to phrenology, Braid thought that the different parts of the brain, through their corresponding connections with bodily organs, could mediate disease and its cure, and that cure was facilitated by the effects on the brain of his hypnotic technique, combined with manipulation of the skull and other body parts.

Whilst dismissing imagination as the explanation for his own results, Braid was very aware of the effects that imagination can have. At the time when Braid was developing his concept of hypnosis, German chemist Karl von Reichenbach claimed to have discovered the 'Odic force'. He first described this in 1845, and in the following year William Gregory, who was Professor of Chemistry at Edinburgh and a friend of Reichenbach, published an annotated English translation of Reichenbach's work. [104] Reichenbach had been researching the alleged physiological and therapeutic effects of magnets and crystals and found that they produced sensations when put close to susceptible sick individuals, and that they emitted 'flame-like emanations' that could be seen only by his sensitive subjects. All objects were susceptible to the Odic force, which, Reichenbach believed, was reinforced by the sun, moon and planets. [105] He believed that he had discovered a new universal force that was identical with so-called mesmeric fluid, and he thought that his own scientific discovery had successfully debunked Mesmer's theory. Braid responded to this in a pamphlet that he published in 1846 after conducting his own experiments with magnets. He found that subjects experienced sensations only if they had been told what to expect, and dismissed the manifestations of the Odic force as being simply the effect of imagination upon sensory perception. [106]

In order to understand Braid's concept of the imagination, particularly following his later association with Garth Wilkinson, it is helpful to discuss the distinction between imagination and fancy, particularly in relation to the concept of imagination that lies within the Western esoteric tradition. [107] 'Fancy' relates to the popular concept of imagination as relating to something that is not real, or, as Coleridge described it, is the result of merely playing with the pre-existing content of memory. [108] This

114

contrasts with the Western esoteric concept of imagination as an active and creative process. The latter concept has been highlighted particularly by Henry Corbin, who described the active imagination as an intermediary between the world of the senses and the spiritual world, a realm which is 'the "place of apparition" of spiritual beings, Angels and Spirits'.[109] The creative power of the imagination was recognized by Paracelsus, for whom imagination was central to the practice of medicine.[110]

Swedenborg also held the concept of active imagination.[111] He described four levels of imagination, the lowest being fantasy and the highest a state of 'active or living imagination, which, in particular, should be called the vision of the prophets'.[112] As a reader of Paracelsus, Coleridge and Swedenborg, Wilkinson cannot fail to have absorbed the esoteric concept of active imagination, and indeed this is clearly displayed in his writing. He believed that thoughts could become physically manifest in the material world. In 1848, the year in which he first met James Braid, Wilkinson wrote:

> I hold that forms of thought, becoming successively grosser and grosser, or clothing themselves into new forms in a series, may and do exist in the outer world; and when there answer through a series of likenesses to their prototypes in the brain, and are referable to them.[113]

In *The Human Body*, Wilkinson applied this concept to illness and healing, developing the idea that imagination could be both the cause and cure of illness, commenting that 'in imagination, what you seem to have, you have; and the body is, among other things, full of imagination'.[114] Wilkinson admitted, and indeed rejoiced in, the proposal that his favoured treatment, homoeopathy, works through the agency of the imagination: 'This imagination, by the wonderful connection of the mind with the body, is not only the prophet, but in part the realization, of a new-born health'.[115]

Braid and Wilkinson first met when Wilkinson was lecturing in Manchester. Wilkinson described Braid's demonstration of his hypnotic technique:

Yesterday afternoon I spent again at Mr Braid's, when he shewed us a
wonderful case: a young lady, who hypnotised herself, and then, in obedience
to our actions upon her, went through the dramatization of the passions and
emotions. To see her in the attitude of prayer, was heavenly and beautiful:
& when Mr B played upon his organ...she joined in voice and attitude, &
constituted a living statue of adoration almost too affecting for us to look at.
To some of the music she danced...I never saw anything so spiritual in this
world...What is odd, Braid disbelieves in all the spirituality and clairvoyance.
'Try her' said he. I asked her where I came from. She replied, 'From over
the water'. 'What water'. 'From France'. 'When was I there'. 'Three months
since'. 'What did I see'. Here a look of speechless horror, which continued, &
she could not utter a word, but at every repetition of the question, cowed with
terror. Braid said it was all gammon, & a mere coincidence. [116]

Wilkinson spent more time with Braid, and described his experience of being hyp-
notized by him:

I tead with Braid, & I saw many sublime and ridiculous experiments. He
hypnotised me three times. It is a dodge far beyond Mesmerism. I don't
know when I have felt so well as this morning, which I am sure, comes
from the tranquil air of the state into which I was thrown. The respiration
is the grand secret. If you can draw that, you pull down any quality of wine
you please from the spiritual cellars of the brain, which in their turn are fed
from the vintage of the skies. It is a powerful curative agent. [117]

By the time that he wrote *The Human Body*, Wilkinson had developed clear
concepts about the way in which hypnosis operated. Like Braid, he believed that
mesmerism and hypnosis were different, with occult phenomena occurring only
during mesmerism. His evidence for believing that hypnosis and mesmerism are two
different phenomena was that hypnosis can be self-induced, whereas mesmerism
required the presence of a mesmerizer who operated on the subject by means of his

magnetic sphere. [118] Wilkinson's concept of the process of hypnosis was psychological and, as such, this differed fundamentally from Braid's physiological explanation. Wilkinson described hypnotic treatment as having two elements:

> 1. Where it produces trance, it has the benefits of the mesmeric sleep, or furnishes so strong a dose of rest, that many cases are cured by that alone. But 2. The suggestion of ideas of health, tone, duty, hope, which produce dreams influential upon the organization, enables the operator by this means to fulfil the indication of directly ministering to that mind diseased, which always accompanies and aggravates physical disorders. We have a direct proof of the continuation of the mind through the body, in the way in which suggestions directed to the mind respecting the organs, operate upon the latter...This order of facts has an important bearing upon the origin as well as cure of disease, rendering it probable that a large number of ills come directly out of the patient's mind...Viewed in this light, many physical changes of structure may be regarded as organic insanities or spells... [119]

In an extensive footnote, Wilkinson showed the generalizability of this concept to other types of medical treatment, an effect that he referred to as 'imagination-treatment'. [120]

In 1851, the year that Wilkinson published these observations, Braid changed his view about the mode of action of hypnosis. He was congratulated about this after giving a lecture on the subject to the Royal Institution:

> [Mr Catlow] congratulated Mr. Braid on having come round to a common sense view...Mr. Braid started originally with the theory that fixed gazing at some object, until the muscles of the eye were strained, was an absolute necessity in the production of these phenomena, and said nothing about the mind. Dr. Hodgson thought Mr. Braid was not to be disparaged for having changed his views after nine years of study, he was rather to be praised for his candour. [121]

In his next published work, Braid quoted extensively from Wilkinson's book, including a verbatim quote from Wilkinson's psychological formulation reproduced above. Braid said that Wilkinson had 'a mind of the *very highest order*, and was, therefore, peculiarly fitted for dealing successfully with the *psychological* part of the question'.[122] In a remarkable turnaround from his earlier views, Braid highlighted the importance of suggestion and imagination in his hypnotic process, and, like Wilkinson, commented on the importance of the same mental phenomena in the effects of other medical treatments. He quoted Scottish philosopher Dugald Stewart:

> it appears to me, that the general conclusions established by Mesmer's practice, with respect to the physical effects of the principle of Imitation and of the faculty of Imagination...are incomparably more curious, than if he had actually succeeded in ascertaining the existence of his boasted fluid...[123]

It is apparent that Wilkinson's concepts had a fundamental effect on Braid's thinking, moving him towards a more psychological formulation that was the forerunner of dynamic psychology.[124]

Another influence on Braid's thinking was William Benjamin Carpenter. Carpenter was the son of the Presbyterian minister at George's Meeting House in Exeter.[125] After training in Bristol, London and Edinburgh, he finally moved to London in 1845.[126] By then he was an established author and had developed the primary themes by which he is still known. He was appointed to the Fullerian Professorship of Physiology at the Royal Institution and was elected Fellow of the Royal Society.

Carpenter was interested in the work of W R Grove who proposed that physical forces are interrelated and interconvertible.[127] In his *Mutual Relations of the Vital and Physical Forces* (1850), Carpenter commented on Grove's work, and argued that the same principle can be extended to include the vital force.[128] He believed that these forces were different manifestations of a single creative will. The universality of the laws and forces governing the universe was, Carpenter thought, entirely compatible with the concept of an eternal and immutable divine will that continues to be active in the created world. He considered this idea to be so obvious that he was unable to understand why science increasingly rejected religion.

Carpenter argued that, in man, the vital force is intimately related to the nervous system, which carries a 'Nervous Agency' generated from the nerve cells. The vital force and the Nervous Agency are not identical, but the Nervous Agency, as its name suggests, acts as the agent of the vital force. This Nervous Agency is related both to the conscious mind and to the bodily organs, and so is an intermediary between the two. Because of this, the mind is an important agent in the generation of disease.

Carpenter is best known for his contribution to the development of psychological theory. This was motivated by his interest in the phenomena of mesmerism and spiritualism. In 1852, Carpenter presented his concept of 'ideo-motor' reflexes, by means of which ideas can give rise to involuntary bodily reactions without the individual having any conscious plan to act. [129] He used this to explain the phenomena of somnambulism, in which subjects passively obey suggestions from a mesmerist without any conscious act of their own will. This, he said, is made possible by the subject allowing their own will to be in abeyance during the mesmeric or hypnotic process; Carpenter maintained that this is not, as was popularly thought, a result of the magnetizer overriding the will of the subject with his own. He also found here an explanation of other phenomena commonly believed to be supernatural, such as the movement of a dowsing rod, and the swinging of a pendulum towards letters on a table, as used sometimes in spiritualist seances. In these cases, Carpenter believed, it is the *expectations* of the subject that lead to movements without any conscious awareness of it.

Carpenter's concept of 'unconscious cerebration' developed out of his idea of the ideo-motor reflex. He used the term 'ego' freely and in the same sense that we now understand it. He noted the strong resistance to the concept of unconscious mental processes that prevailed in Britain at that time:

> To affirm that the Cerebrum may act upon impressions transmitted to it, and may elaborate Intellectual results...*without any consciousness* on our own parts, is held by many Metaphysicians, more especially in Britain, to be an altogether untenable and even a most objectionable doctrine. [130]

He gave examples that he believed proved the existence of unconscious cerebration, including temporary forgetfulness of something that returns to conscious awareness only when we focus on a different topic; solutions to problems that appear after sleep; and scientific insights that appear to come from nowhere. He pointed out that not only thoughts but also emotions can be carried outside of conscious awareness, and that memories of emotionally distressing events can remain hidden from conscious-ness until their recurrence is triggered by circumstances. [131]

Was William B Carpenter influenced by Swedenborg? John S Haller, in his book on Swedenborg and mesmerism, asserts boldly that Swedenborg's ideas were 'unknown' to Carpenter. [132] This is not correct: not only was Carpenter a personal friend of Garth Wilkinson, whose main aim in life was to promote and interpret Swedenborg's ideas, but also he discussed Swedenborg explicitly in his essay 'On the fallacies of testimony in relation to the supernatural'. [133] It is plain from this discussion that Carpenter was familiar with, and valued, Swedenborg's scientific works, whilst rejecting the validity of his later spiritual experiences. Therefore, we are at liberty to examine the possible influence that Swedenborg had upon Carpenter.

In his *Principia*, Swedenborg puts forward the idea that all the forces of nature originate from a single point which is the latent energy of the whole universe. [134] The *Principia* was well known to the scientifically orientated followers of Swedenborg, including Garth Wilkinson, but for those who might find the book heavy going, R M Patterson, described as a 'late Professor of the University of Pennsylvania', had provided a simple summary:

Descending from 'The First Natural Point,'—a term by which pure motion is designated, Swedenborg defines the phenomena of heat, light, magnet-ism, and the elementary substances themselves, as so many graduated manifestations of Infinite Activity. [135]

In his subsequent work, *Outlines of a Philosophical Argument on the Infinite and Final Cause of Creation*, which was translated by Wilkinson, Swedenborg extended this idea to include the soul, the life force of the body. [136] We thus have a formulation from Swedenborg's scientific works that is not merely consistent with, but is similar in detail to, Carpenter's much-quoted later thesis that all forces, including the vital force, are representations of one single active power.

The concept of 'unconscious cerebration', to use Carpenter's term, is also central to Swedenborg's psychology. According to Swedenborg, spiritual influx into the human brain, either immediate from the Lord or mediate from spirits, occurs without our being aware of it, and yet it has a fundamental effect upon human thinking and behaviour. Of course, this is different from Carpenter's thesis, which emphasizes the effect of sensory rather than spiritual input to the brain. Examples closer to Carpenter's thinking can be found in Wilkinson's works. For example, Wilkinson recalled an acquaintance who denied the reality of ghosts and apparitions, whilst at the same time feeling 'a cold steam down the back'. [137] Wilkinson differentiated between 'mental faith'—the conscious awareness of an idea or belief—and 'corporeal faith', which is a belief not in conscious awareness which gives rise to bodily effects. [138] He claimed the beneficial effects of such treatments as charms, mesmerism and homoeopathy can be brought about by means of a 'corporeal faith' even when a person's reason denies the possibility of benefit. Corporeal faith is 'fundamental or organic', and its vehicle is the imagination: not the conscious imagination, but the imagination that is 'a body and a structure'. [139] If the term 'unconscious cerebration' is substituted for 'corporeal faith', then we have the elements of Carpenter's concept of the ideo-motor reflex, published by Wilkinson a year before Carpenter's groundbreaking lecture on the subject.

A recent scholarly article on ideo-motor action affirms that research in psychology has focused on a question that was hitherto unanswered: 'How is the mind able to use the body to achieve its goals, without any notion of the anatomy and neurophysiology of its functioning'? [140] Whilst this question may be difficult for modern science to answer, it is readily answered by the ancient formulation that includes the notion of the soul as a formative agent. Garth Wilkinson, following Swedenborg, was clear that the soul has its seat in the brain, from where it extends to all parts of the body; the body is constructed specifically for the purpose of being the agent of the soul in the material world. Wilkinson believed that the medium for the transmission of the soul throughout the body is the 'nervous fluid' that is produced by the cells of the cerebral cortex. This concept resonates precisely with Carpenter's theory of a 'Nervous Agency' that is produced by the brain cells and which acts as an intermediary between the mind and the body.[141]

It was Wilkinson, not Carpenter, whom Braid credited with developing the psychology of hypnosis.[142] Carpenter, like Braid, quoted extensively from Wilkinson's *The Human Body*, and referred to Wilkinson as 'an intelligent friend, who has paid special attention to the psychological part of this enquiry'.[143] It has been suggested that Carpenter was the intellectual leader of a small informal group of 'physiological psychologists' who included Benjamin Collins Brodie, Robert Dunn, Henry Holland, Thomas Laycock, John Daniel Morell and Daniel Noble.[144] Wilkinson not only collaborated with Carpenter, but was also an 'intimate and excellent friend' of John Daniel Morell.[145] Carpenter, Wilkinson and Morell dined together, and Morell attended lectures at the Swedenborg Association.[146] It is clear that Garth Wilkinson should be included in the august list of 'physiological psychologists' who are regarded as forming the vanguard of modern psychology.

— 5 —

The Other World: Garth Wilkinson's Adoption and Rejection of Spiritualism

The Spiritual Manifestation Movement is shaking all minds here. I know it is the Earthquake of this Age...Revelations continuous with Swedenborg's, & far more important for this Age, are come, & are coming.
Garth Wilkinson, writing in 1855[1]

spiritist informations tell us nothing. They are only continua of the earthly senses, which are nowhere continuous with the spiritual or the heavenly. They are brainless of the upper realm.
Garth Wilkinson, writing in 1885[2]

Fig. 5: One of a series of spirit photographs owned by Wilkinson.
Swedenborg Society Archive K/126 (a).

I n 1848, mysterious rapping noises began to disturb the occupants of a small wooden farmhouse in Rochester, New York. The house was the home of John D Fox, his wife Margaret, and their two younger daughters Margaretta (Maggie) and Catherine (Kate), aged fifteen and twelve. The rappings were attributed to a peddler who was reputed to have been murdered in the cellar of the house, and the girls claimed to have established communication with the supposed spirit. They became famous locally and began travelling to demonstrate their powers of communication with spirits.[3] Other spirit mediums emerged, the phenomenon spread rapidly in America, and spiritualism arrived in England in 1852 when Mrs Hayden, the wife of a New England journalist, began holding seances in London.

This is the standard history of the beginning of so-called 'modern spiritualism', which is better termed 'American spiritualism'. Whilst academic writers today recognize that there were important antecedents for modern popular spiritualism, this was not widely understood in Victorian England. The author William Howitt, a friend of Wilkinson, observed in 1863 that spiritualism 'has almost universally in this country been regarded as an entirely new phenomenon'.[4] This view, he said, was the result of 'profound ignorance' of the history of spirit manifestations, for 'American spiritualism is but the last new blossom of a very ancient tree, coloured by the atmosphere in which it has put forth'.[5] He gave examples of earlier spiritual contact, including that of

Emanuel Swedenborg, whom he regarded as 'perhaps the greatest spirit-medium that ever appeared'.[6] Even the rapping that was characteristic of American spiritualism was no new phenomenon; in an addendum to her husband's translation of Ennemoser's *History of Magic*, William's wife Mary Howitt described some of her own researches into earlier spirit phenomena, including spirit rappings heard in the Wesley household in 1716, when John Wesley was thirteen years old.[7] For the Howitts, like many intellectuals of the day, the atmosphere into which the new spiritualism had been put forth was suffused with animal magnetism and Swedenborgianism.[8]

Garth Wilkinson regarded mesmeric somnambulism as the beginning of modern spiritualism, and he offered his own potted history of spiritualism:

> Spiritualism began in its present form, in this country... under the guise of Mesmerism... But out of Clairvoyance, or Mesmerized Sight, arose a second spiritual wave,—of minds impressed, and speaking by impression, or, as it used to be called, Prophesying... Then came the third and greater wave, of Spirit-rapping and Table-moving. The table tipped to the letters of the alphabet, and spirits spelt out messages to those around the board. By-and-by, instead of the table, the hands of certain individuals were chosen to communicate the messages of the spirits, by involuntary writing.[9]

Garth Wilkinson here identifies three successive waves of modern spiritualism, but there was another current that was based on magical practices. This related to the ritual summoning of spirits for magical purposes, a practice that has ancient roots.[10] This practice, condemned by the Christian church, had always tended to be secretive. Nevertheless, the magical tradition continued into the nineteenth century. One of the leading proponents of this practice in the early nineteenth century was Frederick Hockley. As a young man, Hockley worked in the occult bookshop of John Denley, where he read the works of the Swedenborgian sympathizer Ebenezer Sibly.[11] Later in life, when discussing Swedenborg's concept of the spirit world and its interaction with man, Hockley used Wilkinson's biography of Swedenborg as his source.[12] Although he engaged with the new wave of American spiritualism—for example, attending the seances of the celebrated medium Daniel Dunglas Home—Hockley preferred the traditional method of communing with spirits by using a crystal ball. [13] In 1853 he founded the 'Croyden circle', a group of spiritualists who received messages from an elite group of spirits presided over by the 'Crowned Angel of the Seventh Sphere'. [14] The utopian socialist Robert Owen, by then an old man, was particularly excited by messages from the Crowned Angel that were directed to him personally, and in his letters Hockley kept Owen updated on these pronouncements. [15]

In 1847, the year before the famous spirit rappings began in America, Garth Wilkinson experienced spirit rappings in his own London home, and he wrote excitedly and at length about it to his friend Henry James, Sr. His grandmother, who Wilkinson described as a strong-minded and controlling person, had died recently.

> Within a fortnight after her decease, our bedroom at Store Street became the theatre of strange noises and tappings. The first time the thing occurred—three taps, most low, yet impressive and commanding—we were both awakened by it simultaneously, and falling asleep again after mutually remarking the singularity of the sounds, we were both equally infested by dreams so heavily uncomfortable, that we were rendered bodily ill by the event for two days afterwards... [16]

When Wilkinson told the taps to stop, the initial response was an increased intensity of the tapping, which then stopped. Wilkinson attempted to find natural explanations for the phenomena:

> I invented several notable hypotheses, every one of which I felt was an attempt at self-deception before I had uttered it. I descanted learnedly upon what a stray mouse might do—upon the natural creaking of old furniture—upon boards and planks, and their uneasy language—upon nothing at all, as having accounted for many things, and therefore worth a trial in this case. My wife, however, was more honest to her own convictions, and from the moment

of the first taps, declared that she knew too well the sound of the old lady's leather-padded stick; and that there was no mistake about the matter.[17]

The rappings were heard by Wilkinson's young son, and also by Garth's brother George who was staying with him. At the same time, rappings were heard at the Veterinary College, where Wilkinson's grandmother had died and where his sister still lived. Later, Fanny Roberts, the sister of his brother George's wife, came to visit, and lodged close to the Veterinary College. Wilkinson said of her that she 'has been for some little time past, one of the most remarkable clairvoyants (saving the Seeress of Provorst) that I have heard of'.[18] Whilst there, she developed 'fits' which Wilkinson and his brother George treated by mesmerizing her. On a subsequent visit to the Veterinary College she suffered a fit so severe that she could not be moved from there, at which time she began to have visions of a spirit:

In the middle of the night all was tranquil, when suddenly she cried out to George: 'Oh what a funny old woman there is, sitting at the bottom of my bed'. George went into her room, and mesmerized her, and the presence then disappeared, and George succeeded in convincing her that it was a delusion. No sooner, however, had he gone, than the visitant was there again, and this time Fanny Roberts sprang out of the bedroom, calling out 'Oh! George, it is no delusion: it is your grandmother'...Five or six times was the visit repeated to the terror stricken patient in the course of that night; and on one occasion the spirit sat upon her legs, which as she said, nearly destroyed her...After this she told us, that from having loved this world too much, the old lady was unresting in the other...and that unless certain things—most trivial things—were attended to at once concerning her effects, she should continue to disturb the family.[19]

Wilkinson was convinced that Fanny had reported information that she could not possibly have known other than through spirit communication, which she said took place by direct transference of thought rather than through natural speech. He was concerned that he had harmed her by mesmerizing her, so he refrained from doing this again, but her experiences of spirit manifestations continued and spread to include communications from other deceased family members. Wilkinson noted that Fanny, when in the normal waking state, could remember only vestiges of her experiences when mesmerized.[20] He believed that the cases of Fanny and the other somnambulists showed that 'mesmerism is doing a Providential Work here, and if it goes on conquering as it has done, it will root out a certain species of scepticism from the land'.[21]

These personal experiences of Wilkinson, together with his central interest in mesmerism and Swedenborg, made him a ready believer in the phenomena of American spiritualism when they reached England. In 1853, the year after Mrs Hayden had arrived in London, Wilkinson wrote to Henry James, Sr that:

> Nothing is talked of here but table movings and spirit rappings. There is, so far as I know, no class of persons of importance who are not penetrated with this odd-looking movement. The only people who are actively contra are the stony materialists and the grassy philosophers: both of them hate this noise which the approaching spiritual world makes with its big toes. The pious Atheists too want Mrs Hayden and her coadjutors to be put in prison: she is, they say, blasphemous; and degrades the mighty dead by summoning them to her table: as if the meanest degradation was not infinitely superior to the annihilation to which man has been condemned by Philosophers and Atheists. For the rest, I really could not have credited that so vast a change of state of mind could have come over a nation, as this which has come to England by this simple means. All classes are opened now about spiritual intercourse; and are beginning to learn that the other world is human in its good, bad, and indifferent.[22]

In England, American spiritualism flowered first in London and in the industrial North. These first strongholds of spiritualism in England map closely to the areas that had earlier embraced the ideas of Emanuel Swedenborg, and some sections of the population of these areas were predisposed to accepting spiritualism, not only because of their understanding of Swedenborg's spiritual experiences, but also by the phenomena of mesmeric somnambulism. In the industrial North, there was a living folk tradition of belief in spirits, and visiting lecturers at the Mechanics' Institutes and other establishments that promoted popular education for the masses had familiarized them with the phenomena of mesmerism. The ideas of Emanuel Swedenborg had been disseminated amongst the factory workers by the Reverend John Clowes, who had a firm belief in the reality of spirit communication.[23] In London, it was the intelligentsia and aristocracy that first adopted spiritualism. Many of these early adopters were followers or at least readers of Swedenborg, and they had already accepted a probable relationship between mesmeric somnambulism and Swedenborg's experiences. The early enthusiasts for spiritualism held their own seances to which friends were invited, and the phenomena demonstrated at these seances were so intriguing that the movement spread rapidly to involve many people who had no knowledge of earlier spirit communication, and who therefore believed, as observed by Howitt, that this was a new phenomenon.

Spiritualism can be seen as a reaction against the increasingly materialist atheism of the day, at a time when traditional Christian belief systems were threatened by the march of scientific discovery and conventional Christian practice was not in keeping with the freethinking individualism of the time.[24] Spiritualism produced observable phenomena that could be regarded as 'scientific proof' of a spiritual dimension, which marked it as a 'spiritual science' that was in keeping with the other empirical sciences. For its adherents, spiritualism formed the basis of a new religious outlook that stressed the possibility of individual self-development without the need for mediation by a priestly class.[25] It had natural affinities with other social movements that carried the same overall philosophy of freedom, individualism and self-improvement, including temperance, vegetarianism, antislavery, antivivisection and Nonconformist religion. Spiritualism also related to the position of women in society.[26] Women were regarded as particularly gifted mediums because they were thought to have a natural feminine trait of passivity. Critics regarded the trance states of mesmerism and spiritualism, in which the will was given over to another, as signs of mental weakness akin to hysteria.[27] On the other hand, becoming a spiritualist medium offered women an opportunity for status and recognition outside of the home, which traditionally had been the only place in which they could exercise moral and spiritual authority. Historian Alex Owen has pointed out that the time of expansion of spiritualism (the 1860s and 1870s) was also a time when issues of sexual equality and women's rights were current, with campaigns for suffrage and improvement in the economic and legal position of women.[28] Logie Barrow, meanwhile, has emphasized the close relationship between spiritualism—particularly 'plebeian spiritualism', as he terms it—and socialism. The spiritual afterworld, which spiritualists termed 'Summerland', was believed to be modelled along socialist lines, and it was thought that millenarian transformation could be brought about in this world by angels.[29] Many early spiritualists were followers of the utopian socialist Robert Owen; one of the earliest groups of adherents in Keighley, Yorkshire included many Owenites, and their magazine, the *Yorkshire Spiritual Telegraph* (1855), was edited by a Swedenborgian follower of Owen, John Garnett.[30] Garth Wilkinson, particularly in his younger years, fully embraced these liberalizing trends in society, and so was naturally drawn to spiritualism against the backdrop of his involvement with mesmerism and Swedenborg.

One of the early groups in London to be inspired by American spiritualism was the circle of Elihu Rich.[31] Rich was a London-based Swedenborgian, who in 1839 had established the 'New Church Mutual Instruction Society' with the aim of systematically studying correspondences.[32] He published a biography of Swedenborg and was joint author and editor of *The Occult Sciences: Sketches of the Traditions and Superstitions of Past Times and the Marvels of the Present Day* (1855), which covered a wide variety of esoteric topics that ranged from fairies and angels to necromancy; talismans and amulets; spiritualism; and mesmerism.[33] By 1854, a group of Swedenborgians organized by Rich gathered in London to listen to the trance utterances of a seeress called Annie.[34] Rich wrote of his experiences with spiritualism, protecting his identity from all but his inner circle by using only his initials, E. R.[35] This spiritualist circle included James Knight, the leader of the local Swedenborgian group in Derby, as well as 'a select few in London'.[36] In his book Rich defended vigorously the practice of spiritualism against critics from within the sectarian New Church. He cited examples from the Bible of spirit communication, and also observed from 'within [his] own knowledge' that Reverend Thomas Hartley, a friend of the elderly Swedenborg, 'might have added the testimony of his own experience'.[37] Rich was also aware that John Clowes had communicated with spirits. He described the spiritual vision of an elderly lady, recently deceased, 'who in her bright, youthful days often acted as amanuensis to Mr. Clowes'.[38] This lady, a few days before her death, reported undergoing a spiritual experience in which she believed herself to be in the presence of angels and the Lord. Rich believed that communication with spirits was not only acceptable to Swedenborgian principles, but was at the very core of them: the believer in spiritualism and mesmerism, wrote Rich, is 'the very man who adheres faithfully to them [the truths revealed by Swedenborg]'.[39]

Rich's medium Annie claimed to obtain her revelations from paradise and from a 'gold and silver garden'.[40] Sophia De Morgan also described a medium who operated from within a 'gold and silver garden'. Echoing Swedenborg's natural, spiritual and celestial degrees, this medium described three levels through which she ascended when experiencing her spiritual revelations: the first was green countryside like that of earth, but 'clearer and brighter and *more real*'; the next was the 'gold and silver garden', and the highest level was a 'jewelled garden'.[41] There is good reason to believe that Garth Wilkinson was also a member of this loosely formed group. In his notes from the period 1854-6 he described seances with an Annie Milner, who was, at various times, in the 'Green Garden' and the 'Gold and Silver Garden'. Annie saw her sitters' presence in the spiritual world as well as in the material world, and some of her pronouncements were very flattering to Garth Wilkinson. In one note, Wilkinson recorded her as revealing that 'I can see you [JJGW]——there are three spirits near. . .I asked for a message for you and had to take it from the Girdle of your dress: Be patient and merciful for thou hast great work to do. . .Jehovah will help you and be by your side. That's all. The Girdle of Purple silk. The message written on silver paper and fastened to it'.[42]

Another medium observed by Wilkinson produced spirit messages that lacked any Swedenborgian context and were more typical in content for that time, particularly amongst mediums from America. The medium, Mrs Newton, transmitted messages from an American Indian spirit guide, who told those present what the 'Great Spirit' had communicated to him, such as 'Great Spirit tell Indian when he weep in sorrow for the wrongs done [by] white brother, he tell him that wrong be black as charcoal, so Indian Spirit tell him in good time that charcoal will become a diamond, if he yield him to nature's laws'.[43]

Wilkinson's friend William Howitt was perhaps the best-known early advocate for spiritualism in England. He was a prominent member of a loosely formed group of spiritualists who held seances in their homes.[44] Recorded members of this group include physician Dr John Ashburner,[45] Augustus and Sophia De Morgan,[46] Mr and Mrs Newton Crossland,[47] Benjamin Coleman,[48] Professor and Mrs Maurice Nenner,[49] Garth Wilkinson, and his brother William Wilkinson and his wife.[50] The Howitts had became interested in spiritualism whilst reading and translating Ennemoser's *The History of Magic*, which includes enthusiastic accounts of animal magnetism, Paracelsus, Jacob Boehme and Swedenborg.[51] In his own book *The History of the Supernatural* (1863) Howitt gives a sweeping overview of spirit manifestations through the ages, and he reviews the revelations of Christian theosophists including Jacob Boehme, John Pordage, Jane Leade, Emanuel Swedenborg and Madame Guyon, all of whom he regarded as having been in contact with the spiritual world. His book, particularly the second volume, has several references to the work of his friend Garth Wilkinson.[52] Howitt and his circle believed they were following the traditions of theosophy, animal magnetism, spirit communication and magic, all interpreted within a Christian framework. This group was interested in what they regarded as the manifestations of God in this world, 'on the throne of his own magnificent universe'.[53] Like Garth Wilkinson, Howitt deplored transcendental idealism; he berated Immanuel Kant for reducing the concept of God to a subjective metaphysical abstraction. Later in life, Mary Howitt rejected spiritualism, saying that it was 'one of the greatest misfortunes that ever visited us; it was false, all false and full of lies. Revelations seemed to come, but they were nothing but the suggestions of devils'.[54] William Howitt, however, remained convinced of the reality of spiritual manifestations, even though he recognized that there were many fraudsters. In a letter to his niece in 1867, Howitt explained that the seemingly banal expressions of the spirits, such as rapping and the manifestation of flowers, were the result of the debased spiritual state of humanity, so that spirits could attract their attention only by these crude physical means; in the future, he believed, the power of the spirit would 'display its ancient glory in healings and teachings'.[55] Later in his life Howitt dismissed the more crude forms of spiritualism, but maintained that 'this dispensation [spiritualism] has been for us the chief fact of our earth pilgrimage'.[56] For William Howitt, spirit manifestations were, quite simply, positive proof of survival after death.

The Howitts were close friends of the socially prominent Cowper-Temples. William Francis Cowper, a Liberal Member of Parliament, later became William Francis Cowper-Temple, first Baron Mount-Temple. He and his wife Georgiana were readers of Swedenborg and their home at Broadlands in Hampshire has been described as a haven for movements that emphasized 'moral purity', such as temperance, homoeopathy, vegetarianism and anti-vaccinationism.[57] Cowper-Temple was a devout Christian with a penchant for preaching, but he was liberal in his spirituality and held other religious systems in high regard. Gladstone described him as having 'the stamp of purity, modesty, gentleness...in a peculiar degree'.[58] His wife Georgiana had been introduced to spiritualism by Mary Howitt, and seances were held at their home by leading mediums, including Daniel Dunglas Home. Thomas Lake Harris was also an honoured guest at the home of the Cowper-Temples at Broadlands, and he was intent on persuading William Cowper-Temple to join his utopian community, the Brotherhood of New Life, at Brocton in New York State.[59] The Cowper-Temples helped to fund this community, but did not make the same mistake as Laurence Oliphant by joining it.[60] Garth Wilkinson's friend and admirer, artist Dante Gabriel Rossetti, who founded the Pre-Raphaelite Brotherhood, was an intimate friend of the Cowper-Temples and attended many of their seances, as did the renowned art critic and social commentator John Ruskin.[61]

Garth Wilkinson was acquainted with Ruskin, but was less impressed with him than most of his contemporaries.[62] Although Ruskin was a believer in spiritualism, his attitude towards it was ambivalent. He had an early interest in the phenomena of spirit drawing and visited the home of Garth Wilkinson in 1857 in order to examine the 'spirit drawings' that had been produced by Wilkinson's young son.[63] Ruskin's active involvement with spiritualist seances was encouraged by Georgiana Cowper-Temple.[64] Ruskin was drawn to spiritualism by his agonizing uncertainty about immortality. He attended his first seance at the home of Mrs Gregory, widow of William Gregory, Professor of Chemistry at Edinburgh University, who was involved in various esoteric pursuits including mesmerism.[65] Ruskin was convinced of the reality of spiritualism after attending seances by Daniel Dunglas Home, but he did not wish his belief to be made public. Despite his acceptance of the phenomena of spiritualism, he reminded Georgiana that such manifestations were predicted to precede the Second Coming of Christ in the Book of Revelation. When asked by Holman Hunt how he had regained his faith in immortality, Ruskin replied that 'what has mainly caused the change in my views is the unanswerable evidence of spiritualism. I know there is much vulgar fraud and stupidity connected with it, but underneath there is, I am sure, enough to convince us that there is personal life independent of the body; but with this once proved, I have no further interest in the pursuit of spiritualism'.[66]

Given the interests of the Cowper-Temples, it is not surprising that Garth Wilkinson was part of their circle. Georgiana attended seances at Garth Wilkinson's house, and in 1869 Wilkinson dined with the Cowper-Temples in the elevated company of Prince George, Duke of Cambridge, as well as Annie Watts (née Howitt) and her husband, and François-Louis Bugnion, a follower of Thomas Lake Harris who called himself Bishop St Paul.[67] In 1888 they wrote inviting the elderly Wilkinson to stay with them, in a letter couched in intimate terms.[68] Unfortunately, William Cowper-Temple died before that invitation could be taken up.

William Wilkinson, Garth's brother, was a leading spiritualist and also Secretary of the Swedenborg Society. He edited *The Spiritual Magazine* and wrote a book about his experiences with spiritualism. In this book, he described how he and his wife became involved with spiritualism following the death of their son at the age of eleven.[69] First his other son, and then his wife, began to receive messages that apparently came from the dead boy, and then William's wife developed the faculty of spirit writing and drawing. Her drawings included flowers and buildings, which she was told represented the progress of her dead son to higher spiritual levels.

Spirit writing and drawing were, and remain, well-recognized phenomena amongst spiritualists.[70] Garth Wilkinson did not write about his sister-in-law's spirit drawings, but it is clear that he accepted the reality of such phenomena. He described a visit from a friend who drew extinct animals including deinotherium, an ancient relative of the elephant. Wilkinson was particularly interested in this medium because the spirits with which he claimed to be in contact were dismissive of other mediums; Wilkinson thought that this 'frees us from all idea of Authority in every such case; and presents the results of mediumship as merely suggestive. This is what the spirit world is to the natural—a perpetual suggestion'.[71] For Wilkinson, even in his early enthusiasm for spiritualism, mediums had no claim to the divine authority that he recognized in Swedenborg. Always eager to find a practical use for new experiences, Wilkinson developed spirit writing to compose poetry, and spirit drawing to picture homoeopathic remedies and to use as a treatment for insanity.[72]

Garth Wilkinson himself edited the short-lived *Spiritual Herald*, which survived for only six months in 1856. The magazine was received positively, although with reservations, by mainstream Swedenborgians in England. The popular Swedenborgian journal, *The Newchurchman*, welcomed the fact that the *Spiritual Herald* was edited by followers of Swedenborg, which they felt would result in it showing 'a degree of common sense and intelligence superior to the ordinary run of such publications'.[73] They observed that:

> As spiritualism is now one of the great facts of the age, and will, in all likelihood prove itself a strong ally, or a desperate enemy of the New Church, it becomes us all, in either case, to make ourselves well acquainted with its character and pretensions; and hence we welcome the 'Spiritual Herald' as a periodical likely from the character of its conductors, to give us a calm and impartial record of those marvellous phenomena which will soon be the talk of Christendom.[74]

Despite this guarded acceptance of Garth Wilkinson's journal, spiritualism was already a controversial topic within the sectarian New Church, and the apparently balanced viewpoint expressed in 1856 would soon turn into an implacable opposition to any manifestation of the spiritualist movement.

Daniel Dunglas Home (1833-86)

Daniel Dunglas Home was perhaps the most famous of the American mediums that came to England. His fame rested upon the unusual nature of the phenomena that he produced. Levitation was standard in his seances; for example, it was reputed that he once floated out of a second-storey window and returned through the window of an adjacent room.[75] Born near Edinburgh in 1833, Home was taken by his aunt to live in America at the age of nine. After achieving some popularity as a medium in America, he arrived in London in 1855. He declared that when his ship docked in England 'I stood there alone, with not one friend to welcome me'.[76] Once in London, he took lodgings which he had been recommended by friends in New York. He quickly became known for his seances, which were attended by the intelligentsia and literati of London, and he was soon invited to stay with Mr J S Rymer, a solicitor in the London suburb of Ealing.[77] According to Home's wife, it was there that Home met Garth Wilkinson, who attended Home's seances in Ealing.[78] Wilkinson was clearly awestruck by the phenomena that he observed there and believed in them without reservation. In a letter to a friend, Wilkinson reported enthusiastically that:

> A curious event occurred the other night. My wife & I went to see a Mr Home, an American medium of some renown. Besides the most extraordinary physical phenomena (which proved to my mind that the power of spirit is actual & tangible,——for I literally grasped the spirit-fingers in my own,——and that bye and bye the upper world will prove to be the grand motive power,)——at the end of the séance, to my wife's astonishment, a spirit requested by Alphabet to speak with her. He spelt out this——'George B., my dear Emma, I live. Imortality [sic] is a great truth. Oh! How I wish my dear Elizabeth had been present.'[79]

In his autobiography *Incidents in My Life* (1864), Home reported that Garth Wilkinson attended many of his seances in 1855.[80] Wilkinson wrote an enthusiastic account of Home's abilities, referring to him as the 'Wizard of the North', in an article that he contributed to the *Morning Advertiser* under the pseudonym of Verax. Home published Garth Wilkinson's long account in full in his autobiography.[81] In this article, Wilkinson describes a variety of phenomena, including the levitation of a large and heavy table; rapping and bells ringing; the materialization of disembodied hands and arms; a piano accordion that played 'God Save the Queen' and 'The Last Rose of Summer' from under the table with no apparent human agent; and spirit messages of a personal nature. Wilkinson regarded Home as a man of the highest moral integrity and he was entirely convinced that the phenomena he had witnessed were authentic manifestations of the spirit world.

At least one of Home's seances was held in Wilkinson's own home, where Home was a guest. It appears that Home suffered from a personal or emotional crisis whilst staying with the Wilkinsons; William Howitt wrote to his niece that Home was 'quite beside himself for a time at the Wilkinson's and in a most pitiable condition'.[82] Home was never proven to be fraudulent, as was the case for so many apparent mediums, and he did not take money for his seances, though he enjoyed the patronage of the aristocracy and was supported by believers from the higher social classes. He was investigated at length by William Crookes, an eminent scientist and Fellow of the Royal Society, who pronounced the phenomena that he observed to be a genuine manifestation of a newly evident 'Psychic force', although he did not accept that the force was derived from the world of spirits.[83] It was William Howitt's belief in Home's mediumistic abilities that sustained his belief in spiritualism even after he had become disillusioned by the level of fraud amongst mediums in general.

A number of notable people were introduced to spiritualism by Wilkinson. Amongst these was the American Romantic novelist, Transcendentalist and Brook Farmer Nathanial Hawthorne, who lived in England with his family from 1853 to 1859.[84] The Hawthorne children were treated for measles homoeopathically by Garth Wilkinson in 1857, and Hawthorne attended an evening reception at Wilkinson's house where he was shown spirit drawings and told of other spiritual marvels such as materializations. Hawthorne was ambivalent about what he had seen and heard, maintaining a highly sceptical attitude whilst acknowledging Wilkinson's 'sanity and integrity'.[85] Wilkinson also introduced his patient Florence Theobald to spiritualism. Florence was the sister of homoeopath Robert Masters Theobald, and of Morell Theobald, a friend of William Howitt, who later wrote of his own experiences of spiritualism in *Spirit Workers in the Home Circle* (1887).[86]

Andrew Jackson Davis (1826-1910)
Some somnambulist mediums, who were not part of the mainstream of popular

spiritualism, attracted the particular attention of Swedenborgians because they claimed to extend his spiritual knowledge. The two most notable examples were Andrew Jackson Davis and Thomas Lake Harris. Andrew Jackson Davis was an apprentice shoemaker in the small town of Poughkeepsie when, in 1843, he was mesmerized by a local tailor who had attended a talk by a travelling lecturer on mesmerism.[87] Subsequently, he developed abilities that were typical for somnambulists, and became known particularly for his ability to diagnose disease. He also claimed to be possessed by a higher intelligence which gave out scientific and philosophical information. In 1844, whilst in the mountains, he claimed to have been visited by the spirits of Galen and Swedenborg, who gave him lengthy instruction. That same year Davis said that 'I have now arrived at the *highest degree* of knowledge which the human mind is capable of acquiring' and wrote his account of the genesis of the universe and the nature of the spiritual world in his book *The Principles of Nature* that was published in 1847, and which he dictated whilst in a mesmeric trance.[88] This, and his later books, were widely read. Wilkinson's initial impression of Davis's work, gleaned from extracts in the *New York Tribune*, was not favourable. He wrote to Henry James, Sr that it was revelation 'not worth the revealing', and that it appeared to be a second-rate version of Swedenborg's revelations: 'verbal coincidences, even paragraph by paragraph, with Swedenborg, or with anyone else, are perhaps curious pieces of psychology, but surely nothing more: there is no advantage in having a poor transcript of what we already have in perfection, imparted to us from the other world'.[89] Nevertheless, he felt that it was good to have more seers emerging, in order to 'tame the arrogance' of the followers of each one, and to reduce any feeling of exclusivity, particularly when their revelations were contradictory.[90] Shortly afterwards, he read Davis's book, and received it enthusiastically, saying that 'in spite of all its shortcomings & negations, it is easy to see that its uses will be immense...The scientific, intellectual, spiritual, and practical value of Davis, is a thing not to be lightly pronounced upon...[there is] more of the second [i.e., intellectual value] than in all the current philosophy'.[91] This opinion was given in the same letter to Henry James, Sr in which he reported the spiritual experiences of his relative Fanny Roberts; it is clear that he was overwhelmed by all this evidence of a new era of communication from the spirit world. In a letter to the Swedenborgian journal, *The New Jerusalem Magazine*, he opined that 'Nothing seems more probable than that we shall have Revelations of this sort, by dozens', although, in this public communication, he was careful to add that any revelation must be subjected to a ' "trial of the spirits" with the same penetratingly affectionate scrutiny as the trial of any of the departments of nature'.[92]

Wilkinson's position here carries a tone of millenarianism. Like all followers of Swedenborg, he accepted Swedenborg's pronouncement that the Second Coming had already occurred in the spiritual world, and he was receptive to any apparent signs of the beginning of a new era in the material world. Elsewhere, Wilkinson made his millenarian position explicit, describing 'divine and positive signs of the End'.[93] He believed that the phenomena of mesmeric clairvoyance and spiritualism were clear signs of a providential change in the state of humanity. The notion that a new millennium was imminent had long been held within Christianity, and the idea was particularly popular during the time of great social and economic change in the late eighteenth and early nineteenth centuries.[94] Sociologist Bryan Wilson describes several approaches taken by millenarians, including the belief in divine, cataclysmic intervention, for which the secular equivalent is social revolution, in contrast to a more gradual, reformist approach which is exemplified by some of the utopian so-cialist movements, and their religious equivalents which postulate change mediated by divine providence rather than secular social reform.[95] The French Revolution, which had been supported by radical Swedenborgians, had been taken as a sign that the world was entering into its last days.[96] The more radical Swedenborgians of the nineteenth century, including Garth Wilkinson, not only accepted mesmerism and spiritualism as providential signs of the new age, but also supported some secular social reformist movements including those with a revolutionary goal, such as the Paris uprising of 1848.[97] The utopian socialism of Charles Fourier was received par-ticularly enthusiastically by followers of Swedenborg, who saw it as a direct secular equivalent of the spiritual new age that had been announced by Swedenborg.[98]

The dissemination of millenarian ideas depended upon charismatic prophets who appeared during the eighteenth and nineteenth centuries. Amongst these were Richard Brothers, who believed that his surname showed that he was descended from

James, the brother of Jesus. He heard the voice of God and experienced heavenly visions, and he believed that he would lead the return of the Jews to the Holy Land in order to rebuild Jerusalem.[99] Another millenarian prophet was Joanna Southcott, who claimed to have been instructed by the voice of God and demonstrated apparent clairvoyant powers. She believed that she had been chosen to be the instrument of the second virgin birth.[100] There was an overlap between the followers of millenarian prophets such as Brothers and Southcott, and those of Emanuel Swedenborg, with some followers shifting their allegiance from one to another. Secular utopian socialism was represented mainly by the systems of Henri de Saint-Simon, Robert Owen, and Charles Fourier, each of whom had a following in England. A millenarian 'prophet' who was a contemporary of Garth Wilkinson was James Elishama ('Shepherd') Smith. He was initially a follower of Joanna Southcott and an associate of Robert Owen, and later developed his concept of 'universalism' which was a combination of religious millenarianism and social radicalism.[101] Garth Wilkinson knew and admired Smith. Like the Swedenborgians, Smith believed that the millennium was a spiritual rather than a physical event, and that there was a perfect analogy between the physical and metaphysical worlds.[102] Wilkinson first met Smith in 1847 in the office of Hugh Doherty, another friend of Wilkinson who was the chief protagonist in England of the doctrines of Charles Fourier. Doherty was the editor of an English Fourierist magazine, *The London Phalanx*, and Smith was assisting him in this enterprise even though, as noted by Wilkinson, the doctrines of Smith and of Fourier had quite different conceptual origins despite their superficial similarities. Wilkinson came to know Smith well through their mutual interest in spiritualism. Although Wilkinson held Smith in high regard personally, he found his speech and writing to be oracular in style, and his basic theosophy to be impenetrable.[103]

One of Andrew Jackson Davis's most ardent early supporters was George Bush (mentioned in the preceding chapter). Bush was a follower of Swedenborg's teachings and believed that mesmerism was part of a divine plan that was aimed at confirming those teachings. He believed that Swedenborg himself had entered into the spirit world in a state of elevated mesmeric trance. Whilst he deplored the use of mesmerism for public demonstration and placed little weight on the utterances that came from most

141

mesmeric somnambulists, he was impressed by the revelations of some individuals. In his book *Mesmer and Swedenborg*, published in 1847, he singled out Davis for special praise. There is little doubt that Bush's favourable assessment of Davis's revelations influenced Garth Wilkinson: in his 1847 letter to *The New Jerusalem Magazine*, Wilkinson wrote in support of Bush's positive view of Davis, a view that was quite contrary to his own first impression.[104] Bush's initial opinion was based on a few pamphlets that Davis had published before his *Principles of Nature*, but his opinion of Andrew Jackson Davis changed dramatically after he had read Davis's book in full. Bush warned against the numerous errors, absurdities and falsities in the book. He said that 'indications are rife of a general demonstration about to be made, or now being made, of the most pernicious delirium breaking forth from the world of spirits upon that of men'.[105] It was in the following year that the Fox sisters began their spirit rappings.

Wilkinson's positive assessment of Davis continued at least until 1850, when he wrote to Henry James, Sr that 'your Davis is one of the most extraordinary phenomena of the world...His powers of analogy and common sense, of imagination or if he please, spiritual observation, are also a clear step beyond all poetry'.[106] Davis never travelled to England, and so Wilkinson did not meet him personally. However, Wilkinson played a much more active role in the promotion of the other major American seer who was adopted by many followers of Swedenborg: Thomas Lake Harris.

Thomas Lake Harris (1823-1906)

Thomas Lake Harris was born in Stratford, England, but emigrated to America with his family whilst still a boy.[107] He trained for the Baptist ministry and then converted to Universalism before coming under the influence of Andrew Jackson Davis, through whom he developed an interest in Swedenborg. He also embraced the utopian socialist ideals of Robert Owen and Charles Fourier. Together with Seventh Day Baptist minister James D Scott, Harris formed the 'Apostolic Circle' which received spirit messages from apostles and prophets including St Paul and Daniel.[108] They established a cooperative agricultural community in Virginia which was guided by their instructions from the spirit world. This venture failed and Harris went on to set up the 'Church of the Good Shepherd' in New Orleans, which professed to follow Swedenborg's teachings although it was unrelated to the official Swedenborgian New Church. In 1859, he announced that he had been called to preach in England. Before Harris visited London, he and Wilkinson had corresponded on spiritual matters. Wilkinson had told Harris of the revelations from the spirit medium Annie, and Harris expressed his excitement about this and said that he would help Wilkinson to publish his experiences. Harris told Wilkinson that he had been unable to write a letter earlier because 'you must have been in the fairy sphere at that time for the attempt brought me into most exquisite contact with the Little People and the letter resolved itself into a Poem'.[109] Wilkinson wrote gushingly to a mutual friend about Harris, saying 'And now, may I ask you to express to Mr. Harris, in the names of myself, my wife and many, many friends, our sense of the delicious gales from inward lands that have blown over us out of the Books which have been given through him. The Epic and Lyric are New World-doors opened, never to be shut again'.[110] Shortly before his visit to England, Harris wrote to Garth Wilkinson, asking him to arrange for suitable venues and audiences in London.[111] When he arrived in London, he stayed at the Wilkinsons' house for some weeks.[112] At that time, Wilkinson believed that whereas Swedenborg had operated at the spiritual level, Harris had opened up the celestial level of understanding, a development which had been predicted by Swedenborg.[113]

The revelations of Thomas Lake Harris were accepted more readily in America than in England, where he was accepted only by those followers of Swedenborg who embraced spiritualism.[114] As well as Garth Wilkinson and Elihu Rich, two key figures in the Swedenborg Society—William Wilkinson and William White—were also supporters of Harris. At that time William Wilkinson was Secretary of the Society, and White was the librarian, agent and bookseller. White began selling the books of Thomas Lake Harris and other writers on spiritualism, and in 1860 the Committee of the Society passed a majority resolution that White should be instructed to stop selling such works from their premises.[115] The ensuing dispute culminated in the dismissal of both William Wilkinson and William White, but White did not accept this and returned to the Swedenborg Society with several strong-arm men in an attempt to take over the premises by force. The dispute was eventually settled by arbitration, but neither William

Wilkinson nor William White returned to their previous positions in the Society. Harris and Garth Wilkinson do not appear to have played any direct role in these events. At that time when the trouble was brewing, Harris was in Norway on a fishing trip, and as the crisis deepened he wrote to Garth Wilkinson from Scotland that:

> I have this night seen the Angel who has been placed over the Swedenborg Society. I am told that our Lord will not permit the Celestial Sense of the Word, as unfolded through me, to be made a bone of contention. I do most fervently hope that our kind friend Mr White will see his way clear to a solution of the present complicated affair with the Swedenborgians. How can he——a man of peace——remain in that Establishment——with the sphere of the Sect continually, and most bitterly, making inroads upon his internal harmony. [116]

Harris returned to America in the spring of 1861, writing to a friend that he had to return hurriedly because 'a crisis has occurred in the spiritual world'. [117] When Harris returned to London some years later, he did not visit Garth Wilkinson, who by that time had become disenchanted with Harris. Harris stayed instead stayed with the Oliphant family. Laurence Oliphant was a successful author and Member of Parliament until, against the advice of Garth Wilkinson, he became involved with Harris, as a result of which he lost his career in Parliament, his reputation and some of his friends, including Garth Wilkinson. [118]

After the William White affair, Garth Wilkinson left the Swedenborg Society and did not rejoin until 1878. During this time, Wilkinson's view turned gradually against spiritualism, and he later condemned it, falling into line with the views of orthodox Swedenborgians. [119]

Why did Garth Wilkinson turn away from spiritualism? In broad terms, his move away from spiritualism mirrored the general trend amongst London intellectuals. Author and professor of psychology Geoffrey K Nelson has proposed three major reasons for the decline of spiritualism in America: the exposure of fraud; the association between spiritualism and socialism; and the strong anti-Christian elements. [120] These same pressures on spiritualism were present in England, particularly amongst

London middle-class spiritualists. Logie Barrow, meanwhile, has drawn attention to the difference between London spiritualists, who were mainly Christian in orientation, and the plebeian spiritualists, mainly in the north of England, who rejected traditional Christianity and who were, in some cases, virulently anti-Christian as well as embracing socialist ideals.[121] After the novelty of the phenomenon wore off, the intelligentsia soon lost interest in the banal content of the utterances of spiritualist mediums. Men whom Wilkinson admired, including Emerson, were dismayed by the banal level of supposed communications from the spirit world.[122] They made stinging criticisms of Wilkinson. Thomas Carlyle mocked Wilkinson's involvement with spiritualism, and his close friend Henry James, Sr believed that participation in spiritualism had sullied Wilkinson's intellect.[123] The poet James Thomson, who was an early advocate for Garth Wilkinson's genius, considered that spiritualism had tarnished his reputation:

> In fine, I am aware of no other living English writer so gloriously gifted
> and so little appreciated except Garth Wilkinson: and Garth Wilkinson has
> squandered his superb genius in most futile efforts to cultivate the spectral
> Sahara of Swedenborgianism, and, infinitely worse, the Will-o'-the Wisp
> Slough of Despond of Spiritualism. . . [124]

Middle-class Londoners who became disillusioned with spiritualism gravitated towards organizations which they regarded as more in keeping with their intellectual approach to the supernatural, such as the Society for Psychical Research. Garth Wilkinson, after accepting that he had been wrong about spiritualism in his younger days, and that Henry James, Sr had been correct, came to believe that scientific investigation of spiritualism was pointless. In 1883 he wrote to William James that:

> I see your father was so absolutely right in his discarding of Spiritism.
> Mankind will not suffer that kind of will o' the wisp immortality to be forced
> into its convictions. Science can never confirm it into solidity. . . [125]

Having previously believed in the revelatory value of spiritualist communications, he now accepted the view of his contemporaries that they were banal and worthless:

> The worst feature of spiritism is, that it leads frivolous persons to ask Tom, Dick and Harry of the 'spirit life', what their views are of God and the universe; and to place importance in the answers because they are spoken from the presumed higher rostrum of the other life. . . [126]

After rejecting spiritualism, Wilkinson retained a strong belief in the reality of the spiritual world, in keeping with his Swedenborgian beliefs. Asked in 1869 to submit evidence to the Committee of the London Dialectical Society which was investigating the claims of spiritualism, he wrote:

> I have been a believer in the spiritual world, and its nearness to the natural world, nearly all my life. And the rareness of communication between the two is to me one of the greatest of miracles; a proof of the economic wisdom, the supreme management, the extraordinary statesmanship of the Almighty. My whole soul, perfectly unconvincible by the other side, knows this for me; and floods me with the power of it every hour. [127]

This is a statement of one of the central doctrines of Swedenborg, that of spiritual influx. Swedenborg warned explicitly against actively seeking to communicate with spirits, a pursuit which he regarded as extremely dangerous. He believed that communication with spirits was permitted for him only because he was under the direct protection of the Lord. [128]

Wilkinson's considered position later in life echoed that of mainstream Swedenborgians, which was that the only spirits we can relate to are those that correspond to our own affections and desires, which, in all but the most spiritually advanced people, are intrinsically evil. [129] Therefore, we will almost certainly attract evil spirits to ourselves if we actively seek to make contact with the spirit world. The following view was attributed to Wilkinson in a biographical sketch published in 1879:

I do not deny, but prize, in their place, spontaneous motions of the spiritual world upon and in the natural world...On the other hand, solicited intercourse with the spiritual world is, to me, a mistake, and, with my convictions, it would be a sin to take part in séances, or in any other means, in such solicitation.[130]

Nevertheless, he felt the need to explain why spiritualism had been permitted at all. His conclusion was that spiritualism emerges when a population has degenerated to the point of crisis, and that it serves the purpose of reminding the masses of the reality of an afterlife:

There is nothing divine in it, for it only reaches to the spirit of the people in which it occurs, and to their corresponding spirits or ancestors; but it commands the masses by authoritative utterances as of gods, and comforts them by promises of supernatural help...Spiritualism seems allowed in this Europe also to enable us, by its key, to unlock the difficulty of gentile subsistence afar from the revealed Father, by spirits, or even angels, manifesting somewhat of a life to come.[131]

Wilkinson's family strove actively to deny his earlier involvement with spiritualism. Towards the end of his life, Wilkinson's wife Emma attempted to suppress any account of her husband's involvement with spiritualism. She wrote to Julian Hawthorne, son and biographer of Nathaniel Hawthorne, asking him to remove reference to her husband's involvement in spiritualism from the next edition of his book:

May I beg of you in any future edition of the Life of your father to leave out your passage upon my husband and spiritualism? He is utterly opposed to it now. On Mr. Home's first appearance in England very remarkable things did occur; but from the first I was a most decided opponent, and by my firmness I have kept all I know and love from having anything to do with it for at least thirty-five years. You may imagine, therefore, I feel hurt at seeing so spiritually minded a man as my husband really is to be mixed up with so evil a thing as spiritism.

You will pardon a faithful wife her just appreciation of his character. One other author took the liberty of using his name in a similar way, and I wrote to him also.[132]

He responded rather ungallantly by publishing her letter. This gives us some further insight into a more prosaic reason for Wilkinson to reject spiritualism—his wife's implacable opposition to it. He was much influenced by her; for example, it was Emma that persuaded him to adopt homoeopathy into his medical practice.

Wilkinson's nephew and biographer, Clement Wilkinson, went even further in his attempts to nullify Garth Wilkinson's involvement with spiritualism. In 1894, Wilkinson had written a letter to John Thomson, a Glasgow bookseller, in which he referred to his friendship with the medium Annie Milner, 'the greatest clairvoyant I have ever heard of'. When writing Wilkinson's autobiography, Clement Wilkinson annotated his uncle's letters in blue pencil, and he scored out the entire passage relating to the mediumship of Annie Milner, noting that this 'had better not be transcribed'. In the published biography, Clement wrote 'It appears that Wilkinson was firm so far as abstaining from attendance at séances was concerned', a statement that is plainly refuted by the information in Wilkinson's papers that Clement had full access to.[133]

Victorian spiritualists recognized the contribution that Garth Wilkinson had made to their cause. An obituary in the spiritualist journal *Light* noted that:

He was the most notable Swedenborgian of his time, a successful homeopathic physician, and a convinced Spiritualist...As a Spiritualist, Dr. Wilkinson, unlike so many other Swedenborgians, was never ashamed to avow his convictions...[134]

The same journal predicted in 1911 that Wilkinson would find an 'honoured place' in the history of spiritualism.[135] However, his contribution to spiritualism, like most of his other achievements, is now unrecognized, and he is given only passing mention in histories of modern spiritualism; indeed, his involvement with spiritualism did much to damage his reputation amongst those men whose opinion he valued most.

– 6 –

The Philosophical Basis of Garth Wilkinson's Medicine

*Man has been truly termed a 'microcosm' or little world in himself,
and the structure of his body should be studied not only by those who
wish to become doctors, but by those who wish to attain to a more
intimate knowledge of God.*

Abū Ḥāmid Muḥammad ibn Muḥammad al-Ghazālī[1]

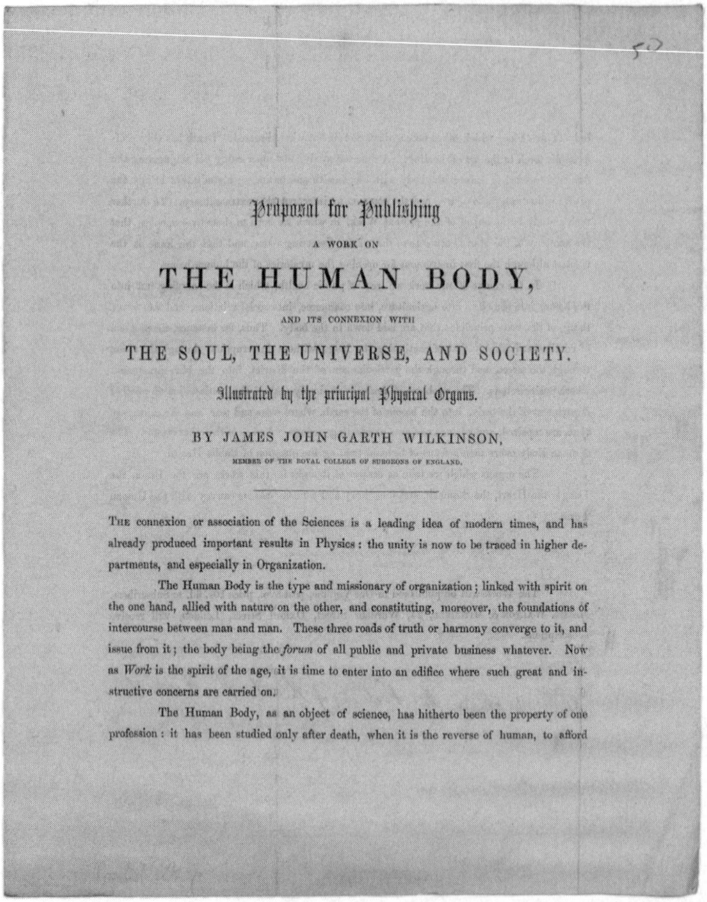

Proposal for Publishing

A WORK ON

THE HUMAN BODY,

AND ITS CONNEXION WITH

THE SOUL, THE UNIVERSE, AND SOCIETY.

Illustrated by the principal Physical Organs.

BY JAMES JOHN GARTH WILKINSON,

MEMBER OF THE ROYAL COLLEGE OF SURGEONS OF ENGLAND.

THE connexion or association of the Sciences is a leading idea of modern times, and has already produced important results in Physics : the unity is now to be traced in higher departments, and especially in Organization.

The Human Body is the type and missionary of organization; linked with spirit on the one hand, allied with nature on the other, and constituting, moreover, the foundations of intercourse between man and man. These three roads of truth or harmony converge to it, and issue from it ; the body being the *forum* of all public and private business whatever. Now as *Work* is the spirit of the age, it is time to enter into an edifice where such great and instructive concerns are carried on.

The Human Body, as an object of science, has hitherto been the property of one profession : it has been studied only after death, when it is the reverse of human, to afford

Fig. 6: Proposal for publishing Wilkinson's book *The Human Body*. On the reverse Wilkinson wrote a letter to J F I Tafel, 26 January 1850.
Swedenborg Society Archive, K/126 (e).

T he two most important philosophies on which medical practice can be based are the mechanist and the vitalist. The mechanist position, which today is overwhelmingly dominant, assumes that all of human physiology and illness can be explained in terms of the laws of physics and chemistry. This extends to the explanation of consciousness itself as a by-product of brain activity. In the more extreme forms of this formulation there is no place for free will or for any spiritual reality outside of the material.[2] Modern empirical science takes this as its starting point, and its methods rely upon detailed observation of the material world and explanations made in terms of material cause and effect. According to this paradigm, medical treatment relies primarily upon physical interventions with drugs or surgery with the aim of correcting the physical pathology causing the illness.

The alternative philosophy, which is vitalist, has been well summarized by medical historian Elizabeth Haigh:

> In its most general sense, vitalism assumes that the study of organic phenomena cannot be reduced to a branch of physics or chemistry. It affirms that the living body possesses some unique entity, a soul, force, faculty or principle which causes it to transcend the realm of inert matter.[3]

This philosophy allows an entirely different approach to medical treatment, one that takes account of a spiritual reality which can be worked upon in order to promote health. This approach has a long and distinguished history, which is perhaps best known historically in the medicine of Paracelsus, and today is expressed in some of the medical approaches that are regarded as 'alternative' or 'complementary', including homoeopathy and hypnosis.[4]

After his break with orthodox medical practice, Garth Wilkinson took a vitalist approach to medicine that was based on Swedenborg's theosophy. Inevitably, he found himself in conflict with the science of his day, which denied the need to consider the presence of an active divinity within all creation.[5] For Wilkinson, science could not be conducted without a focus on the sacred. True science, according to Wilkinson's concept, saw no distinction between science and the sacred, and was based upon knowledge of an immutable metaphysical order, the understanding of which is the true aim of a valid science.[6] Wilkinson's a priori metaphysics was of course that of Swedenborg. He defined true science as the 'Art of Knowledge'.[7] This type of 'science' represents such a different paradigm that it requires a different world view. A mind schooled in materialist science finds it difficult to adopt the world view that is associated with this model, which is generally rejected as unscientific. Swedenborg was regarded by Wilkinson as the originator of the 'true' scientific paradigm within which he operated, and Wilkinson's version of this science was based upon his interpretation of Swedenborg combined with other influences from his reading and his experience, particularly that of mesmerism.

Wilkinson dismissed the materialistic science of his day as 'scientism'.[8] True science, for Wilkinson, recognizes an ultimate spiritual reality without which there can be no understanding of the material world. This spiritual reality centres upon the Divine Human as the archetype of creation. Scientism, for Wilkinson, consists of funnelling down into greater and greater detail, whereas true science seeks higher spiritual truths by reasoning upwards from empirical observation. To be a true scientist requires a capacity for spiritual perceptions, the ability to reason analogically, and an 'ear for the harmony which principles play as they move over the varied and very difficult chords of nature'.[9] He considered scientism as 'intelligence gathered out of self-love and the love of the world', and therefore inherently sinful according to his Swedenborgian precepts.[10] Wilkinson's rejection of scientism and adoption of 'true science' lay explicitly at the root of many of his interests, most obviously in his opposition to vivisection, but also in less obvious intellectual fields including Fourierism and the state control of medicine.[11]

The history of vitalism

Garth Wilkinson's vitalism meant that he could not accept any suggestion that matter could give rise to life of its own accord. The debate about this issue can be traced back to classical times and Wilkinson was familiar with the ancient arguments. The mechanistic concept of life was represented in early Greece by the theory of atomism. Greek atomism began with Leucippus (5th century BC), but the most lucid account is that given by Epicurus (341-270 BC) and this was developed further by Lucretius (*c.* 99-*c.* 55 BC).[12] The atomists believed that matter derived from atoms (indivisible particles) in a void. Atoms collide at random and aggregate to form the whole of creation including living beings. Garth Wilkinson thought that it was absurd to suggest that the cosmos and its inhabitants could have been created by blind chance, even over infinite time. Adopting a mocking tone, he said Epicurus believed that 'When the primordial atoms had diced forth a man, he stood his ground, and if woman were accidentally added, a race was initiated'.[13]

Aristotle is regarded as the founder of later vitalist theories.[14] The Aristotelian view is that a rational soul can be present only when there is an organized body, and so there must be an intrinsic organizing vital force that causes the body to be formed in the first place. The rational soul or *nous* is unique to man, and it alone exists externally and is immortal. The lower parts of the soul constitute the vital force.[15] Wilkinson thought that Aristotle's philosophy contained a shadow of the truth, but that this 'goes no higher than to the inhabitation of man's passions in specific organs of the body'.[16] Aristotle's concept of an eternal, uncreated world with an impersonal 'unmoved mover' as the first cause was not compatible with Wilkinson's Swedenborgian beliefs. He believed that after the revelations of Swedenborg, systems of metaphysics that make no reference to the human form as the divine archetype of the cosmos had become an anachronism.[17]

Plato took an animist view of the relationship between the body and the soul.[18] In his view the body is merely an instrument of the soul, and it is fashioned by the soul for that purpose. For Plato, the soul animates the body, and the same soul functions as pure intellect. Pure intellect is the true nature of the soul, but this is corrupted by the imprisonment of the soul in the body. Wilkinson regarded Plato's view to be correct in part, but he believed that Plato was 'ineffectual' because he was not a visionary. Whereas Swedenborg had actually been to the world of spirits, and thus received knowledge by direct observation, Plato was only able to make inferences about the other world.[19] In particular, Wilkinson followed Swedenborg in believing that the soul is no prisoner in the body; he held that since Swedenborg's insights, 'body and soul are no longer two, but one in their harmonies'.[20]

During the sixteenth and seventeenth centuries, natural philosophy underwent major changes that would lead to the development of modern science; this was the so-called 'scientific revolution'.[21] Prior to that period, Aristotelian philosophy had dominated the study of natural philosophy, and conclusions about the operation of nature were drawn by reasoning from Aristotelian first principles. During the Renaissance, there was a resurgence of interest in Platonic, Neoplatonic and Hermetic texts, which provided an alternative philosophical framework to that of Aristotle, and this was incorporated into scientific thinking.[22] The major change in thinking during the scientific revolution was an increasing emphasis on the importance of the empirical method, which was promoted particularly by Francis Bacon. Discoveries based on observation, such of those of Galileo Galilei increasingly challenged the Aristotelian position because they were incompatible with it.[23]

In the seventeenth century, mechanism found a new credibility with the rise of scientific thinking that was based on mechanics and mathematics. The work of Descartes was a watershed in the development of a mechanistic physiology. His separation of body and soul, with a mechanical body plus a mind that thinks and imagines, but does not animate the body, made it easy to neglect the soul completely when considering human physiology.[24] Under these influences, mechanistic physiology took a firm hold on medical thinking during the seventeenth century.

Despite this, there was still a strong current of vitalism that ran alongside the conventional mainstream. This was promoted by Joan Baptista van Helmont, a follower of Paracelsus.[25] He held the Paracelsian concept of a formative *archeus*, the vital principle or force that pervades the whole of nature from minerals to man. Nevertheless, by the start of the eighteenth century, most physicians were mechanists.[26] Herman Boerhaave, who was Professor of Medicine at Leiden, was the most renowned and influential European physician in the first half of that century.[27] Boerhaave accepted the existence of a soul as well as a body, but he emphasized the need to limit medicine to empirical observation only, and so avoid undue speculation.

As the eighteenth century progressed, vitalist concepts again became fashionable.[28] As one English observer put it early in the nineteenth century:

> When mechanical philosophy began to lose its novelty, it was in some
> measure supplanted as a fashionable study by a peculiar species of
> metaphysics...During the progress of this enticing science, physiologists
> laid hold of its notions and doctrines, and two opposite systems were
> produced, the more ancient explaining every thing by the action of a *living
> principle*, and the more modern by a principle somewhat indefinite, to
> which they gave the name of *irritability*.[29]

The concept of irritability had been promoted by one of Boerhaave's students, Albrecht von Haller.[30] Haller was famous for distinguishing between irritability and sensibility as characteristics of living tissues. He identified irritability with the ability to contract, and confined the concept to muscle fibres.[31] Sensibility, on the other hand, was found only in those body parts with a nerve supply, which in humans 'upon being touched [transmit] the impressions of it to the soul'.[32] Furthermore, the nervous system, he believed, was the means by which the soul communicates back to the body. He described the soul as 'a being which is conscious of itself, represents to itself the body to which it belongs, and by means of that body the whole universe'.[33]

Vitalism in Britain

At the end of the eighteenth century, two significant books on vitalist physiology were published in Britain. The first of these was by English physician, astrologer and Swedenborgian sympathizer Ebenezer Sibly whose *Key to Physic* was published in 1795.[34] He regarded it as obvious that matter of itself is dead, and must be animated by 'some other being, more powerful than matter'.[35] This 'other being' is the *Anima Mundi*, the living spirit of the natural world, which is a secondary cause in the service of the primary Deity. Both matter and the *Anima Mundi*, according to Sibly, have existed for eternity. Humans alone have a personal soul which is 'the *eternal* essence or Tincture of the Divinity'.[36] Sibly believed that the soul is incapable of acting on the body, or the body on the soul.[37] He subscribed to the concept of the 'great chain of being', describing a hierarchical order from God through the angels to the *Anima Mundi* and so to the celestial bodies and all of nature on earth, with correspondences between the different levels.

The second English text on vitalist physiology published at the end of the eighteenth century was written by Richard Saumarez. Saumarez had been a pupil of John Hunter, who was an important influence on the promotion of vitalism in England.[38] Hunter, regarded as 'the greatest living exponent of scientific surgery' in Britain at that time, believed that the vital force is carried in the blood.[39] This is the same John Hunter that taught medicine to John Benoit de Mainauduc, who had promoted mesmerism amongst members of the Theosophical Society in the 1780s.[40] Hunter did not publish his vitalist ideas, and it was left to one of his students, John Abernethy, to transmit them.[41] Writing in the early years of the nineteenth century, Abernethy cited 'Mr Hunter's opinion' that life results from a 'subtile, mobile, invisible substance' superadded to living tissues, and that mind is superadded to life.[42]

Richard Saumarez acknowledged his debt to Hunter when he published his *A New System of Physiology* in 1798.[43] Saumarez ridiculed the mechanical paradigm of nature, saying that 'Nothing else than a crooked zigzag way of thinking could have led these *philosophers* to have ascribed to matter, independent of the participation of life, the power of organization, and to this organization the source of life as its cause'.[44] He described three principles of human life: the living principle (that is, the vital spirit), by means of which 'there is harmony and consent between all the parts' of the body; the sentient principle, through which animals gain knowledge of the external world through their sense organs; and the rational principle, by which 'the different voluntary parts are made to act and are directed to their proper end'.[45]

Vitalism in England in the nineteenth century

At the start of the nineteenth century, the view in England was that 'The physiological works published in the eighteenth century were few and unimportant, and were chiefly written in Latin and German'.[46] It was felt that that the only significant volume on physiology at that time was *First Lines of Physiology* by Haller, which had been translated into English by William Cullen in Edinburgh in 1786. This was the standard text in England at the turn of the nineteenth century, and it focused on Haller's theories of irritability and sensibility.[47] Thereafter, research moved towards explaining the functions of life through the usual laws of physics and chemistry.[48] Even if a more generalized concept of a vital force was entertained, this was not regarded as a valid topic for physiological investigation or speculation. At the international Göttingen Congress of Physiologists in 1854, 'it is said that not one physiologist out of 500 present raised his voice in favour of a special soul-substance'.[49]

True vitalism nevertheless retained a foothold in England in the early nineteenth century, primarily through the lectures and books of John Hunter's student John Abernethy. He published a series of lectures, *An Enquiry into the Probability and Rationality of Mr. Hunter's Theory of Life* in 1814, and this went into several editions.[50] Following Haller's reduction of vitalism to irritability and sensibility, and the experiments in 1791 of Luigi Galvani who showed that electrical sparks can produce twitching in the legs of frogs that were otherwise apparently dead, it appeared that irritability, a cardinal part of vitality, had been linked to electricity.[51] Abernethy adopted this idea enthusiastically, saying that the vital principle is 'of a similar nature' to electricity.[52] At that time, the mathematics of electromagnetism had not been formulated; electricity and magnetism could still be regarded as mysterious and immaterial forces that could be invoked as analogous to, or even identical with, the life force within the paradigm of vitalism as opposed to materialism. There was considerable interest in the relationship between physical and vital forces, which was stimulated by the publication in 1850 by Wilkinson's friend William B Carpenter of *The Mutual Relations of the Vital and Physical Forces*.[53] He believed that all these forces were different manifestations of a single creative will:

> Force...emanating from the Divine Will...manifests itself in electricity, magnetism, light, heat, chemical affinity, and mechanical motion; but... when directed through organized structures, it effects the operations of growth, development, chemico-vital transformation, and the like.[54]

As discussed in Chapter 4, Carpenter believed that the vital force in man is expressed through a 'Nervous Agency' that is transmitted by the nervous system and which acts as an intermediary between the conscious mind and the bodily organs.

Contemporary comment shows that Carpenter's hypothesis raised great interest in the mid-nineteenth century, not only amongst intellectuals but also in the popular mind.[55] It is clear that Garth Wilkinson's lectures on physiology at the Mechanics' Institutes and their subsequent publication as *The Human Body* was not an isolated eccentricity, but reflected a current of thought that was very lively and topical at the time.

Even though the dominant view of physiology as the nineteenth century moved into its second half was one of physico-chemical mechanism rather than vitalism, several prominent individuals maintained a vitalist approach, and Garth Wilkinson contributed actively to the debate. These individuals tended to belong to the subculture that also embraced mesmerism, phrenology and other unorthodox approaches. One such was William Gregory, Professor of Chemistry at Edinburgh,[56] who had been a student of Justus von Liebig at the University of Giessen in Germany. Liebig accepted the concept of a vital principle, although he adopted the familiar position that physiology should limit itself to investigation of the laws underlying physical phenomena.[57] Gregory maintained Liebig's vitalist views, and he translated into English many of Liebig's works, which were published in Cambridge in 1847. In the introduction to the 1850 edition of his translation of Liebig's *Researches on the Motion of the Juices of the Animal Body*, Gregory made his own vitalist views explicit, remarking that 'it is…obvious, that…mechanical and chemical causes are not alone sufficient to explain the phenomena of animal life, since they are present equally in a dead and a living body'.[58] Gregory took an active interest in phrenology, mesmerism and spiritualism, for which he was ridiculed by his academic colleagues.[59] In 1851, Gregory published *Letters to a Candid Inquirer, on Animal Magnetism*. In this work he discusses clairvoyance, including the use of crystals and magic mirrors, as well as conversations with spirits held during the mesmerized state.[60] He was familiar with the works of John Dee and Emanuel Swedenborg. Like others before him, he was struck by the similarities between the spiritual experiences of 'magnetic ecstatics' and those described by Swedenborg, whom he described as 'a man of prodigious ability and learning'.[61] He declared that 'a great proportion of those things which are called magic, witchcraft, divination, &c., obviously depend on those principles of Animal Magnetism'.[62]

A prominent physician who continued to support the vitalist position during its fallow period was Lionel Smith Beale, a Fellow of the Royal College of Physicians and Physician to the Royal Free Hospital in London. In 1870 he published *Protoplasm: or Life, Force and Matter*. His summary of orthodox medical opinion at that time illustrates how far the pendulum had swung towards a mechanistic view:

> The idea that life is a power, force, or property of a special and peculiar kind, temporarily influencing matter and its ordinary forces, but entirely different from, and in no way correlated with any of these, has been ridiculed, and is often spoken of as if it were too absurd to require refutation.[63]

For Beale, the notion that human life is the result of complex but undefined molecular machinery was an unproven dogma supported by authoritative opinion only. He also dismissed the idea that matter can arrange itself into a configuration that is alive without being acted upon by some organizing power. He thought that the existence of a vital force is self-evident, but that this force is not accessible to empirical observation and experiment. Mechanists, he believed, had a 'desire to chain the mind so tightly to the material that it shall no longer exercise one of its remarkable endowments—that of stretching towards regions into which the senses cannot penetrate'.[64]

Beale's book was written mainly in reaction to the work of Thomas Henry Huxley, an eminent biologist, who became Hunterian Professor at the Royal College of Surgeons and President of the Royal Society, and who was a supporter of Charles Darwin. He was a confirmed mechanist who believed that the basic building block of all matter is protoplasm, a substance that is found in all cells. In 1868, he gave an address at the invitation of a group of Scottish Presbyterians, in which he set out his views in lay terms:

> Protoplasm, simple or nucleated, is the formal basis of all life. It is the clay of the potter: which, bake it and paint it as he will, remains clay, separated by artifice, and not by nature, from the commonest brick or sun-dried clod.[65]

Protoplasm, in Huxley's view, is formed when carbonic acid, water and nitrogenous salts come together 'under certain conditions'.[66] Protoplasm first forms plants, from which animals must obtain it. He believed that even the higher mental faculties of man are the product of mechanism.

Huxley's address expressed his views in terms understandable to the general public, and following publication they became very well known. Such views inevitably incurred the wrath of Garth Wilkinson. He criticized Huxley for his 'triumphant Scientism' which proclaims the 'Material antichrist', an unknowable God, and the baselessness of conscience.[67] Wilkinson summarized the protoplasm theory thus:

> the protoplasm of modern thought is the doctrine of a primordial matter or stuff from which all organizations take their origin, and which reaches in its upward course from organific cells by developments of shapes through animals to mankind, being therefore a præ-seminal continent of the forces of life. In fact, it is Nature itself regarded as a lake of seed.[68]

Wilkinson regarded the protoplasm theory as an extension of Greek atomism:

> The advanced evolutionist also holds that chemical atoms, or metaphysi-
> cal Lucretian atoms, though apparently unvital, can become sufficiently
> alive to form protoplasm, which is the road to all vegetable, animal, and
> human existence.[69]

With obvious reference to Huxley's analogy between protoplasm and clay,
Wilkinson said that Huxley's protoplasm is a 'clay mind. . .actively shunting the pot-
ter'.[70] The theory, he said, supposes the building of organisms 'from below upwards',
and is 'emptied of the belief in a Creator having purposes'.[71] Wilkinson believed
that, contrary to the protoplasm theory, 'ideas and plans in divine manform, not
protoplasms, are the beginnings of all things'.[72] He regarded the idea that people
depend upon plants for their protoplasm as absurd:

> No childhood but dribbling senility of science, it leaves out, as unworthy of
> notice, the fact that men and women make men and women, and that the
> lake of primordials inside any conceivable organism is made in an analo-
> gous way. . .[73]

Wilkinson was concerned that education of the public should offer them an opportunity for spiritual development, and he regarded Huxley's lecture as a serious
threat to the public good.[74]

Interest in vitalism was revived at the end of the nineteenth century by the work
of Gustav von Bunge.[75] His lectures were first published in English translation in
1890, and the introductory lecture on 'Vitalism and Mechanism' proved to be highly
influential, because it openly expressed the doubts that many people had felt about
the prevailing 'scientific' approach. He ended this essay provocatively by asking
'May it not be possible that every cell and every atom is really a conscious being,
and that all life is conscious life?'[76] During the last decade of the nineteenth century,
publications relating to neo-vitalism mushroomed in orthodox medical journals,

and this trend continued into the early twentieth century. Though this development is of great interest in the history of medicine, it occurred very late in Wilkinson's life. He must have been aware of the direction of medical thinking around him, but he made no mention of neo-vitalism in his later works.

Vitalism and the esoteric concept of 'living nature'

The concept that every part of the natural world is alive within a 'complex, plural, hierarchical entity that is continuously animated throughout by a living energy or soul', referred to as 'living nature' for short, is a core tenet of the Western esoteric tradition which was set out by Antoine Faivre.[77] Jane Williams-Hogan has pointed out that, according to Swedenborg, nature is essentially dead, and therefore the inclusion of his work in the corpus of Western esotericism should be questioned.[78] As we have seen, Garth Wilkinson also believed that nature has no intrinsic power to form itself *ab initio*, and that all the forms and functions of nature are extrinsic in origin. He expressed this by saying unequivocally that nature is dead: 'Nature, to the walls of her, to the *flammantia mœnia Mundi*, is dead, the footstool of God, but not the throne'.[79] He regarded the concept of an intrinsically living nature as akin to primitive animism, in which volcanoes spew lava by intent and even stones have awareness and volition.[80] He pointed out the dire spiritual consequences of such beliefs. If life is intrinsic to nature, then soul and God become optional extras, matters of belief rather than necessity, and they can be discarded without negating life in nature. This, thought Wilkinson, is the path to atheism, or at least to a polytheism in which different aspects of nature become gods. Also, Wilkinson pointed out the conflict that would occur if nature was intrinsically living and also perfused by a higher soul, 'there would *ab initio* be two souls in it, and not reception of life, but confusion'.[81]

Wilkinson followed Swedenborg in believing that all of 'dead nature' is enlivened by spiritual influx:

The intercourse of soul with body, and of spirit with nature, lies then in the similarity of each with each: it depends upon a scale of divine wants,

162

by which spirit must come down into nature, and soul into body, for the purpose of carrying life throughout the possible forms of the creation.[82]

Because of this influx, nature shows wisdom down to the molecular level:

> nature exhibits the marks of transcendent intelligence...could she be sup-
> posed to act of herself, she would deserve credit for the highest wisdom...
> the molecules of matter, and the organic unities of living beings, operate
> with a wisdom which is the same with that of the human mind, though not
> self-conscious...[83]

On the topic of 'living nature', Wilkinson's views were close to those of both his master Swedenborg, and the *Naturphilosophe* Lorenz Oken. This is readily illustrated by comparing some brief quotes from each of these authors:

> [From Wilkinson] nature herself is dead, and without the continued influx
> of divine life, would neither move, nor breathe, *nor be*.[84]
> [From Swedenborg] The spiritual from its origin has life in itself, but
> the natural from its origin has nothing of life in itself...there is in every
> created thing in this world a spiritual and a natural,...a spiritual as the
> cause and a natural as the effect...not the least thing is possible or can be
> possible in nature in which there is not a spiritual.[85]
> [From Oken] There is in the universe no vital force of its own; the individ-
> ual things lie not there some time and await the polarizing breath, but they
> first *become* through the breath of God...There is nothing properly dead in
> the world; that only is dead which is not, only the nothing...Everything in
> the world is endowed with life; the world itself is alive, and continues only,
> maintains itself, by virtue of its life...[86]

For our three philosophers, life is inextricably tied to the very existence of nature; nature *must* be alive, for without the continuous influx of the creative life force it would not exist at all.[87] It is clear that Jane Williams-Hogan's assertion that, because Swedenborg said that nature is essentially dead, his philosophy cannot be regarded as meeting the criterion of 'living nature' according to Faivre's criteria for Western esotericism, is one that requires some finessing. What was meant by Swedenborg—and also Wilkinson and Oken—is that nature cannot *self-generate* life; the concept that nature can have life *of itself* is essentially materialistic, or at best a primitive animism. They believed that life is a spiritual, not a material, phenomenon. It is plain that the concepts of Wilkinson, Swedenborg and Oken are entirely compatible with—and indeed exemplars for—the Western esoteric concept of living nature.

The explicitly theistic vitalism of Swedenborg, Oken and Wilkinson carries clear implications for the study of anatomy and physiology. Within this theistic framework, experiments carried out on living animals cannot lead to an understanding of the life of man, because of perceived differences in the nature of their souls.[88] Dissection of the dead, whilst useful to understand the tool used by the spirit or soul, cannot in itself provide information on first causes without reasoning upwards by analogy. Nevertheless, the study of anatomy can be used as the starting point for an understanding of deity, by those who hold to the Judaeo-Christian teaching that man was made in the image of God.

As a young man, Garth Wilkinson was particularly excited by Swedenborg's physiological works; he has been characterized as 'the first major student of Swedenborg's pre-theological writings'.[89] He believed that the study of these works would make him 'a far more able professor of medicine', and indeed Swedenborg's philosophy, particularly as expressed in his physiology, became the yardstick against which Wilkinson measured the validity of his future medical practice.[90]

Swedenborg's search for the soul

Garth Wilkinson made it clear that he had obtained his basic ideas on physiology from Swedenborg. He commented later in life that:

All the physiological knowledge that I have which transcends the text books, is derived from the Treatises of Swedenborg, THE ANIMAL KINGDOM,

CONSIDERED ANATOMICALLY, PHYSICALLY, AND PHILOSOPHICALLY, and THE ECONOMY OF THE ANIMAL KINGDOM, which I translated 51 and 48 years ago, and which I now read with wonder.[91]

Swedenborg wrote these books immediately before his revelatory spiritual experiences, and in them his thinking shows a clear pattern of development. In the introduction to *The Economy of the Animal Kingdom* (1740), the first of the two books to be written, Swedenborg emphasizes that knowledge of truth can begin only from observation and not from abstract reasoning; when truth is reached it is accompanied by 'a certain cheering light' in 'some sacred temple in the brain'.[92] Some people have a special gift for putting together many observations and developing a general truth from them; plainly he regarded himself as being amongst those that are gifted in this way. He explains that he will focus initially on the blood, because it is 'the complex of all things that exist in the world, and the storehouse and seminary of all that exist in the body'.[93] Thus, everything that we assimilate from the environment, whether this is food, air, or indeed pollutants, finds its way into the blood and so provides the material that is used in the structure and function of the body.[94] Swedenborg pointed out that in the body the soul arrives 'at the ultimate end which it had represented to itself'.[95] However, 'the soul has her residence in a place so sublime and eminent, that we cannot ascend to her'.[96] Swedenborg indicates that we must begin by the study of the structure and function of the body, because this is an exact representation of the soul in every aspect, and it is all that we have immediate and reliable access to.[97] Science, not philosophy, must be our starting point if we are to avoid error. Only then can we proceed to higher levels of understanding by applying the doctrine of series and degrees, according to which, as summarized by Martin Lamm, 'nature becomes a giant organism in which each part is a reflection of the whole'.[98] Swedenborg conceived that everything is arranged in a series; for example, there are series within the mineral, vegetable and animal worlds, which are constituents of a still higher series that begins with the 'first substance of nature'.[99] This concept can be applied to the process by which the soul descends to the body in a series of manifestations which are discretely different from each other, yet

GARTH WILKINSON-CHAPTER 6

correspond to each other and are all manifestations of the soul, which is the 'first substance' of the body. In man:

> next to the soul, in the order of forces and substances, is the spirituous fluid;
> next, the purer blood; and next, the red blood; which last is thus as it were
> the corporeal soul of its own little world. [100]

Thus, the red blood becomes in its turn the 'first substance' of the body, and hence the appropriate focus for study. From the blood come the building materials and the vitality that are necessary for the body to develop and function. Swedenborg believed that the spirituous fluid, the purest 'soul fluid' that is only one step away from the soul itself, is produced in the 'cortical glands', which we would now recognize as the cell bodies of the cerebral cortex. [101] This fluid vitalizes the blood, and is also the mode by which the will is transmitted through the nerves and sensation is brought to conscious awareness. By means of this, the soul can 'know' the material world. Swedenborg tells us that the soul 'builds a brain, in order that the things perceived by the senses may penetrate even to itself, the soul'. [102] Above all is life and wisdom that originates from God and flows into us, the understanding of which is 'infinitely above the sphere of the human mind'. [103]

In the prologue to his next physiological work, *The Animal Kingdom* (1744-5), Swedenborg again made it clear that his purpose was to attain knowledge of the soul. He regretted his haste in attempting to develop higher truths from consideration of the blood alone. He now recognized that the whole of human anatomy must be considered. In order to achieve this, he would 'examine thoroughly the whole world or microcosm which the soul inhabits', because the soul 'is represented in the body, as in a mirror'. [104] He had become more circumspect about the source of true knowledge, regarding this less as the special ability of a gifted person, but more as something given from a higher source. He again emphasized that the *only* way that embodied man can reach an understanding of higher principles is by reasoning from empirical observation. Higher principles can be formulated from information gained through the senses. Then, 'In proportion as by these means we ascend to truths, in the same proportion truths descend to us...truth is...infused into our minds from its heaven'.[105] Swedenborg related this to the state of contemplation described by Plato, by means of which he acknowledged 'himself as a part of a higher world' in which 'The soul, freed as it were from the body, ascends and is enlightened; descending again, it is obscured, but it is afterwards purified and reascends'.[106] Swedenborg recognized that 'this may perhaps appear like a mere fable, to those who have not experienced it'.[107] It is well documented that Swedenborg, from an early age, entered into meditative states that were associated with reduction or cessation of respiration.[108] It is apparent that Swedenborg is here describing a method of finding truth by starting with empirical observation of human anatomy, then using reason to define higher order principles, and finally using a meditative technique to attain still higher knowledge that is 'infused' from heaven.[109]

Swedenborg's *The Animal Kingdom* contains a detailed account of anatomy as it was known at the time, with heavy reference to the most authoritative anatomical texts then available. He makes few spiritual speculations based on these anatomical facts.[110]

At the time when he wrote his physiological works, Swedenborg had not yet formulated his concept of the Divine Human as the archetype for all of creation and for human anatomy and physiology.[111] This revelation came to him shortly after completing these works. His later followers, when they addressed the topic of human physiology, were able to incorporate this concept into their thinking. Significantly, Swedenborg retained his focus on the value of sensory information as the starting point for knowledge even after he began to experience the spirit world, although information from spirits came directly into his sensorium, with no need for mediation by the sensory organs.

In his theological works, Swedenborg recognized correspondences between human organs and aspects of mental function, and through them with the Divine Human with its spiritual and angelic communities. In this way, the human body corresponds to heaven:

Moreover, the states of spirits and angels, together with all their varieties, can in nowise be understood without a knowledge of the human body, for the Lord's kingdom is like a man...[112]

Humans can receive divine love and wisdom through their higher mental faculties of will and understanding. Will and understanding have their seat in the brain, and extend to the whole body by means of correspondences. These mental faculties are represented specifically in the body by the heart and the lungs, and in heaven by the celestial and spiritual realms:

in any one man, in his spiritual world called his spiritual man, there are two kingdoms, one of the will and the other of the understanding...These kingdoms indeed correspond to the kingdoms of the heart and the lungs in the body. It is the same in the heavens. The celestial kingdom is the voluntary part of heaven, and the good of love rules there. The spiritual kingdom is the intellectual part of heaven and truth rules there, all this corresponding to the functions of the heart and lungs in man.[113]

Swedenborg said that this was demonstrated to him by angels, and that in heaven, as in a spiritually enlightened man, there is a 'marriage' of love and wisdom.[114] Love can be impure and directed to worldly pleasures, but true wisdom comes from the Lord only. In the human body, impure blood from the heart is purified when it passes through the lungs. This represents the purification of love by wisdom, so that love is directed to the Lord rather than to earthly pleasures:

That the blood in the lungs purifies and nourishes itself correspondently to the affections of the mind is as yet unknown, but is very well known in the spiritual world...From this correspondence it comes that man is purified in respect of his love if he loves wisdom, and is defiled if he does not love it. Moreover, all purification of man is effected by truths of wisdom, and all defilement by falsities opposed to the truths of wisdom.[115]

The esoteric physiology of John Clowes

Whilst Garth Wilkinson was the main author to follow Swedenborg's approach to physiology, he was not the first. John Clowes also wrote on human anatomy, though with the disadvantage that he had no medical training and little anatomical knowledge. His book *Letters on the Human Body* was first published in 1826 and reprinted in 1862. This book considers human physiology from a Swedenborgian viewpoint. He begins by observing that the human body, being made in the image of God, contains 'volumes of instruction', which we cannot look at 'if we look with attentive eyes, without seeing a reflected Image of our HEAVENLY FATHER'.[116] He pays particular attention to the physical senses and their conscious perception, which he regards as fundamental to the understanding of Swedenborg. The sensory organs can physiologically transmit sensations to the brain, but unlike lower animals humans also have a conscious perception which is brought about 'by virtue of a faculty—not inherent in those things themselves, nor yet in the organ by and through which they gain admission—but implanted in every man by the GREAT CREATOR; being the constant and wonderful result of the life which every human being receives continually from God'.[117] He contrasts the bodily eye that can see the world of the natural sun with the 'intellectual eye' that can see the world of the spiritual sun 'with all its various inhabitants and objects'.[118] People who do not use the intellectual or spiritual eye see only the '*husk* and *shell* of things' and so have no idea of their spiritual correspondences.[119] He goes on to make a similar analysis of the other senses. He points out that nature is brought alive only when it becomes consciously present in the human mind.[120] Without consciousness, nature is unreal; it is lifeless and meaningless. This was the broad conclusion of both Clowes and Tulk, although they differed in their beliefs regarding the reality of nature in the absence of conscious awareness, with Tulk taking a more hardline idealist perspective.

Clowes goes on to discuss other bodily organs, but his limited grasp of anatomy prevented him from making any detailed analysis. Garth Wilkinson, as a trained physician, did not have this disadvantage.

Garth Wilkinson's Psychological Physiology

The term 'Psychological Physiology' was used by Garth Wilkinson to mean the soul (*psyche*) in its manifestation or *logos* as the living physical body. He believed that Swedenborg had been 'commissioned' by the Lord to found this discipline, which requires 'an even or equated knowledge of the body and the soul: the soul being a complete and in nowise a disembodied man within the known embodied man, and having therefore a superiorly substantial or spiritual physiology'.[121]

Wilkinson's book on esoteric physiology, *The Human Body and its Connection with Man* (1851) was his first major work. Like many others in his day, he argued against the compartmentalization and exclusivity of academic knowledge, and believed that all knowledge should be publicly available. Choosing physiology as an ideal candidate for this type of public dissemination, he deplored the scientific approach of reaching down into ever more detailed material investigation which he believed would reach such a level of smallness that it would result in annihilation.[122] Instead, he believed that empirical observation should lead upwards into greater and broader truths. Writing from an avowedly Swedenborgian perspective, he regarded himself as examining the book of nature, in which 'our Lord is written down in the pages of nature herself as the truth of her whole creation'.[123] He criticized the 'scientific natural theology' that regards God as a mere craftsman who created the cosmos, and made it clear that his goal was to uncover the spiritual reality that underpins the natural world.[124]

Wilkinson had access to more recent and accurate anatomy than that which had been available to Swedenborg, and he also had the benefit of the later insights that Swedenborg had attained as a result of his experiences in the spirit world. Although Wilkinson did give an outline of contemporary anatomy and physiology, he also made extensive use of analogy to offer a broad interpretation of these facts, extending them not only into spiritual areas but also into consideration of social organization and medical practice. Like Swedenborg, he devoted a chapter to each organ, and he summarized his thesis thus:

> The brain gives it [the human body] life or ends, which are the lords and masters of organization. The lungs give it motion, without which life would be futile. The heart gives it substance, without which motion and work

would be impossible. The stomach gives it supplies, without which, moving substance, subject to wear and tear, could not last. And the skin gives new ends, or individuality, without which the whole would evaporate.[125]

There is nothing especially remarkable in this formulation; nothing here would be expected to win the high praise that this book was given by some commentators. However, a later important chapter addresses the relationship between the body and the soul, and here Wilkinson draws some more global conclusions.

Wilkinson, like Swedenborg, took the classical view that the soul forms the body and then makes use of it for its own ends. Wilkinson envisaged a cosmic cycle, which begins when:

The soul commences with the commencement of nature, and flies down, weaving and constructing, through all her kingdoms. The brain is the home that it makes on its own plan, of the solar fires, and the brain is the soul of the body anew, and the sun of the microcosm. . . The nerves are the next construction of the dramatic soul. . . making ether and magnetism into pathways for the processions of thought and will. . .[126]

The soul is thereby identified as the *real* body, and every bodily organ is ensouled by it through the nervous system. The first bodily essence that receives the soul is the 'nervous fluid' that is produced in the cells of the cerebral cortex and distributed through the body through the nerves and blood vessels. Without this, 'the soul could not be incarnate, nor the body animate'.[127] This nervous fluid transmits thought and will throughout the body. The work of ensoulment then continues beyond the body by means of the five senses. The human senses are the means by which knowledge of nature is brought to the mind and thence the soul; as Wilkinson puts it, for example, 'the ear is the hearing-trumpet of the real body [i.e., the soul], which would otherwise be deaf to the music of nature'.[128] By means of the nervous system, the soul can descend into nature and bring it back to live in the human mind:

For the soul running downwards from the brain to the skin, never ending in the end begins anew, and reattaches death to life by the standing wonder of the fivefold senses...And as the soul descended, the senses reascend...[129]

Here Wilkinson is describing the physiological plot of a cosmic drama in which the principal character is the brain as the home of the soul, and the other organs play supporting roles.[130] The result of this process is that life is brought to nature, which is dead without human awareness of it.

Wilkinson believed that the body is fashioned for the sole purpose of becoming the external, physical expression of the soul. Accordingly, the physical body is as alive and as spiritual as the soul; it is the external working through which the soul is in correspondence with the material world. The soul is not imprisoned in a dead body as envisaged by Plato, but confers life upon it so that they can be in harmony:

This connection of soul with body is no chaining of the living to the dead... but it is the live man freely working with the finest tools of nature, the chief musician in continual play upon the choicest instrument of music...the immortal confers his own life upon his mortal bride...[131]

The harmony between soul and body is the result of correspondence, which is a causal principle of creation:

Correspondence comes from above downwards...[it] is causation relatively in its own right...The causation lies in the thing above introducing itself into the sphere below, and presenting itself there through the rules of that lower sphere.[132]

Wilkinson believed that correspondence between the spiritual and the physical worlds is the causal force behind the whole created cosmos. Everything in the created world has its spiritual counterpart, and everything in the mineral, plant and animal world is created because it has a spiritual use. Man is above all in having the divine purpose of returning the whole cosmos to its divine origin through his own spiritual regeneration. The use of correspondence in creation is 'to bring the Divine Creation down; to ultimate and fix it [in the material world]; and through man, his regeneration, and ascension into heaven, to complete the circle, and cause all things to rise representatively to their centre and fountain in the Lord'.[133] Spiritual regeneration of man will thus result in the return of nature to its previous state of perfection.[134]

Following Swedenborg, Wilkinson placed particular emphasis on the role of the brain, lungs and heart. He recognized that 'From the oldest times the sympathy between the mind and the heart has been acknowledged. The records of disease likewise show, that the heart is affected and altered by the state of the mind, and *vice versa*'.[135] The particular emotional correspondence with the heart is love; not, of course, love in the sexual sense, but rather meaning that to which the person is most attracted. The highest level of love is found in God: 'And as ancient chiefs traced their lineage to the Gods, we follow their figure, and track up the heart loves until they claim parentage from the God of love'.[136] Again adopting Swedenborg's thesis, Wilkinson described the correspondence between the understanding and the lungs. Breathing is affected by (and thus represents) the senses and the passions. Because respiration is particularly related to the intellect, it can be used to control the senses and the passions:

because the mind has power over the lungs, it can handle the senses by their means, and prevent the floods of worldliness from penetrating to the upper sensoria. So also it can stop the mounting passions. This it does by suspending the breath, and cutting off the supplies of sense and animality.[137]

This give rise to a trance state, during which, according to Wilkinson, the intellect is free to ascend to higher spiritual planes and there receive celestial wisdom:

Nor do we know a limit to the excursions of the intellect on these holidays, when it visits its celestial birthplace, secure of finding its lungs and factories ready to start into reciprocation at a moment's notice on its re-arrival.[138]

Wilkinson's much later work *The Soul is Form and Doth the Body Make* (1890) is primarily devoted to developing further his concepts of correspondence between body and mind. He restates his view that mind and body are not separate, but rather the body *is* the mind in physical representation, 'the very *obsequium* or compliance or obedience of the mind'.[139] As empirical evidence in support of this spiritual truth, Wilkinson put forward the well-known effect of states of mind on the function of bodily organs. He saw this as an influx into correspondent organs of spirits which can 'assail, arrest, or pervert their functions'.[140] Wilkinson derived further evidence for his position from the ancient use of language in which psychological states were regarded as being embodied in various organs. He quoted with approval a long fragment of *Confessio Amantis*, a poem by early English poet John Gower, which details these associations and which purported to be part of the instruction that Aristotle gave to his pupil Alexander the Great. Wilkinson regarded this use of language as 'a survival from the primeval Churches and their Revelations'.[141] Towards the end of his life, Wilkinson summarized his concept of spiritual physiology, formulated in terms of Swedenborgian correspondences:

The gate whereby Theology enters the sciences of the body of man is already given in the fact that man is to be an image and likeness of God; and finitely to correspond to the infinite Creator. This law of Correspondence, an omnipresent image-and-likeness-law, descends through every degree of his being...If this be so, then every natural organ...has a spiritual organ within it uniting it to correspondent faculties next above it; and by private degrees of ascent to the soul and the Creator. So considered, theology will be at home in physiology.[142]

In *The Human Body*, Wilkinson displayed some further developments in his early thinking. He saw parallels between the individual human body and human society as a whole:

[Humankind] has its brains in those who are the presiding influences of the social universe; its lungs are in those who are the practical intellect of the ages, and the voice of truth to the world; its heart is the thousandfold love that carries the races to their goals...its belly is the whole schooling of mankind, all the men...that hunger and thirst to receive infants and savages, and convert them into angels. Its skin is in those who are the bonds of their state, which are nothing more than... inviolable law. [143]

Wilkinson was already developing a strong interest in the social concepts of Charles Fourier, the French utopian socialist and philosopher, whose views on society were regarded by Wilkinson and many other Swedenborgians as being analogous to Swedenborg's philosophy of the human body. [144] In *The Human Body* Wilkinson also shows a keen interest in the human mind, which, as he says, is 'in every part of the body, co-extensive and co-intensive with the organism...We are solid statues of consciousness'. [145] He developed these ideas further in his collaboration with James Braid, the father of hypnosis. [146]

In an article on 'Correspondences' that was published two years before *The Human Body* and so relates to the same period of Wilkinson's thinking, he addresses the importance of human physiology for the process of creation:

the great movement of the universe enters his [man's] body, and becomes his constitution. The world lives in him, and fits him to live in the world. Not a stone, or a plant, or a living creature, but carries up its heart's thread into his loom, there to be wound into human nature, and...to obey the progress of his own immortal destinies. For...while creation is the work of God, modification is the function of man; or, in other words, the world is continually created by God through man... [147]

The notion that 'the world is continually created by God through man', so that the design of creation is modified as it passes through man, is one that would have been acceptable to Tulk. It is a philosophy that carries profound implications for the origin of the adverse aspects of the created world, such as illness, plagues and pestilences, famine and environmental disaster. Wilkinson would return to these issues in the context of his views on the relationship between health and the human spiritual condition, which are discussed in the next chapter.

— 7 —

Healing the Spirit: Garth Wilkinson's Medicine

[A man] becomes a physician only when he knows that which is unnamed, invisible, and immaterial, and yet efficacious.

Paracelsus[1]

Fig. 7: 'Diagram of the uses of mistletoe', from Wilkinson's few surviving notes on his homoeopathic practice and remedies.
Swedenborg Society Archive, A/150 (a).

I llness was a major preoccupation of the Victorians. The advent of the Industrial Revolution, with its overcrowded and insanitary living conditions, harsh working environments and poverty, led to an upsurge of diseases, including cholera, dysentery and typhus, as well as occupational diseases associated, for example, with work in coal mines and cotton mills. [2]

Garth Wilkinson's revulsion by the orthodox medical practice of his day has already been noted and I have argued that his adoption of Swedenborg's philosophy, as well as his social background, predisposed him to follow the alternative therapeutic approaches of his day, including homoeopathy, mesmerism, hydropathy and herbalism (the 'big four' alternative treatment approaches of the nineteenth century, as described by historian Roger Cooter). [3] Wilkinson's primary approach was homoeopathy, and he applied his other interests to his homoeopathic practice in novel and surprising ways.

Swedenborg on illness and healing

Even though medicine was not a major focus of interest for Swedenborg, he did offer views on the origin of illness and suitable approaches to treatment in several of his works, both scientific and theological. Throughout these works he maintained a clear focus on the importance of the mind as the primary cause of illness.

In his scientific works, Swedenborg divided diseases into three broad types that relate to the three vital fluids: those of the red blood, which relate to the body; those of the purer blood, which relate to the animus or animal mind; and those of the spirituous fluid, which relate to the rational or intellectual mind. Illness of the body can be caused by the harmful effects of either the external world or a disturbed mind. Swedenborg proposed that these causes include an excessive quantity or poor quality of food; harmful components of respired air (including 'pestiferous vapours'); the absorption through the skin of toxins, which enter the red blood indirectly after first being absorbed into the 'purer blood' or animal spirits; a disturbed state of the higher mind which arouses passions in the animus and hence bodily dysfunction; and external trauma such as cuts and bruises.[4] Treatments for bodily illnesses include the regulation of diet, taking proper rest and sleep, having a tranquil mind, and taking medicines derived from natural sources.

Illnesses of the purer blood, the diseases of the animus, show themselves as mental disorders such as anger, melancholy, fluctuation of mood and impairment of memory. Such conditions can be the result of either bodily disease, acting from below, or abnormalities of will and judgment in the intellectual mind, which act on the animus from above. Effective treatments for these conditions, thought Swedenborg, include convivial company and the study of moral philosophy, as well as medicines derived from nature.

Diseases of the purest blood, the spirituous fluid, which is 'the external form of the soul', are not the usually recognized illnesses of the body or mind, but are moral in nature, such as 'loves of self, vain ambitions, misanthropy, hatreds, [and] excessive desires for depravity'.[5] Treatment for this includes attention to the illnesses that result from the secondary effects of a disturbed intellectual mind on the animus and body, as well as paying primary attention to restoring moral function by means of instruction from a suitable master and a study of theology, both natural and revealed.

It is plain from this account that Swedenborg emphasized the primacy of mental symptoms, the use of treatments derived from nature, and the importance for health of moral rectitude. He described essentially a hierarchy of causes of disease, from the intellectual mind through the animus to the body. He also posited an even higher ultimate cause of all illness, the nature of which was unknown to him at that time, and which he said 'come[s] from some other source, nor do we know whence'.[6] Shortly after writing this, Swedenborg had his revelatory experiences and realized that all diseases ultimately are spiritual in origin.

In his theological works, Swedenborg built on the ideas that he had described in his scientific works.[7] He proposed three broad categories of illness: those that are inherited; those that relate directly to spiritual influx; and those that have apparently natural causes.

Swedenborg believed that character traits are inherited from the paternal side, which furnishes the soul to the foetus.[8] These pass from generation to generation, and any tendency towards those states of mind that can generate illness will potentially cause illness in the offspring. However, this is not inevitable and can be modulated if the individual who inherited those tendencies follows a worthy spiritual path.

According to Swedenborg, every person is attended by both good and evil spirits during life in the material world. People are not conscious of these spirits, which act at a level higher than the reasoning mind.[9] The spirits produce inclinations towards good or evil behaviour that enter into the conscious mind and can be accepted or rejected by using reason.[10] Whether the influences of angelic or infernal spirits are accepted depends upon the internal state of the person: that is, whether his primary desire is for heavenly or for worldly things. If we accept evil inclinations, then we come more under the control of the infernal spirits that cause illness. All human diseases are the result of a correspondence between the spirits of hell and the 'evil desires and cravings of the lower mind' such as envy, hatred, intemperance and overindulgence in bodily pleasure.[11] Each disease is associated with the spirits of the dead who felt the same passion as the patient.[12] When a person has such feelings, infernal spirits become conjoined with the internal man. These spirits cause blockage of the finest invisible tubules that reach into the inner man, and this in turn has damaging effects down the chain of vessels and throughout the physical body, resulting in disease. The infernal spirits, which were previously confined to the internal man, are then able to enter into the diseased parts of the body.[13]

Swedenborg continued to accept that diseases can result from apparently natural causes, just as he had described in his scientific works. However, in his spiritual works this was reframed by his belief that noxious influences from the natural world are the result of the sinful state of man.[14] He also continued to believe that naturally derived medications can and should be used in the treatment of illness, because they have been made available by divine providence.[15]

Swedenborg's thesis emphasizes the psychological aspects of illness and healing. A person who is fully committed to a sensual life (relating to love of self and the world) is not only attracted to worldly pleasures, but also freely uses his intellect and reason to justify that position. Inevitably, such a person is prone to both mental and physical illness.[16] Healing, Swedenborg says, is the result of faith in the omnipotence of the Lord.[17] He cited the many biblical examples of healing by faith, as well as other miracles that are possible to those of faith. Therefore, although illness can be alleviated symptomatically by means of physical treatments, real cure as well as the prevention of future illnesses depends upon an altered mental attitude, and ultimately on the moral state of the patient. It follows that any physician seeking effective treatment must pay primary attention to these issues.

Parallels have been drawn between Swedenborg and Paracelsus, and it has been suggested that some of Swedenborg's terminology was influenced directly or indirectly by Paracelsus.[18] Garth Wilkinson's ideas show much more striking parallels with those of Paracelsus, and there is evidence that as a young man Wilkinson was aware of the work of Paracelsus.[19] Both men rejected the conventional medicine, as well as the academic authorities, of their day. They both believed that much medical wisdom can be obtained from the folklore of the common people, and both believed that medical knowledge should be made accessible to the general population. More importantly though, their actual medical theories showed many commonalities, including the central importance of the mind in the production and treatment of disease, and the spread of contagious disease through sin.

Garth Wilkinson's practice of medicine

After he had rejected the practices of conventional medicine, Garth Wilkinson adopted a concept of health that derived from his Swedenborgian concepts, and which echoed much more ancient ideas:

Health, in short, by the old definition (and we know of no better), is
harmony in its most considerable meaning—harmony of the parts of
the body with themselves—harmony of the mind with the body—and
harmony of both with the circumstances and ordinances into which we are
born: harmony also of the human frame with the climate that it inhabits,
and with external nature in its variety.[20]

Wilkinson's concept of the origin of disease mirrored his generally Swedenborgian
concept of the world: everything material corresponds to a higher spiritual reality,
and the world was created perfect by God but is modified by the sins of man, which
give rise to noxious elements of the earth such as poisonous plants and dangerous
animals. In parallel with this, all disease has a spiritual origin and is fostered by the
evil in the mind of man. The catastrophes of the world—not just disease epidemics,
but also other disasters such as earthquakes and volcanic eruptions—are the product
of the same human evils, and hence correspond to disease in the human body. As
Wilkinson puts it, 'All disorders are spiritual disorders first, then mental depravities,
then bodily diseases, and then mundane catastrophes'.[21] Wilkinson was aware that
some diseases are associated with bacteria and with chemical abnormalities (such
as those causing gout), but he regarded these as secondary effects of the disease
rather than as physical causes. For Wilkinson, there was only one disease, which
is of the mind, and the way in which this is expressed in the body depends on the
nature of the mental aberration, together with the susceptibility of the organs due
either to heredity or to misuse (as in gluttony leading to a vulnerability to stomach
complaints). Bacteria are the desperate attempt of the diseased body to set up a new
life, and since they are the repository of the disease they have some capacity to cause
secondary illness in other predisposed people. It was clear to Wilkinson that bacteria
were not the primary cause of disease, because, he argued, people had not always
been on the earth, so the first person to contract a disease could not have contracted
it by transmission of bacteria from another person.[22] Regarding the social body
more generally, Wilkinson regarded depraved individuals as the bacteria of society.
Extending his concept to particular social groups, and echoing the social attitudes

183

of his time, he believed that some groups were predisposed to certain illnesses. His example of this was Russian influenza, which he believed affected only the upper social classes, compared with cholera in the lower classes. They are essentially the same disease, resulting in each case from people craving for things beyond their reach, but they affect different parts of the body: the intestines in the 'abdominal people' of the lower classes, and the head and lungs of the more intellectual upper classes. [23] Whole nations could be susceptible to particular illnesses because of their sinful proclivities, and nations could export illnesses along lines that Wilkinson called 'teledemes' by analogy with the telegraph. Transmission occurs from the powerful 'mental races' of the West to the weaker 'bodily races' of the East. [24] Here America was the biggest culprit, because 'The lust of eating everything up' as the ruling passion leads to a failure of nutrition (cholera) in the deprived nations. [25]

Applying the 'doctrine of spheres', Wilkinson postulated that when a person is diseased then the sphere around that person is also diseased, and hence they should be left at home so that others are not exposed to their diseased sphere during transit. In particular, they should not be transported to hospitals which worsen disease by inducing fear, and which transmit disease over a wide area because of the collective spheres of the sick. [26]

Wilkinson believed that medicine, like the human race in general, had degenerated since ancient times. Ancient man, he believed, lived in complete harmony with himself and his environment and so did not suffer illness. When the earliest degeneration set in (as the result of sin), men still had an instinctive awareness of the properties of herbs and other natural remedies, and of their correspondence with the human body, so that they could use them to ward off disease. By Wilkinson's time, so he believed, this knowledge was present only in rudimentary form and had been replaced by the crude treatments of allopathic medicine, such as bleeding and the use of poisonous and debilitating medicines.

Wilkinson's view was that to be effective, a physician must not only recognize the source of disease in human evil, but must also have a personality which inspires faith and hope. The healer must be 'full of light' which will illuminate the dark spots of the patient. [27] He attacked the elitism of medical specialists. Echoing his criticism of 'scientism' which he thought funnelled down into vanishingly small detail rather than expanding upwards to higher truths, he thought that physicians who specialized in a single disease were often men of 'one book; maybe, their own on the subject'.[28] They were generally regarded as the medical aristocracy to whom general practitioners should refer complex cases, but Wilkinson reversed this argument by proposing that 'The greatest men have been universal specialists—specialists in generals and universals'.[29] Since body and mind are an indivisible unity, the physician needs to take a holistic view. He regarded homoeopaths as 'anti-specialists' who could often effect cure where specialist physicians had failed. He took on board the criticism that cure could have taken place because the patient had more faith in the homoeopath than in the orthodox physician, but he regarded that as a positive assertion about homoeopaths:

> Perhaps the quack, apart from his simple means, had faith in himself and not in the material means alone, and imported his faith to the patient. Perhaps he laid hold of the mind in the body, which can work such wonders there.[30]

Because Garth Wilkinson's medical practice was informed directly by his Swedenborgian beliefs, he had a strong emphasis on vitalist approaches and the primacy of the mind. Although homoeopathy was his main approach to healing, Wilkinson was eclectic. He was an early adopter of mesmerism and used this in his medical practice.[31] He was also an advocate of other methods of natural healing that were popular in his day. He recommended the system of hydropathy that had been promoted by Vincenz Priessnitz, whose methods included cold baths, the consumption of large amounts of water, avoidance of alcohol, a plain diet, exercise and fresh air.[32] Wilkinson believed that 'The system of Preissnitz [*sic*] belongs to a group of sciences which include the whole of the four elements of the ancients, and apply them to the healing art. Earth, air, fire and water are the basis of outward hygiene'.[33] Wilkinson took the water cure himself, writing to Henry James, Sr in 1849 that:

For some weeks past I have been privately inflicting on myself the cold water cure, and with both benefit and bane. I had long felt the evils of continual indigestion, and the curse of all stimulants, but the thing got at last so bad that I was a nuisance to myself, and to everybody else: so I made up a mind like iron, to become a rigid abstinent henceforth, and to mulch the devil by water in its various forms...This is 5 weeks since; and though I am weaker for my change of diet, yet I am more continuous, better tempered, happier, and sleepier.[34]

Wilkinson also used magnets; although he did not write about this in his published works, he endorsed an advertisement for 'Darlow's Flexible Magnetine Appliances', saying that he used them often in his practice, and that he found them effective for 'low vitality in the great nervous centres, or in the principal organs of assimilation, nutrition, and blood purification'. These devices were magnetic belts, breast shields and patches for flexible use.[35]

The principles of homoeopathy

Homoeopathy was by far the most dominant aspect of Wilkinson's therapeutic approach. Before discussing the details of Wilkinson's homoeopathic practice it will be helpful to outline some of the more basic concepts that underpin this system of healing. Homoeopathy was developed by Samuel Hahnemann (1755-1843), a physician who had been appalled by the brutality and lack of effectiveness of the medical treatments that were then in use. Hahnemann developed the ancient Hippocratic concept of *similia similibus curantur*, or 'like cures like'. This contrasted with allopathy, the use of medicines to act *against* symptoms, which was the prevailing therapeutic concept at that time. Homoeopathic medicines are tested, or 'proved', by administering very small doses of them to healthy individuals and recording the symptoms that are produced. The medicine is then used to treat people that have the same symptoms as those produced by that medicine. Another fundamental principle is that of the *minimum dose*, which in practice means that the medicines are used in extremely high dilutions.

Homoeopathy derives directly from the vitalist tradition, which was the dominant concept of life at the time when Hahnemann was studying and practising medicine. However, when he first developed his theory, Hahnemann made little direct reference to the concept of a vital force. He regarded himself as an empiricist, guided only by observable results. Later in his career, when he felt the need for a theoretical underpinning of the observed effects, he focused more on the concept of a vital force, which he called the *dynamis*.[36] He set this out in the fifth edition of his *Organon*, which was translated in 1849 by Robert Ellis Dudgeon, a close friend of Garth Wilkinson:

> In the healthy condition of man, the spiritual vital force (autocracy), the dynamis that animates the material body (organism) rules with unbounded sway, and retains all the parts of the organism in admirable, harmonious, vital operation. . . The material organism, without the vital force, is capable of no sensation, no function. . . When a person falls ill, it is only this spiritual, self-acting (automatic) vital force, every where present in his organism, that is primarily deranged by the dynamic influence upon it of a morbific agent inimical to life. . .[37]

Hahnemann proposed that the effectiveness of homoeopathic remedies was due to them having more power than the disease, so that the natural disease was displaced by a medicinal disease with similar symptoms; but, as the medicinal disease has only a short duration of action, the vital force could more easily overcome it, leaving the vital force ultimately free from both the medicinal and the natural illnesses.[38] Hahnemann said that this action of homoeopathic remedies depends on their spiritual powers.[39]

The notion of a 'spirit-like' treatment resonates with Swedenborg's belief that all illness has a spiritual origin. Swedenborg made several statements that can be taken as a direct endorsement of the homoeopathic principles that 'like cures like', and that more refined preparations of medicines act at a higher level of disease. In *Divine Love and Wisdom* he tells us that 'These things which do injury to man are called uses because they are of use to the evil in doing evil, and are also conducive

187

to absorbing malignities, and thus to curing them'.[40] He gave more detail about this in his *Adversaria*:

> Things unclean are wiped off by something equally unclean; the bite of a scorpion and of serpents is removed by their ashes or dust. Likewise in spiritual things unclean spirits take away unclean things.[41]

Swedenborg also emphasized the notion that toxic plants can become therapeutic to the body when given as tinctures, whereas their volatile essences have a 'spiritual' effect:

> every plant contains a use, a spiritual use in the spiritual world, and both a spiritual and a natural use in the natural world. The spiritual use is for the various states of the mind, and the natural use is for the various states of the body. It is well known that minds are refreshed, recreated, and stimulated, or on the other hand that drowsiness, sadness, or fainting is induced, by the odors and flavors of different kinds of plants; also that the body is healed by the various solutions, purgations, and remedies made from plants, and on the other hand, is destroyed by the poisons extracted from them.[42]

Homoeopathy and American Swedenborgians

The first practising homoeopath in America, Hans Burch Gram, was a Swedenborgian who had trained with Hahnemann.[43] Homoeopathy rapidly became the preferred treatment amongst American Swedenborgians.[44] From their perspective, Hahnemann's system of medical treatment plainly required a more adequate theoretical framework, and they attempted to develop a spiritual rationale for the efficacy of homoeopathic treatment. This was a matter of lively debate in the years immediately preceding the publication of Wilkinson's *The Human Body*.

In 1844, Swedenborgian homoeopath William E Payne made an early formulation of the supposed affinities between the doctrines of homoeopathy and those of Emanuel Swedenborg.[45] Starting from the Swedenborgian premise that nature is created by the Lord but modified through man, he described a 'healthy' state in which infernal spirits pass unimpeded through man, terminating in animals, plants and minerals. These recipients of infernal spirits develop evil characteristics so that they become a suitable receptacle for the spirits. Thus animals become ferocious, plants and minerals become poisonous, or other evil characteristics develop. Disease arises when the passage of infernal spirits through man is blocked, so that the spirits lodge in the organ to which they correspond. The organ is then altered so as to better accommodate the spirit, and disease ensues. Treatment is by presenting the spirit with a more favourable lodging in the form of a homoeopathic remedy, then the spirit can continue its journey out of the body. Very dilute homoeopathic remedies work because the 'spiritual property is the only active property of matter'. However, the remedy must maintain some material association so that it can work on the same plane as the diseased organ.

This issue became a topic of lively exchange in the columns of the *New Church Repository* in 1850. This began with an article by homoeopath Richard DeCharms, written in response to an anonymous article critical of homoeopathy that had been published in the *New York Tribune*.[46] The central position taken by DeCharms was that homoeopathy works because infernal spirits that are causing disease will pass willingly into inferior but corresponding hellish habitats. He described what he called a 'law of derivation', according to which the effects of disease-inducing spirits would be cured by enticing the spirit into another corresponding habitat of a lower degree, which is preferred by the inverted value system of such spirits. Thus, the effects of animal poisons can be cured by vegetable, and vegetable by mineral. He complicated this model by describing an alternative system of cure, in which the reverse can happen:

> But there may be a cure of disease by the Lord's *elevation* of the activities of man's life from a lower to a higher plane. Hence, in the cure of a mineral poison by a vegetable one, or of a vegetable poison by an animal one, there is, probably, a quiescence of the activity of the more infernal spirits in the more ultimate poison . . . [47]

For DeCharms, this is the principle by which moral approaches can cure disease, by bringing infernal spirits into a state of quiescence. In this way, DeCharms felt able to explain a cure that proceeded either in the direction of animal-vegetable-mineral, or its complete reverse. Furthermore, he offered no explanation for the use of homoeopathic dilutions. This was a deeply unsatisfactory formulation, and not surprisingly it was promptly attacked in a subsequent edition of the same journal by the Swedenborgian physician William Henry Holcombe, who was practising allopathically at that time.[48] Holcombe pointed out that influx of evil spirits takes place only into animal forms, and that vegetables and minerals carry evil only through their uses. These evils become manifest only when the plant or mineral is associated with an animal. The affinity of infernal spirits with poisonous substances 'is entirely connected with the noxious relations of these substances *to man*'. Holcombe also observed that if infernal spirits gravitated by choice to the vegetable and then to the mineral kingdoms, then 'the whole infernal world would be precipitated into the mineral kingdom'. He proposed his own model that supported allopathic treatment. Following Swedenborg, he suggested that diseased tissues act as 'matrices' or moulds for the influx of infernal spirits, and that the way to expel such spirits is to treat the diseased tissue and thus render it unreceptive to them. At a higher level, it is necessary to receive the influx of divine love, so that infernal spirits cannot gain a foothold. At both levels, these approaches illustrate the allopathic principle of *contraria contrariis curantur*, or 'opposite cures opposite'. Another Swedenborgian allopath who rejected the notion that Swedenborg's teaching supports homoeopathy was William M Murdoch. He wrote that:

> I am not able to find a single principle, and scarcely a single expression, in the works of Swedenborg that can be construed into the support of the notion that LIKE CURES LIKE, 'similia similibus curantur'. Indeed, this seems to me, to be that very principle which our Lord repudiated, when he taught that it was impossible to cast out devils by Beelzebub the prince of devils.[49]

This was the climate in which Wilkinson developed his own concept of homoeopathy. It is especially noteworthy that these earlier commentators had focused on the correspondence between homoeopathic remedies and spirits, and did not discuss the primacy of mental symptoms which Swedenborg had stressed as the highest cause of illness. This development was made by Wilkinson, and it would become a central theme of later theories of homoeopathy.

Wilkinson's homoeopathy

Wilkinson had learned of homoeopathy from Henry James, Sr, to whom he wrote that 'You, more than any other man, led me into Homoeopathy',[50] but it was his wife Emma that finally drove him to practise homoeopathy. In a very personal account, Wilkinson describes the illness of his eldest child, then a baby, who was suffering from bronchitis. He prescribed an allopathic dose of ipecacuanha as an emetic, but his wife refused to administer it, and an argument ensued. In Wilkinson's words, Emma told him that 'for long... she had felt a repugnance to all my practice, and that this very occasion was sent, partly to oblige me to look into that new thing called Homoeopathy'.[51] She administered a dose of ipecacuanha 'such as would pass through the eye of a needle' and the child rapidly recovered. Understandably moved by this experience, Wilkinson introduced homoeopathy into his medical practice, which began to flourish. In 1852 he wrote to his father:

> My business increases beyond expectation... Homoeopathy, into which
> Emma compelled me, has for the first time caused me really to love my
> noble Profession.[52]

In 1853 Wilkinson received an honorary MD from the College of Homeopathic Medicine of Pennsylvania,[53] and this has led some commentators mistakenly to conclude that he studied there.[54] At that time, such awards were issued to physicians who already held a recognized medical degree, without the need for attendance or examination.[55] Wilkinson's only visit to America was much later, in 1869.

Although popular with patients, homoeopathy was anathema to conventional physicians at the time when Wilkinson took it up. This was expressed vividly by a friend of Wilkinson's who adopted homoeopathy at about the same time:

> my heresy offended many of my valued medical and other friends, and excluded me from all professional interchange of opinions and consultations with the leaders in medicine, and from all orthodox medical societies; and on social and scientific grounds this was a great loss to me.[56]

Wilkinson's early formulation of the principles of homoeopathy is set out in *The Human Body* (1851). He regarded the homoeopathic principle of 'like cures like' as being based firmly on the 'science' of correspondences, as set out by Swedenborg:

> The practical blessings of the New Medicine are dependent, as we conceive, firstly upon the science of correspondence, which bringing poison and disease together with a completer fitness, poisons the disease, and kills it; and secondly, upon the smallness of the doses, or we would rather say, the use of the spirit and not the body of the drugs.[57]

He paid particular attention to the way in which such minute doses of medication, so small that 'we are obliged to desert the hypothesis of their material action', might act.[58] He regarded homoeopathic remedies as acting within an 'invisible world which is especially versed about organization' which contains 'forces and substances whose minuteness excludes them from our vision'.[59] Homoeopathic remedies 'deal with the spirits of things, which are their potential forms, gradually refining massy drugs, until they are likened to those sightless agents which we know to be the roots of nature, and feel as the most powerful in ourselves'.[60] Such agents have a presence throughout the body, and gain strength through this dissemination.[61] He thought of homoeopathic medicines as 'curative personalities, who take our shape upon them to battle in us with our ills'.[62]

Wilkinson's focus on psychological mechanisms has already been noted in relation to his work on hypnosis, and this focus is no less apparent in his system of homoeopathy. If homoeopathic remedies are to be regarded as 'curative personalities', then necessarily to be effective they must have some affinity with the personality of the patient, in a relationship similar to that between the mesmerizer and his subject. He believed that the practice of homoeopathy needed to be changed in order to reflect this:

> Homoeopathy requires many changes, and new brains of the
> Hahnemannian order, before it will do itself justice according to the con-
> ception of its founder...Among the first of these, we reckon that natural
> pathogenesis which the powers intrinsic to the body daily exercise upon it:
> viz., the powers of the mind, soul, and the inner man. By eliciting this, we
> shall get at the leading idea of pathogenesis, and also obtain rules for the
> succession of symptoms and states as welling from a single fountain head.
> Otherwise, unless our eyes be thus armed by these greater knowledges, the
> various symptoms that drugs evoke in different parts of the frame, will seem
> to have no connection with each other... [63]

He believed that 'morbid states of mind have the effects of true poisons upon the body, and must be regarded as spiritual drugs, each having a pathological history of its own'. [64] Clearly, a spiritual medication was required to counteract this.

Wilkinson held to a central concept that groups of symptoms can all be referred to particular states of mind, and that these mental inclinations are the true origin of those symptoms. He believed that this was the key to the effective use of homoeopathic remedies:

> For not only are all the symptoms to be recorded and grouped in their
> places round the organs, but a head symptom must be found which is their
> common denominator; a principal fact from which the remainder flow.
> When this is done, you will have in your mind a portrait of the drug, as the

painter has with him an instinctive limning of the faces of the intellects
and passions; and you will then become acquainted with your pharmacy,
be enabled to divine symptoms by insight without cumbersome catalogues
of them impossible to remember, and to apply them with something like
genius to the moving facts of each case as it arises.[65]

In Wilkinson's view, the potential benefits of homoeopathy went far beyond the cure
of diseases. Wilkinson saw a correspondence between homoeopathy and the function
of assimilation in the alimentary system, which he related further to a higher order
concept of assimilation. The assimilation of food requires it first to be broken down
into its finest constituents, which then, via the blood, replenish and renew the organs
according to their needs. Extending this into the spiritual realm, Wilkinson said that:

The possibility of assimilation lies in the fact, that the universe runs man-
ward from its source...The use of assimilation consists in renewing all
things upon their highest models, and by their best examples. Accordingly
in the physical man, it is the bringing together of the ends of the earth, to
be built in the temple of the body. In the mind, it is the translation of nature
into thought, and of matter into spirit.[66]

In an elaboration of this theme that has clear alchemical undertones, Wilkinson
described this process as 'the conversion of all brass into gold...of men into spirits'.[67]
In short, it is nothing less than transmutation. He suggested that homoeopathy would
ultimately have a redemptive effect for humanity in general. This would be effected
through the eradication of hereditary diseases, which result from past sins: 'what
another gain it will be, when hereditary maladies begin to be displaced...What virtues
may we not expect, when with all higher helps to good, the body itself seconds the
monitions of the soul!'[68] This concept has a millenarian flavour, heralding a new
spiritual age of conformity between the external man and his soul.

Very few of Wilkinson's notes on his practice of homoeopathy have survived. However,
amongst this material are drawings and notes that relate Wilkinson's homoeopathic

practice directly to his interest in mesmerism and contacting the spirit world. He developed a method of pictorial expression of homoeopathic remedies, saying that:

> This mode of representing Uses is new, and will be useful: it originates from a Spiritual Society who love the Hieroglyphics of Uses, and who think they have a method of dignifying them, which will serve the purposes of good men on Earth.[69]

Plainly, Wilkinson believed that this method of expression had been given to him through spiritual influx from the world of spirits. He produced abstract drawings of homoeopathic remedies (see Fig. 7) and two things become apparent from these representations. Firstly, Wilkinson interpreted the action of homoeopathic remedies in physiological terms that were based on Swedenborgian concepts. Secondly, that the accompanying texts to the drawings are attributed in two different ways, for example, either 'Hahnemann' or '† Hahnemann' with an obelus indicating the person is deceased. This suggests strongly that Wilkinson believed himself to be under the spiritual direction of Hahnemann when he produced these drawings and texts.[70]

Also surviving amongst these papers are a diagram and notes relating to a patient, 'Miss Taylor'. The diagram purports to represent her heart, but plainly it is not an anatomical representation; for example, it has teeth. Given Wilkinson's acceptance of the more esoteric claims for mesmerism, it is probable that this drawing represents a 'mesmeric diagnosis' made through clairvoyance by Wilkinson himself. His notes relate to an anatomical diagnosis of aortic aneurysm, with proposed homoeopathic remedies. Enigmatically, he adds the footnote 'Hahnemann will Listen' and makes a note to himself that 'Hahnemann' and 'Listen' would be good starting points for poems, presumably to be composed using his technique of improvisation. This note is dated 4 April 1857, and the pieces are in a bundle that also contains notes for poems. This dates the material to the period when Wilkinson was actively involved with spiritualism and was seeking inspiration from direct spiritual influx.[71]

Wilkinson regarded some of his patients as being beyond the action of homoeopathic remedies because they were spiritually possessed. In his notes on a 'Mrs Philpot', he wrote:

She is in a state of extreme obstinacy of will, which depends upon spiritual possession. This is not susceptible to the action of homeop. Let her have the Mother of Tincture of Agaric.[72]

It is characteristic of Wilkinson that he attempted to integrate all the areas of his intellectual activity into a single conceptual schema. This required that they should be applied to the development of homoeopathic remedies, and this produced some surprising bedfellows for homoeopathy, including Icelandic lore, herbalism, veterinary practice, vaccination, fairies and spiritualism.

On one of his trips to Iceland, which were stimulated by his fascination for Scandinavian history and folklore, Wilkinson learned that animals grazing near the volcanic Mount Hekla, in fields that were contaminated by volcanic ash, developed bony overgrowths and other conditions.[73] This immediately raised the possibility of producing a homoeopathic remedy. Wilkinson obtained some of the ash, and found that in homoeopathic dosage it was effective against diseases of the bones and teeth.[74] This homoeopathic remedy is still in use today.

Wilkinson had a strong interest in herbal remedies. In *Epidemic Man and His Visitations*, Wilkinson quotes with approval from the poem 'Man' by George Herbert, an English poet of the 'metaphysical school', which expresses the homoeopathic principle of *similia similibus curantur*: 'Herbs gladly cure our flesh because that they/ Find their acquaintance there'.[75] In 1852, he told Henry James, Sr that his main intellectual pursuits at that time were medical botany and the Northern (Scandinavian) languages.[76] In the same year he wrote to his father that 'Homoeopathy has led me to the study of the Old Herbals of various countries, and I see in them an unlimited extension of the Homoeopathic medicine. England is particularly rich in this kind of lore'.[77] He made use of homoeopathic preparations of traditional herbal treatments and saw no need for formal provings of these ancient remedies:

> I find that the Old Herbals give note of a number of plants and the like, useful for certain maladies; and the use descended from ancient time, and well attested. Now what but pedantry should prevent anyone from curing by

this prestige? Why not prepare the herbs Homeopathically, and use them by tradition? When they have also been proved upon the healthy, so much the better; but why wait for that?[78]

In 1854, Wilkinson proposed to the Hahnemann Medical Society some new homoeopathic remedies which derived from his interest in the apparent success of vaccination against smallpox by using the vaccinia (cowpox) virus.[79] He believed that 'it is our duty to see what other animal diseases run parallel with human diseases' in order that medicines might be prepared from them.[80] Wilkinson had observed equine diseases at the Royal Veterinary College, where his uncle William Sewell was Professor. He was struck particularly by the disease glanders, which causes lung nodules and ulceration of the respiratory tract, and farcy, a variant of glanders which leads to ulcerated nodules in the skin. He suggested that nosodes (homoeopathic remedies made from diseased tissues) prepared from infected horse tissues, and rendered harmless by homoeopathic dilution, might be effective for the treatment of 'consumption, caries of the nasal bones, chronic abscesses, and other maladies', and he added that his own preliminary trials of these nosodes had been encouraging.[81] In his enthusiasm, Wilkinson believed that he had found a potential cure and preventative treatment for consumption.

Wilkinson's essay, published in *The British Journal of Homoeopathy*, was followed immediately by a commentary from John James Drysdale, one of the editors of the journal, who said that he had developed the same idea independently, but that he had found nosodes prepared from animals with glanders and farcy to be ineffective.[82] Criticizing isopathy (a homoeopathic practice that makes use of nosodes), he said that 'certain unreflecting men have brought the whole subject into discredit by the erection of a quite premature and unsubstantial system'.[83] His criticism of Wilkinson's idea included the observation that the animal diseases are transmitted by self-replicating viruses, and therefore any homoeopathic preparation will either contain viruses, in which case it would be pathogenic rather than homoeopathic, or it would not, in which case it could be expected to treat quite different symptoms. He concluded that 'we have little to hope from further experiments in the way recommended by Dr. Wilkinson'.[84] There is no record of Wilkinson's reaction to his dismissal as an 'unreflecting man', but his nosodes are still in use today, for conditions similar to those that he suggested.[85]

A suggestion from Wilkinson that caused even more controversy was his proposal to use spiritualism in the treatment of insanity.[86] This surprising proposal stemmed from the popular belief at that time that involvement with spiritualism can cause insanity.[87] He noted that whilst there were homoeopathic treatments for brain disease, there were none for the mind, and developed his thesis that '[spiritualism] is one of the Lord's plants for curing insanity'.[88] He had his own view of how spiritualism can lead to insanity:

> The privilege of speaking with the unseen world exalts the conceptions, and
> sometimes the sense of importance of its recipient. Excited attention, played
> upon by unexpected influences, carries the mind off its balance, and control
> of reason grows feebler, until a paroxysm of artificially induced insanity
> sometimes concludes the experiment. This is a very rare result...Where
> there has been no organic disease, I have never yet known any permanent
> state to result from these crises of excitement: they pass off in a few days, or
> a few weeks, and leave the medium calmer than before.[89]

However, the situation is different if the paroxysm of insanity is suppressed and not allowed to run its proper course, as happens when such people are taken into asylums. The source of insanity then remains in the patient, who remains insane until it is released. In short, Wilkinson's basic assumption was that 'the patients are mediums presumptive' whose pronouncements have been misunderstood and repressed.[90] He proposed the therapeutic use of involuntary drawing of the kind common at that time amongst spiritualist mediums. If not art, then writing (especially poetry), dance or any other mode of artistic expression would be equally useful.

> By this means the inward experiences and troubles of the whole of these
> patients will be brought to the surface; the patients will be taught that an-
> other spirit than their own is in the process; they will gradually transfer their

madness to that other agent; and their pictures or products will become the scapegoat of their states. . . Then will fear and suspicion, which are the two door-keepers of the madman's mind, die of the new permission to develop freely his madness on the canvas.[91]

Wilkinson claimed that art of this kind can be shown to be produced by a spirit rather than by the imagination, because it is produced without the will of the patient 'with a feeling of unself'.[92] He was quite prepared to accept the criticism that it might be the patient's own spirit that was emerging rather than an alien one, but he thought it must be a spirit of some kind. There is no record of this treatment being put into practice, although Wilkinson evidently maintained an interest in insanity and was in correspondence with several asylum doctors even towards the end of his life.[93]

Not surprisingly, Wilkinson's proposal was greeted with outrage by the asylum doctors, who were anxious to remove any vestiges of supernaturalism from their speciality and instead join the ranks of the scientists.[94] The response, written in their professional journal, *The Asylum Journal of Mental Science*, is a 36-page condemnation of both spiritualism and homoeopathy.[95] Nevertheless, the author conceded that drawing and writing in the insane can act to 'drain the internal malady away by sapping its root and strength, viz., inward brooding, fear, and suspicion'.[96] This is remarkably similar to Wilkinson's summary of the beneficial effects to the insane of artistic expression, albeit set within a very different explanatory paradigm.

Always ready to consider new ideas, however outlandish, Wilkinson also practised the system of 'electrohomoeopathy' which had been developed by an Italian, Count Cesare Mattei.[97] This approach, which became very popular in the late nineteenth century, claimed to harness the therapeutic properties of electrical charges contained in homoeopathic extracts of medicinal herbs. These 'Electrical liquids', designated by various colours, were to be taken internally, or applied externally, for the treatment of various illnesses including syphilis and cancer.[98]

Even more on the fringes of esoteric medicine was Wilkinson's concept of 'fairy medicines' that act at a higher spiritual level than homoeopathic remedies. He described 'celestial' medicines that he said were gathered by fairies. Amongst his papers is a drawing of a 'bottle' in which there can be seen a central figure of a fairy, in a heart that signifies 'her love in her work'.[99] This is surrounded by four 'eyes' that represent 'her fourfold light: light of Fairy Heaven, Fairy Etherland, Fairy Earthland and Human Earth or Body'. The celestial medicines derive 'not from plants or herbs, but from sympathies and loves, which take this form'. Here, Wilkinson focuses on the curative value of properly directed 'sympathies and loves', as a form of healing that is above the spiritual or natural-spiritual nature of homoeopathic remedies.[100]

Commentators on homoeopathy commonly draw a distinction between two types of homoeopathy: one that is more materialist in outlook, and another more spiritual form of homoeopathy that Peter Morrell has termed 'transcendental homeopathy'.[101] Morrell regarded transcendental homoeopathy as characterized by a belief in isopathy, the use of higher potencies (which, in the inverted conceptual framework of homoeopathy, means higher dilutions), and the theory of miasms (contaminations that enter the body through the skin and spread to cause generalized illness). It is plain that Garth Wilkinson belonged to this camp. He was a high-potency prescriber, and regarded extreme dilutions as spiritual in nature:

> Fact shows that the attenuation of medicines may go on to such a point,
> and yet their curative properties be preserved, nay, heightened, that we are
> obliged to desert the hypothesis of their material action, and to presume
> that they take rank as dynamical things.[102]

Wilkinson's homoeopathy was extreme even by the standards of transcendental homoeopathy, and in the early days of his practice this approach was out of step with the leading English homoeopaths of that time, particularly those that were medically qualified such as Richard Hughes and Robert Ellis Dudgeon. They preferred to use less dilute preparations of homoeopathic remedies, which still had the potential to exert pharmacological effects. Dudgeon, who nonetheless remained a friend of Wilkinson, was particularly scathing about isopathy and very high-potency (high dilution) prescribing. In 1854 he published his *Lectures on the Theory and Practice of Homoeopathy*, and he went on to observe that:

we see some nominal partisans of homoeopathy developing the doctrines of Hahnemann into the most absurd extravagancies, carrying their dilutions to the most preposterous height, and gravely publishing so-called provings of absolutely inert substances, such as loaf-sugar and skim-milk, or pretending to treat their patients with dynamized thunderbolts and diluted moonshine.[103]

He squarely blamed Constantine Hering, one of the early pioneers of homoeopathy in America, for introducing such practices:

our transatlantic and sometimes transcendental friend Dr. Hering, one of whose transcendentalisms consists in taking up every point of Hahnemann's doctrines where Hahnemann himself judiciously left off, and pursuing it beyond the extreme limits of probability, and for some short distance into the domain of absurdity—Dr. Hering, I say, gravely asserts that the addition of one miserable globule will make a whole trough of water medicinal.[104]

Dudgeon also blamed Hering for 'having introduced isopathic heresies' that he had 'raked up from the dust and rubbish of antiquity'.[105]

The division amongst homoeopaths in nineteenth-century Britain reflected the wider social context. The dominant group in the middle of the century were the low-potency (low dilution) prescribers, who rejected any esoteric aspects of homoe-opathy and who wished to be identified with 'scientific' and respectable medicine. They supported the old social order and believed that the practice of homoeopathy should be restricted to qualified doctors. This type of practitioner is typified by Frederick Foster Quinn, who had made his name treating the Whig aristocracy. On the other hand, transcendental homoeopaths were more likely to include lay healers and young radical doctors from the same group that adopted phrenology and other unorthodox approaches. In embracing a transcendental concept of homoeopathy, Wilkinson allied himself with the non-medical homoeopaths, even advocating the complete deregulation of medicine. He was part of a more general movement in

Victorian England that was termed at the time 'physical puritanism', by analogy with religious Puritanism. [106] This movement embraced lifestyle and therapeutic approaches to health that were based on vegetarianism, hydropathy, mesmerism, phrenology, teetotalism, homoeopathy and herbalism. These approaches to health were not the exclusive province of professionals, but could be learned and used by everyone. Historian J F C Harrison has highlighted the association between this 'physical puritanism' and social reform movements of the nineteenth century that focused on increased democracy, social equality and opportunities for social mobility. [107] This reflected an increased mood of self-reliance and the wish for an egalitarian society that rejected authoritarianism and adopted socialist principles. Through his lectures and publications, Wilkinson must be seen as a leading figure in this movement, though his contribution is characteristically ignored. [108]

Several practitioners of transcendental homoeopathy found that they had an affinity with the occult and magical organizations that were established later in the nineteenth century. There is no evidence that Garth Wilkinson was ever a member of any such group, though he evidently had sympathies with some of those that did join. For example, Wilkinson was a family friend of homoeopath and spiritualist Robert Masters Theobald, who was a member of a magical order, The Golden Dawn. [109]

Towards the end of his life, in 1893, Wilkinson was still pondering the mode of action of homoeopathic remedies. He wrote to William Boericke that:

> Through my dear R.E. Dudgeon, I have just reperused the *Organon* translated by him; but Hahnemann's explanation of Homeopathy is not a likely one, for how can the slight motion of an infinitesimal dose be a more powerful state than the diseased action which it fronts and routs, David's pebble from the Brook which smote Goliath was not naturally stronger than he, but spiritually. So Homeopathy needs a spiritual or natural-spiritual explanation...A doctrine of regeneration is needed...To follow this Swedenborgian opening will be the work of future time. I want to think of it, if my time allows. [110]

Wilkinson's last attempt to make such a formulation was published in 1895 in an open letter to Robert T Cooper, a homoeopath of the materialist and 'scientific' school. Wilkinson outlined the Swedenborgian world view and the relationship of homoeopathy to it. He described Swedenborg's 'Doctrine of Degrees', according to which there are ascending spiritual levels in man. He asserted that:

> our Founder's infinitesimal medicines, from the third to the two hundredth dilution, and onwards...meet in the diseased body this Doctrine of Degrees...the various dilutions at certain steps represent different phases of spiritual effort according to the number so to speak of the fibre to which they are level...Hahnemann had himself, as my friend Dr. Dudgeon informs me, a view that infinitesimals did put on in some way a spiritual power. They were inventions of his doctrinal faith walking along experience....[111]

Wilkinson became accepted by the wider homoeopathic community in Britain, and was elected as President of the British Homoeopathic Congress in 1885.[112] He was also honoured by American homoeopaths, not only by the presentation of an MD from the College of Homeopathic Medicine of Pennsylvania, but also more personally by William Boericke of Boericke & Tafel, the leading American homoeopathic pharmacists and publishers of the time. Boericke's esteem for Wilkinson was so great that he named his son, who eventually became Professor of Therapeutics at the Hahnemann Medical College in Philadelphia, Garth Wilkinson Boericke in honour of his friend. Wilkinson's letters show that he took a close interest in the progress of his young namesake.[113] The regard in which Wilkinson was held amongst American homoeopaths was also expressed by William Holcombe, who quoted from Wilkinson's 'luminous writings, which coruscate athwart the darkness of his age like the fire of heaven'.[114]

James Tyler Kent (1849-1916)
Transcendental homoeopathy, developed in America under Swedenborgian influences, did not begin to gain ground in Britain until the 1870s.[115] It was developed and

systematized subsequently in America by James Tyler Kent, who had a considerable influence on British homoeopathy.[116] Kentian homoeopathy was seen as faithful to Hahnemann's later ideas, and his followers regard it as the 'orthodox' approach.

Kent was converted to homoeopathy after his wife had been cured of a serious illness by a homoeopath in 1876, and later he became a follower of Swedenborg's philosophy. He did not become prominent in the world of homoeopathy until the mid-1880s.[117] Kent's ideas show a strong concordance with those of Wilkinson. The most striking of these is the concept that mental symptoms have primacy.[118] Kent believed that because the primary symptoms are personal and psychological in nature, the disease and its treatment can be regarded as having a personality. The 'artistic prescriber' builds up a mental catalogue of 'sick images' which can be related to the 'sick personality' of the patient, so that a remedy of similar 'personality' can be chosen.[119] Garth Wilkinson's description in *The Human Body*, published decades earlier, of homoeopathic remedies as 'curative personalities' whose 'portraits', based upon the mental characteristics of the patient, must be painted by the physician, is a plain statement of the position that would later define Kent's homoeopathy. Kent systematized this idea into a practical method of history-taking for homoeopaths, which began with eliciting 'the loves and hates, or desires and aversions' of the patient, with much less attention paid to the actual physical symptoms that the patient was experiencing.[120] The choice of homoeopathic remedy was to be based more on mental than on physical symptoms. Other aspects of Kent's homoeopathy, such as his belief that disease is the result of sin, and his use of high potencies (high dilutions) of homoeopathic remedies, were also informed by his Swedenborgian beliefs, though they had been put forward by other Swedenborgian homoeopaths and so were by no means original. Although Wilkinson believed that the practice of homoeopathy needed to be changed by 'new brains of the Hahnemannian order' in order to reflect this truth, this change was not systematized until the publication of Kent's homoeopathic works.

There is no direct evidence that Kent took his idea of matching the 'personality' of the remedy to that of the disorder from Wilkinson, but, given the fame of Wilkinson amongst American homoeopaths, it is likely that Kent was aware of Wilkinson's earlier ideas, which had been expressed in his *The Human Body*, a book widely read by followers of Swedenborg in America.

British homoeopathy today

During the past two decades, one branch of British homoeopathy has developed beyond the so-called 'classical' homoeopathy of Kent, by incorporating a variety of contemporary spiritual practices and concepts that reflect New Age spirituality. This has included the 'proving' of homoeopathic remedies by using meditation. One group that pursues this approach is the Guild of Homoeopaths. This is a loosely formed group of homoeopaths that meditate together after taking, or simply holding, a homoeopathic remedy. After the meditation, they each describe their experiences. Remedies are linked to particular chakras. Chakras, a concept derived from Indian medicine, are vortices of energy in the body. These practitioners regard chakras as relating to the vital force of homoeopathy. A *New Materia Medica* has been produced by using the meditative method. [121] This approach, which is increasingly popular, has been attacked by other homoeopaths on the grounds that it lacks credibility. Some homoeopaths now hold the belief that homoeopathic remedies can be effective simply by writing them on a slip of paper as a talisman, or even merely by thinking them. [122] Remedies proved in this fashion have become increasingly abstruse, including, for example, the remedies named 'Berlin Wall' and 'Rainbow'. This is a recrudescence of Dudgeon's 'dynamized thunderbolts and diluted moonshine'. So far, nobody has emulated Garth Wilkinson's attempt to treat insanity with homoeopathic spiritualism, but such an approach would probably find favour with some homoeopaths today.

How does Wilkinson's homoeopathy relate to the concepts of today's homoeopathy? It can be noted in passing that in Wilkinson's depiction of phosphorus, the three transverse lines representing its sites of action, which Wilkinson took to be the 'chest, abdomen and generative organs', are analogous to the heart, solar plexus and base chakras used by some of today's homoeopaths. [123] Two of these chakras—the solar plexus and the base—are noted as sites of action of phosphorus in the *New Materia Medica*. [124] More generally, Wilkinson's method of 'improvisation', a process that he regarded as allowing divine influx to be unimpeded by human reason, can be regarded as a form of meditation. Although his depiction of the results of his meditation is different from that of today's homoeopaths, Wilkinson's method is nonetheless a variant of meditative proving. Just as with Kent, there is no evidence that these practices were based on Wilkinson's ideas, and indeed these twentieth-century practitioners of homoeopathy are unlikely to be familiar with his works, but it can be said at least that Wilkinson was well ahead of his time.

– 8 –

From Philosophy to Social Activism

*Nature has placed mankind under the governance of two
sovereign masters,* pain *and* pleasure.
Jeremy Bentham[1]

*Evil was not created by God but introduced by man, because
man turns the good which continually flows in from God
into evil, by turning away from God and turning towards himself.
When this happens, the pleasure given by good remains, but it now
becomes the pleasure given by evil. . .*
Emanuel Swedenborg[2]

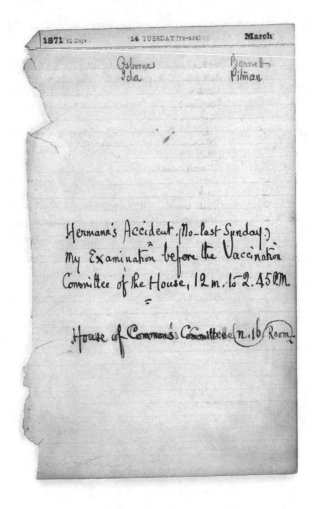

Fig. 8: Fragment from Wilkinson's no longer extant diary for 1871, noting his appointment with the Vaccination Committee of the House of Commons. Swedenborg Society Archive A/152 (d).

G arth Wilkinson was a young man struggling to find his identity in the rapidly changing social environment of the nineteenth century. As a doctor educated outside of the traditional establishments, he was a member of the new middle class, and he espoused the liberal values typical of that group. As he moved into middle life, Wilkinson became increasingly active in several of the social and political causes of his day.

It is useful at this point to outline some of the broad Swedenborgian doctrines that related to his political views. One such was Swedenborg's doctrine of 'uses', which concerns the purposes for which the world was created and how they are ordered with regard to their use for man, through whom they are uses to the Lord. For example, food and clothing are uses serving the material needs of man, and Sacred Scripture is a use which serves spiritual needs.[3] Wilkinson related this to the utilitarianism of Jeremy Bentham, which is regarded as a cornerstone of early nineteenth-century English liberalism. In his 'principle of utility' Bentham related the utility of any object or action to its tendency to produce 'benefit, advantage, pleasure, good, or happiness' or to prevent the occurrence of 'mischief, pain, evil, or unhappiness'. This can refer to the effects on an individual or on the whole body of society, and the actions not only of individuals but also of governments.[4] Bentham's utilitarianism came under criticism for its apparent promotion of selfishness, rather than a moral foundation for society.[5] Wilkinson echoed this criticism. He regarded Bentham's principle of utility as a secular version of Swedenborg's doctrine of uses, but he felt that Bentham's thesis was deficient because it ignored the higher human faculties, particularly those relating to morality:

> This [doctrine], however well brought forward by Bentham and others, has rather limited use than advanced it, because the current doctrine of utility regards the highest parts of man's capacity as not only useless, but fallacious; whereas Swedenborg's doctrine of uses includes these as the main and everlasting field of utility. . .[6]

Another component of Wilkinson's Swedenborgian belief system was the emphasis placed on freedom of personal choice. Human beings, according to Swedenborg, are placed under the equal influence of good and evil spirits, and they are endowed with reason through which they can make a choice between the two—a choice that determines their fate in the afterlife.[7] In an extension of this idea, many followers of Swedenborg have placed great importance on individual freedom of choice in all areas of life. This plainly resonated with the individualism of Victorian liberalism. One area where choice was regarded as particularly important related to the sanctity of the human body, which Swedenborgians, like mainstream Christians, believe to be created in the image of the Lord. This led to their tendency to mistrust orthodox medicine, with its heroic treatments that were aimed only at the physical body, and their preference to opt instead for heterodox approaches such as homoeopathy that were regarded as spiritual, or in harmony with nature.[8]

Especially important for Wilkinson was Swedenborg's concept of correspondences. His mind readily appreciated analogy, and he was quick to apply the Swedenborgian doctrine of correspondence between the spiritual and the natural worlds to other areas, particularly the correspondence between the human body and the structure of society. This resonated with the shift in British political ideology in the second half of the nineteenth century, which increasingly came to see society as an evolving organism. This conceptual shift ran in parallel with the acceptance of Darwin's theory of evolution, although it is simplistic to suggest that Darwin's theory was the main catalyst for the recrudescence of the concept, which is an ancient one that can be traced back to the philosophers of Greece.[9] Another stream of thought that came into play after 1865 was British idealism. This philosophy followed Hegel's system of absolute idealism, but with a religious orientation. Hegel regarded the concept of a God that is self-sufficient in his transcendence as an error, because God needed to create in order to realize himself.[10] Thus creation, including human society, is an expression of God, so that 'moral progress is literally the progressive manifestation of the divine'.[11] British idealism found fertile ground in Liberal Anglicanism, a movement which sought to emphasize the commonalities rather than the differences between Christian sects in order to establish a national church under the umbrella of Anglicanism, promoting the notion of a moralized state rather than one based on self-interest.[12] One, perhaps extreme, statement of the influence of religion on national politics in the second half of the nineteenth century is that 'All the pregnant concepts of the modern theory of the state are secularised theological concepts'.[13]

The concept of society as a unitary organism found credibility amongst followers of Swedenborg who saw the Divine Human as the archetypal model for the whole of creation. Wilkinson was no exception and, in the context of contemporary politics, he built upon Swedenborg's linking of the Divine Human to the structure of society. Wilkinson discussed social structures, using the term 'organic society' to describe them.[14] In doing so, he was in tune with the political trends of his time, though giving them a Swedenborgian slant. The notion of an organic state was interpreted in diverse ways according to political persuasion; thus, it was used both as an argument against state intervention (thereby allowing society to grow by itself), and as an argument in favour of state intervention (for example, to support the poor who were seen as victims of the structure of society rather than their own failings).[15] Wilkinson was resolutely against state intervention, partly because of his commitment to freedom of personal choice, and partly because he believed that changes in society were unfolding as a result of a divine plan consequent upon the Last Judgment which, according to Swedenborg, had occurred in 1757 in the spiritual world.[16] Since Wilkinson believed that the spiritual world is the determinant of the material world, it was therefore inevitable that similarly radical changes would take place here. His notion of how this would take place changed during his life, in parallel with his politics more generally; as a young man, he took a revolutionary stance, but later he expected, like most mainstream Swedenborgians, that change would take place gradually. In 1882 he wrote that:

A gifted friend said to me, 'I have not the slightest idea of the direction in which the world is going. Have you any?' I told him, Yes. That we were living in the first days of the Second Coming of Christ in a new Divine religion upon earth...That heaven, the Lord enthroned within it, and hell, on new terms of human liberty and rationality, are the real combatants behind the events of the modern drama, and that heaven in the long run is bound to win every battle, in so far as men can be won to heavenly ways...That all things are to be made new; all business, all property, all relations; all that has sprung out of the old natural mind, and which has to be carefully reconstituted, not destroyed, by the descent of the new heavens into the natural mind, and its regeneration in the Divine Image.[17]

Wilkinson thought that since the Last Judgment in 1757 there had been many signs of the new age, including the break-up of the old hierarchy, revolutions, the new political liberalism, the new freedoms achieved by women, and the mental freedom to seek spiritual development in new and individualistic ways. In Wilkinson's view, the new age would be characterized by the successful conclusion of a variety of contemporary causes that he supported, including campaigns against vivisection, compulsory vaccination, and the regulation of medicine:

The time [the post-Second Coming] will belong to the ages of inspiration transcending genius. Evil methods will pass away. Medicine will have new insights and capacities because it will have new honesty, bravery, tenderness and virtue from the Lord...Surgical homicide will cease, and hospitals will not be the educational laboratories in which the poor are the clay which the doctor moulds into the costly and mortal chalice of orthodox practice for the rich...Vivisection will be penal through the length and breadth of the land... Huge fees for surgery will be forbidden, as being rank baits to cutting and mutilating. The contamination of men by inoculation of diseases from man or beast will be scouted as heinous...Medicine will be disestablished, shorn of power borrowed from the State, so that cases of death and injury may have fairplay before juries. All men and women will be free to practise with this justice over them...These seem to be results that will come directly out of a religion that demands that evils are to be shunned as sins before God.[18]

In the context of Wilkinson's belief system, his social and political campaigns were not related simply to worldly values, but were part of the working out of the new age or 'new church' of humanity; he was, he thought, engaged in nothing less than the conquest of the evils of hell.

Wilkinson's millenarianism also informed his economic position. He believed that Swedenborg's doctrine was that 'the people of this earth are fundamentally <u>commercial</u>, or existing and flourishing in the interchange of commodities between all countries'.[19] He referred to liberal philosopher John Stuart Mill as asserting that commerce is an intrinsic part of human society. However, in Wilkinson's view the aim of commerce was not selfish personal gain. Rather, he believed that 'wealth must descend from the upper ranks' instead of them spending it on 'luxury, vanity...and personal indulgence', and be used to clear the London slums; this, in turn, would bring increased revenue to the upper classes, which they could again use to improve the lot of the poor.[20] He regarded this redistribution of wealth as a form of spiritual redemption for the rich, and believed that it would start to occur as a natural consequence of the Last Judgment, without the need for state intervention. It would replace charity, which he regarded as mere 'leakages of wealth'.[21] Wilkinson was at pains to point out that this was not communism, because the current social order would be retained, but with a voluntary circulation of wealth between the higher and the lower social classes.

The Paris uprising

As a young man, Garth Wilkinson's political beliefs led him into the radical political arena of republicanism. Following in the footsteps of earlier radical followers of
Swedenborg who had supported the French Revolution, Garth Wilkinson and his
brother William were amongst a small group of Swedenborgians who supported the
Paris uprising of June 1848, which was in protest against a perceived turn towards
conservatism by the Republic.[22] On 23 June 1848, the day that the uprising started,
he left for Paris, where he met his friends Hugh Doherty and Lord Wallscourt.[23]
Wallscourt had set up a socialist commune on his estate in Ireland, and was a
member of the Irish Confederation, a nationalist independence movement.[24] Whilst
in Paris they met up with several other radical socialists, including the elderly Robert
Owen, Albert Brisbane and Charles Anderson Dana, Fourierist editor of the *New York
Tribune* whom Wilkinson had befriended during a visit to England. They were in
the thick of the action and Wilkinson wrote graphically to his wife about the noise of
musketry and artillery, and the 'whizz of iron' near his head.[25] He was greatly moved
by the massacre of the French workers and watched prisoners being brought in. He
plainly sided with the workers, and regarded socialism as the dominant political
force of the future:

> They have their hands tied behind their backs, and march in the midst of the
> troops with a sad, heroic air. It is one of the most melancholy sights that the
> world presents: intelligent, brave hunger compressed and crushed by the bay-
> onets of the upper Classes. Many atrocities have of course been committed...
> So ends the first skirmish between Socialism and the old Civilization...
> Judging the beginning of Socialism by the beginning of Liberal Politics, how
> vast is the preponderance of force in favour of the former.[26]

Back in England, revolutionary zeal was focused in the Chartists, whom Wilkinson
observed remotely, but with interest (a position that was typical of the radical middle
class at that time).[27] He lamented that the London newspapers catered for the conservative middle classes and gave no information about either 'the spirit of modern

France', or the views and activities of the Chartists, until the eve of their meeting in London when 'the *Times* proclaimed that the terror was at hand'.[28] The Chartists had planned their demonstration for 10 April 1848, and on the evening prior to that Wilkinson hosted a dinner for several family members, including his brothers William and George and his uncle Professor William Sewell, as well as friends, including John Reynell Morell, who had translated into English Fourier's *Passions of the Human Soul*, and Thomas Cooper, the Chartist poet.[29] Cooper had been an active supporter of the Chartists, but by this time he had distanced himself from them and moved in London's literary circles.[30] Wilkinson watched the preparations of the Chartists from a distance. Before the Chartist meeting he noted that 'London is in a state of panic. . . for myself, nothing that happened would in the least degree surprise me: I expect a Revolution within 2 years: there may be one within 3 days'.[31] After the Chartist meeting, which had been controlled rigidly by very large numbers of police and had passed without incident, Wilkinson was less sanguine about the possibility of a revolution in England, remarking that 'As to social reform, I fear that England is one of the last countries that will adopt any high form of it'.[32] He left for Paris shortly after this and showed no positive inclination towards revolution after he had witnessed events there. Instead, Wilkinson adopted the more usual Swedenborgian position that social change would come about gradually rather than through revolution.

Utopian socialism

Many followers of Swedenborg found a natural affinity with the utopian socialisms of Robert Owen, Henri de Saint-Simon and Charles Fourier, which mirrored their concept of the social structures that would be expected consequent upon the Second Coming in the spiritual world.[33] Robert Owen was a deist, believing that the cosmos was created by a God who played no further part in the affairs of the world. He believed that the way in which individuals developed was fashioned entirely by their education and by the influences of the society in which they lived.[34] Owen's solution was a new system of education and government, and he attempted to put his ideas into practice, most notably in a community for the workers at a cotton mill in New Lanark, Scotland, and at the New Harmony community in America, which Owen bought in 1825 from its founder Johann Georg Rapp.[35] Both of these ventures failed, but Owen's social theories remained highly influential, resulting for example in the cooperative movement that still exists today. Owen's views antagonized many Christians in his day, particularly because of his denial of free will, as well as the anti-Christian tracts that were published by his followers. Despite this, some Swedenborgians adopted his views, particularly in America, perhaps because his expectations of the new society were millenarian in nature.[36]

The obvious ambiguity about Owen's position, that human fate is determined entirely by their education and society, is that he was educated and lived within that same society yet somehow was able to rise above this in order to set out the conditions through which other people could be similarly elevated. Later in life, and somewhat in contradiction of his deist beliefs, he developed a sense of divine mission.[37] He also adopted spiritualism and developed a relationship with the occultist Frederick Hockley, who transmitted to Owen messages from the 'Crowned Angel of the Seventh Sphere'.[38] Owen, no doubt disenchanted by the failure of his worldly attempts to establish a community, came to believe that good and 'superior Spirits' would influence governments to accept his ideas.[39]

Garth Wilkinson did not accept Owen's philosophy, and when the two men met in 1848, late in Owen's life, Wilkinson regarded him as a sorry figure, writing to his wife that Owen was:

> a nice quiet old citizen of the world, wedded most amusingly to his circum-
> stances & parallelograms, & for the rest, putting his conceit aside, a humble
> enough specimen of Man. He always thinks the morrow is to see Owenism
> prevalent over the world, and that all his failures have been successes. There
> is something in a man who has received a life of stripes, & still does not
> know that he is beaten.[40]

By the time that Wilkinson met Owen, many of those Swedenborgians who had earlier been Owenites had turned to Fourierism.[41] Fourier believed that modern civilization caused unhappiness because of fraud, waste and exploitation.[42] He criticized the inefficiency of 'isolated households'. He believed that world history moved in epochs and that the current state of society which he called 'Civilization' would move through several further stages to reach a condition of 'Harmony' in which the human passions, which are fundamentally good but corrupted by the current social system, would be allowed their natural expression. He envisaged that the harmonious society would comprise communities or phalanxes of 1620 people balanced according to their leading passions and their productive abilities. Over two million such communities would ultimately cover the world in a harmonious net-work. This would lead to the end of diseases and would promote total sexual liberty. He described correspondences between human passions and the phenomena of nature, such that when the passions were harmonized there would be beneficial changes in the climate. Some of Fourier's more bizarre ideas, including the notion that humans would evolve prehensile tails, were suppressed by his followers in America, but were seized upon by his opponents, particularly Karl Marx and Friedrich Engels.[43]

Swedenborgians were quick to note similarities between the doctrines of Fourier and those of Swedenborg, and these were set out by American Swedenborgian homoeopath Charles Julius Hempel.[44] Hempel regarded Fourier's doctrine as the practical application of Swedenborg's theories, and believed that the New Church would be the vehicle for putting Fourier's ideas into practice. When that had happened, human society in this world would mirror heavenly society. In a summary that clearly relates to the socialist ideal, Hempel listed the characteristics of a heavenly society as outlined by Swedenborg, which he thought should include the following: 1. Unity of interests: that is, each exists for the good of all (this does not imply that everybody is the same: diversity is necessary for effective function); 2. Guarantee of subsistence: people should work unwaged for the community in accordance with their abilities, and in return be provided with food, shelter, clothing and other necessities of life; 3. Labour should be carried out by groups of individuals of like ability, not forced on individuals regardless of their aptitude; 4. Women's rights should be equal to those of men; 5. Children should learn because they wish to do so, in a manner that is concordant with their own proclivities, and should not have teaching forced upon them; 6. There should be no slaves or servants; 7. A worldly paradise should be restored, for example by draining marshes, digging irrigation canals, warming the poles, and establishing a power 'by means of which the meteors will be controlled, and the atmospherical movement universally regulated'.[45] Everybody should have a productive use, which would exclude aristocrats, who simply live off their wealth, and those engaged in commerce, which accumulates wealth that is not used for the benefit of the community, as well as the armed forces, lawyers and doctors, who would no longer be necessary in the ideal society. Hempel saw this society as closely analogous to that described by Fourier.

In a popular book on Fourier's doctrines published in 1844, the American journalist and admirer of Swedenborg Parke Godwin described 'the most exact and wonderful co-incidence' between Fourier's doctrine of universal analogy and Swedenborg's doctrine of correspondences: Fourier, he thought, was working in 'the sphere of science' and Swedenborg in 'the sphere of spiritual knowledge'.[46] He described Fourier's analogies between the structure of the human body, the human passions and the structure of an ideal phalanx. The alleged similarity between the doctrines of Swedenborg and Fourier was not generally welcomed amongst sectarian New Church Swedenborgians. Their journal, *The New Church Magazine*, accused Fourierists of distorting Swedenborg's philosophy to fit in with their own views.[47] They were particularly outraged by Fourier's views against marriage and in favour of sexual freedom.

An important boost was given to Fourierism by the community at Brook Farm, under the leadership of Transcendentalist George Ripley. This utopian Transcendentalist community, which was a departure from Emerson's individu-alist Transcendentalism, aimed 'To establish the external relations of life on a basis of wisdom and purity; to apply the principles of justice & love to our social organization in accordance with the laws of Divine providence'.[48] The community was organized on a basis of social equality and cooperation; labour on the farm was rewarded directly and proportionately with board and lodging, and education and medical care was provided to all. Fourier's ideas, which had been brought to America by Albert Brisbane in his book *Social Destiny of Man; or, Association and Reorganization of Industry* (1840), were adopted during the 1840s by the leaders of Brook Farm. Although Brook Farm followed no official religious creed, some prominent members were admirers of Swedenborg's philosophy, whilst remaining non-sectarian. The doctrines of both Fourier and Swedenborg were promoted in the influential journal of Brook Farm, the *Harbinger*. For example, John Sullivan Dwight, an editor of the *Harbinger*, wrote that 'In religion we have Swedenborg; in social economy Fourier; in music Beethoven'.[49] Another prominent Brook Farmer and friend of Garth Wilkinson, Charles Anderson Dana, wrote in the *Harbinger* that 'The chief characteristic of this epoch is, its tendency, everywhere apparent, to unity in the universality; and the men in whom this tendency is most fully expressed are Swedenborg, Fourier and Goethe'.[50] Brook Farmers disparaged the lack of social involvement of the sectarian members of the Swedenborgian New Church. Dwight wrote that:

> The Swedenborgians seldom look out of their own church for movement. As a sect. . .they are quietists and exclusivists. They are not active reformers, but accepting literally the revelations of their master they cling to their small community of a New Church. . .[51]

Dwight described the Swedenborgian journal *The New Jerusalem Magazine* as 'altogether theological and simplistic-spiritual', focusing on 'the common details of individual private life' rather than supporting social causes.[52]

Garth Wilkinson's friend Henry James, Sr was an influential intellectual and financial supporter of Fourierism, to which he was converted in the 1840s after visiting Edmund Tweedy, treasurer of the American Union of Associationists.[53] Tweedy had earlier visited Garth Wilkinson whilst on a trip to England, and James's visit to Tweedy in New York had been prompted by Wilkinson, who hoped that James would interest him in the doctrines of Swedenborg.[54] James became interested more generally in utopian socialism, writing in 1850 that 'Every one who trusts in a living and therefore active God. . .behooves to acquaint himself forthwith with the marvellous literature of Socialism, above all with the writings of CHARLES FOURIER'.[55] Like many others, James melded the philosophy of Fourier with that of Swedenborg. In doing so, he went further than many would venture, accepting for example Fourier's doctrine of free love, which he regarded as consistent with Swedenborg's support for concubinage in his work *Conjugial Love*.[56]

Garth Wilkinson's early mentor Charles Augustus Tulk made the acquaintance of the leading proponent of Fourierism in England, Hugh Doherty, who was a convert from Owenism. According to Tulk, Doherty at that time was researching the similarity of the doctrines of Fourier and those of Swedenborg, long before Hempel published in America his influential comparison of their ideas.[57] Doherty published a Fourierist journal, and Wilkinson noted in 1842 that 'The Fourierists are taking considerable notice of Swedenborg's doctrines in their Journal, the *London Phalanx*'.[58] Later, Wilkinson engaged in a long correspondence with Henry James, Sr on the subject of Fourierism. Initially, Wilkinson was unimpressed with Fourier's doctrines, remarking that Fourier 'does not grow in my affections', and that his system of Association was an unproven theoretical prototype.[59] He thought that Fourier's criticism of the contemporary state of society was likely to be flawed:

> I cannot help suspecting that our Fourierite friends have come too hastily
> to the conclusion that the present civilization, in its improvability, does
> not contain harmonic, orderly, intellectual verities: surely the great
> international links of commerce, &c. &c. &c., and the complex of existing
> human relations, are something very stupendous: and before giving
> adhesion to the Phalanstery, one would like to see whether these (I don't
> mean their abuses) are not a Divine Order in present society.[60]

Unlike Fourier, he believed that society should be based on family units, and he abhorred the sexual freedom that Fourier championed. He also deplored the American Fourierists' reluctance to publish his works in translation from the original French.[61] Nevertheless, he went on to make a deeper study of Fourier's beliefs, particularly in relation to Swedenborg's doctrines, and he became more convinced that Fourier had described the worldly equivalent of the Swedenborgian heaven. In July 1847, he wrote to Henry James, Sr that 'All you say of the Association movement I echo from my heart. It is the morning brightness of the world's day, and has all my sympathies; in fact, I believe it, and its human founder, far more than I tell everybody'.[62] Wilkinson's conversion was so complete that Emerson, after visiting Wilkinson in London in 1848, wrote that 'Wilkinson my Swedenborgian sage is to my surprise a Fourierist'.[63] In the same year, Wilkinson declared that it was his 'mission' to bring together the philosophies of Swedenborg and Fourier and 'cement them into one harmony'.[64] He thought that Swedenborg's work *Conjugial Love* was 'destined to be the point of fusion between the Swedenborgian and the Fourieristic truths', though no doubt with an interpretation different from that of Henry James, Sr.[65]

As with so many of Wilkinson's youthful enthusiasms, his attitude to Fourier shifted as he grew older. Already by 1850 he had declined an invitation by Albert Brisbane to translate more of Fourier's works into English because 'it would interfere with my usefulness in other things, to be known as a translator of Fourier'.[66] At that time he thought that Fourier's descriptions of the human passions were 'really the greatest contributions yet made to an exact science of Human Nature', but he rejected socialism, which he said 'bears no relation whatever to the Divine Verities'.[67] In later years he still regarded Fourier as a man of genius, but declared that his system could never be achieved in practice without the influence of divine influx, which Fourier had altogether neglected.[68] This aligned him with a view popularly held by mainstream Swedenborgians, and which was expressed in 1891 by the Swedenborgian writer and friend of Wilkinson, Rudolph Leonard Tafel.[69] Echoing Garth Wilkinson's earlier formulation, Tafel deplored the current inequalities of wealth and looked forward to a society in which wealth would be distributed according to the level of use that individuals are to society. Any surplus wealth would be deployed for the benefit of all. Knowledge and learning would not be valued unless it was put to use. The family unit would be at the heart of the new society. Natural science as it is now taught would give way to the spiritual science of correspondences. Such changes, thought Tafel, cannot be brought about by the external social changes proposed by socialism, but must come from the hearts of people inspired by divine influx to turn away from the love of themselves and the world and towards the love of God. Nevertheless, he thought that some parts of the new society would bear an external resemblance to a socialist society. For example, Tafel foresaw that private enterprises would be administered instead by the state and the principle of cooperation would be adopted in farming, industry and shops.

Environmentalism

The notion that all of humanity is a unitary organism is allied closely to the idea that the world is a similar entity. In Wilkinson's Swedenborgian concept, the world was created perfect, in correspondence with the Divine Human, but was then modified by man. Spiritually, this modification takes place because the spirits of humans who commit evils are the building blocks of hell, which, like heaven, has its material correspondences, which in this case are the noxious elements of the natural world. Wilkinson recognized that humans can also have a directly physical damaging effect on the world, which again is driven by their impulses to evil. Wilkinson gave one example of an environmental catastrophe in his book *On Human Science*: insects in Scandinavia eat the trees but are kept in check by birds. The birds migrate to southern Europe where they are shot in large numbers. As a result, the birds will no longer keep the insects in check, they will destroy the trees, and the forests will die leaving bare sand that is washed away by the rain. At that time, such ideas were not widely accepted, and Wilkinson realized that it would seem strange 'that man with his small stature can thus modify the great globe, and all that inhabits it'.[70] In the same work, Wilkinson mentions how impressed he was when he read *The Earth as Modified by Human Action* by George Perkins Marsh, who is regarded as America's first environmentalist. Marsh described human physical damage to the planet, whilst Swedenborg had described spiritual damage resulting from the influences of hell reflecting human evil. Wilkinson regarded 'Earthquake, cyclone, pestilence and all kinds of plague and ruin' as being the results of that evil influence.[71]

Wilkinson's concern was not merely to preserve the environment, but to facilitate the enjoyment of it by those who were currently excluded from the open countryside. Showing his concern for the working class and his antipathy to the landed gentry, he railed against the greed of landowners who sequestered large tracts of open moorland in Derbyshire so that they and their friends could shoot grouse, whilst workers in the grimy industrial cities were forbidden to take exercise and fresh air on the moors.[72]

Like his social concepts, Wilkinson's concern for the environment was informed by his millenarianism. He believed that the risk of total destruction of the earth by man had passed since the Last Judgment, and that the damage already done would be reversed because hell had been defeated. One of his particular concerns was the hunting of animals, which he believed would be abolished in the new age of humanity:

> Destruction of animals for sport and skill would be questioned by the religious conscience, which it seldom is in any pulpit yet. . .And especially the raid of travellers upon the great lives of the hippopotamus, the giraffe, the ostrich, the elephant, and other such creatures, would be forbidden. . . This will come to be the tone of British opinion. . . [At the present time] Parliaments laugh when humanity to animals is under discussion. . . conserve as much as you can with all possible conscience; waste no beasts, great or small; destroy no species. . .[73]

Deregulation of medicine

Most of the liberal causes taken up by Wilkinson were related to medicine.[74] Prominent amongst these was his opposition to the Medical Act of 1858, which legislated for the compulsory registration of doctors who had passed examinations in approved Medical Colleges and permitted the removal from the register of doctors who were involved in criminal or unprofessional behaviour.[75] The Act also stipulated that only registered doctors could hold public medical office. The Act was plainly to the advantage of qualified doctors and the great majority of them supported it in principle, although there was concern within the elite of the medical profession that their status might be impaired. Prior to the introduction of the Act, membership of the Royal College of Physicians was the most prestigious medical qualification, and was mainly restricted to graduates of Oxford and Cambridge. Doctors educated at these universities, according to one contemporary source, had 'the same education as those who fill the highest stations in life; they are brought up with those persons, and afterwards become physicians'.[76] The Royal College of Surgeons was less exclusive, and the Society of Apothecaries was of considerably lower status. Those who were educated by apprenticeship in the provincial medical centres, such as Garth Wilkinson, commonly held Membership of both the Royal College of Surgeons and the Society of Apothecaries, and the majority of them, including Garth Wilkinson, were general practitioners who dispensed their own medicines. Many supporters of the Medical Act, such as Thomas Wakley, the editor of *The Lancet*, regarded themselves as radicals with a mission to level the medical playing field. Wakley and others also campaigned for the outlawing of heterodox medical practices such as homoeopathy, which they regarded as quackery. They failed in this aim, perhaps because politicians were aware that the public tended to fear and distrust (and often could not afford) the orthodox medical treatment of that time, and so they made considerable use of heterodox practitioners. In opposing the Medical Act, Wilkinson was clearly out of step with the great majority of qualified doctors. However, there are obvious personal reasons for his stance, particularly his adoption of the 'transcendental' homoeopathy favoured at that time by lay practitioners. [77] This, together with an emphasis on the importance of human freedom of choice, led Wilkinson inexorably to oppose the Act. In doing so, he demonstrated a radicalism that was far beyond that of Wakley. Not content with levelling the status of qualified medical practitioners, he sought to place all healers on the same legal footing. His most vigorous attack on the new legislation was set out in his tract *Unlicensed Medicine* (1855). [78] Here, he declared that every man is a physician by virtue of the healing powers of the soul, which can be used also to help other people. The new medicine is liberal, in the sense of putting public service before private gain. The old medicine, a monopolistic medical despotism protected by the state, which draws its practitioners from the privileged classes and which excludes the public from decisions about their own health, is bound to wither in this new spirit of liberalism. Members of the public should be educated to care for their own health, principally by means of homoeopathy. True, doctors are expert at diagnosis, but there is no need for diagnosis in early, mild cases and even in cases that have progressed further it is not difficult to make diagnoses. Possession of a diploma is no guarantee of healing powers, and most quackery is to be found amongst conventional doctors. Healers should be recognized on merit only: 'what we want, is...the acceptance on independent, merit principles, of any and every man who can heal'.[79] He mocked a recent article by Wakley in *The Lancet* which said that knowledge of the 'science of medicine' is necessary 'for judging of the effects of medicinal agents upon the human frame in health and disease'. If that was true, said Wilkinson in his customary acerbic style, then only doctors would know whether they were ill or not: 'No man could know whether his stomach-ache had been removed until at the end of an entire curriculum of medical studies'.[80] The most highly qualified doctors would be in a state of living hell because they would experience illnesses that others could not feel. Wilkinson despaired of influencing Parliament, and proposed instead direct appeals to the public by advertising the appropriate homoeopathic remedy for whichever disease was prevalent at the time, though he showed some ambivalence by suggesting that a doctor should be in charge of the advertising campaign!

The Anti-vaccination campaign

Wilkinson also became a prominent campaigner against vaccination. Early in his life he had supported vaccination, and indeed vaccinated his own family against smallpox.[81] At that time, he espoused a view popular then amongst homoeopaths that vaccination demonstrated the homoeopathic principle of 'like cures like'. In 1854 he read a paper to the Hahnemann Medical Society, in which he put forward the view that vaccination 'has virtually added two years to the life of every man, woman, and child' and that it 'keeps our women's faces clean and handsome, and has therefore much to do with the beauty and vigour of the human breed'.[82] Later in life he became a vociferous opponent of vaccination, pointing out that the principle of vaccination is in fact antithetical to that of homoeopathy, which never 'aims to give the disease', whereas vaccination 'is unsuccessful unless it gives the disease'.[83] He was led to this change of heart through the intervention of the Countess de Noailles, who used her wealth to support several of the causes espoused by Wilkinson, including anti-vaccination, antivivisection and the repeal of the Contagious Diseases Act.[84] She had been instrumental in setting up the Ladies' National Association for the Diffusion of Sanitary Knowledge in 1858. The group, which specialized mainly in distributing health-related tracts aimed at self-help, had a number of medical advisors including Garth Wilkinson, whom the Countess tried to interest in the anti-vaccination campaign. When first approached about this in 1865 Wilkinson dismissed the question as relatively unimportant, but after more study he decided that vaccination was 'one of the greatest and deepest forms [of social wickedness], abolishing the last hope and resort of races, the new-born soundness of the Human Body'.[85] Later, the Countess said that 'the only one who lent an ear to the sad tale was Dr. Garth Wilkinson, who began mildly, but afterwards waxed valiant in fight. May he and the little band which his genius has helped to bring into the field "soon put to flight the armies of the aliens" '.[86] Wilkinson and the Countess became personal friends, and he was a frequent guest at her house in Eastbourne.[87]

The campaign against vaccination was primed by the Compulsory Vaccination Act of 1853, which mandated that all children should be vaccinated against smallpox. The Act became a focus for protests about control of the population by the state and by professionals. Opposition to vaccination came from all classes: the working class because of their personal experience of state oppression; and the middle class from their political platform of liberalism. Although the anti-vaccination movement crossed class boundaries, it was predominantly a working-class issue, because it was enforced amongst them much more vigorously than for the middle classes. It was claimed that vaccination not only poisoned the blood but often caused visible deformities including skin eruptions and rotting flesh. When bovine lymph was used for vaccination, it was feared that children might take on the mental or physical characteristics of cattle. More common amongst the poor was the use of arm to arm vaccination, in which fluid from the vesicles of a vaccinated child was used to vaccinate other children. It was believed that this could spread a variety of hereditary and contagious diseases, particularly syphilis.

Wilkinson believed that vaccination was ineffective and could even promote the spread of smallpox. Supporters of compulsory vaccination offered as evidence of its efficacy the reduction in the rate of infection that followed shortly after successive Acts of Parliament introducing stricter enforcement, but Wilkinson pointed out that each Act had been introduced during an epidemic, and the natural history of the disease was to abate following an epidemic, regardless of vaccination. He believed that vaccination produced a 'vaccine disease' that was mild in the person vaccinated, but which could spread as smallpox to their contacts, describing vaccination as 'compulsory artificial small-poxing'.[88] He recommended that vaccinated people should be quarantined; and in his caustic manner proposed that medical men who carry vaccine in their pockets should be isolated together with their patients.[89] He took the view that vaccination was a cynical ploy to cover up the real causes of smallpox epidemics amongst the poor, which were related to 'bad habits, depressed minds, and filthy slums'. The remedy for this was to provide better housing for the poor rather than the Government spending money on the rich.[90] In an echo of his republican days, he proposed that the royal wealth might usefully be spent on this project.

The anti-vaccination movement was allied closely to other liberalizing move-ments of the time, such as the campaigns for women's rights and for repeal of the Contagious Diseases Act.[91] Anti-vaccinationists rejected the scientific validity that was claimed for vaccination and which emphasized the elitism of the medical profession, and in turn they were accused of being anti-scientific in their attitude. They tended to favour the heterodox healing approaches popular amongst the working classes, including medical botany, homoeopathy and hydropathy, that were regarded as 'natural' and did not require any specialized scientific knowledge for their use.[92] The anti-vaccination movement was also associated with antivivisectionism, both of which practices were regarded as an expression of the brutality of the medical profession. Feminists saw a link between medical and sexual violation. Rejection of traditional authority, particularly where this impinged upon the freedom of the individual, was reflected also in the religious views of anti-vaccinators, who tended to be atheists or Nonconformists; some were also active in the socialist move-ment. Prominent amongst the ranks of the active anti-vaccinators were several of Swedenborg's followers and sympathizers, including not only Garth Wilkinson, but also William White; Francis William Newman, brother of the Cardinal and a reader of Swedenborg; and Henry Pitman, editor of the *Co-operator and Anti-Vaccinator*, and brother of the prominent Swedenborgian and inventor of shorthand, Isaac Pitman. There was also an association between anti-vaccinationism and a wider 'physical puritanism' movement which also embraced teetotalism and vegetarianism. Most of the causes promoted by Garth Wilkinson can be found within this complex tapestry of interwoven conceptual threads. Notable exceptions to this are teetotalism and vegetarianism, both of which Wilkinson rejected.[93]

Wilkinson co-edited a collection of tracts against vaccination that was published in 1892. In his introduction to the tracts he observed that 'The history of medicine, rife in delusions. . .supplies no instance comparable to the absurdity of vaccination'.[94] His primary objection to vaccination was moral: he regarded compulsory vaccination as 'an intolerable tyranny' whether the vaccine works or not, but the more so in that it does not work and spreads other diseases such as syphilis.[95] He quoted Sir James Paget, Surgeon Extraordinary to the Queen, as saying that vaccination produces 'a permanent morbid condition' of the body.[96] Paget regarded this as beneficial, but Wilkinson saw it as a pathology that would have dire consequences. He used the analogy of syphilis, which first causes a local chancre that heals, only to give rise to long-term serious illness in later life. So too, thought Wilkinson, with the vaccination scab; the resulting 'permanent morbid condition', he thought, renders the individual more susceptible to other diseases, including tuberculosis and cancer. In short, 'The whole race is fouled with diseases to allay its panic about one disease', and this would be passed on as an hereditary trait to future generations.[97] This view resonates with Swedenborg's view of hereditary illness.[98] Expressing a view that was held widely amongst anti-vaccinationists, Wilkinson declared that smallpox should instead be treated by natural, herbal remedies.[99] This approach, he said, can be used by 'Any good nurse. . .without medical assistance', and patients can be treated in their own homes.[100]

Antivivisection

The anti-vaccination campaign and the movement against vivisection were allied closely and often involved the same people, including Garth Wilkinson.[101] Like vaccination, vivisection was regarded by most doctors as an example of progress by means of science. Many antivivisectionists were concerned that science had lost its moral compass, and some, like Garth Wilkinson, rejected the fundamental philosophy of modern science. Vivisection became the focus of a perceived conflict between religion and science, although the terms of that debate are far from simple. The commonly held view that vivisection was at that time supported by the tenet of Christianity that man has dominion over all the animals, whereas Darwin's theory of evolution facilitated the antivivisection movement because of its emphasis on the kinship of all animals, has been questioned.[102] The notion of a common ancestry for all animals and hence the kinship between man and other animals had been prevalent long before Darwin, whose contribution was to explain the process by using the concept of natural selection. Darwin himself was a supporter of vivisection for the sake of gaining knowledge, and the concept that human beings are at the pinnacle of creation and therefore superior to other animals was used as a justification for the practice. In contrast, many prominent Christians, particularly Nonconformists and evangelicals, opposed vivisection on the grounds that cruelty to God's creatures is an abomination.

The debate about vivisection was predicated, then as now, on the question of whether animals have sentient awareness. If the bodies of animals are anatomically and physiologically similar to those of humans, then we can learn about human physiology by dissecting animals. However, if animals have a human-like self-awareness of pain and suffering, then there would be a moral imperative against vivisection.[103] Garth Wilkinson took a different position that has been neglected by historians of the vivisection debate. Although he abhorred the cruelty involved in vivisection, which he regarded as 'the last debauchery' of a science which has lost all sight of the soul and the Creator, he believed that this in itself was not sufficient reason to oppose vivisection.[104] Following Swedenborg, he had studied human physiology in order to understand the soul and therefore the Lord, in whose image, he believed, the soul and ultimately the human body are made. He regarded soul and body as a unity. Because the human soul and body are as one with the Lord, whereas those of animals are not, Wilkinson thought that it was quite impossible to learn about human physiology by studying animals. Human physiology, he believed, cannot be understood without reference to a higher, primary, spiritual physiology which lower animals lack entirely:

> There is only the most trifling analogy between animals and men,
> reasoning from below upwards...all that is distinctively human outlies the
> animal...On the other hand there is complete and illuminating analogy
> between men and animals when the mind moves rationally from above
> downwards...you can learn about animals, and unlock their secrets, from
> human life, if you have the genius to do it; but you cannot learn anything
> of the life of man from animals.[105]

Animal organs may look similar to those of men, said Wilkinson, but, for example, human lungs are governed by divine inspiration whereas the lungs of animals, in addition to their basic physiological function, represent their own peculiar life and instinct. The reality of human organs is ultimately spiritual, not physical. To understand human anatomy and physiology requires the use of 'spiritual genius'; animal physiology can be understood only by dissecting a dead animal and applying one's knowledge of the animal's life and habits to anatomical observations.[106] There is nothing that can be learned from vivisection about human or animal functions which could not have been discerned from the dissection of the dead and the use of creative imagination, which comes 'by influx from the source of life, which is God'.[107]

It was this consideration—the misleading futility of vivisection related to its lack of a spiritual dimension—which was Wilkinson's primary reason for opposing it. Although some antivivisectionists extended their concern for animal welfare into the practice of vegetarianism, Wilkinson's beliefs did not lead him in that direction.[108]

Contagious Diseases Act

Another of Wilkinson's major campaigns was for the repeal of the Contagious Diseases Act. The social dislocation that was brought about by the Industrial Revolution was associated with an increase in prostitution. This was a matter of great social concern and it brought about a variety of responses that depended upon the social and political outlook of the commentators.[109] For example, conservative members of the old hierarchy regarded the lower classes in general as a threat to social stability, and prostitutes were seen as conduits for bringing disease to respectable society. In contrast, socialists pointed to prostitution as an example of the oppression of the working class by the higher social classes, and the degradation and poverty of the working class consequent upon capitalist industrialization. Evangelicals saw the root of prostitution as sin and their focus was on saving fallen women, for example by opening refuges, whereas the newly emerging feminist groups pointed to the oppression of women by male authority figures.

These different positions resulted in a wide range of social and political responses to prostitution. Part of the conservative response was the introduction of the Contagious Diseases Acts of 1864, 1866 and 1869. These Acts were introduced because of concern about an apparent rise in sexually transmitted diseases amongst servicemen, and they mandated the compulsory medical examination of prostitutes who operated close to military bases in the south of England. Women were subjected to fortnightly internal examination and, if infected, they were transferred to a 'lock hospital' which had wards for the treatment of venereal disease. In an era where venereal disease was still seen as divine punishment for licentious behaviour, the lock hospitals carried a heavy stigma. Their atmosphere was religious and strictly disciplined. [110]

The introduction of these measures inevitably aroused the ire of those with a liberal or socialist outlook, and by the 1870s opposition to the Acts coalesced into the repeal movement, which has been characterized as 'a coalition of middle-class nonconformists, feminists, and radical working men'. [111] The campaign against the Contagious Diseases Acts touched on a variety of more general issues within Victorian society, including the extension of state power to control the poor and disadvantaged, the role of women in political activism, and other issues relating to the emerging feminist agenda.

The most prominent group within the repeal movement was the Ladies National Association for the Repeal of the Contagious Diseases Act (LNA), a feminist organization that was led by Josephine Butler. [112] Butler, whose father was an antislavery campaigner and whose mother was a devout member of the Moravian Church, was a charismatic leader and public speaker. She had been moved by the plight of destitute women in the workhouses of Liverpool, where she had moved with her husband, an Anglican clergyman. Board members of the LNA, which was open only to women, were primarily provincial middle-class radical liberals who were religious Nonconformists. LNA members regarded the repeal campaign as one aspect of a broader movement to improve women's rights, and they also supported a wider liberal agenda including the anti-vaccination and antivivisection movements. They were attracted to the new heterodox medical approaches such as water cures, partly as a reaction to the materialism of male-dominated orthodox medicine.

Judith Walkowitz has noted that excessive focus by historians on Josephine Butler has led to a neglect of male supporters for the reform movement. Despite their own middle-class origins, the women of the LNA, when seeking male support for their cause, tended to ally themselves with working-class men rather than those of the higher social classes, whom they regarded with some suspicion. Given the social and political agenda of the LNA, Garth Wilkinson was a natural ally with their cause, and correspondence between Butler and Wilkinson suggests that this natural affinity was recognized and valued by Josephine Butler.

In 1870, at a time when repealers were seen as eccentrics with no chance of success, Wilkinson published a tract against the 'forcible introspection of women' that was permitted under the Act.[113] The tract was addressed to the Home Secretary, and began by asking him how he would like the women in his own family to be subjected to this indignity. Far from preventing disease, said Wilkinson, the speculums used in the process of internal examination, which were not properly washed, spread disease from one woman to another. He pointed out that many of the women thus forcibly examined 'but for accident of birth might have been presented for the first time at the Queen's last Drawing Room'.[114] He concluded that the men who promote this practice have two motives: a general love of power, and a specific 'medical lust of handling and dominating woman'.[115] He reprinted the text of a letter that he had received from Josephine Butler, which included this account from one of the registered women:

It is such awful work; the attitude they push us into first is so disgusting and so painful, and then these monstrous instruments,——often they use several. They seem to tear the passage open first with their hands, and examine us, and then they thrust in instruments, and they pull them out and push them in, and they turn and twist them about; and if you cry out they stifle you with a towel over your face'.[116]

Butler pointed out that even in genteel women who are examined with their consent and with the utmost care, the procedure is painful and humiliating, and quoted another woman's lament against the treatment that she had received at the hands of men:

It is *men, men, only men*, from the first to the last that we have to do with! To please a man I did wrong at first, then I was flung about from man to man. Men police lay hands on us. By men we are examined, handled, doctored, and messed on with. In the hospital it is a man again who makes prayers and reads the bible for us. We are had up before magistrates who are men, and we never get out of the hands of men till we die.[117]

Other letters from Josephine Butler show that she enlisted Garth Wilkinson's practical help for her campaign, and that she supported his stance on heterodox medical practice. In 1873 she asked Wilkinson to help her return a cheque for £1000 to the Countess de Noailles.[118] Apparently the people of Liverpool had taken this contribution as a rebuke, and several rich local gentlemen came forward with money to support the building of 'an industrial home for unemployed women to fit them for emigration'. The project had been taken over by these men (including 'men with whom it would be impossible for me to work'), and if the cheque from the Countess de Noailles was accepted, then the LNA would have no control over what was done with it. In another letter, Butler lamented the state of medicine, saying that the physician should be 'a person who looks upon a human being as a being of <u>soul</u> as well as matter... [There is] a possible error which men have fallen upon, of taking into account not the soul but the <u>matter</u> only, not only of the patient but of the <u>physician</u>'.[119]

Wilkinson's affinity for feminist causes is shown also by his support for Ursula Mellor Bright, an advocate of women's suffrage. In 1870 he signed her petition in

233

support of married women's property rights, which he said was in the interests of 'bare justice to married women, and consequently to homes'.[120] Ursula Mellor Bright and her husband, Member of Parliament Jacob Bright, also opposed compulsory vaccination, and some years later Wilkinson upbraided Jacob Bright for keeping his own views private and not speaking up against it in Parliament.[121]

Wilkinson had no formal political allegiance. In 1867 his friend Francis William Newman had described Garth Wilkinson as a republican,[122] and yet in 1845 Wilkinson had described himself as 'a hanger on of the Radical party in England'.[123] The Radicals were never a formal political party. Harriet Martineau summed up the state of British politics in 1830 by saying that:

> the Tories thought it was their duty to govern the people (for their good) as a
> disposable property; that the Whigs thought it their duty to govern as trustees
> of the nation, according to their own discretion; and that there were persons
> living, and effectually moving in the world of politics, who thought that the
> people ought to govern themselves through the House of Commons.[124]

The Radicals supported free trade and parliamentary reform, including universal male suffrage, and, as Carlyle put it in 1840, they should have been 'speakers for that great dumb, toiling class which cannot speak'; although, in Carlyle's view, they manifestly failed in this objective.[125] It is natural that Wilkinson, with his views on the freedom and rights of the individual, would have been drawn to this group. He was a supporter of Sir Robert Peel, who, although leader of the Tory Party (which transmuted into the Conservative Party under his leadership), came to support the Factory Act (1844), which limited working hours for women and children, and the repeal of the Corn Laws in 1846, which by removing restrictive practices antagonized the landowners.[126] Wilkinson's support for Peel puts him at the more conservative end of the Radical movement, despite his early flirtation with revolutionary politics. After Peel's death, which was much lamented by Wilkinson, his followers, known as Peelites, eventually made a political alliance with Whigs and Radicals in 1859 to form the Liberal Party. Reflecting his shift towards the centre ground of politics,

Wilkinson described himself in 1885 as a Conservative, and said that he had been 'made such by Beaconsfield's [Benjamin Disraeli, Earl of Beaconsfield] statesmanship, and then by Gladstone's iniquities'.[127] As examples of these iniquities, he cited Gladstone's role in the Battle of Majuba Hill in the first Boer War; the Irish problem; and British policy in the Sudan which led to General Gordon's defeat in the Siege of Khartoum.[128] In 1888, his friend Mr Matheson confusingly summed up Wilkinson's complex politics as 'a certain radically liberal conservatism'.[129] Wilkinson's flirtation with revolutionary politics as a young man had shifted in middle life to social activism within liberal protest movements against Government interference; later in life, without losing his liberal outlook, he became a more conservative follower of Swedenborg's philosophy.

– 9 –

Mythology

*The mythological process does not have to do with natural
objects, but rather with the pure creating potencies whose original
product is consciousness itself.*
Friedrich Wilhelm Joseph Schelling[1]

*In [Norse] mythology we have an element which is prominent
and supreme. . .namely spirit-speaking. Without such influx,
Mythology is impossible. . .*
James John Garth Wilkinson, writing in 1897[2]

Fig. 9: A pressed flower enclosed in Wilkinson's notebook containing his
travel log of a trip to Norway in 1871.
Swedenborg Society Archive A/150 (c).

I n his *The Human Body*, Garth Wilkinson pointed to a correspondence be-tween the circulation of the blood and the human life cycle.[3] He saw the right atrium, which is the chamber of the heart to which circulating blood returns and from which it begins its circulatory journey, as representing the family home: Wilkinson quoted William Harvey as saying that the right atrium is 'the first part of the heart to live, and the last to die'.[4] From here the blood returning from the body is first pumped through the right ventricle of the heart around the lungs, where, in Wilkinson's thinking, it receives the oxygen of wisdom and understanding. The blood then returns to the heart, from where it is pumped around the body. Having absorbed oxygen from the lungs and then nutrients assimilated from food in the intestines, and so completing its 'education', the blood assumes a new role: it becomes the agent for dispersing oxygen and nutrients around the body, analogous, thought Wilkinson, to the use of wisdom and assimilated knowledge in the wider world of public service. Finally, the blood, now old and spent, returns to its family heartland in the right atrium. Wilkinson's own life resembles this pattern, with his school education followed by an introduction to Swedenborg's works, and mentoring from Charles Augustus Tulk, Henry James, Sr and others; then his medical and political campaigns; and finally his retreat from public life and his return in old age to greater dependence on his family and to his intellectual origins in Swedenborg's philosophy.

The false paths Wilkinson felt he had taken as a young man, such as spiritualism, gave way in old age to his steadfast and undeviating following of Swedenborg.

As he became less involved in public life, Wilkinson turned his attention increasingly to a new interest: the Swedenborgian interpretation of mythology. In seventeenth- and eighteenth-century England, interest in Egyptian, Babylonian and Chaldean history was fuelled by a belief that the Jews had learned their religious customs from the Egyptians, and that Greek philosophy had also originated in Egypt.[5] The Hermetic texts were regarded as expressing this ancient Egyptian knowledge and Egyptian hieroglyphics were regarded as representing an ancient universal Adamic language. It was believed that myth and imagery were used to conceal the spiritual mysteries from the masses, but that ultimately the underlying truth was forgotten, leading to idolatry. Prominent intellectuals, including Isaac Newton and his friend William Stukeley, were fascinated by mythology.[6] Following further archaeological exploration and discovery, interest in mythology reached a new high during the nineteenth century and there was a new focus on theories of how myth had arisen. Historians of myth have discussed these theories in some detail, but with little emphasis on the wider social and political associations that accompanied the various theoretical positions regarding the origin of myth, and with scant discussion of their relationship to heterodox interests, such as spiritualism, mesmerism and homoeopathy, that were so popular in the nineteenth century.

A prominent theme in the discussion of the reception of myth in the nineteenth century is the relationship between myth and science. A leading author on this topic, Robert A Segal, asserts that the typical opinion in nineteenth-century Britain was that myth and science were incompatible.[7] Both were seen as attempts to explain the operation of the physical world, but it was thought that whereas science searched for material explanations that rested on observation and verifiable experiment, myth simply explained events in the world as resulting from the decisions and actions of gods. The fundamental belief within the scientific framework was that the trajectory of humankind had been one of progress, moving from a condition of primitive savagery where mythical explanations prevailed into more rational and civilized modes of thinking and behaviour. Hence, myth was regarded simply as the result of primitive thinking amongst people who had yet to develop a scientific culture, and it was believed that the progress of science would ultimately lead to the demise of myth as an explanatory paradigm.

The two leading protagonists of the idea that myth was merely a primitive attempt to explain the world were James George Frazer and Edward Burnett Tylor. Both of these authors applied the method of comparative anthropology. Anthropology had developed during the nineteenth century as a result of the increased availability of ethnographic information relating to aboriginal and tribal people. Also, the discovery of geologically dated ancient human remains demonstrated a very long human prehistory and forced a reassessment of the history of humanity. The culture of the early ancestors of Europeans was equated with that of the 'savage races' still living in other parts of the world. A concept developed of ancient beliefs and practices surviving into later societies where they lost their original meaning. Edward Tylor, in his *Primitive Culture* (1871), defined survival as those 'processes, customs, opinions, and so forth, which have been carried on by force of habit into a new state of society different from that in which they had their original home, and they thus remain as proofs and examples of an older condition of culture out of which a newer has been evolved'.[8] The existence of seemingly irrational mythical beliefs was thus regarded as proof of an earlier culture. Frazer's comparative method, meanwhile, was to focus on a myth that appeared absurd, and to relate that to similar myths in other cultures with the aim of finding a unifying explanation. Frazer assumed that all cultures go through similar stages of development, so that it was acceptable to make comparisons between the belief systems of ancient European cultures and those of existing tribal cultures in other parts of the world. In his popular work *The Golden Bough* (1890), Frazer described three stages for the development of human culture: an Age of Magic (which he thought remained the state of the Australian aboriginals), an Age of Religion, and finally, at the most advanced level, an Age of Science. He believed that different cultures evolved at different speeds, which from his perspective meant that European culture had developed particularly rapidly in order to reach its present scientific stage.

This perspective had significant social and political connotations.[9] If Europe was the most highly evolved society, then Europeans had a responsibility to help backward

cultures evolve to their level. Thus, Frazer's theory supported the imperial domination of other countries; Europeans had not only the right, but the duty, to take up the
'white man's burden' of civilizing backward societies. It was proposed that even within
one society there were different levels of social evolution. This notion supported the
maintenance of class structures in Britain. The scientific intelligentsia were regarded
as the most highly evolved section of society, and the clergy and religious people had
at least evolved out of barbarism. However, the greater part of the population was
the workers, whom Frazer regarded as representing the Age of Magic because of their
superstitions and lack of scientific knowledge. He regarded them as a threat to the
more civilized sections of society, and believed that this justified their control by the
upper social echelons in order to prevent them from reverting to savagery.

Whilst the theories of Tylor and Frazer supported social control, their unashamed
scientism did not support a society that conformed to traditional social hierarchies.
If social policy should be determined on the basis of scientific principles, then the
aristocracy had no automatic right of domination within society, unless they were
also scientists. Also, the tenets of comparative anthropology cast doubt upon Christian
myths just as much as on those from classical times, and clergy and religious believers
were assigned to a subculture that was less advanced than that of scientists. Because
of this, churchmen who might have been Frazer's natural allies against spiritualism
and magical practices were instead outraged by his theory.

Although the general view in the nineteenth century was that myth was a kind
of 'nature poetry' or primitive natural philosophy, it came to be recognized that
myth was inspired not only by the natural world, but also by human passions and
emotions.[10] This view was first promoted by George Grote, who wrote that Greek
mythology was 'a special product of the imagination and feelings, radically distinct
both from history and philosophy'.[11] Grote believed that myth came to be regarded
as literally true because it was in harmony with human emotion. Before Grote, most
scholars had regarded Greek mythology as a distorted account of history.[12]

Grote was a friend and follower of Jeremy Bentham.[13] He edited Bentham's book
Analysis of the Influence of Natural Religion on the Temporal Happiness of Mankind
(1822), which Bentham had written under the pseudonym of Philip Beauchamp. Grote

was also a friend of James Mill, father of John Stuart Mill, who was a boy of twelve when Grote first met his father. The younger Mill became a lifelong friend of Grote. Grote was a Member of Parliament from 1832-41, where he was one of the Benthamite 'Philosophical Radicals'. Grote's political agenda included reduction of taxation (particularly for the poor), reduction of public expenditure, removal of restrictions on trade, and universal education. [14] His primary political campaign related to the ballot, with the aim of extending suffrage and enabling secret voting.

Grote's analysis of Greek mythology did not lead him to hold it in respect. Instead, in his view, the state of mind that gave priority to human feelings and imagination was primitive compared to the rationality which came later and which, for Grote, represented progress. In keeping with his Benthamite outlook, Grote believed that the influence of myth and religion from earlier times had been damaging to Athenian democracy, and that aristocratic Greeks had made use of this to maintain their power. He thought that although the ancient Greeks had regarded their mythology as historical, it was in fact a pseudo-history. [15] By challenging the historical validity of the Greek myths, Grote was also implicitly challenging the validity of biblical stories.

Walter Pater is considered to have followed in the footsteps of Grote by adopting the view that mythology reflected human passions and emotions. Pater was a critic of the arts who took a subjective approach to his work, seeking to feel the effect of the inner 'virtue' of an art work. [16] He regarded the work of the aesthetic critic as analogous to that of a chemist, who seeks the elemental foundation of a compound; though in the arts, the elemental foundation is a virtue that has a subjective effect on the observer. The notion that a person experiencing a work of art might be moved by its influence and thus be transported involuntarily to a new subjective place was commonly regarded as potentially dangerous or degenerate in the late nineteenth century. Jeffrey Wallen has described how this potential influence of art was likened to that of mesmerism, susceptibility to which was also regarded as a sign of personal weakness. [17] Pater took a similarly subjective approach to his study of mythology, relating myths to human emotion and personality. For example, he described the mythical figure Dionysus as 'the projected expression of the ways and dreams of primitive people, brooded over and harmonised by the energetic Greek imagination'.[18] Despite his penchant for subjectivity, Pater wrote from a position of scientific naturalism and explicitly rejected the possibility that supernatural agencies can act in the material world.[19]

Pater's opposition to any hint of the supernatural was shared by other students of mythology who prided themselves on taking a scientific approach. Their attitude towards spiritualism, which requires a belief that the mind can exist without the body, is a good barometer for assessing this, because belief in spiritualism is closely allied to belief in other esoteric phenomena. As historian Frank Turner has observed, 'With a few notable exceptions...men of science...dismissed hypnotism, mesmerism, telepathy, and spiritualism...The scientific reductionism of...naturalistic writers...made them ill-disposed to consider that mind might exist separately from its physical organism'.[20] Of course this is a generalization; spiritualism appealed primarily to those with heterodox belief systems, but it was also used by more conservative intellectuals who wished to preserve a religious outlook in the face of the prevailing scientific materialism. They attempted to place spiritualism within the realm of science by using 'scientific' methods to investigate spiritualism, for example through the Society for Psychical Research.[21]

The public attitude of Tylor and Frazer towards spiritualism was predictably negative. Tylor wrote that modern spiritualism was 'in great measure a direct revival from the regions of savage philosophy and peasant folklore', and this was the tone of his attitude towards spiritualism in all his published works.[22] For Tylor, this meant that savage modes of thinking and behaviour remain stubbornly ingrained despite the progress of civilization. However, there is evidence that his private evaluation of spiritualism was much less negative. Tylor's private diaries have been examined by the American scholar George W Stocking, who noted that Tylor attended many spiritualist seances in the latter part of 1872, including those held by prominent mediums like Daniel Dunglas Home, Kate Fox and the Reverend Stainton Moses.[23] He was also a friend of leading proponents of Victorian spiritualism such as the Howitts. In most cases he dismissed the phenomena that he observed as being the result of fraud or gullibility, but some of what he saw gave him pause for thought. After observing a seance by Kate Fox, he noted in his diary that 'Last night for the first time I saw and heard what deserves further looking into if I get the chance', and he was left 'in wonder' at the 'spiritual gifts' of Stainton Moses.[24] He admitted to himself that there was 'a prima facie case [for spiritualism] on evidence' and said that he could 'not deny that there may be a psychic force causing raps, movements, levitations &c', although he thought that the case for this was much weaker than the spiritualists claimed in their publications.[25] He appears to have been influenced by his assessment of the character of the mediums, particularly Stainton Moses, whom he regarded as 'a gentleman and apparently sincere'.[26] It must have been difficult for Tylor to reconcile this opinion of Moses with his view that modern spiritualism was an expression of primitive savagery which was liable to subvert civilized society. Although Tylor accepted privately the possible existence of a previously unrecognized 'psychic force' (which presumably would be accessible to scientific investigation), there is no doubt that his bias was against such phenomena. He recorded that the medium at a seance that he attended, who claimed to be controlled by the spirit of Mesmer, talked 'the usual spiritualistic and anti-vaccination cant'.[27]

The primitive practices that Frazer envisaged as characterizing his Age of Magic included 'homoeopathic magic' that operated according to laws of similarities and which was used, amongst other things, to treat illness.[28] Although Frazer did not make the point explicitly, this related directly to the modern practice of homoeopathy that was popular in his day. Frazer declared that homoeopathic and other varieties of sympathetic magic were 'familiar. . .to the crude intelligence not only of the savage, but of ignorant and dull-witted people everywhere'.[29] Telepathy, the belief that the mind can operate at a distance from the body, was similarly dismissed by Frazer as being one of the first principles of magical thinking.[30] Primitive and unscientific thinking of this kind plainly needed to be kept under control by scientific hegemony in order to avoid the whole of civilized society lapsing into barbarism.

Benthamites, amongst whom we must include George Grote, took a predictably dim view of spiritualism and other esoteric pursuits. In a letter to William Thomas Thornton, Grote's friend John Stuart Mill wrote:

Since in all that relates to the communicators with spirits, the men are manifestly imposters, why should one feel any difficulty in believing them

to be so altogether, & their apparent marvels to be juggling or other tricks?
Their exploits certainly would never do anything to shake my total disbelief
in clairvoyance, of which apart from its extreme antecedent improbability,
I have never read of any case the evidence of which did not leave the most
obvious loopholes for fraud.[31]

It is clear that an academic interest in mythology did not presuppose any particular
political outlook; mythology was interpreted to accord with all the political frameworks
of the time, ranging from Benthamite utilitarianism to conservatism and imperialism. A similar adaptation of mythical stories to support current social and political
movements can also be found within the popular mythology of the time, and historian
Stephanie Barczewski argues convincingly that nineteenth-century interpretations
of the popular legends of King Arthur and Robin Hood reflected the social concerns
of that time.[32] For example, Robin Hood was regarded as a Saxon hero, so that his
myth represented the fight for freedom in the face of Norman oppression, and thus
resonated with liberal notions of individual freedom as well as emphasizing the
inherent racial superiority of an Anglo-Saxon nation.

Whilst the dominant nineteenth-century approach to mythology took the
position of scientific naturalism, and the interpretation of mythology was used
to support diverse political and social aims, other students of mythology regarded
it as an expression of perennial spiritual truths. Mythology, when regarded as a
story hiding layers of deeper spiritual meaning, can be seen as the ideal vehicle for
transmitting esoteric knowledge. Antoine Faivre has pointed to the foundational
importance of myth for *philosophia occulta*, alchemy, theosophy, *vis imaginativa*
and other aspects of Western esotericism.[33] The allegorical and spiritual interpretation of the literal word is ancient and widespread. It was used by the Neoplatonists
and was adopted by early Christians in order to interpret the Old Testament in
conformity with the revelation of Christ in the New Testament.[34] It was also used
to 'Christianize' ancient and pagan texts.[35] Whilst some early Christians did this
simply for the purpose of religious conversion, there was a stream of Christian
thinking that regarded some ancient and pagan texts as reflecting a *prisca*

theologia, an ancient theology that was based on true divine revelation. This tradition began with the early Christian Fathers and was revived in the Italian Renaissance, particularly by Marsilio Ficino.[36] However, from the Middle Ages onwards, the mainstream Church had sought to condemn all mythologies other than its own as pagan and idolatrous, although Greek and Roman myths were allowed for their historical interest. The Christian myth of the Fall of humanity was dominant in the eighteenth century, but by the second half of the nineteenth century intellectual opinion generally favoured the thesis that human culture was a progressive evolution out of primitive savagery.[37]

The notion that there was once a 'Golden Age' of humanity is ubiquitous throughout different cultures and historical periods, but it was largely ignored by nineteenth-century academic historians of mythology, who adopted the prevailing positivist, evolutionary and anti-religious ethos.[38] Golden Age mythologies all subscribe to the notion of 'living nature', in which the cosmos is a living whole and humans are the link 'between the inner dimension of spirit and the outer world of form'.[39] This theme was developed by Mircea Eliade in the mid-twentieth century. He maintained that the common feature of paradisaical mythology is the proposal that heaven at that time was readily accessible by humankind, either because heaven was on earth or because heaven could be reached easily, for example by climbing a tree or a mountain.[40] It was thought that in the Golden Age, humans were sages who were in communication with the whole of nature and could perform miracles such as flying. They were in harmony with the divine will and continuously in the presence of the Divine. Food was present in abundance without the need for work; there was no death or disease; and there was complete harmony between man, animals and nature in general. Humans were regarded as having a responsibility to maintain the whole of nature, every part of which was regarded as sacred. The myths generally go on to describe a sequence of ages followed by a final apocalyptic cleansing with a subsequent return to paradisaical conditions.[41]

Concepts of a Golden Age and the subsequent decline of humanity were still popular in the eighteenth century, so it is unsurprising that they were adopted by Swedenborg. He described a series of spiritual epochs in human history using the term 'Churches'.[42] The first of these he referred to as the 'Most Ancient' or 'Adamic' Church, which was the period before the biblical Flood. At first this was a Golden Age, but this went into spiritual decline before the Flood.[43] In accord with the popular opinion of his day, Swedenborg believed that at that time, humankind lived in complete harmony with the Divine. He explained that they made no dualistic distinction between the spiritual and material worlds, because their perceptions were processed as correspondences:

> For the member of the Most Ancient Church there was no other worship
> than internal such as is offered in heaven, for among those people heaven
> so communicated with man that they made one...Thus, being angelic
> people, they were internal men. They did indeed apprehend with their senses
> the external things that belonged to the body and to the world, but they paid
> no attention to them. In each object apprehended by the senses, they used
> to perceive something Divine and heavenly. For example, when they saw
> any high mountain they did not perceive the idea of a mountain but that of
> height, and from height they perceived heaven and the Lord.[44]

This innate faculty of perceiving through correspondences was lost when humankind turned from the love of God to the love of self and the world, and their ancient awareness was then externalized as mythology: 'the knowledge of correspondences... spread to Greece, but there it was converted into myths'.[45]

At this time idolatry also developed:

> The ancient people who possessed the science of correspondences made
> themselves images to correspond to heavenly ideas...not so as to worship
> them, but to call to mind the heavenly ideas they stood for...Once the
> knowledge of correspondences had been wiped out, their descendents started
> to worship as holy, and finally as deities, the images and statues their
> ancestors had erected...[46]

The worship of nature—the sun, trees, and so forth—was regarded by Swedenborg as having the same origin. Polytheism, meanwhile, developed mostly as a result of transforming the attributes of God into individual deities:

> in ancient times people gave the Supreme Deity, or the Lord, various
> illustrious names. They used these in accordance with His attributes...
> But after the Church fell away from goodness and truth, and at the same
> time from such wisdom, they started to worship as many gods as there were
> descriptive names of the one God...[47]

Swedenborg's Most Ancient Church was followed by four other epochs or 'Churches': the Ancient, Jewish, Christian and New. These relate loosely to the world ages described by Hesiod and Ovid, with the addition of the 'New Church', by which Swedenborg meant the present spiritual epoch, which he believed had begun after the Last Judgment had taken place in the spiritual world in 1757 initiating a period of spiritual awakening.[48]

The notion of a Golden Age in which there was no dualistic separation between the mundane and the divine is an expression of the absolute idealism of *Naturphilosophie*, and therefore it is not surprising that Schelling took an active interest in this epoch and the subsequent development of mythology.

Schelling's work has been neglected by historians of mythology. He argued that in prehistorical times human consciousness was fundamentally different from that of today.[49] In those times, he thought, humanity was unified and consciousness related to the inner, spiritual man that was removed from the material world. When humanity separated into races, the nature of consciousness altered fundamentally and related instead to the external physical world. Mythology, according to Schelling, is the expression of a primordial universal religion which rests upon 'an *actual*, real relation of the human essence to God', and which is independent of human thought.[50] After separation of the races, each race received a revealed religion suited to their culture, which was mediated rather than directly inspired. According to Schelling, the widely held view that humanity has made steady progress from the earliest times is incorrect, and in fact the process had been one of decline.

The strong influence that Swedenborg had on Schelling's writing has been noted by Friedemann Horn, although he does not cite their views on mythology as an example of their congruence of thought.[51] However, Schelling's thesis regarding the state of consciousness of ancient humanity and the decline of humanity since the most ancient times accords strongly with Swedenborg's view. Whilst it is tempting to regard this as a further example of Swedenborg's influence on Schelling, the concepts were not original, and so both men may have developed their theme independently from other sources.

One of Schelling's pupils who was influential on the nineteenth-century interpretation of mythology was Friedrich Max Müller, a German-born scholar who lived in England, where he was Professor of Comparative Philology at Oxford. The young Müller went to Berlin in 1844 with the primary purpose of attending Schelling's lectures on mythology.[52] He held detailed discussions with Schelling on the subject and later visited the elderly philosopher several times.[53] Müller held an apparently idealist philosophy, saying that 'As we have made and defined the two words and concepts, matter and spirit, they are now inseparable; and the two systems of philosophy, materialism and spiritualism, have no sense by themselves but will have to be merged into the higher system of idealism'.[54] However, as his formulation implies, he believed that this situation was the result of the use of words, rather than a position derived from higher philosophical argument. Müller's analysis of the origin of myth also diverged from the views of his former mentor and was again based on a philological, rather than a philosophical, premise. He believed that myths, originally allegorical, were eventually misunderstood by the ancients, who took them literally. He proposed that an original Aryan root language had no abstract nouns and instead used descriptions of the attributes of an object, such as 'the giver of warmth' or 'the shining one' for the sun, or 'the runner' for a river. The simple description of nature in these terms gave rise to a poetry; but more than that, if he was distressed then 'the ancient poet had...the heart of nature to commune with, and in her silent suffering he saw a noble likeness of what he felt and suffered within himself'.[55] Thus, Müller regarded early mythology as the expression of an intuitive knowledge of the correspondence of nature with human thought and emotion, which is why it had an enduring appeal at a fundamental level, even though the appellations lost their original meaning and became personalized as gods.

The idea that there had once existed a prototypal Indo-European or Aryan race with its own language had been put forward earlier by William Jones, and this fuelled Müller's comparative mythology. Müller, who was a Sanskrit scholar, saw affinities between European and Indian mythologies. He championed Indian traditional thinking, with the result that he was opposed both by those who regarded Indians as an inferior and unimprovable race, as well as by those who believed that Indian culture would benefit from being Europeanized.[56] A distinction was made between Indo-European, Semitic and Turanian (Ural-Altaic) races, with Indo-Europeans regarded as the most talented and successful group. The Indo-Europeans were regarded as having spread knowledge and culture to lesser peoples, thus justifying imperialism. It was widely believed that the original inhabitants of India were black and that the caste system was invented in an attempt to prevent the blood of the original blond, blue-eyed Aryan invaders from being sullied by that of the indigenous population. Inevitably, though, the blood lines mixed and the Aryan culture disintegrated in India.[57] For his part, Müller argued against any classification of humanity that was based on physical appearance, asserting that the only true classification must be based on language, religion and nationality. He regarded Indians as 'Aryan brethren' and opposed the extremes of colonialism. He took the view that the affinity between Europeans and Indians would facilitate the Europeanization of India without the need for oppression. Garth Wilkinson adopted the view that the British and Indian races were of common origin, and suggested that 'the two ends of the Aryan Race' would be reunited by the divine word as revealed by Swedenborg.[58]

Müller was a family friend of the Liberal Prime Minister William Ewart Gladstone, and Gladstone too had a keen interest in mythology.[59] Gladstone took the traditional view of mythology as the remnant of a golden or paradisaical era, writing that in Homeric myth there were 'vestiges of a real traditional knowledge, derived from the epoch when the covenant of God with man...had not yet fallen within the contracted forms of Judaism for shelter, but entered more or less into the common consciousness, and formed a part of the patrimony of the human race'.[60]

Belief in a Golden Age and subsequent fall, particularly if based on the biblical account, necessarily encompasses a belief in spirits and the spirit world. This stands in direct contrast to the materialistic interpretations of mythology that became dominant in the nineteenth century. Swedenborg, of course, was immersed in the world of spirits and Schelling also wrote of spirits and their world within his non-dualistic formulation of creation.[61] Gladstone had a firm belief in spirits, and was involved with spiritualism and other esoteric pursuits of his day. He attended several seances, saying that he approached spiritualism with a 'contented reserve'.[62] After attending one seance on 29 October 1884, Gladstone was quoted in a report in the *Morning Post* to have said that:

> there were subtle forces with which our 'puny minds' could not deal, and which he could not comprehend; he held the attitude, therefore, not of a scoffer, but of a student...his recent experiences of thought-reading were sufficient to show that there were forces in nature which were not generally recognised...he spoke at length about his own observations in the domains of clairvoyance and electrobiology.[63]

Gladstone was upset that comments which he considered to have been made in private were published in this way. In keeping with the Christian belief system that underpinned his politics, Gladstone was opposed to Benthamite utilitarianism, on the grounds that actions should be judged on the grounds of their moral worthiness, not merely their utility for the promotion of happiness in the majority.[64]

It is thus apparent that there were two competing modes of interpretation of mythology in the nineteenth century: firstly, the predominant 'scientific' model which regarded mythologies as vestiges of primitive explanations of the world; and, secondly, the notion that mythologies represent a perennial philosophy that had been known to a select few throughout the history of humanity. The first, 'scientific' mode of interpretation of mythology is broadly incompatible with belief in the supernatural, although it allows the possibility that there exists a previously unknown natural force that could be studied scientifically when it had been properly identified. In contrast, ideas of a Golden Age of revelation or a perennial philosophy readily accommodate, or indeed presuppose, belief in the supernatural, and so are compatible with a belief in spirits and other esoteric phenomena.

Garth Wilkinson had long had an interest in mythology, particularly that of the Icelandic Norsemen, but he did not begin publishing on this topic until later in life. By then, he was a confirmed Swedenborgian, so that his interpretation of mythology necessarily followed Swedenborgian lines. The same path was followed also by the American Swedenborgian Carl Theophilus Odhner. Both authors interpreted mythological texts by using Swedenborgian correspondences. Like the myth of the Fall of humanity, the concept of correspondences between the spiritual and material worlds had been prevalent in the eighteenth century when Swedenborg was producing his theological works. For example, the Scottish theologian Andrew Michael 'Chevalier' Ramsay wrote that 'In the state of pure and exalted nature, the intelligent images and material pictures, tho' quite different substances, must have necessary resemblances to each other'. Recognizing this, the ancient sages 'looked upon the material universe and all its parts as shadows, emblems, and pictures of the intellectual world; and so made use of the properties, virtues, and qualities of the one, to design, indicate and represent the powers, attributes, and faculties of the other'.[65] Isaac Newton, whose lectures on physics Swedenborg attended as a young man, took a particular interest in correspondences in his own exegesis of the Bible. He suggested, for example, that birds, animals and insects were used to represent 'kingdoms and bodies politic, fire to signify warr wch [sic] consumes them, the sun moon and stars to signify the king and his people'.[66] It is plain that Swedenborg's fundamental concepts and his method of biblical exegesis were in step with the intellectual climate of his day.

Wilkinson published his first work on mythology in 1887 and in the following year Odhner gave a series of lectures on the subject in America.[67] Wilkinson went on to publish two more books on mythology, whilst Odhner published his perspective on mythology in the Swedenborgian journal *New Church Life* before publishing books on *The Correspondences of Canaan* (1911), *The Golden Age* (1913) and *The Mythology of the Greeks and Romans* (1927).[68] Both men followed Swedenborg's thesis that there had been a succession of 'Churches' which began with a revelation and then went into spiritual decline. Odhner discussed the Golden Age explicitly in Swedenborgian terms.[69] He described this as a time in which humans had immediate spiritual perception of correspondences and a direct interaction with the celestial angels of heaven to whom they were akin. Intercourse with angelic spirits, thought Odhner, was safe at that time, because until then all spirits were good. After the Fall, the spirit world became dangerous because it was inhabited by the demonic spirits of fallen humans who could deceive and harm any person who came into contact with them. Odhner was astonished that nobody outside of New Church circles was aware of Swedenborg's account of the Most Ancient and Ancient Churches, which, for Odhner, solved the mystery of the origin of mythology. He supposed that this knowledge was denied to the majority of people because they were not yet in a fit state spiritually to receive it.

Garth Wilkinson believed firmly in Swedenborg's spiritual epochs or 'Churches', which commenced with the Adamic Golden Age, and which each began with a new revelation, followed by a period of spiritual decline, vestigial remains of those revelations manifesting themselves as mythology.[70] Wilkinson distinguished between two types of mythology: 'residual religion which had still some guidance in it, and a mythology which now belonged to the imagination'.[71] He denied the Darwinian view that humans had evolved from primitive ancestry. In his view, there was no such thing as prehistoric man. The first men, whom he regarded as the sons and daughters of God, 'did not pass their heart's babyhood, its infancy, or its nursery days, among cave-bears and hairy rhinoceroses'.[72] Despite basing his arguments on a spiritual, rather than a literal, interpretation of the Book of Genesis, he felt the need to comment on the fossil evidence for prehistoric man. He argued that fossils thought to be prehistoric man are not actually human, and explained the lack of archaeological evidence for his own theory by suggesting that the bones of the first Adamic men 'were not ossified and not fossilizeable like ours'.[73] Savagery was a later, degenerate state of humanity, not its starting point. He pointed to savages within contemporary society, represented in 'the mass of helpless and decaying people, who…exist in all ranks and classes…but in multitude at the lowest end'.[74] They are characterized by their uselessness, and by the fact that their lines die out.[75]

Wilkinson believed that eventually evidence would be found to prove the spread of humanity from a common starting place, which he identified with biblical Eden. He regarded Egypt and India as sites of the second, or Noahtic Church. As this church degenerated it seeded individual mythologies that developed separately. Heathen religions, thought Wilkinson, contain 'remainders' of revelation which were mythologized and added to from the local culture. He proposed, for example, that serpent myths were a remainder from the Adamic Church, whilst the 'heathenisms' of Egypt, Greece and Rome were remainders from the Noahtic Church.[76] The concept of mythology as a pre-scientific attempt to understand nature was, for Wilkinson, an invention not of primitive savages, but of professors. Rather, he believed that mythology was based upon a true spiritual understanding of the world which ultimately reflects the correspondence between the spiritual and the material realms. In Wilkinson's view, it was the task of comparative mythology to trace 'the likeness and parallelism of Myths in various races and ages', and purge 'the true mythological body from the accretions of fancy and imagination'.[77] He emphasized the need to separate mere allegories (such as the kennings of early Norse literature) from true correspondences, which are spiritual.[78]

Wilkinson's first published attempt to give a Swedenborgian exegesis to a specific mythology was his work on the myth of Oannes that had been recorded by Berossos, a Babylonian priest who was born between 330 and 323 BC.[79] The English archaeologist Austen Henry Layard led archaeological expeditions to Assyria and Babylon in 1845-7 and 1849-51. His books based on these expeditions, *Ninevah and its Remains* (1849) and *Discoveries in the Ruins of Ninevah and Babylon* (1853) were bestsellers. Whilst there, he discovered fragments of clay tablets which contained the Mesopotamian creation myth. This mythology was known already from fragments of writings by Berossos, but the level of antiquity of this myth was unknown until Layard's discoveries. Striking similarities were noted netween the Babylonian myth and the first two chapters of Genesis, and it was widely believed that the authors of Genesis had used the Babylonian mythology as source material.[80] It was thought that archaeology, as well as providing evidence for the historicity of the Bible, was able to show that there was a continuous tradition connecting the primeval world with the civilized nineteenth century.[81] The first published account of the Mesopotamian creation story was George Smith's *The Chaldean Account of Genesis* (1876), republished soon afterwards in an edition revised by Reverend Archibald Henry Sayce, Professor of Assyriology at the University of Oxford.[82] Babylonian mythology remained popular in the second half of the nineteenth century and was expounded, for example, by Sayce in his work *Lectures on the Origin and Growth of Religion as Illustrated by the Religion of the Ancient Babylonians* (1887), which was one of Wilkinson's sources.[83]

Oannes was a fish-god who had a human head beneath his fish head and feet joined to his tail. He spoke with the voice of a man and he was credited with rising from the sea to teach humanity about writing, mathematics, agriculture, law-making and building. Wilkinson gave a Swedenborgian analysis of the myth, for example, citing the correspondence between factual knowledge and fish.[84] Wilkinson regarded Oannes as cognate with the biblical Noah.[85] However, he faced the problem that in the Babylonian account of the Flood that is attributed to Berossos, Oannes is not mentioned. Wilkinson deals with this difficulty by simply transposing the fragments of Berossos, which is contrary to scholarly opinion then and now. He says that this is permissible, because Berossos was a priest of Babylon and was therefore likely to have 'naturally assigned the first place to Babylon in the events of the days of old'.[86]

Wilkinson's major work on mythology was his Swedenborgian interpretation of the Icelandic poem *Voluspa*, which dates from the late tenth century, a time when Christianity was replacing ancient pagan religion.[87] In the eighteenth century, Thomas Percy had published his *Northern Antiquities* (1770), which included commentary on Norse mythology and translations of some of the *Edda*.[88] This went into several editions and revisions, such as the highly popular 1847 edition revised by J A Blackwell, which became the standard work on the subject.[89] The *Poetic* and *Prose Edda* became the subject of public lectures. Several other translations and commentaries were published, including works aimed at children. Secondary myths were built around the recorded Norse myths, for example, the typically Victorian suggestion that the *Edda* had been composed originally in the Western Isles of Britain and transmitted to Iceland from there. In 1886 William Morris listed the *Poetic Edda* as the fourth out of 100 of the world's greatest books.[90]

Wilkinson had been an Icelandophile since he had travelled there as a young man. It is during one of these journeys that he was alerted to the potential homoeopathic use of Hekla lava.[91] Wilkinson was part of what has been described as an 'invisible college' of more academically inclined Iceland enthusiasts.[92] Two leading figures were Icelanders based in Britain: Guðbrandur Vigfússon in Oxford, and Eiríkur Magnússon in Cambridge. Wilkinson engaged in correspondence with Guðbrandur in order to establish the best way of organizing regular shipments of Hekla lava to England.[93] Another member of this circle was Jón Hjaltalin, an Icelandic academic, parliamentarian and Swedenborgian, who spent time in Edinburgh and in London, where he and Wilkinson studied the *Edda* together.[94] It was from Hjaltalin that Wilkinson learned Old Icelandic, so that he could read the *Edda* in their original language. Hjaltalin later wrote to Florence Pertz, Wilkinson's granddaughter, that he:

> first made the acquaintance of my oldest and dearest friend in Great Britain, your grandfather, on board the mail-steamer Arcturus on a voyage from Reykjavik to Grangemouth in Scotland during August 6th-11th 1866. He had taken great interest in Sweden on account of Swedenborg, and travelled there and learned Swedish. In Copenhagen he had been introduced to Icelandic and the Icelandic literature, and taken great interest in them at once. This led him to take a trip to Iceland, and he liked travelling on pony's back, and to Thingvellir, the place of the old Icelandic Althing...[95]

Wilkinson introduced Hjaltalin to the works of Swedenborg, and Hjaltalin suggested generously that he 'had much more to learn from [Wilkinson] as to the inner meaning of these old songs, than he had to learn from me except as far as the language was concerned'.[96]

The *Voluspa* purports to be an account given by a seeress who had knowledge of the whole history of the world, from its creation through to its destruction. Wilkinson's early interest in this work coincided with the time when he was involved with spiritualism. During a visit in 1855 to a Dr Kahl at Lund in Sweden, he described a message received through an English medium from the 'Icelandic heaven', in which the seeress had claimed that the *Voluspa* was the word of the Lord which had been given to her in ancient times.[97] When he wrote his commentary on the *Voluspa* in 1897, Wilkinson still believed that this work was divinely inspired.[98] He made his own translation from the Old Icelandic into English, using as his source an edition transcribed from the Codex Regius, which had been published in Germany by Theodor Möbius in 1860. His interpretation was based on correspondences and he declared that his spiritual understanding of the *Voluspa* would have been quite impossible without the insights that he had gained from Swedenborg.[99]

Wilkinson's interpretation of the *Voluspa* owes much to his highly active imagination, and his poetic style of writing makes a secondary interpretation of Wilkinson's own words necessary before even a summary snapshot of his work can be offered. Although Wilkinson's interpretation of the *Voluspa* spanned the whole text, he gave particular emphasis to an exegesis of the Icelandic story of the creation of man, saying that no previous commentator had put this into context adequately.[100] Norse mythology describes the destruction of the primordial giant Ymir by Odin and his two brothers, who formed the world from Ymir's body.[101] Ymir's blood formed the sea and his body formed earth and rocks. From this material, dwarves were formed by the gods. Wilkinson regarded these dwarves as 'mineral men' who were 'divine caskets' waiting to be filled with life and soul.[102] The infusion of life and soul into 'mineral man' is described thus in Wilkinson's translation of *Voluspa*:

> And then three Aesir from that band, able and loving, came to a house. Found on the land Ask and Embla, good for little; out of fate. Spirit they owned not, mind they had not, blood nor bearing, nor good complexion. Odin gave spirit, Haenir gave soul, Lodur gave blood and good complexion.[103]

The Aesir are Norse gods, who 'represent Elohim the divine Truth, God-Man, founding humanity upon the *earth*, and surrounding its corporeal sensual faculties and last reactions with spiritual powers'.[104] Ask and Embla, names which are taken as referring to Ash and Elm trees, are, for Wilkinson, no more real trees than the dwarves are real dwarves; they are correspondences: whilst the dwarves represent caskets waiting to be filled, Ask and Embla are 'infant humans' who have now been given 'the seeds of future faculties'. [105] These faculties—of will and understanding—are endowed by Yggdrasil, a mythical Norse tree with branches and roots that reach into all layers of creation including the abodes of the gods, humans and the dead. Wilkinson regards this as the Tree of Life, and through it comes fate and the freedom to act within that fate. Odin used this freedom to seek knowledge of the future, in return for which he gave one of his eyes. According to the myth, this eye is in the well of Mimir at the foot of Yggdrasil. Wilkinson interpreted this to mean that Odin had forfeited his inner, spiritual eye in return for terrestrial knowledge. As a result, his intellect was no longer divinely inspired. Wilkinson regarded Odin not as a man or a god, but as a spiritual epoch during which humanity had become debased by seeking sensual rather than celestial knowledge.

The *Voluspa* goes on to give accounts of war, and ultimately Ragnarok, the Norse Armageddon that is described as a battle between the gods. For Wilkinson, Ragnarok had occurred in 1757, the year in which Swedenborg believed the Last Judgment had occurred in the world of spirits, heralding the New Church. Wilkinson believed that the *Voluspa* made reference to Swedenborg in the stanzas describing the world reborn after Ragnarok, which refer to an eagle that 'goes to fish on the mountain fells'. [106] Wilkinson related this to Swedenborg's own declaration that he was a spiritual fisherman. Wilkinson did not give a detailed exegesis of Ragnarok, commenting that he would leave that to his successors. He evidently believed that he was blazing a trail, but it is a trail that nobody has yet followed.

Wilkinson continued working on the interpretation of ancient mythology until the time of his death in 1899. His last excursion into the mind of the ancients focused on Egypt. The way to understanding ancient Egyptian hieroglyphics had been opened up by the discovery in 1799 of the Rosetta Stone, which was finally deciphered in the 1820s. Wilkinson's views on Egyptian hieroglyphics are detailed in an unpublished manuscript, in which he explains that hieroglyphs are 'correspondential writing' which reflect the correspondence between the natural and the spiritual which had been handed down as 'unbroken tradition from a remote past' when Egypt was a member of the Ancient Church.[107] Echoing Swedenborg, Wilkinson believed that the spiritual sense of hieroglyphics had been gradually lost, leading to idolatry in which, for example, sun worship was practised:

> The Ancient Church understood nothing else by the sun but the Lord, and the Divine-Celestial of His Love. Wherefore they had the rite of praying to the rising Sun; not even thinking of the sun. But after their posterity had lost this altogether...they began to worship the mere sun and moon...[108]

He described Egyptian mythology as 'a chaos with gold and precious stones in it, waiting...to be disinterred in a resurrection such as the mummies expected, but with a spiritual sense to it'.[109]

His last book on mythology was an exposition of an Egyptian funerary text, the 'Book of Respirations', which was published shortly after Wilkinson's death in 1899. This text evidently appealed to Wilkinson because of Swedenborg's thesis that respiration is a core part of human physiology that has correspondences throughout the material cosmos and the spiritual world, and he explained in detail Swedenborg's views on the correspondence between the lungs and the understanding. He regarded Swedenborg's work on respiration as a direct successor to the Egyptian work, a 'Swedenborgian or Second Book of Respirations'.[110]

It is plain that, at the end of his life, Wilkinson saw Swedenborg as the bringer of a wisdom that formed the core of a much more ancient tradition. This was a perennial philosophy that stemmed from the Most Ancient Church, in which all people lived simultaneously in both the material and spiritual worlds, and each had an intuitive understanding of the primary spiritual significance of everything in the sensible world, just as Swedenborg claimed for himself. Wilkinson fully expected that he was living in an era when this blissful state would be restored to humanity.

− 10 −

Afterword

Fig. 10: J J G Wilkinson in September 1888, aged 76.
Swedenborg Society Archive, section M.

In the Preface, I observed that Wilkinson's fame dwindled as he grew older, which begs the question of why this happened, and why his work is virtually unknown today. Several reasons for this can be put forward. Firstly, even the greatest enthusiast for Wilkinson's literary merit would not suggest that his style of writing makes for easy reading; his tendency to use flowery language couched in metaphor and hyperbole often serves to obscure his underlying message. Even those who penetrate the verbiage find a message that seems alien to today's readers. This is partly because his basic conceptual framework is that of the Western esoteric tradition, transmitted through the writings of Emanuel Swedenborg which are known to few people today. Also, he was very much a product of the social and political conditions of his day, and without some awareness of those currents his interests and enthusiasms can appear to be disjointed and unrelated.

A more prosaic reason is that Wilkinson suffered from a malady common to people of outstanding but restless and impatient intellect: failure to take any one idea through to its completion. Wilkinson provides several ready examples of this tendency. He was centrally involved with early spiritualism, but dropped this, and ultimately condemned it because of a combination of social pressures and his growing ideological dependence on a pure, unmodified and mainstream interpretation of Swedenborg's writings. He did not follow some of his intellectual contemporaries into the scientific investigation of paranormal phenomena because he believed that pursuit to be worthless or even spiritually dangerous. His close involvement with mesmerism and hypnosis led him to the brink of understanding unconscious mental mechanisms, but he gained no credit because he chose to interpret his understanding in Swedenborgian, rather than purely psychological, terms. Instead, he fed ideas to those who are now much better known in the field, including James Braid and William Benjamin Carpenter. In his homoeopathy Wilkinson was ahead of his time, for example in his emphasis on the primacy of mental symptoms, but he kept this within his own practice and did not systematize it into a method that could be adopted by his contemporaries. This was left to James Tyler Kent, who is now famous in homoeopathic circles. Also, Wilkinson's homoeopathy was sullied by his tendency as a young man to adopt methods that were regarded as so much beyond the pale that they could never be accepted, such as the notion of fairy medicines and his proposal to treat insanity with 'homoeopathic' doses of spiritualism. His involvement with the utopian socialism of Charles Fourier, at first enthusiastic and tinged with a sense of mission, faded when he decided that it lacked the spiritual dimension that would be demanded by his Swedenborgian beliefs. His *magnum opus*, *The Human Body*, contained spiritual wisdom that was lost to all but the most persistent readers because his complex insights were clouded by his obscure style of writing. This work was seen by at least one of his contemporaries as standing in the tradition of German *Naturphilosophie*, a claim that Wilkinson would have refuted vigorously because of his prejudice against anything that he perceived as being related to philosophical idealism. He did not develop his physiological insights further and the work that he intended as follow-up, *The Soul is Form*, was a more straightforward account of Swedenborg's system without any real development on Wilkinson's part.

Wilkinson's early career was summed up perceptively by Emerson, writing in 1856:

Wilkinson, the editor of Swedenborg, the annotator of Fourier, and the
champion of Hahnemann, has brought to metaphysics and to physiology
a native vigor, with a catholic perception of relations, equal to the highest

attempts, and a rhetoric like the armory of the invincible knights of old. There is in the action of his mind a long Atlantic roll not known except in deepest waters, and only lacking what ought to accompany such powers, a manifest centrality. If his mind does not rest in immovable biases, perhaps the orbit is larger, and the return is not yet: but a master should inspire a confidence that he will adhere to his convictions, and give his present studies always the same high place.[1]

It is now clear that the 'manifest centrality' of Wilkinson's thought was Swedenborgian theosophy, to which he adhered with increasing fidelity as he aged. The breaking wave of his Atlantic roll left behind the jetsam of many youthful enthusiasms, such as socialism and spiritualism; some of his other interests, including homoeopathy and opposition to vivisection, were still afloat later in life, but only insofar as they were supported by a pure wave of Swedenborgianism. As he said towards the end of his life: 'I confess myself a Swedenborgian, a name which, a quarter of a century ago, I should have repugned'.[2]

Because Swedenborg claimed to communicate with angels and other inhabitants of the spiritual world, he has been regarded as insane by many of my fellow psychiatrists, beginning with Henry Maudsley in the nineteenth century. What matters, though, is not whether Swedenborg was technically insane according to today's criteria—and I do not believe that he was—but rather the quality of his theosophy. If one looks beyond the narrow viewpoint of medical diagnosis, Swedenborg's philosophy is revealed as one that is not only logical and consistent, but also one that has real practical applications. What has struck me forcibly about Garth Wilkinson was the way in which he used Swedenborg's philosophy as an explanatory and motivating driver for action within his own social context.

Why is Garth Wilkinson of particular interest today? A general reason is that the study of Wilkinson's life and works within his social context makes a significant contribution to the historiography of the nineteenth century, particularly in relation to the pervasive influence of Swedenborg's theosophy on some of the major movements of that time such as spiritualism, homoeopathy and mesmerism. An overview of Wilkinson's life also highlights the way in which his passion for the latest fashionable 'spiritual' movements such as nineteenth-century spiritualism and mesmerism diverted him from the spiritual path that he started on and eventually returned to; perhaps this can be regarded as reflecting a general tendency for the young to explore popular 'alternative' and 'radical' ways before settling on a path that is possibly more mainstream. Wilkinson's politics reflected the same pattern, moving from republican to liberal socialist to conservative.

In our time there are many fashionable spiritual movements on offer, and there is little doubt that Wilkinson would have explored them had he been alive today. Two examples are New Age religion and practices derived from Eastern religion. The New Age movement offers many diversions including the channelling of spirits, esoteric forms of healing, strategies for personal growth, and neopaganism. The indebtedness of some New Age thought to Swedenborg's theosophy has been proposed but not fully explored.[3] New Age philosophy and practices have been developed within the context of today's individualism, and the common focus on self-improvement would appear to be the antithesis of the approach taken by Swedenborg and other Christian mystics, for whom a focus on the self is regarded as a hindrance to a proper focus on God. Eastern religion, particularly Zen Buddhism, has also entered popular awareness. Whilst the true practice of Zen meditation in its proper context can be regarded as a profound and demanding spiritual discipline, there is also a 'pop Zen' movement in which, once again, Zen is regarded as a vehicle for personal development. A plethora of 'mindfulness' approaches have been developed, which, though derived originally from Buddhist meditation practices, are divorced from their original spiritual context and presented as means to overcome psychological problems—again, a form of self-improvement, which is as alien to Buddhists as it is to Christian mystics. If Wilkinson was alive today, would he have followed the same pattern of exploring these and other contemporary spiritual movements, relating them to Swedenborg's theosophy, and then rejecting them? We can only speculate.

We can perhaps be more certain of Wilkinson's political allegiances if he was alive today. He was a very early adopter of many of the leading social and political movements of today. We can point for example to his concern for the environment, his belief in the right of everybody to roam the countryside, his views against vivisection and the hunting of animals, his support for the women's rights movement, and his opposition to state intervention in the life of individuals. His certainty in the rectitude of all these causes was bolstered by his Swedenborgian belief system. Swedenborg's theosophy remains as socially relevant today as it was for Garth Wilkinson.

Endnotes

—

Bibliography

—

Index

ENDNOTES

Introduction

[1] Clement John Wilkinson, *James John Garth Wilkinson; A Memoir of his Life, with a Selection from his Letters* (London: Kegan Paul, Trench, Trübner & Co., 1911).

[2] Henry James, Jr, letter to William James, 31 October 1909, in *The Correspondence of William James*, ed. Ignas K Skrupskelis and Elizabeth M Berkeley, 12 vols. (Charlottesville and London: University Press of Virginia, 1992-2004), vol. 3, pp. 402-5 (p. 405).

[3] Frederick H Evans, *James John Garth Wilkinson: An Introduction* (Reprinted privately: Mrs Frank Claughton Mathews, 1936).

[4] Logie Barrow, 'An Imponderable Liberator: J.J. Garth Wilkinson', in *Society for the Social History of Medicine Bulletin*, no. 36 (June 1985), pp. 29-31; Francis Treuherz, 'The Origins of Kent's Homeopathy', in *Journal of the American Institute of Homeopathy*, vol. 77, no. 4 (1984), pp. 130-49.

[5] Wilkinson's handwritten autobiography is held in the Swedenborg Society Archive A/149 (e), and was reproduced in the biography of him written by his nephew Clement Wilkinson, *James John Garth Wilkinson*, pp. 1-12.

[6] Richard Lines, 'Charles Augustus Tulk—Swedenborgian Extraordinary', in *Arcana*, vol. 3, no. 4 (1997), pp. 5-32 (p. 5).

Chapter One

[1] James John Garth Wilkinson, *Emanuel Swedenborg: A Biography* (London: William Newbery, 1849), p. 1.

[2] J J G Wilkinson, letter to Ralph Waldo Emerson, 3 January 1874, in Swedenborg Society Archive K/125 (3). Wilkinson was never a member of the sectarian New

Church, but came to regard himself as a Swedenborgian in the sense that he accepted Swedenborg's precepts.

3   The legal role of special pleader is now defunct; their job was to write statements of case for use in court proceedings, without themselves appearing in court.

4   Wilkinson took a close interest in his genealogy, and the information that he recorded is preserved in the Swedenborg Society Archive A/151 and A/153. His father told him that the family was of Danish extraction, and Wilkinson believed that this probably accounted for his attraction to Scandinavian languages: J J G Wilkinson, letter to his granddaughter Florence Pertz, 26 April 1896, in Swedenborg Society Archive A/153.

5   Clement Wilkinson, *James John Garth Wilkinson*, p. 2, which reproduces J J G Wilkinson's manuscript autobiography held in Swedenborg Society Archive A/149 (e). (The manuscript autobiography switches between being written in the third and the first person.)

6   Clement Wilkinson, *James John Garth Wilkinson*, p. 2.

7   Ibid., p. 6.

8   Ibid., p. 7.

9   Ibid.

10   Ibid., p. 8.

11   Ibid., p. 12.

12   Wilkinson says little directly about his father, who appears to have been emotionally distant and authoritarian. As a young man, Garth wrote a poem entitled 'The Lawyers: what of them?' (the law being his father's profession) in which he described them as a 'Bench of fools' who 'spoil the nation's wit': James John Garth Wilkinson, *Improvisations from the Spirit* (London: William White, 1857), pp. 215-16.

13   Donald Leinster-Mackay, *The Rise of the English Prep School* (London and Philadelphia: The Falmer Press, 1984), p. 28.

14   Totteridge was a well-to-do village outside London, which is now part of Greater London.

15   Norman G Brett James, *The History of Mill Hill School, 1807-1907* (London: Melrose, [1909]), p. 71.

16   It is recorded, for example, that two pupils who absconded and were found that evening asleep in a local cake shop, were flogged and expelled, a punishment that was regarded as severe even by the standards of the time: Norman G Brett James, *The History of Mill Hill School*, p. 71.

17   Clement Wilkinson, *James John Garth Wilkinson*, p. 14.

18 The indenture was signed on the 4 June 1828, at a cost to Wilkinson's father of £500: Swedenborg Society Archive K/124 (b), folio 50. Thomas Leighton was appointed surgeon to the Newcastle Infirmary in 1803. He was described as 'a spruce, tidy, red-faced little gentleman, closely shaved and scrupulously clean, dressed in a dark blue coat, cut away in front and decorated with double gilt brass buttons, yellow waistcoat and white cravat, with frilled front shirt, drab knee britches, top boots with brown tops and a black beaver chimney pot hat': from 'Newcastle Infirmary Timeline' at <http://research.ncl.ac.uk/nsa/tl2.htm>, accessed 2 November 2013.

19 M Jeanne Peterson, *The Medical Profession in Mid-Victorian London* (Berkeley: University of California, 1978).

20 George Haliburton Hume, *The History of the Newcastle Infirmary* (Newcastle-upon-Tyne: Andrew Reid & Co., 1906), p. 42.

21 The medical staff are listed in Hume, *The History of the Newcastle Infirmary*, pp. 142-8.

22 This is discussed in Chapter 8.

23 T M Greenhow, *Cholera, as it Recently Appeared in the Towns of Newcastle and Gateshead* (Philadelphia: Carey & Lea, 1832), pp. 122-3.

24 See Chapter 7. Wilkinson later referred to hospitals as 'the educational laboratories in which the poor are the clay which the doctor moulds into the costly and mortal chalice of orthodox practice for the rich': James John Garth Wilkinson, *Swedenborg Among the Doctors. A Letter to Robert T. Cooper. M.D.* (London: James Speirs, 1895), p. 43.

25 This theme occurs several times in Wilkinson's works, most particularly in his *War, Cholera, and the Ministry of Health. An Appeal to Sir Benjamin Hall and the British People* (Boston: Otis Clapp, and Crosby, Nichols, & Co., 1855).

26 The information in this and the next paragraph is taken from letters, mostly undated but from June 1832 until 1833, from Wilkinson to his father, James John Wilkinson, in Swedenborg Society Archive K/124 (b).

27 James Syme, 'The Address in Surgery', in *British Medical Journal*, vol. 2, no. 241 (12 August 1865), pp. 142-9 (p. 143). There was no anaesthesia at that time.

28 Syme, 'Address', p. 146.

29 'Walking the wards' in one of the London hospitals, a largely self-directed process in which the student was permitted to take advantage of any clinical experience and practical teaching that was available, was a mandatory requirement for the qualifications that Wilkinson sought: see Keir Waddington, *Medical Education at St. Bartholomew's Hospital, 1123-1995* (Woodbridge, Suffolk: The Boydell Press, 2003), p. 49.

30   Clement Wilkinson, *James John Garth Wilkinson*, p. 140.

31   J J G Wilkinson, letter to his fiancée Emma Marsh, 10 December 1839, in Swedenborg
      Society Archive K/124 (e).

32   See Chapter 2 for more examples of this.

33   J J G Wilkinson, letter to Henry James, Sr, 18 September 1847, in Swedenborg Society
      Archive K/123. The latitudinarian movement within the Church of England em-
      phasized the role of reason applied to the essential truths of the Bible, and thus
      de-emphasized the importance of imposed church doctrine: see Martin Fitzpatrick,
      'Latitudinarianism at the Parting of the Ways: A Suggestion', in *The Church of
      England c. 1689-1833: From Toleration to Tractarianism*, ed. John Walsh, Colin
      Haydon and Stephen Taylor (Cambridge: Cambridge University Press, 1993), pp.
      209-27.

34   J J G Wilkinson, letter to Henry James, Sr, 18 August 1853, p. 5, in Houghton Library,
      Harvard University, at <http://nrs.harvard.edu/urn-3:FHCL.HOUGH:12249590>,
      accessed 11 June 2014.

35   J J G Wilkinson, letter to Mrs Cockerill, 5 May 1896, in Swedenborg Society Archive
      K/125 (12).

36   J J G Wilkinson, letters to his fiancée Emma Marsh, 9 June 1836 and 25 July 1836,
      in Swedenborg Society Archive K/124 (e). Melancholia was a recurring burden for
      Wilkinson; in 1846 he wrote to his friend Henry James, Sr that he had been depressed
      for weeks following a bout of influenza, and that he could not write anything formal
      for fear of insulting James 'with the most inept twaddle'. He had stopped all his
      usual occupations and felt it 'impossible spiritedly to resume them': J J G Wilkinson,
      letter to Henry James, Sr, 1 December 1846, in Swedenborg Society Archive K/123.
      Wilkinson regarded mental depression as a disconnection from the Lord, leading to
      the feeling that we are living for no purpose, though he recognized that there were
      misanthropists who delighted in this form of misery, and others again who became
      distressed when they recognized the evil in themselves: letter to his fiancée Emma
      Marsh, 10 September 1839, in Swedenborg Society Archive K/124 (e).

37   J J G Wilkinson, letter to his fiancée Emma Marsh, 20 May 1839, in Swedenborg Society
      Archive K/124 (e).

38   J J G Wilkinson, letter to his fiancée Emma Marsh, 15 March 1839, in Swedenborg
      Society Archive K/124 (e).

39   Richard Lines, *A History of the Swedenborg Society 1810-2010* (London: South
      Vale Press, 2012), p. 35.

40   J J G Wilkinson, letter to his fiancée Emma Marsh, 9 October 1838, in Swedenborg Society Archive K/124 (e).

41   J J G Wilkinson, letter to the Publishing Committee, 4 October 1838, in Swedenborg Society Archive K/75.

42   J J G Wilkinson, letter to his fiancée Emma Marsh, 20 May 1839, in Swedenborg Society Archive K/124.

43   J J G Wilkinson, letter to the Publishing Committee, 4 October 1838, in Swedenborg Society Archive K/75.

44   J J G Wilkinson, letter to Henry James, Sr, 18 November 1847, in Swedenborg Society Archive K/123.

45   J J G Wilkinson, letter to Henry James, Sr, 25 January 1850, in Swedenborg Society Archive K/123.

46   J J G Wilkinson, letter to Henry James Sr, 8 February 1850, p. 8, in Houghton Library, Harvard University, at <http://nrs.harvard.edu/urn-3:FHCL.HOUGH:12249590>, accessed 11 June 2014.

47   J J G Wilkinson, *Emanuel Swedenborg*, p. 1. Wilkinson set the scene for this biography of Swedenborg by saying on the first page that 'We are no followers of Swedenborg. . . The truth, we believe, is not arrested or contained by any man'. In the second edition of this work, published in 1860, this phrase was modified to read 'We are no blind followers of Swedenborg'.

48   J J G Wilkinson, letter to Henry James, Sr, 2 August 1850, in Swedenborg Society Archive K/123.

49   For an outline of the history of this publication, see William Ross Woofenden, 'Preface to the Second Edition' and 'Preface to the 1977 Edition', in Emanuel Swedenborg, *Swedenborg's Journal of Dreams 1743-1744*, tr. J J G Wilkinson, ed. William Ross Woofenden, introd. Wilson Van Dusen, 2nd edn. (London: Swedenborg Society and Bryn Athyn, PA: Swedenborg Scientific Association, 1989), pp. vii-ix and x-xiv.

50   J J G Wilkinson, letter to John Thomson, 7 October 1894, in Swedenborg Society Archive K/125 (15).

51   Ibid.

52   J J G Wilkinson, letter to Henry James, Sr, 1 February 1844, in Swedenborg Society Archive K/123. Swedenborg's manuscripts were obtained from the Royal Academy of Sciences in Stockholm, where they were held.

53   J J G Wilkinson, letter to Henry James, Sr, 2 May 1845, in Swedenborg Society Archive K/123.

54 James John Garth Wilkinson, 'From our London Correspondent' (letter dated 3 April 1847), in *The New Jerusalem Magazine* (Boston), vol. XX, no. CCXXXVII (May 1847), pp. 377-9 (p. 378). John Daniel Morell (1816-91) was a close friend of Wilkinson. Morell was castigated by Wilkinson for his omission of Swedenborg's philosophy from the first edition of his work; Wilkinson was instrumental in persuading Morell to include this in subsequent editions: J J G Wilkinson, 'From our London Correspondent' (letter dated 3 June 1847), in *The New Jerusalem Magazine* (Boston), vol. XX, no. CCXL (August 1847), p. 542. John Abraham Heraud (1799-1887) edited *The Monthly Magazine*, with content that has been described as 'freely-mixed popularizations of post-Kantian philosophy, esoteric mystical commentary, literary effusions, and idealistic calls for child-centered education and communitarian socialism': Charles Capper, *Margaret Fuller: An American Romantic Life, Volume I: The Private Years* (New York: Oxford University Press, 1992), p. 332.

55 J J G Wilkinson, 'From our London Correspondent' (letter dated 3 July 1847), in *The New Jerusalem Magazine* (Boston), vol. XX, no. CCXL (August 1847), p. 544. At that time, Wilkinson had three manuscripts from Stockholm which the Association could not afford to publish: J J G Wilkinson, letter to Henry James, Sr, 18 December 1847, pp. 6-7, in Houghton Library, Harvard University, at <http://nrs.harvard.edu/urn-3:FHCL.HOUGH:12249590>, accessed 15 February 2016.

56 John Spurgin (1796-1866) was Chairman of the Swedenborg Society almost continuously between 1827 and 1864: see Lines, *A History of the Swedenborg Society 1810-2010*, pp. 27-9. He was a highly regarded physician who, doubtless influenced by Swedenborg's physiological works, practised an eclectic brand of medicine, emphasizing the primacy of the blood and the importance of mental influences on physical conditions. He was an opponent of homoeopathy, which he regarded as illogical, lacking in judgment and acceptable only to the credulous: see John Spurgin, *Cure of the Sick: Not Homoeopathy, not Allopathy, but Judgment* (London: John Churchill, 1860). Wilkinson credits Spurgin with advocating the translation of Swedenborg's physiological works: J J G Wilkinson, 'From our London Correspondent' (letter dated 3 March 1847), in *The New Jerusalem Magazine* (Boston), vol. XX, no. CCXXXVI (April 1847), pp. 331-3 (p. 331).

57 A book review in a leading medical journal of the day concluded that *The Economy of the Animal Kingdom* 'cannot fail to interest all who have leisure to peruse a production which, having been long since superseded by later and more sound writers, has lost all practical utility': *The Medico-Chirurgical Review and Journal of Practical Medicine*, vol. 49 (1846), p. 479.

58   J J G Wilkinson, letter to his fiancée Emma Marsh, 8 October 1839, in Swedenborg
     Society Archive K/124 (e).

59   Wilkinson went back to Swedenborg's original sources; his British Library lending slips
     show that he read all of the classic authors on anatomy including Haller, Leeuwenhoek,
     Morgagni, Swammerdam and Vesalius: Swedenborg Society Archive A/57.

60   J J G Wilkinson, letter to his fiancée Emma Marsh, 8 October 1839, in Swedenborg
     Society Archive K/124 (e).

61   James John Garth Wilkinson, *The New Jerusalem and the Old Jerusalem. The Place
     and Service of the Jewish Church among the Aeons of Revelation with other essays*
     (London: James Spiers, 1894), p. 205.

62   Clement Wilkinson, *James John Garth Wilkinson*, p. 123.

63   The edited posthumous works were: *Doctrina Novæ Hierosolymæ de Charitate*; *De
     Domino, et de Athanasii Symbolo*; and *Canones, seu Integra Theologia, Novæ
     Ecclesiæ. De Deo uno et infinito. De Domino Redemptore; et de redemptione.
     De Spiritu Sancto. De Divina Trinitate* (all London: James S Hodson and William
     Newbery and Manchester: Edward Baylis, 1840).

64   Wilkinson's friendship with Henry James, Sr is discussed in detail in Chapter 3.

65   This was the period between June 1849 and December 1850: Clement Wilkinson,
     James John Garth Wilkinson, p. 76. During this period, Wilkinson included in his
     letters to Henry James, Sr the pieces that were intended for publication. It seems that
     James was allowed carte blanche to edit and use this material as he saw fit, and it
     often appeared anonymously. In the present work I have used Wilkinson's letters as
     the primary source for his views.

66   Clement Wilkinson, *James John Garth Wilkinson*, p. 42.

67   Ralph Waldo Emerson, 'Swedenborg; or, the Mystic', in *Representative Men: Seven
     Lectures* (Boston: Ticknor and Fields, 1861), pp. 95-145 (pp. 112-13).

68   Harold Silver, *The Concept of Popular Education; A Study of Ideas and Social
     Movements in the Early Nineteenth Century* (London: MacGibbon and Kee, 1965),
     pp. 210-26.

69   J J G Wilkinson, letter to Emerson, 15 October 1849, in Swedenborg Society Archive
     K/125 (3).

70   Clement Wilkinson, *James John Garth Wilkinson*, p. 82.

71   Elizabeth Palmer Peabody, *Lectures in the Training Schools for Kindergartners*
     (Boston: D C Heath & Company, 1893), p. 157.

72   Henry D Thoreau, *Journal*, cited by Jeffrey S Cramer in an Afterword to Thoreau,

Walden, ed. Jeffrey S Cramer (New Haven: Yale University, 2006), p. 371.

[73] Henry James, Sr, letter to J J G Wilkinson, 9 September 1851, quoted by Clement Wilkinson, *James John Garth Wilkinson*, p. 183.

[74] Harold Aspiz, 'Whitman's "Poem of the Road" ', in *Walt Whitman Quarterly Review*, vol. 12, no. 3 (Winter 1995), p. 175.

[75] 'Art. V.- *The Human Body and its connexion with Man, illustrated by the Principal Organs*. By JAMES JOHN GARTH WILKINSON. London, 1851', in *The North British Review*, vol. XVII, no. XXXIII (May 1852), pp. 131-44 (pp. 132, 141, 140).

[76] Thomas Carlyle, letter to Joseph Neuberg, 25 July 1851, in *The Carlyle Letters Online*, at <http://carlyleletters.dukejournals.org/cgi/content/full/26/1/lt-18510725-TC-JN-01>, accessed 12 August 2015.

[77] The importance of Swedenborg as a forerunner of the New Age movement has been affirmed by Wouter J Hanegraaff in his *New Age Religion and Western Culture* (Albany, NY: SUNY Press, 1998), pp. 424-9. Dimitrije Mitrinović (1887-1953), now little known, was a Serbian émigré to England who lived in Bloomsbury. He was active in the early days of the New Age movement and referred to Swedenborg frequently in his works. He adopted the concept from the esoteric tradition, including that expressed by Swedenborg, of a 'Universal Human' as the blueprint for both individual man and the cosmos. He looked forward to the coming of a 'Universal Socialism of Humanity' in which the Universal Human would become expressed as a state of social harmony: Harry C Rutherford, *The Religion of Logos and Sophia: From the Writings of Dimitrije Mitrinović* (Sausalito, CA: The Society for Comparative Philosophy, 1973). The library of Mitrinović, part of which is now housed at the University of Bradford, includes copies of several of Wilkinson's works including *The Human Body* which he has closely annotated.

[78] Wilkinson's publication of Blake's poems is discussed in detail in Chapter 3.

[79] Wilkinson's association with Tulk and his ideas is discussed in detail in Chapter 3.

[80] J J G Wilkinson, *Improvisations from the Spirit*, pp. 397-8. The sexologist Havelock Ellis (1859-1939) pointed out that this technique was a forerunner of Sigmund Freud's method of free association: Havelock Ellis, 'Psychoanalysis in relation to Sex', Essay XVIII, in *The Philosophy of Conflict and Other Essays* (London: Constable & Co., 1919), pp. 212-13. Ellis's assertion stung Freud sufficiently to provoke a response. He said that Wilkinson's work had no influence 'on the choice of psycho-analytic technique': Sigmund Freud, 'A Note on the Prehistory of the Technique of Analysis', in Sigmund Freud, *Collected Papers*, ed. J Riviere and J Strachey, 5 vols. (London:

Hogarth Press and Institute of Psychoanalysis, 1950), vol. V, pp. 101-4. This implies that Freud was at least aware of Wilkinson's work.

[81] James Thomson, *Biographical and Critical Studies*, ed. Bertram Dobell (London: Reeves and Turner and Bertram Dobell, 1896), pp. 298-371 (pp. 317, 369).

[82] Ibid., pp. 350, 318.

[83] Ibid., p. 298 n.

[84] Alexander Gilchrist, *The Life of William Blake*, 2 vols. (London: MacMillan, 1880), vol. I, pp. 427-8.

[85] Ralph Waldo Emerson (ed.), *Parnassus* (Boston: James R Osgood and Company, 1875), pp. 34, 509.

[86] J J G Wilkinson, letters to his fiancée Emma Marsh, 23 October 1838 and 2 October 1839, in Swedenborg Society Archive K/124 (e). Wilkinson's association with Thomas Carlyle is discussed in detail in Chapter 3.

[87] Wilkinson attended the first performance of Browning's play *Strafford* on 1 May 1837, together with some three dozen companions including Dow and Wilkinson's brother William: J J G Wilkinson, letter to his fiancée Emma Marsh, 5 May 1837, in Swedenborg Society Archive K/124 (e).

[88] Wilkinson's involvement in the social and political issues of his day are discussed in detail in Chapter 8.

[89] Wilkinson's involvement with mesmerism and spiritualism are discussed in full in Chapters 4 and 5 respectively.

[90] Henry James, Sr, letter to Emerson, 1856, quoted in Ralph Barton Perry, *The Thought and Character of William James*, 2 vols. (London: Oxford University Press, 1936), vol. I, pp. 83-6 (p. 85).

[91] Alfred Habegger, *The Father. A Life of Henry James, Sr* (Amherst: University of Massachusetts Press, 1994), p. 240.

[92] J J G Wilkinson, letter to Henry James, Sr, 17 June 1846, in Swedenborg Society Archive K/123.

[93] Clement Wilkinson, *James John Garth Wilkinson*, p. 38. Wilkinson had attended a course of lectures at the Veterinary College and lived with his uncle for a short time: J J G Wilkinson, letter to William Boericke, 2 November 1894, in Swedenborg Society Archive K/125 (2).

[94] J J G Wilkinson, letters to Henry James, Sr, 18 October 1847, in Swedenborg Society Archive K/123, and 30 April 1847, in Houghton Library, Harvard University, at <http://nrs.harvard.edu/urn-3:FHCL.HOUGH:12249590>, p. 9, accessed 11 June 2014.

95 J J G Wilkinson, letter to Henry James, Sr, 22 March 1849, p. 6, in Houghton Library, Harvard University, at <http://nrs.harvard.edu/urn-3:FHCL.HOUGH:12249590>, accessed 11 June 2014.

96 J J G Wilkinson, letter to Henry James, Sr, 30 April 1847, p. 8, in Houghton Library, Harvard University, at <http://nrs.harvard.edu/urn-3:FHCL.HOUGH:12249590>, accessed 11 June 2014.

97 Wilkinson's practice of homoeopathy and its relation to his Swedenborgian beliefs is discussed in detail in Chapter 7.

98 J J G Wilkinson, letter to Henry James, Sr, 8 November 1850, p. 1, in Houghton Library, Harvard University, at <http://nrs.harvard.edu/urn-3:FHCL.HOUGH:12249590>, accessed 11 June 2014.

99 J J G Wilkinson, letter to his father James John Wilkinson, 2 December 1850, in Swedenborg Society Archive K/124 (b).

100 J J G Wilkinson, letter to his father James John Wilkinson, 28 January 1852, in Swedenborg Society Archive K/124 (b).

101 At least one of his daughters, Emma, was later sent away to school in Calais: J J G Wilkinson, letter to Henry James, Sr, 18 August 1853, p. 8, in Houghton Library, Harvard University, at <http://nrs.harvard.edu/urn-3:FHCL.HOUGH:12249590>, accessed 11 June 2014.

102 J J G Wilkinson, letter to his father James John Wilkinson, 22 April 1856, in Swedenborg Society Archive K/124 (b).

103 Wilkinson made two trips to Iceland, in 1866 and 1868, and notebooks relating to these trips are preserved: Swedenborg Society Archive A/150.

104 Clement Wilkinson, *James John Garth Wilkinson*, p. 86.

105 See Chapter 9.

106 J J G Wilkinson, Travel Diary (1869), p. 2, in Houghton Library, Harvard University, at <http://nrs.harvard.edu/urn-3:FHCL.HOUGH:12249596>, accessed 11 June 2014. Longfellow is known to have attended spiritualist seances: see J M Peebles, *What is Spiritualism? Who are these Spiritualists? and What can Spiritualism do for the World?*, 5th edn. (Battle Creek, MI: Peebles Publishing, 1910), pp. 93-4.

107 J J G Wilkinson, Travel Diary (1869), p. 38 (the first of two pages numbered 38 by Wilkinson in the original manuscript).

108 Ibid. Wilkinson's views on James's concept of the Divine Natural Human is discussed in Chapter 3.

109 J J G Wilkinson, Travel Diary (1869), p. 38.

[110] Ibid., pp. 42-3.

[111] Ibid., p. 44. Decades later, Wilkinson rebuked America for its greed, which he believed was a spiritual cause of cholera in less fortunate nations; see Chapter 7.

[112] The sons, Fritz and Edward, both became engineers: J J G Wilkinson, letter to Henry James, Sr, 11 December 1880, p. 4, in Houghton Library, Harvard University, at <http://nrs.harvard.edu/urn-3:FHCL.HOUGH:12249590>, accessed 11 June 2014.

[113] Clement Wilkinson, *James John Garth Wilkinson*, p. 115. Wilkinson had a large collection of newspaper articles and maps of the theatre of war: Swedenborg Society Archive L/403.

[114] John Robinson, *The Attwood Family, with Historic Notes and Pedigrees* (Sunderland: Published privately, 1903), pp. 11, 127-8.

[115] James John Garth Wilkinson, *Epidemic Man and His Visitations* (London: James Speirs, 1893).

[116] Francis Claughton Mathews and Benjamin St John Attwood-Mathews were cousins.

[117] 'England Marriages, 1538-1973', index, *FamilySearch*, at <https://familysearch.org/pal:/MM9.1.1/N6SV-T74>, accessed 26 Mar 2014. James John Wilkinson and Eliza Hackett Ford, 04 Jul 1867; citing St Mary's, Kingswinford, Stafford, England, reference; FHL microfilm 1040006.

[118] Clement Wilkinson, *James John Garth Wilkinson*, pp. 117, 119.

[119] Cecilia Payne-Gaposchkin, *An Autobiography and Other Recollections*, ed. Katherine Haramundanis, 2nd edn. (Cambridge: Cambridge University Press, 1996), p. 81. Cecilia was also impressed by one of Wilkinson's stranger books, written under the pseudonym of John Lone, in which he advocated that artists should paint with both hands simultaneously in order to produce a three-dimensional effect. This idea was stimulated by the popularity of the stereoscope, which had been invented in 1838: see John Lone (pseud. J J G Wilkinson), *Painting with Both Hands; or, the Adoption of the Principle of the Stereoscope in Art, as a Means to Binocular Pictures* (London: Chapman and Hall, 1856). Cecilia was left-handed, which was not tolerated at school in those days, and she was stimulated by her great-grandfather's book to practise using both hands, with the result that she became not only ambidextrous but also able to write 'backwards, upside down, and upside down backwards': Payne-Goposchkin, *Autobiography*, p. 92.

[120] Payne-Gaposchkin, *Autobiography*, pp. 81-2. The other daughter of Emma Pertz née Wilkinson was Florence who was a professional pianist and a close friend of the younger Henry James: Payne-Gaposchkin, *Autobiography*, p. 83. Henry James, Jr's letters to Florence Pertz are housed in the Harvard University library MS Am 1237.18.

[121] The contribution of Swedenborgian thought to the exegesis of ancient mythology in the nineteenth century, which is discussed in detail in Chapter 9, has been neglected entirely by historians of mythology.

[122] J J G Wilkinson, letter to Henry James, Sr, 11 December 1880, pp. 3-4, in Houghton Library, Harvard University, at <http://nrs.harvard.edu/urn-3:FHCL.HOUGH:12249590>, accessed 11 June 2014.

[123] Clement Wilkinson, *James John Garth Wilkinson*, p. 263.

[124] James John Garth Wilkinson, *The Book of Edda Called Voluspa: A Study in Its Scriptural and Spiritual Correspondences* (London: James Speirs, 1897).

[125] Clement Wilkinson, *James John Garth Wilkinson*, p. 132.

[126] Ibid., pp. 125-6.

[127] J J G Wilkinson, Address Book 1892, in Swedenborg Society Archive A/183 (r).

[128] J J G Wilkinson, letter to his daughter Florence Attwood-Mathews, 14 March 1879, pp. 1-2, and letter to William James, 16 Dec 1882, in Houghton Library, Harvard University, at <http://nrs.harvard.edu/urn-3:FHCL.HOUGH:12249589>, accessed 11 June 2014.

[129] One of these was the famous opera singer and actress Geneviève Ward (1837-1922), whom Wilkinson referred to as his neighbour and family friend: J J G Wilkinson, letter to Henry James, Sr, 11 December 1880, p. 2, in Houghton Library, Harvard University, at <http://nrs.harvard.edu/urn-3:FHCL.HOUGH:12249590>, accessed 11 June 2014.

[130] <http://www.readysteadybook.com/Article.aspx?page=henrysutton>, accessed 17 November 2013.

[131] For information on Wyld's association with Blavatsky see George Wyld, *Notes of My Life* (London: Kegan, Paul, Trench, Trubner & Co., 1903), pp. 71-4. Despite these associations, there is no evidence that Wilkinson was ever involved directly with the Theosophical Society.

[132] The same sentiment led to the involvement of early Swedenborgians in the antislavery movement: see Chapter 2.

[133] According to his biographer, Blyden was 'keenly interested in the views of Swedenborg' on Africa and its people: Hollis R Lynch, *Edward Wilmot Blyden, Pan-Negro Patriot 1832-1912* (London: Oxford University Press, 1967), p. 82. Wilkinson dedicated his book *The African and the True Christian Religion* to Blyden, saying that he had made 'large use' of Blyden's work *Christianity, Islam and the Negro Race*: see James John Garth Wilkinson, *The African and the True Christian Religion, his Magna Charta. A Study in the Writings of Emanuel Swedenborg* (London: James Speirs, 1892), pp. v-viii (p. v). Blyden expressed the view that African Muslims would read

Wilkinson's works 'with avidity and attention': Edward Blyden, letter to J J G Wilkinson, in J J G Wilkinson, *The African and the True Christian Religion*, pp. 243-5 (p. 244). At Wilkinson's invitation, Blyden delivered a lecture to the Swedenborg Society in 1892 in which he highlighted Swedenborg's views on Africa and commended New Churchmen for their early and enthusiastic support of the antislavery movement: *Eighty-Second Report of the Swedenborg Society* (London: Swedenborg Society, 1892), pp. 25-40. Another African deeply impressed by Wilkinson's *The African and the True Christian Religion* was Robert Grendon (*c.* 1867-1949), a mixed-race African poet, educator and social activist who was much influenced by Swedenborg's teaching. He believed in the transformative power of education, saying that 'The native is undergoing tuition, and the educated fellow is destined to play a mighty part in the uplift of his ruder brother': Grant Christison, 'African Jerusalem: The Vision of Robert Grendon', Ph.D. Thesis (University of KwaZulu-Natal, 2007), at <https://www.yumpu. com/en/document/view/19304820/african-jerusalem-the-vision-of-robert-grendon-researchspace->, accessed 18 February 2013. The quote is from Timothy J Couzens, 'Robert Grendon: Irish Traders, Cricket Scores and Paul Kruger's Dreams', in *English in Africa*, vol. 15, no. 2 (October 1988), p. 82.

The World's Parliament of Religions in Chicago in 1893, which was intended to create a dialogue of faiths, was targeted by the New Church which gave several presentations there: L P Mercer (ed.), *The New Jerusalem in the World's Religious Congresses of 1893* (Chicago: Western New-Church Union, 1894).

[134] These entries perhaps relate to Wilkinson's published work on the relationship between spiritualism and insanity: see Chapter 7.

[135] G T, [Obituary], source unidentified, p. 90, in Swedenborg Society Archive A/183 (i).

Chapter Two

[1] Abbé Barruel, *Memoirs, Illustrating the History of Jacobinism*, tr. Robert Clifford, 4 vols. (New York: Cornelius Davis, 1799), vol. IV, pp. 81-2, 93.

[2] Robert Hindmarsh, *Rise and Progress of the New Jerusalem Church, in England, America, and other Parts*, ed. Edward Madeley (London: Hodson & Son, 1861), p. 142.

[3] Peter James Lineham, 'The English Swedenborgians 1770-1840: A Study in the Social Dimensions of Religious Sectarianism', Ph.D. Thesis (University of Sussex, 1978), pp. 13-14.

[4] Marsha Keith Schuchard, 'Swedenborg, Jacobitism, and Freemasonry', in *Swedenborg and His Influence*, ed. Erland J Brock (Bryn Athyn, PA: Academy of the New Church,

1988), pp. 359-79; 'Jacobite and Visionary: the Masonic Journey of Emanuel Swedenborg (1688-1772)', in *Ars Quatuor Coronatorum*, vol. 115 (2003), pp. 33-72.

5   From A Kahl, 'On the Influence of the New Church in Sweden', quoted in R L Tafel, 'Swedenborg and Freemasonry', in *New Jerusalem Messenger* (New York), vol. XVII, no. 17, 27 October 1869, pp. 266-7 (p. 267). See also Edwin S Crandon, 'Swedenborg and Masonry', in *Morning Light*, vol. 31 (1908), pp. 458-9, 469-70, 478-9. It can of course be argued—and indeed Schuchard makes the point—that sectarian historians of the New Church have a vested interest in suppressing any involvement of Swedenborg with Freemasonry.

6   Marsha Keith Schuchard, *Why Mrs Blake Cried: William Blake and the Sexual Basis of Spiritual Wisdom* (London: Century, 2006), pp. 59-83.

7   Cyriel Odhner Sigstedt, *The Swedenborg Epic* (London: Swedenborg Society, 1981), p. 189; Emanuel Swedenborg, *Spiritual Diary*, tr. George Bush, John Smithson and James F Buss, 5 vols. (London: James Speirs, 1883-1902), vol. V, §6081, p. 202.

8   Marsha Keith Schuchard, 'Dr. Samuel Jacob Falk: A Sabbatian Adventurer in the Masonic Underground', in *Millenarianism and Messianism in Early Modern European Culture: Jewish Messianism in the Early Modern World*, ed. M D Goldish and R H Popkin (Dordrecht: Kluwer Press, 2001), pp. 203-26; Hermann Adler, 'The Baal Shem of London', in *Transactions of the Jewish Historical Society of England*, vol. 5 (1902-5), pp. 148-73; Gordon P G Hills, 'Notes on Some Contemporary References to Dr. Falk, the Baal Shem of London, in the Rainsford MSS. at the British Museum', in *Transactions of the Jewish Historical Society of England*, vol. 8 (1915-17), pp. 122-8.

9   Lineham, 'The English Swedenborgians', p. 44; Sigstedt, *Swedenborg Epic*, p. 383.

10   Christopher Walton, *Notes and Materials for an Adequate Biography of the Celebrated Divine and Theosopher William Law* (London: The Author, 1854), p. 597.

11   Thomas Hartley's preface to Emanuel Swedenborg, *A Theosophic Lucubration on the Nature of Influx*, tr. Thomas Hartley (London: M Lewis, 1770), p. xx.

12   The significance of these individuals is discussed later.

13   Schuchard, *Why Mrs Blake Cried*, pp. 144-5.

14   Alfred Gabay, 'The Reverend Jacob Duché and the Advent of the New Church in England', in *The New Philosophy*, vol. 109 (July-December, 2006), p. 381.

15   Lineham, 'The English Swedenborgians', p. 49.

16   Robert Hindmarsh, in a letter to G J Billberg of 28 November 1796, noted that 'During the life-time of Swedenborg, I believe that only two or three individuals cordially embraced his writings; among whom was the late Rev. Mr Thomas Hartley, who

visited and corresponded with him': Swedenborg Society Archive K/143.

[17] Except where otherwise indicated, biographical information on Clowes is taken from Theodore Compton, *The Life and Correspondence of the Reverend John Clowes M.A.* (London: Longmans, Green & Co., 1874).

[18] Thomas Robinson, *A Remembrancer and Recorder of Facts and Documents illustrative of the Genius of the New Jerusalem Dispensation* (Manchester: Robinson, 1864), p. 12.

[19] Ibid., p. 246.

[20] Joy Hancox, *The Queen's Chamelion: The Life of John Byrom—A Study of Conflicting Loyalties* (London: Jonathan Cape, 1994).

[21] Ibid., p. 15. Montpellier at that time was a premier medical school which was known for its iatrochemical approach that was based upon Paracelsian medicine; see Allen G Debus, *The French Paracelsians* (Cambridge: Cambridge University Press, 1991), pp. 143-6. It had not yet become famous for the vitalist medicine that was promoted by Boissier de Sauvages (1706-67) in the 1730s and 1740s; see Elizabeth A Williams, *A Cultural History of Medical Vitalism in Enlightenment Montpellier* (Aldershot: Ashgate, 2003), pp. 80 ff.

[22] Aside from its purely practical value, the use of encrypted and symbolic writing has fascinated people with esoteric inclinations throughout the ages, whether as a means of keeping esoteric knowledge secret, as a means of communication with spiritual powers, or in the search for an ancient, primal, symbolic language such as that which was thought to be contained in Egyptian hieroglyphics. Examples include the steganography of Johannes Trithemius (1462-1516), discussed in Noel L Brann, *Trithemius and Magical Theology* (New York: SUNY Press, 1999), pp. 135-47. Isaac Pitman (1813-97), originator of the famous Pitman shorthand, was a Swedenborgian; see Alfred Baker, *The Life of Sir Isaac Pitman* (London: Pitman & Sons, 1908), pp. 26-7.

[23] Amongst Byrom's pupils were Charles and John Wesley, with whom he discussed theological issues: Hancox, *The Queen's Chamelion*, p. 215.

[24] Stephen Hobhouse, *William Law and Eighteenth Century Quakerism* (London: George Allen & Unwin, 1927), pp. 112, 115.

[25] Hancox, *The Queen's Chamelion*, p. 125.

[26] John Byrom, *The Private Journal and Literary Remains of John Byrom*, ed. Richard Parkinson, 2 vols. (Manchester: Chetham Society, 1854-6), vol. I, part I, pp. 616-19; vol. II, part I, pp. 106, 112-13. These conversations took place in 1735-7, which is the

period during which Law became a follower of Boehme: Arthur Versluis, 'Law, William', in *Dictionary of Gnosis and Western Esotericism*, ed. Wouter J Hanegraaff, Antoine Faivre, Roelof van den Broek et al. (Leiden: Brill, 2006), pp. 677-9. The *Dictionary of Gnosis and Western Esotericism* is hereafter referred to as *DGWE*.

27   *A Catalogue of the Library of the late John Byrom* (London: privately published, 1848).

28   Byrom, *The Poems of John Byrom*, ed. Adolphus William Ward, 3 vols. (Manchester: Chetham Society, 1894-1912), vol. II, part II, p. 600.

29   Paul Kléber Monod, *Solomon's Secret Arts. The Occult in the Age of Enlightenment* (New Haven and London: Yale University Press, 2013), p. 214.

30   Adam McLean, comment on *Alchemy Website*, at <http://www.alchemywebsite.com/a-archive_nov99.html>, accessed 5 May 2011. The cryptic markings include, for example, 'Khun. tab. 2' and 'Fl. Tom. II. p235', which are interpreted by McLean as references to illustrations in Heinrich Khunrath's 'Amphitheatrum', and Robert Fludd's 'Utriusque cosmi...historia Tome II'. Joy Hancox, who discovered the drawings, has interpreted them as including blueprints for the Globe Theatre, the Rose and other Elizabethan theatres, with features that linked back to older buildings including Westminster Abbey and King's College Chapel in Cambridge and even further back to the imagined construction of the Temple of Solomon: Joy Hancox, *The Byrom Collection: and the Globe Theatre Mystery* (London: Jonathan Cape, 1997). This interpretation of the drawings has been dismissed by other scholars. For example, see reviews of the earlier hardback edition of *The Byrom Collection* (which had a slightly different title but the same content): John Orrell, 'The Byrom Collection: Renaissance Thought, the Royal Society and the Building of the Globe Theatre', in *Modern Language Review*, vol. 88, no. 4 (October 1993), pp. 943-5; Michael Hunter, '*The Byrom Collection: Renaissance Thought, the Royal Society and the Building of the Globe Theatre* by Joy Hancox', in *English Historical Review*, vol. 110, no. 437 (June 1995), pp. 751-2. Unfortunately these drawings remain in private ownership, so they are not readily available for scrutiny by other scholars.

31   In Byrom, *The Private Journal*, vol. I, part I, Byrom recounts several meetings with Stukeley, both at the Royal Society (pp. 101, 111, 118, 122, 204) and, in 1726, at Stukeley's home (p. 203).

32   The two major biographies of Stukeley, which provided background material for this account, are Stuart Piggott, *William Stukeley: An Eighteenth-Century Antiquarian* (London: Thames and Hudson, 1985), and David Haycock, *William Stukeley: Science,*

Religion and Archaeology in Eighteenth-Century England (Woodbridge: Boydell Press, 2002).

33 Abury was commonly used as the name for Avebury.

34 David Boyd Haycock, 'Ancient Egypt in 17th and 18th Century England', in Peter Ucko and Timothy Champion (eds.), *The Wisdom of Ancient Egypt: Changing Visions through the Ages* (London: UCL Press, 2003), pp. 133-60; Antoine Faivre, 'Egyptomany', in *DGWE*, pp. 328-30.

35 Haycock, 'Ancient Egypt', p. 152.

36 Ibid., p. 145.

37 W C Lukis, *The Family Memoirs of the Rev. William Stukeley, M.D. and the Antiquarian and other Correspondence of William Stukeley, Roger & Samuel Gale, etc.* (London: Whittaker & Co., 1882), p. 220.

38 Ralph Cudworth, *The True Intellectual System of the Universe*, 2 vols. (Andover and New York: Gould & Newman, 1837-8), vol. I, pp. 721 ff. This Christianizing tendency remained a prominent feature of the neo-Druidry that was established in the late eighteenth century. Ronald Hutton, *Blood and Mistletoe. The History of the Druids in Britain* (New Haven: Yale University Press, 2009), pp. 86-102, discusses Stukeley's role in the development of neo-Druidry. Neo-Druidry is discussed from the perspective of the Western esoteric tradition by Joanne E Pearson, 'Neopaganism', in *DGWE*, pp. 828-34 (pp. 831-2).

39 Lukis, *Family Memoirs of Stukeley*, p. 78.

40 Haycock, 'Ancient Egypt', p. 140.

41 Compton, *Clowes*, pp. 8-9.

42 Exactly when Clowes first read William Law is unclear, though Clowes's later recollection is that this was after he had taken up the post at St John's (Compton, *Clowes*, p. 8). This must have been very early in his ministry; his patron Edward Byrom installed Clowes at St John's with the specific intention of promoting Law's doctrines, and it is recorded in Robinson, *Remembrancer and Recorder*, p. 247, that Clowes's sermons reflected Law's theosophy very early in his ministry.

43 John Newton, letter to Richard Houghton, 18 November 1762, in Byrom, *The Private Journal*, vol. II part II, pp. 637-9.

44 Compton, *Clowes*, p. 16.

45 Ibid.

46 In Swedenborg's thinking, the *Divinum Humanum* is the form of the Lord that is the template for heaven, the created cosmos and human beings, each of which

corresponds with all the others.

[47] Compton, *Clowes*, p. 18.

[48] Ibid., pp. 18-20.

[49] Ibid., p. 25. We have no date for this meeting, which must have taken place between Clowes's meeting with Houghton in 1773 and Hartley's death in 1784.

[50] Ibid., p. 26.

[51] Ibid., p. 25. It is noteworthy that Hartley himself had remained a cleric within the Anglican Church despite his adoption of Swedenborg's theosophy; apparently Swedenborg had not seen any problem with this during their association.

[52] Ibid., p. 39.

[53] John Clowes, letter to Robert Hindmarsh, 29 September 1799, in Compton, *Clowes*, pp. 63-4. This letter was gleefully reproduced by nineteenth-century spiritualists, under the title of 'Rev. John Clowes a Spiritualist', in the supplement to *The British Spiritual Telegraph*, vol. III, no. 9 (1 April 1859), p. 189.

[54] Carl Theophilus Odhner, *Annals of the New Church with a chronological account of the life of Emanuel Swedenborg* (Bryn Athyn, PA: Academy of the New Church, 1904), vol. I, pp. 117, 120.

[55] This area of Northern England, now known as Greater Manchester, has a long history of esotericism that has not been investigated systematically. John Dee lived in Manchester from 1596 to 1605 as warden of Christ's College. Dee's stay in Manchester is particularly well covered by Charlotte Fell-Smith, *John Dee (1527-1608)* (London: Constable, 1909). Based on Dee's diaries, Fell-Smith concludes that books from his library were 'constantly in request' during his time in Manchester. This included the use of Dee's library by people who were searching for witches, leading to the trial and execution of the Lancashire witches at Pendle Hill in 1612. Pendle Hill was also the site where George Fox, founder of the Quakers, had his vision in 1652: see Rufus M Jones, *The Remnant* (London: Swarthmore Press, 1920), p. 130. It is possible that Dee left a legacy that helped to lay the foundation for the later Behmenist and Swedenborgian movements there.

[56] John Harland and T T Wilkinson, *Lancashire Folk-Lore: Illustrative of the Superstitious Beliefs and Practices, Local Customs and Usages of the People of the County Palatine* (London: John Heywood, 1882), pp. 49-61.

[57] Harland and Wilkinson, *Lancashire Folk-Lore*, pp. 105-6.

[58] For example, a nineteenth-century wise man in Worsley, Lancashire known as 'Owd Rollinson' owned Agrippa's *Three Books of Occult Philosophy* in J Freake's 1651

translation; William Lilly's *Christian Astrology* (1659); John Gadbury's *Thesaurus Astrologiae* (1674); Ebn Shemaya's *The Star* (1839); Zadkiel's *Grammar of Astrology* (1849); and Christopher Cook's *A Plea for Urania* (1854): see Harland and Wilkinson, *Lancashire Folk-Lore*, p. 124. 'Cunning-folk' are discussed by Owen Davies, 'Cunning-Folk in England and Wales during the Eighteenth and Nineteenth Centuries', in *Rural History*, vol. 8 (April 1997), pp. 91-107.

59 Ralph Mather, 'A List of some Names and the Places of Abode of Persons, in whose Minds the Light of God has Arisen, or is graciously rising', in Walton, *Notes and Materials*, pp. 595-6. 'Teresa' is presumably a reference to Saint Teresa of Ávila (1515-82), a Carmelite mystic.

60 Clarke Garrett, *Origins of the Shakers: From the Old World to the New World* (Baltimore: Johns Hopkins University Press, 1998), p. 267.

61 Some Moravian communities, which were popular in Lancashire, also developed from these Behmenist groups: Garrett, *Origins of the Shakers*, p. 145.

62 A Member of the Old Church, *An Inquiry into the Commission and Doctrine of the New Apostle, Emanuel Swedenborg* (Manchester: Thomson, 1794), p. 14. Antoinette Bourignon de la Porte (1616-80) was a Flemish mystic who had followers in Britain in the late seventeenth and early eighteenth centuries: see John Cockburn, *Bourignianism Detected: or the Delusions and Errors of Antonia Bourignon and her Growing Sect* (London: Brome, 1698). On p. 14 of *An Inquiry...*, the author refers to 'Mrs. Leese' as a Shaker; this is likely to be an erroneous reference to Ann Lee (1736-84), the leader of the Shaker movement.

63 James Dakeyne, 'Samuel Dawson', in *The New Church Magazine* (London), vol. IX, no. 103 (July 1890), pp. 316-25. Dawson claimed that the medicinal properties of individual plants had been revealed to him during an intense spiritual experience, and he had 'a somewhat extensive practice among the working classes', p. 322. He also sold 'mystic poultices'.

64 Compton, *Clowes*, p. 22.

65 Ibid., p. 37.

66 Ibid., p. 38.

67 Ibid., p. 41.

68 Hindmarsh, *Rise and Progress*, p. 23.

69 James Hogg, *De Quincey and His Friends* (London: Sampson Low, Marston and Company, 1895), p. 29.

70 Compton, *Clowes*, p. 84.

71 Hindmarsh wrote articles condemning practices that stemmed from the Western esoteric tradition; for example, see Robert Hindmarsh, 'Observations on Astrology, the Science of Palmistry, and the Transmigration of Souls', in *The Intellectual Repository for the New Church* (London), vol. V, no. XXXIX (January-March 1819), pp. 305-14.

72 Lineham, 'The English Swedenborgians', p. 136.

73 Carl Th. Odhner, *Robert Hindmarsh: A Biography* (Philadelphia: Academy Book Room, 1895), p. 6.

74 Hindmarsh, *Rise and Progress*, p. 23.

75 Ibid., p. 67.

76 William White, *Emanuel Swedenborg: His Life and Writings*, 2 vols. (London: Simpkin, Marshall & Co., 1867), vol. II, pp. 601-2.

77 Ibid., p. 603. The New Church minutes for this period were destroyed. Early extracts from *Conjugial Love*, which were translated into English by John Augustus Tulk, contained sexually explicit references that were condemned by the conservative members of the New Church. There is good evidence that concubinage was supported not only in theory but in practice by some New Church members at that time: see E P Thompson, *Witness Against the Beast* (Cambridge: Cambridge University Press, 1993), pp. 136-8.

78 E P Thompson, *Witness Against the Beast*, p. 140. The secretary of this Society was Henry Servanté, supported by John Augustus Tulk (1756-1845), Benedict Chastanier (1739-1816?), Carl F Nordenskiöld (1754-1828) and Carl B Wadström (1746-99).

79 'To the Public', in *The New-Jerusalem Magazine, or A Treasury of Celestial, Spiritual, and Natural, Knowledge* (June 1790), pp. 255-6.

80 White, *Swedenborg*, vol. II, p. 610.

81 Odhner, *Hindmarsh*, p. 46. Cowherd declared himself to be 'the most extraordinary man living'. He had established a breakaway group, the 'Bible Christians', who were required to be strict vegetarians and teetotallers.

82 Ibid., p. 55.

83 White, *Swedenborg*, vol. II, p. 612. In 1860 White was involved in a serious dispute with the Swedenborg Society in London when he offered spiritualist books for sale in the Society's bookshop, of which he was the proprietor at the time. This is discussed in detail in Chapter 5.

84 John Benoit de Mainauduc, *The Lectures of J. B. de Mainauduc, M.D.* (London: Printed for the Executrix, 1798), pp. iii, iv.

85 Schuchard, 'Dr. Samuel Jacob Falk', p. 216; John Timbs, *English Eccentrics and*

Eccentricities, 2 vols. (London: Richard Bentley, 1866), vol. I, p. 136. John Hunter's vitalism is discussed in detail in Chapter 6.

[86] Tim Fulford, 'Conducting the Vital Fluid: The Politics and Poetics of Mesmerism in the 1790s', in *Studies in Romanticism*, vol. 43, no. 1 (2004), pp. 57-78 (p. 67).

[87] Robert W Rix, 'Healing the Spirit: William Blake and Magnetic Religion', in *Romanticism on the Net* (online journal), no. 25 (February 2002), at <http://www.erudit.org/revue/ron/2002/v/n25/006011ar.html>, accessed 31 May 2010.

[88] Fulford, 'Conducting the Vital Fluid', p. 67.

[89] Austin Dobson, *At Prior Park and Other Papers* (London: Chatto & Windus, 1912), p. 101.

[90] Philippa Faulks and Robert L D Cooper, *The Masonic Magician. The Life and Death of Count Cagliostro and his Egyptian Rite* (London: Watkins, 2008), p. 97.

[91] Dobson, *At Prior Park*, p. 108.

[92] Mary Pratt, *A List of a Few Cures Performed by Mr and Mrs De Loutherbourg, of Hammersmith Terrace, Without Medicine* (London: The Author, 1789), p. 9.

[93] Dobson, *At Prior Park*, p. 119; Anthony Pasquin, *Memoirs of the Royal Academicians* (London: H D Symonds, 1796), p. 80.

[94] Nicolas Flamel (*c.* 1330-1418) was a French manuscript copier who amassed a considerable and unexplained fortune. He was reputed to have been an alchemist, but the works attributed to him were written much later; see Frank Greiner, 'Flamel, Nicholas', in *DGWE*, pp. 370-1. According to Marsha Keith Schuchard, Tulk's inscribed author's copy of the *Testament of Nicholas Flamel* (London: Hodson, 1806) is held with a collection from the library of Eric Benzelius in Linköping, Sweden; see Schuchard, *Why Mrs Blake Cried*, p. 401 n. 5.

[95] Schuchard, *Why Mrs Blake Cried*, p. 316.

[96] The Book of Enoch is an ancient Jewish text that was known to early Christians but then lost to the West until the eighteenth century. The first English translation was published in 1821. It is remarkable for its account of the origin of evil and of mystical visions. See Margaret Barker, *The Lost Prophet. The Book of Enoch and its influence on Christianity* (London: SPCK, 1988); *The Book of Enoch*, tr. R H Charles (Mineola, NY: Dover, 2007).

[97] Schuchard, *Why Mrs Blake Cried*, pp. 316-17. The association between Hermes and Enoch (identified also with the Koranic Idris) had been made in the seventh century by the Hermetic Sabian sect in Harran, Northwestern Mesopotamia; see Brian P Copenhaver, *Hermetica: The Greek* Corpus Hermeticum *and the Latin* Asclepius *in*

a New English Translation, with Notes and Introduction (Cambridge: Cambridge University Press, 1992), pp. xlv-xlvi.

98 Adam McLean, 'General Rainsford. An Alchemical and Rosicrucian Enthusiast', in *Hermetic Journal*, vol. 13 (1990), pp. 129-34.

99 Marsha Keith Schuchard, 'Blake's "Mr. Femality": Freemasonry, Espionage, and the Double-Sexed', in *Studies in Eighteenth-Century Culture*, vol. 22 (1993), pp. 51-71 (p. 64).

100 Benedict Chastanier (1739-1816?). Sources give different dates for Chastanier: Lineham, 'The English Swedenborgians', p. 141 gives 1739-1818; Alfred J Gabay, *The Covert Enlightenment: Eighteenth-Century Counterculture and its Aftermath* (West Chester, PA: Swedenborg Foundation, 2005), p. 9 gives *c*. 1728-1806; Jean-François Mayer, 'Swedenborgian Traditions', in *DGWE*, pp. 1105-10 (p. 1107), gives 1739-1816? I have opted for the dates given in the *DGWE*, which are close to those of Lineham.

101 Monod, *Solomon's Secret Arts*, p. 311.

102 James Hyde, 'Benedict Chastanier and the Illuminati of Avignon', in *The New-Church Review* (Boston), vol. 14, no. 2 (April 1907), pp. 181-205 (p. 205).

103 Ibid., p. 186. According to Hyde (p. 186), Chastanier translated Georg von Welling's alchemical text *Opus Mago-Cabbalisticum et Theosophicum*.

104 Hyde, 'Chastanier' p. 187.

105 Robert Rix, 'William Blake and the Radical Swedenborgians', in *Esoterica*, vol. V (2003) p. 103, at <http://www.esoteric.msu.edu/VolumeV/Blake.htm>, accessed 29 January 2016; Schuchard, *Why Mrs Blake Cried*, p. 167. Dr Husband Messiter (*c*. 1720-85), whom we have met as a visitor and physician to the elderly Swedenborg, collaborated with Chastanier in this venture: see Gabay, 'The Reverend Jacob Duché', p. 391. The relationship between the London Universal Society that was founded in 1776, and the later Universal Society for Promotion of the New Jerusalem Church that was founded in 1789, is unclear, but Chastanier was a leading member of both societies and it is likely that the second society was a continuation of the first, but with a new constitution.

106 Marsha Keith Schuchard, 'The Secret Masonic History of Blake's Swedenborg Society', in *Blake, an Illustrated Quarterly*, vol. 26, no. 2 (Fall 1992), pp. 40-8. That Chastanier's 'system of Illuminated Theosophists' was introduced into London in 1767 is supported by Masonic sources: see Gordon P G Hills, 'Notes on the Rainsford Papers in the British Museum', in *Ars Quatuor Coronatorum*, vol. 26 (1913), pp. 93-129 (p. 110).

[107] Gabay, 'The Reverend Jacob Duché', p. 391. Robert Rix, 'William Blake and the Radical Swedenborgians', comments that, at the time of the First General Conference of the New Jerusalem Church in 1789, 'the backbone of Swedenborgianism in England was the Universal Society' (p. 107).

[108] Rix, 'William Blake and the Radical Swedenborgians', pp. 105-6.

[109] Lineham, 'The English Swedenborgians', p. 185.

[110] Ibid., p. 174.

[111] William Spence, *Essays in Divinity and Physic...with an exposition of animal magnetism and magic* (London: Robert Hindmarsh, 1792), p. 56.

[112] Ibid., pp. 52-3.

[113] Ibid., p. 54.

[114] Gabay, 'The Reverend Jacob Duché', pp. 386-7.

[115] Clarke Garrett, 'Swedenborg and the Mystical Enlightenment in Late Eighteenth-Century England', in *Journal of the History of Ideas*, vol. 45, no. 1 (1984), pp. 67-81 (p. 72). John Payne (?1700-87) was a bookseller who later became Chief Accountant at the Bank of England: see Samuel Johnson, *The Rambler*, 3 vols. (Philadelphia: Abraham Small, 1831), vol. I, p. 2.

[116] Jacob Duché (1738-98) was a friend of John Clowes, having been introduced through mutual friends. The two men were united in their opposition to a sectarian Swedenborgian church separate from mainstream Anglicanism: see Lineham, 'The English Swedenborgians', p. 165. On a visit to Manchester, Duché took a particular interest in the reported spiritual experiences of the Lancashire Swedenborgians: see Compton, *Clowes*, p. 37.

[117] Garrett, 'Swedenborg and the Mystical Enlightenment', p. 73.

[118] M L Danilewicz, ' "The King of the New Israel": Thaddeus Grabianka (1740-1807)', in *Oxford Slavonic Papers*, new series, vol. 1 (1968), pp. 49-73. See also Gabay, *Covert Enlightenment*, pp. 55-62; Nicholas Goodrick-Clarke, *The Western Esoteric Traditions. A Historical Introduction* (Oxford: Oxford University Press, 2008), pp. 146-7.

[119] Jan A M Snoek, 'Illuminés d'Avignon', in *DGWE*, pp. 597-600.

[120] Jan A M Snoek, 'Pernety, Antoine-Joseph', in *DGWE*, pp. 940-2.

[121] Clarke Garrett, *Respectable Folly: Millenarians and the French Revolution in France and England* (Baltimore and London: John Hopkins University Press, 1975), pp. 101-2.

[122] Garrett, *Respectable Folly*, p. 118.

[123] Hyde, 'Chastanier', p. 194.

[124] Lineham, 'The English Swedenborgians', p. 198; Garrett, 'Swedenborg and the Mystical Enlightenment', p. 75. At this meeting, Bousie was asked by his fellow Masons to gather information for them about Falk, Swedenborg and the alchemist and Fellow of the Royal Society James Price (1752-83) who had recently committed suicide by poisoning in front of a group of chemists who had asked him to give a practical demonstration of the transmutation of mercury to gold, which he claimed to have achieved: see Gordon P G Hills, 'Notes on the Rainsford Papers', pp. 97, 105, 106.

[125] Hindmarsh, *Rise and Progress*, pp. 41-2. According to Schuchard, Hindmarsh was himself initiated into Grabianka's Masonic system: Schuchard, 'The Secret Masonic History', p. 47 n. 35.

[126] Hindmarsh, *Rise and Progress*, p. 45.

[127] Ibid.

[128] Ibid., p. 47.

[129] Garrett, 'Swedenborg and the Mystical Enlightenment', p. 76.

[130] Chastanier, letter to General Rainsford, July 1785, cited in Garrett, 'Swedenborg and the Mystical Enlightenment', p. 75. This view was reflected in the pages of *The New-Jerusalem Magazine* (1 April 1790), pp. 175-6 where it was noted that the Avignon Society had 'degenerated' into worship of the Virgin Mary and belief in the Athanasian Creed.

[131] Garrett, 'Swedenborg and the Mystical Enlightenment', p. 76.

[132] William Bryan, *A Testimony of the Spirit of Truth concerning Richard Brothers. . .* (London, 1795); John Wright, *A Revealed Knowledge of Some Things That Will Be Speedily Fulfilled in the World. . .for the Good of All Men* (London, 1794).

[133] Hyde, 'Chastanier', p. 196.

[134] Fulford, 'Conducting the Vital Fluid', pp. 69-70; Hindmarsh, *Rise and Progress*, p. 47.

[135] John Timbs, *English Eccentrics and Eccentricities*, vol. I, p. 208.

[136] Wright, *A Revealed Knowledge*, p. 19.

[137] Information on the Stockholm Society is from Gabay, *Covert Enlightenment*, pp. 85-92.

[138] Odhner, *Hindmarsh*, p. 12.

[139] Wadström's activities are discussed by P L Johnson, *Carl Bernhard Wadström: In Search of the New Jerusalem*, Swedenborg Society Transactions no. 9 (London: Swedenborg Society, 2013).

[140] The Marquis de Thomé, like many other followers of Swedenborg, distanced himself from

the activities of Mesmer, who he believed was working in blind ignorance of the principles outlined by Swedenborg, and who was therefore ineffectual or even dangerous: see Marquis de Thomé, 'Remarks by the Marquis de Thomé, On an Assertion of the Commissioners appointed by the King [of France] for the Examination of Animal Magnetism', in *The Intellectual Repository*, vol. 2, no. XII (October-December 1814), pp. 191-7.

141 Gabay, *Covert Enlightenment*, p. 88.

142 Garrett, 'Swedenborg and the Mystical Enlightenment', p. 77.

143 A reviewer in the *Monthly Review* (May 1787), quoted in Rix, 'William Blake and the Radical Swedenborgians', p. 99.

144 Fulford, 'Conducting the Vital Fluid', pp. 57-8.

145 The wider context of the Masonic conspiracy theory after the French Revolution is discussed by Norman Cohn, *Warrant for Genocide: The Myth of a Jewish World-Conspiracy and the Protocols of the Elders of Zion* (London: Eyre & Spottiswoode, 1967), pp. 25-7; and Daniel Pipes, *Conspiracy: How the Paranoid Style Flourishes and Where It Comes From* (New York, Free Press, 1997), pp. 66-72.

146 Abbé Barruel, *Memoirs*, vol. IV, pp. 81-2.

147 Ibid., p. 93.

148 John Robison, *Proofs of a Conspiracy against All the Religions and Governments of Europe, Carried on in the Secret Meetings of the Free Masons, Illuminati, and Reading Societies* (Edinburgh: William Creech, 1797), p. 6.

149 Seth Payson, *Proofs of the Real Existence, and Dangerous Tendency, of Illuminism* (Charlestown: The Author, 1802).

150 Rix, 'William Blake and the Radical Swedenborgians', pp. 109-10.

151 Hindmarsh, *Rise and Progress*, p. 132.

152 Odhner, *Hindmarsh*, p. 13; Hindmarsh, *Rise and Progress*, p. 144.

153 Placido de Titi, *Astronomy and Elementary Philosophy, translated from the Latin of Placidus de Titus...the whole carefully revised by M. Sibly* (London: W Justins, 1789). Placido (1603-68) popularized the system of astrological houses that was named Placidian after him. It has been alleged that Sibly plagiarized this translation from a manuscript that he had borrowed: see Martin Gansten, 'Placidean teachings in early nineteenth-century Britain: John Worsdale and Thomas Oxley', in *Astrologies: Plurality and Diversity. Proceedings of the Eighth Annual Sophia Centre Conference 2010*, ed. Nicholas Campion and Liz Greene (Lampeter: Sophia Centre Press, 2011), at <http://www.martingansten.com/pdf/WorsdaleOxley2011.pdf>, pp. 2-3 n., accessed 25 September 2011.

[154] Placido de Titi, *Astronomy and Elementary Philosophy*, p. 4.

[155] Ebenezer Sibly, *A Key to Physic, and the Occult Sciences. Opening to mental view, The SYSTEM and ORDER of the Interior and Exterior HEAVENS; The analogy betwixt ANGELS, and SPIRITS of MEN...* (London: Champante and Whitrow, 1795; 5th edn. London: G Jones, 1814); Allen G Debus, 'Scientific Truth and Occult Tradition: The Medical World of Ebenezer Sibly (1751-1799)', in *Medical History*, vol. 26, no. 3 (July 1982), pp. 259-78. Sibly's contribution to medical thinking in late eighteenth-century England is discussed in detail in Chapter 6.

[156] Ebenezer Sibly, *A New and Complete Illustration of the Celestial Science of Astrology* (London: printed for the proprietor, and sold by W Nicoll, M Sibly, and E Sibly, 1784). Some later editions appeared with a different title, e.g., *A New and Complete Illustration of the Occult Sciences: or, the Art of foretelling future Events and Contingencies...in Four Parts* (London: printed for the author, 1790).

[157] Gordon P G Hills, 'Notes on some Masonic Personalities at the end of the Eighteenth Century', in *Ars Quatuor Coronatorum*, vol. 25 (1912), pp. 141-64 (p. 158); Adam McLean, 'Bacstrom's Rosicrucian society', in *Hermetic Journal*, no. 6 (1979), reprinted at <http://www.levity.com/alchemy/bacstrm1.html>, accessed 15 March 2011.

[158] McLean, 'Bacstrom's Rosicrucian society'. For more on Bacstrom see Monod, *Solomon's Secret Arts*, pp. 281-8.

[159] Lineham, 'The English Swedenborgians', pp. 141-2.

[160] Patrick Curry, *A Confusion of Prophets: Victorian and Edwardian Astrology* (London: Collins and Brown, 1992), pp. 48-9.

[161] Edward Bulwer-Lytton, *Zanoni*, 2 vols. (Philadelphia: J B Lippincott & Co., 1862), vol. I, p. ix.

[162] Joscelyn Godwin, 'Bulwer-Lytton, Edward George', in *DGWE*, pp. 213-17.

[163] Curry, *A Confusion of Prophets*, p. 49. A letter from Coleridge to Denley, 5 March 1818, which is not included in the standard collections of Coleridge's letters, was recently sold privately by auction at Christie's in London. In this letter Coleridge asks Denley for books on 'Star-craft, Witch-craft, Necromancy, Ghosts and the like': See <http://www.christies.com/LotFinder/LotDetailsPrintable.aspx?intObjectID=266033>, accessed 19 June 2011.

[164] Joscelyn Godwin, *The Theosophical Enlightenment* (Albany, NY: SUNY Press, 1994), p. 118.

[165] Ibid., p. 115.

166   Donald Tyson, 'On the *Occult Philosophy*', in Henry Cornelius Agrippa of Nettesheim, *Three Books of Occult Philosophy*, tr. James Freake, ed. Donald Tyson (Woodbury, MN: Llewellyn, 1993), pp. xxxix-xliii (p. xl); Alison Butler, 'Beyond Attribution: The Importance of Barrett's Magus', in *Journal for the Academic Study of Magic*, no. 1 (2003), pp. 7-32 (p. 21).

167   Robert A Gilbert, 'Barrett, Francis', in *DGWE*, pp. 163-4.

168   Lines, 'Charles Augustus Tulk', pp. 5-6.

169   Clowes, letter to Charles Augustus Tulk, 22 March 1813, in Compton, *Clowes*, p. 137.

170   R McCully, 'Benedict Chastanier: An Early New Church Worthy', in *The New Church Magazine*, vol. IX, no. 107 (November 1890), p. 530.

171   Ibid. McCully has here translated into English part of a footnote from the 'Discours Préliminaire' in *Abrégé des Ouvrages d'Em. Swedenborg* (Stockholm, 1788), pp. lxvi-lxvii (McCully erroneously gives the source as p. lxv). McCully is clearly of the persuasion that Chastanier was the author of the *Abrégé*, but it is usually credited as being the work of Daillant de la Touche.

172   H J Jackson, ' "Swedenborg's *Meaning* is the truth": Coleridge, Tulk, and Swedenborg', in *In Search of the Absolute—Essays on Swedenborg and Literature*, ed. Stephen McNeilly (London: Swedenborg Society, 2004), pp. 1-13 (p. 2); Lines, 'Charles Augustus Tulk', p. 12.

173   Jackson, 'Coleridge, Tulk, and Swedenborg', p. 3; Thomas McFarland, 'Coleridge and the Charge of Political Apostasy', in *Coleridge's Biographia Literaria: Text and Meaning*, ed. Frederick Burwick (Columbus: Ohio State University Press, 1989), pp. 191-232 (p. 215).

174   S T Coleridge, *Marginalia*, ed. H J Jackson and George Whalley, 6 vols. (Princeton: Princeton University Press, 1980-2001), vol. V, p. 427, quoted in Jackson, 'Coleridge, Tulk, and Swedenborg', p. 7.

175   Friedemann Horn, *Schelling and Swedenborg: Mysticism and German Idealism*, tr. George F Dole (West Chester, PA: Swedenborg Foundation, 1997).

176   F W J Schelling, *Clara, or, On Nature's Connection to the Spirit World*, tr. Fiona Steinkamp (New York: SUNY Press, 2002), pp. 55-6.

177   Schelling, *Stuttgart Lectures* 481, quoted in Horn, *Schelling and Swedenborg*, p. 79.

178   Coleridge, letter to Charles Augustus Tulk, 20 January 1820, in *Collected Letters of Samuel Taylor Coleridge*, ed. Earl Leslie Griggs, 6 vols. (Oxford: Clarendon Press, 1956-9), vol. V, p. 19.

179   Jackson, 'Coleridge, Tulk, and Swedenborg', pp. 2-3.

McFarland, 'Coleridge', p. 215.

181 'On the Fidelity of the Translations of the Writings of Swedenborg, and on an Attempt to introduce into the New Church the Doctrine of the Ancient Docetae or Phantasiasts, and the Opinions of Modern Idealists. No. II', in *The Intellectual Repository*, New Series, no. XIX (July 1828), pp. 185-95 (pp. 188-90). Nicolas Malebranche (1638-1715), a French Carthusian monk, was a substantial influence on Berkeley; it is likely that the two men met: see A A Luce, *Berkeley and Malebranche: A Study in the Origins of Berkeley's Thought* (London: Oxford University Press, 1934), pp. 1-12, 208-10.

182 Charles Augustus Tulk, letter to J F I Tafel, 15 June 1840, in Swedenborg Society Archive K/4.

183 Charles Augustus Tulk, *Aphorisms on the Laws of Creation, as displayed in the Correspondencies that subsist between Mind and Matter* (London: William Newbery, 1843), pp. 27-8.

184 Charles Augustus Tulk, letter to his 'pupils', 12 September 1832 , in a bound hand-written volume, 'Tulk's Continuation of Spiritual Christianity and Correspondence', in Swedenborg Society Archive A/9.

185 Charles Augustus Tulk, *Aphorisms*, p. 34.

186 Ibid., p. 16.

187 Charles Augustus Tulk, 'To the Editors of the New Jerusalem Magazine', in *The New Jerusalem Magazine and Theological Inspector* (London: Thomas Goyder), no. 6 (June 1828), pp. 188-99 (p. 191).

188 Charles Augustus Tulk, *Spiritual Christianity. Collected from the Theological Works of Emanuel Swedenborg; with an Illustrative Commentary* (London: William Newbery, 1846), pp. 9-10.

189 Ibid., p. 185.

190 Ibid.

191 Kenneth P Winkler, *Berkeley: An Interpretation* (Oxford: Clarendon Press, 1989), p. 138. Berkeley recognized the difficulty of this position, which by extension means that nothing exists unless it is perceived. He dealt with this by developing the notion that perception can be not only by man, but also by God who is omnipresent: see G J Warnock, *Berkeley* (Oxford: Blackwell, 1982), pp. 86-109. This begs the question of the means by which God 'perceives'.

192 Charles Augustus Tulk, *Spiritual Christianity*, p. 182.

193 Charles Augustus Tulk, 'Remarks Respecting Double Consciousness, &c.' (dated 8

October 1845), in *The Intellectual Repository*, vol. VI, no. 71 (November 1845), pp. 418-21 (p. 420).

194 John Clowes, letter, in *The Intellectual Repository*, New Series, no. XIX (July 1828), pp. 236-7 (p. 237).

195 'True Explanation of the Terms "Gnostic," "Phantasiast," and "Pantheist"', in *The Intellectual Repository*, New Series, no. XIX (July 1828), pp. 195-216 (pp. 195-6).

196 Richard McCully, 'Mr. Tulk on the Divine Humanity', in *The New Church Magazine*, vol. IX, no. 101 (May 1890), pp. 202-8.

197 William Blake, *A Vision of the Last Judgment*, in *Blake Complete Writings*, ed. Geoffrey Keynes (Oxford: Oxford University Press, 1972), pp. 604-17 (p. 617).

198 Sheila A Spector, 'Blake, William', in *DGWE*, pp. 173-7 (p. 174).

199 Kathleen Raine, *Blake and the New Age* (London: George Allen and Unwin, 1979), pp. 15, 151-79.

200 G E Bentley (ed.), *William Blake: The Critical Heritage* (London: Routledge & Kegan Paul, 1975), pp. 36-9; Henry Crabb Robinson, *Diary, Reminiscences, and Correspondence of Henry Crabb Robinson*, ed. Thomas Sadler, 2 vols. (London: Macmillan, 1872), vol. II, p. 18.

201 Aileen Ward, 'William Blake and his Circle', in *The Cambridge Companion to William Blake*, ed. Morris Eaves (Cambridge: Cambridge University Press, 2003), pp. 19-36.

202 The claim made by Blake's early biographers that he was raised in a Swedenborgian family has been comprehensively refuted by David Erdman, 'Blake's Early Swedenborgianism: A Twentieth-Century Legend', in *Comparative Literature*, vol. 5, no. 3 (Summer 1953), pp. 247-57.

203 Raymond H Deck, Jr, 'New Light on C. A. Tulk, Blake's Nineteenth-Century Patron', in *Studies in Romanticism*, vol. 16, no. 2 (1977), pp. 217-36.

204 Robert W Rix, 'Healing the Spirit'; Odhner, *Hindmarsh*, pp. 26-30.

205 Jon Mee, 'Blake's Politics in History', in *The Cambridge Companion to William Blake*, pp. 133-49.

206 Ibid., p. 138. In *The Marriage of Heaven and Hell*, Blake says that 'Swedenborg boasts that what he writes is new; tho' it is only the Contents or Index of already publish'd books. . .Any man of mechanical talents may, from the writings of Paracelsus or Jacob Behmen, produce ten thousand volumes of equal value with Swedenborg's': *Blake Complete Writings*, pp. 157-8.

207 Morton D Paley, ' "A New Heaven is Begun": Blake and Swedenborgianism', in

Harvey F Bellin and Darrell Ruhl (eds.), *Blake and Swedenborg: Opposition is True Friendship* (West Chester, PA: Swedenborg Foundation, 1985), pp. 15-34.

[208] G E Bentley, *Blake Records* (Oxford: Clarendon Press, 1969), p. 38.

[209] Raine, *Blake and the New Age*, p. 35.

[210] Kathleen Raine, 'The Human Face of God', in Bellin and Ruhl (eds.), *Blake and Swedenborg*, pp. 87-101.

[211] Blake, *Milton*, in *Blake Complete Writings*, p. 506.

[212] Corbin's concept of the *mundus imaginalis* is discussed in Henry Corbin, *Swedenborg and Esoteric Islam*, tr. Leonard Fox (West Chester, PA: Swedenborg Foundation, 1995), pp. 1-33.

[213] Blake, *A Vision of the Last Judgment*, in *Blake Complete Writings*, pp. 605-6.

[214] Blake, *The Everlasting Gospel*, in *Blake Complete Writings*, p. 748.

[215] Kathleen Raine, *The Human Face of God: William Blake and the Book of Job* (London: Thames and Hudson, 1982), pp. 9-24 (p. 11).

[216] Robert W Rix, 'Healing the Spirit'.

[217] Blake, *Milton*, in *Blake Complete Writings*, p.509. The spiritual correspondences of bodily organs, particularly the heart and lungs, are a central theme of Swedenborg's theology; see, for example, Emanuel Swedenborg, *Angelic Wisdom Concerning the Divine Love and Wisdom*, tr. Clifford Harley and Doris H Harley (London: Swedenborg Society, 1987), §§362-432, pp. 156-204, where content can be found that correlates directly with the anatomical references in *Milton*.

[218] Deck, 'New Light on C. A. Tulk', p. 219.

[219] Ibid., pp. 220-1.

[220] Bentley, *Blake Records*, p. 25.

[221] Deck, 'New Light on C. A. Tulk', pp. 225-6.

[222] Ibid., pp. 228-32.

[223] Ibid., p. 221. At that time only a small number of copies of *Songs of Innocence and Experience* had been printed privately by Blake himself, using an acid-etching process that he had invented: see 'Biographical Notes', in Bellin and Ruhl (eds.), *Blake and Swedenborg*, p. 6.

[224] Coleridge, letter to Revd H F Carey, 18 February 1818, in *Collected Letters of Samuel Taylor Coleridge*, vol. IV, p. 833.

[225] [Charles Augustus Tulk], 'The inventions of William Blake, painter and poet', in *London University Magazine*, vol. 2 (March 1830), pp. 318-23; repr. in Bentley (ed.), *William Blake: The Critical Heritage*, pp. 199-205. The article, though originally published anonymously, is now attributed to Tulk: Deck, 'New Light on C. A. Tulk', p. 223 and n.

[226] The circumstances leading to this publication are discussed in detail in Chapter 3.

[227] Curry, *A Confusion of Prophets*, p. 27.

[228] Ibid., p. 24.

[229] Robinson, *Remembrancer and Recorder*, p. 353.

[230] Garrett, 'Swedenborg and the Mystical Enlightenment', p. 81.

[231] The place of mythology within Illuminism is discussed by Christine Bergé, 'Illuminism', in *DGWE*, pp. 600-6 (pp. 603-4).

Chapter Three

[1] George Berkeley, *A Treatise Concerning the Principles of Human Knowledge... First Printed in the Year 1710* (London: Jacob Tonson, 1734), p. 40.

[2] James John Garth Wilkinson, 'Introductory Remarks by the Translator', in Emanuel Swedenborg, *Outlines of a Philosophical Argument on the Infinite, and the Final Cause of Creation; and on the Intercourse Between the Soul and the Body*, tr. James John Garth Wilkinson (London: William Newbery, 1847), pp. ix-xxx (p. xix).

[3] Martin Lamm suggests that Milton's *Paradise Lost* was a major influence on Swedenborg's work *The Worship and Love of God*, which was written during Swedenborg's transition from his scientific to his theological period: see Martin Lamm, *Emanuel Swedenborg: the Development of his Thought*, tr. Thomas Spiers and Anders Hallengren (West Chester, PA: Swedenborg Foundation, 2000), pp. 184-92. Milton also inspired William Blake, who illustrated Milton's poems extensively and wrote and illustrated his own epic poem *Milton* between 1804-10. Blake believed that he was visited by the spirit of Milton; on one occasion Milton's spirit asked Blake to correct an error in *Paradise Lost*, which Blake declined to do because he was too busy with other things: Pamela Dunbar, *William Blake's Illustrations to the Poetry of Milton* (Oxford: Clarendon Press, 1980), p. 1. Towards the end of his life, when he was a unswerving follower of Swedenborg, Wilkinson was uncomplimentary about *Paradise Lost*, pointing out that it was 'devoid of the true centre written of in the Word' and that it contained factual errors such as the idea that devils are fallen angels: James John Garth Wilkinson, *The Combats and Victories of Jesus Christ* (London: James Speirs, 1895), pp. 73-92 (p. 73).

[4] The term 'idealism' has been used within philosophy in multiple and changing ways. For discussions of the problems of formulating a general definition of idealism, see Stephen Gersh and Dermot Moran, 'Introduction', in *Eriugena, Berkeley, and the Idealist Tradition*, ed. Stephen Gersh and Dermot Moran (Notre Dame, IN: University

of Notre Dame Press, 2006), pp. 1-13 (pp. 1-2), and A C Ewing, *Idealism: A Critical Survey* (London: Methuen, 1934), pp. 2-6.

In this chapter 'idealism' is used to mean the doctrine that there is a non-material or spiritual primary reality which forms a template for, or organizes, the material or natural world. This primary reality is generally regarded as a 'mind', whether human or non-human (such as God or the Neoplatonic *nous*). Within this definition, the material world has been regarded by different philosophers as being either real or as illusory.

Not surprisingly, there are many variants within this broad definition of idealism. For more on non-subjective idealism, see: Vasilis Politis, 'Non-Subjective Idealism in Plato (*Sophist* 248e-249d)', in Gersh and Moran (eds.), *Eriugena*, pp. 14-38 and Jean Pépin, 'Saint Augustine and the Indwelling of the Ideas of God', in Gersh and Moran (eds.), *Eriugena*, pp. 105-22. For more on subjective idealism, see: Winkler, *Berkeley. An Interpretation*; G J Warnock, *Berkeley*, pp. 86-109. For more on transcendental idealism, see: Roger Scruton, *Kant* (Oxford: Oxford University Press, 1992); A C Grayling, 'Scepticism', in *Philosophy: A Guide Through the Subject*, ed. A C Grayling (Oxford: Oxford University Press, 1995), pp. 43-60 (p. 53). For more on absolute idealism, see: Frederick C Beiser, *German Idealism* (Cambridge, MA: Harvard University Press, 2002), p. 353. The *Naturphilosophie* of Friedrich Wilhelm Joseph Schelling (1775-1854) and his follower Lorenz Oken (1779-1851) is an example of absolute idealism: Beiser, *German Idealism*, pp. 349-51. For more on German idealism, see: *The Cambridge Companion to German Idealism*, ed. Karl Ameriks (Cambridge: Cambridge University Press, 2000), pp. 1-17.

5   Garland Cannon, *The Life and Mind of Oriental Jones* (Cambridge: Cambridge University Press, 1990); David Kopf, *British Orientalism and the Bengal Renaissance: The Dynamics of Indian Modernization 1773-1835* (Berkeley, CA: University of California Press, 1969), pp. 34-41.

6   Urs App, 'William Jones's Ancient Theology', in *Sino-Platonic Papers*, no. 191 (July 2009), pp. 1-125 (p. 9). The concept of *prisca theologia* embodies the concept that all esoteric traditions originated from a single divine source and were transmitted through inspired individuals such as Moses, Hermes Trismegistus and Plato: see Nicholas Goodrick-Clarke, *The Western Esoteric Traditions*, pp. 7, 9. Garth Wilkinson regarded Swedenborg as being part of this transmission of ancient knowledge, saying that '[Swedenborg] was one of the links that connect bygone ages with to-day, breathing for us among the lost truths of the past': J J G Wilkinson, *Emanuel Swedenborg*, p. 67.

7   For example, in his *Hymn to Náráyena*, Jones writes, 'Delusive Pictures! unsubstantial

shows!/ My soul absorb'd One only Being knows,/ Of all perceptions One abundant source,/ Whence ev'ry object ev'ry moment flows': Quoted in App, 'William Jones', p. 21. Jones's father, mathematician William Jones (1675-1749), was a Fellow of the Royal Society and a friend of Isaac Newton and William Stukeley: David Boyd Haycock, *William Stukeley*, p. 50. As a young man, Jones was particularly moved by the poems of John Milton: Cannon, *Oriental Jones*, p. 24.

[8] Emma Anne Marsh (1813-86), the daughter of William and Mary Marsh, was born on 20 March in Diss, Norfolk, and Christened in the local Wesleyan Methodist Church: 'England Births and Christenings, 1538-1975', index, *FamilySearch*, at <https:// familysearch.org/pal:/MM9.1.1/NPZZ-5T5>, accessed 15 April 2014, Emma Ann Marsh; citing WESLEYAN METHODIST, DISS, NORFOLK, ENGLAND, reference; FHL microfilm 0596996 (RG4 642).

[9] The major biographies of Swedenborg which outline his life and ideas, and on which this account is based, are: Ernst Benz, *Emanuel Swedenborg: Visionary Savant in the Age of Reason*, tr. Nicholas Goodrick-Clarke (West Chester, PA.: Swedenborg Foundation, 2002); Lars Bergquist, *Swedenborg's Secret* (London: Swedenborg Society, 2005); Martin Lamm, *Emanuel Swedenborg: The Development of His Thought*; and Sigstedt, *Swedenborg Epic*.

[10] Benz, *Swedenborg*, pp. 30-8.

[11] In Swedenborg's day, these topics were regarded as Natural Philosophy; I use the term science because that is how this phase of Swedenborg's life is usually characterized.

[12] Steven Shapin, 'Descartes the Doctor: Rationalism and its Therapies', in *The British Journal for the History of Science*, vol. 33, no. 2 (June 2000), pp. 131-54.

[13] Hugo Lj. Odhner, *The Human Mind, its Faculties and Degrees: A Study of Swedenborg's Psychology* (Bryn Athyn, PA: Swedenborg Scientific Association, 1969), pp. 21-2.

[14] Lars Bergquist, *Swedenborg's Dream Diary*, tr. Anders Hallengren (West Chester, PA.: Swedenborg Foundation, 2001).

[15] Emanuel Swedenborg, *The True Christian Religion*, tr. John Chadwick, 2 vols. (London: Swedenborg Society, 1998), vol. 1, §163, pp. 221-2.

[16] Swedenborg, *Divine Love and Wisdom*, §§14-16, p. 7.

[17] Ibid., §§282-4, pp. 118-19. Swedenborg noted that Descartes also held the concept of God as 'substance in itself'; he recorded in his notebook (written between 1741 and 1744) Descartes' statement that 'substance which has no need whatever of any other thing, can be understood only as being the one only substance, namely God.

As to all other substances, we perceive that they can exist solely by the aid of God's concurrence': Emanuel Swedenborg, *A Philosopher's Notebook*, tr. Alfred Acton (Pennsylvania: Swedenborg Scientific Association, 2009), p. 324.

[18] Emanuel Swedenborg, *The Economy of the Animal Kingdom, Considered Anatomically, Physically, and Philosophically*, tr. Augustus Clissold, 2 vols. (New York: The New Church Press, 1919), vol. II, §§579-652, pp. 5-60. Swedenborg's philosophy at this stage of his thinking, and the influences that gave rise to it, are discussed by Lamm, *Swedenborg*, pp. 65-94.

[19] Swedenborg, *Economy*, vol. I, §253, p. 224.

[20] Mary Louise Gill, *Aristotle on Substance: The Paradox of Unity* (Princeton: Princeton University Press, 1989), pp. 141-4; Frank A Lewis, 'Aristotle on the Unity of Substance', in *Form, Matter, and Mixture in Aristotle*, ed. Frank A Lewis and Robert Bolton (Oxford: Blackwell, 1996), pp. 39-81. Medieval Christian followers of Aristotle—the Schoolmen—recognized the inherent difficulty of reconciling the Aristotelian concept of the soul—which as the form of the body must be inseparable from it—with the Christian doctrine of the survival of the soul after death. Most Schoolmen regarded the human soul as a unique kind of spiritual substance, created by God, which is incomplete without the human body through which it can exercise its functions, but which can also exist separately. Descartes, in contrast, regarded this idea as irrational and proposed that both the body and the soul are complete even when separate: Marleen Rozemond, *Descartes's Dualism* (Cambridge, MA: Harvard University Press, 1998), pp. 139-71. Swedenborg's position is closer to that of the scholastics than that of Descartes, and carries with it some of the same tensions.

[21] Lamm, *Swedenborg*, p. 70; Inge Jonsson, *Visionary Scientist: The Effects of Science and Philosophy on Swedenborg's Cosmology* (West Chester, PA: Swedenborg Foundation, 1999), p. 58. An excellent primary source for the influences on Swedenborg from 1741-4 is his *A Philosopher's Notebook*. Originally published in 1931, this work is an edited translation of the manuscript Codex 36 which is held at the Academy of Sciences in Stockholm. This has been used widely as a source document by Swedenborg scholars. It includes Swedenborg's notes and comments on a wide variety of classical and contemporary philosophers and theologians.

[22] Swedenborg, *Economy*, vol. II, §§275-80, pp. 252-62.

[23] Lamm, *Swedenborg*, pp. 74, 76; Emanuel Swedenborg, *The Economy of the Animal Kingdom, Considered Anatomically, Physically, and Philosophically... Transaction III The Medullary Fibre of the Brain and the Nerve Fibre of the*

Body..., tr. Alfred Acton (Philadelphia: Swedenborg Scientific Association, 1918; repr. Bryn Athyn, PA: Swedenborg Scientific Association, 1976), §§267-8, pp. 193-4.

24 Emanuel Swedenborg, *A Hieroglyphic Key to Natural and Spiritual Mysteries by Way of Representations and Correspondences*, tr. J J G Wilkinson (London: William Newbery, 1847), pp. 7, 12.

25 Benz, *Swedenborg*, pp. 351-62; Wouter J Hanegraaff, *Swedenborg Oetinger Kant: Three Perspectives on the Secrets of Heaven* (West Chester, PA: Swedenborg Foundation, 2007), pp. 3-11.

26 Emanuel Swedenborg, *The Universal Human and Soul-Body Interaction*, tr. and ed. George F Dole (New Jersey: Paulist Press, 1984), p. 104. At this point it is important to clarify the concepts of the Divine Human and the Universal Human in Swedenborg's thought. The Divine Human is the Lord (or God-Man), which is *Esse* and *Existere* and was incarnated as Jesus Christ. The Universal Human (also called the Grand Man or *Maximus Homo*) is heaven, and is in correspondence with the Divine Human. Because the two correspond, they are as one, yet still distinct. See Hugo Lj. Odhner, *Principles of the New Philosophy*, 2nd edn. (Bryn Athyn, PA: Swedenborg Scientific Association, 1986), p. 26; Bergquist, *Swedenborg's Secret*, p. 255; Swedenborg, *Universal Human*, p. 104.

27 Swedenborg, *Universal Human*, p. 70.

28 Swedenborg, *Divine Love and Wisdom*, §§382-3, pp. 168-9.

29 Swedenborg, *Universal Human*, p. 96.

30 Emanuel Swedenborg, *Heaven and Hell*, tr. J C Ager, rev. Doris H Harley (London: Swedenborg Society, 1989), §§131, 363, 422, pp. 89, 264, 311.

31 Swedenborg, *Divine Love and Wisdom*, §330, p. 138.

32 Ibid., §§331-3, pp. 138-9.

33 Emanuel Swedenborg, *The Worlds in Space*, tr. John Chadwick (London: Swedenborg Society, 1997), §18, p. 11.

34 Swedenborg, *Divine Love and Wisdom*, §298, p. 125.

35 Ibid., §§336-9, pp. 141-2.

36 Emanuel Swedenborg, *Arcana Caelestia*, tr. John Elliott, 12 vols. (London: Swedenborg Society, 1983-99), vol. VIII, §6128.2, p.184.

37 Ibid., §5850, p. 42.

38 Swedenborg, *Heaven and Hell*, §297, p. 200.

39 Ibid., §112, p. 75.

40 Swedenborg, *Universal Human*, pp. 253-5.

41 José Antonio Antón-Pacheco, *The Swedish Prophet: Reflections on the Visionary Philosophy of Emanuel Swedenborg*, tr. Steven Skattebo (West Chester, PA: Swedenborg Foundation, 2012), pp. 6-8.

42 Charles Augustus Tulk, copy of a letter to his sister, of uncertain date, in a handwritten bound document, 'Tulk on the Lord's Prayer and Correspondence', p. 96, in Swedenborg Society Archive A/8. It does seem that Tulk had Swedenborg on his side in this argument. Swedenborg said that, 'As the world is to man, so is man to God: from which it follows, that God passes through man into the world, or that God has nothing in common with nature excepting through man: hence that the perfection of nature depends upon the perfection of man': Swedenborg, *Hieroglyphic Key*, p. 12.

43 J J G Wilkinson, letter to Henry James, Sr, 2 September 1845, in Swedenborg Society Archive K/123.

44 J J G Wilkinson, letter to his fiancée Emma Marsh, 25 July 1836, in Swedenborg Society Archive K/124 (e).

45 J J G Wilkinson, letter to his fiancée Emma Marsh, undated, in Swedenborg Society Archive K/124 (e).

46 J J G Wilkinson, letter to Henry James, Sr, 2 September 1845, in Swedenborg Society Archive K/123.

47 Ibid.

48 Ibid.

49 J J G Wilkinson, letter to Henry James, Sr, 29 November 1845, pp. 3-4, in Houghton Library, Harvard University, at <http://nrs.harvard.edu/urn-3:FHCL. HOUGH:12249590>, accessed 11 June 2014. In the same letter, Wilkinson pointed out that Tulk's detractors had also made errors of interpretation of Swedenborg's philosophy.

50 Editorial, in *The Intellectual Repository*, vol. V, no. LX (November 1839), pp. 661-2. The article says of Wilkinson that 'Whether his peculiar opinions have undergone any recent change, we know not; but we have been informed that he was avowedly an Idealist, a disciple of Berkeley and certain German metaphysicians. We know that he has eulogized Mr. C. A. Tulk' (p. 662).

51 J J G Wilkinson, 'Introductory Remarks', in Swedenborg, *Outlines of a Philosophical Argument on the Infinite, and the Final Cause of Creation*, p. xix. Immanuel Kant (1724-1804) was a contemporary of Swedenborg. He wrote a scathing criticism of Swedenborg's experiences of the spirit world, which he regarded as the product of a

sick mind: see *Kant on Swedenborg. Dreams of a Spirit-Seer and Other Writings*, ed. Gregory R Johnson, tr. Gregory R Johnson and Glenn Alexander Magee (West Chester, PA: Swedenborg Foundation, 2002). Kant was widely misinterpreted as a Berkeleyan idealist: Karl Ameriks, 'Idealism from Kant to Berkeley', in Gersh and Moran (eds.), *Eriugena*, pp. 244-68. The central thesis of David Hume (1711-76) was that all we can be certain of is our own mental perceptions, and we cannot assume the real existence of an external, mind-independent world: Antony Flew, *David Hume, Philosopher of Moral Science* (Oxford: Blackwell, 1986), p. 25. It is therefore evident that Wilkinson here was railing against immaterialist subjective idealism.

[52] J J G Wilkinson, 'Introductory Remarks', in Swedenborg, *Outlines of a Philosophical Argument on the Infinite, and the Final Cause of Creation,* p. xx. Ralph Waldo Emerson described this article as 'much the best piece of criticism on Modern Opinions, especially Transcendentalism, which has been written': Emerson, letter to Margaret Fuller, 29 August 1847, in *The Letters of Ralph Waldo Emerson*, ed. Ralph L Rusk, 6 vols. (New York: Columbia University, 1939), vol. III, p. 414.

[53] Emanuel Swedenborg, *Posthumous Tracts*, tr. James John Garth Wilkinson (London: William Newbery, 1847) contains 8 short works and fragments that were written by Swedenborg in 1739 and 1741 as part of planned future volumes in *The Economy of the Animal Kingdom* series that were ultimately left unpublished by the author.

[54] J J G Wilkinson, 'From our London Correspondent' (letter dated 3 May 1847), in *The New Jerusalem Magazine* (Boston), vol. XX, no. CCXXXVIII (June 1847), pp. 412-15 (p. 414).

[55] Ibid., p. 414.

[56] Ibid.

[57] Swedenborg, *Outlines of a Philosophical Argument on the Infinite, and the Final Cause of Creation*, pp. 110-12.

[58] J J G Wilkinson, letter to Emerson, 23 June 1848, in Swedenborg Society Archive K/125 (3).

[59] J J G Wilkinson, letter to Henry James, Sr, 18 November 1847, in Swedenborg Society Archive K/123.

[60] Ralph Waldo Emerson, *Nature*, in *Nature and Selected Essays*, ed. Larzer Ziff (New York: Penguin, 2003), pp. 35-82 (pp. 62-63).

[61] Ralph Waldo Emerson, 'The Transcendentalist', in *Nature and Selected Essays*, pp. 239-58 (pp. 239, 246).

[62] James Spilling, 'Emerson and Dr. Wilkinson', in *The New Church Magazine*, vol. VI,

no. 71 (November 1887), pp. 529-33 (pp. 529, 530).

63   James Spilling, 'Dr. Wilkinson's Reminiscences of Carlyle', in *The New Church Magazine*, vol. VII, no. 75 (March 1888), pp. 107-12 (p. 107). *Sartor Resartus* is a philosophical work, whimsical yet with serious intent, that purports to be a commentary on a fictitious German philosopher called Diogenes Teufelsdröckh ('God-born devil-dung'). It is perhaps best known for its 'philosophy of clothes' which posits that the created universe is merely the external clothing of the soul: see J Macmillan Brown, *The 'Sartor Restartus' of Carlyle. A Study* (Christchurch: Whitcombe and Tombs, n.d.), pp. 96-117. According to the early feminist sociologist Harriet Martineau (1802-76), this book was 'in the hands and hearts of many Swedenborgians in the United States': Harriet Martineau, letter to J J G Wilkinson, transcribed by Wilkinson in a letter to his fiancée Emma Marsh, 23 October 1838, in Swedenborg Society Archive K/124 (e). Carlyle was an important influence on the American Transcendentalists, particularly Emerson: see Arthur Versluis, *The Esoteric Origins of the American Renaissance* (New York: Oxford University Press, 2001), pp. 130-4.

64   Thomas Carlyle, letter to J J G Wilkinson, 28 September 1839, from *The Carlyle Letters Online*, at <http://carlyleletters.dukejournals.org/cgi/content/full/11/1/lt-18390928-TC-JJGW-01>, accessed 21 March 2016.

65   J J G Wilkinson, letter to Henry James, Sr, 1 February 1844, in Swedenborg Society Archive K/123. The so-called 'doctrine of work' posits that the highest goal of worldly work is that it should be carried out not only for material needs but also from the highest spiritual motives: see Thomas Carlyle, *Sartor Resartus*, ed. Archibald MacMechan (Boston and London: Ginn and Company / The Athenaeum Press, 1902), pp. 206-7.

66   Thomas Carlyle, letter to Emerson, 13 November 1847, in *Carlyle Letters Online*, at <http://carlyleletters.dukejournals.org/cgi/content/full/22/1/lt-18471113-TC-RWE-01>, accessed 29 March 2016.

67   For a useful overview of Carlyle's mystical philosophy, see Charles Frederick Harrold, 'The Mystical Element in Carlyle (1827-34)', in *Modern Philology*, vol. 29, no. 4 (May 1932), pp. 459-75.

68   J J G Wilkinson, letter to Henry James, Sr, 25 January 1850, in Swedenborg Society Archive K/123. Swedenborg's views on the 'ages of man' are detailed in P L Johnson, *The Five Ages: Swedenborg's View of Spiritual History* (London: Swedenborg Society, 2008).

69   J J G Wilkinson, letter to Henry James, Sr, 3 May 1850, p. 8, in Houghton Library, Harvard University, at <http://nrs.harvard.edu/urn-3:FHCL.HOUGH:12249590>,

accessed 11 June 2014. (The letter is mis-recorded here as '3 Mar 1850'.)

[70] Thomas Carlyle, letter to Joseph Neuberg, 25 July 1851, in *Carlyle Letters Online*, at <http://carlyleletters.dukejournals.org/cgi/content/full/26/1/lt-18510725-TC-JN-01>, accessed 29 March 2016.

[71] Thomas Carlyle, letter to Joseph Neuberg, 31 May 1852, in *Carlyle Letters Online*, at <http://carlyleletters.dukejournals.org/cgi/content/full/27/1/lt-18520531-TC-JN-01>, accessed 29 March 2016.

[72] Thomas Carlyle, letter to John A Carlyle, 26 March 1858, in *Carlyle Letters Online*, at <http://carlyleletters.dukejournals.org/cgi/content/full/33/1/lt-18580326-TC-JAC-01>, accessed 29 March 2016.

[73] Spilling, 'Dr. Wilkinson's Reminiscences of Carlyle', p. 111.

[74] Emanuel Swedenborg, *Oeconomia Regni Animalis* (Amsterdam: Francis Changuion, 1740-1), featuring annotations by S T Coleridge, in Swedenborg Society Archive L/67.

[75] A Realist (pseud. J J G Wilkinson), 'Passages from the Oeconomia Regni Animalis, and de Cultu et Amore Dei, of Swedenborg, with original comments thereon, by the late Samuel Taylor Coleridge', in *The Monthly Magazine*, vol. V (1841), pp. 607-20.

[76] Ibid., p. 618.

[77] J J G Wilkinson, letter to Henry James, Sr, 3 March 1845, in Swedenborg Society Archive K/123.

[78] Michel Malherbe, 'Bacon's Method of Science', in Markku Peltonen (ed.), *The Cambridge Companion to Bacon* (Cambridge: Cambridge University Press, 1996), pp. 75-98.

[79] Emanuel Swedenborg, *The Animal Kingdom*, tr. James John Garth Wilkinson, 2 vols. (London: W Newbery, 1843-4), vol. I, §§1-23, pp. 1-15.

[80] James John Garth Wilkinson, *The Human Body and its Connection with Man* (Philadelphia: Lippincott, Grambo and Co., 1851), p. 279 n.

[81] Francis Bacon, *New Atlantis. A Worke unfinished*, in his, *Sylva Sylvarum: or A Naturall Historie. In Ten Centuries* (London: William Lee, 1627).

[82] For a literal interpretation, see Rose-Mary Sargent, 'Bacon as an Advocate for Cooperative Scientific Research', in Peltonen (ed.), *The Cambridge Companion to Bacon*, pp. 146-71; for an esoteric interpretation, see Frances A Yates, *The Rosicrucian Enlightenment* (London: Routledge and Kegan Paul, 1972), pp. 164-9.

[83] James John Garth Wilkinson, 'Introductory Remarks by the Translator', in Swedenborg, *The Animal Kingdom*, pp. xv-lxiv (pp. xlviii-xlix).

84 Wilkinson's friendship with Alfred Tulk (b. 1820) is referred to in James John Garth Wilkinson, *Remarks on Swedenborg's Economy of the Animal Kingdom* (London: Walton and Mitchell, 1846), p. 41 n.

85 Peter Hanns Reill, *Vitalizing Nature in the Enlightenment* (Berkeley: University of California Press, 2005), p. 314 n. 16.

86 Dietrich von Engelhardt, 'Natural Science in the Age of Romanticism', in Antoine Faivre and Jacob Needleman (eds.), *Modern Esoteric Spirituality* (London: SCM Press, 1993), pp. 101-31.

87 Antoine Faivre, 'Naturphilosophie', in *DGWE*, pp. 822-6.

88 Beiser, *German Idealism*, p. 483.

89 Ibid., pp. 506-7, 548-9.

90 Ibid., pp. 516-7.

91 Alfred Tulk, Translator's Preface to Lorenz Oken, *Elements of Physiophilosophy*, tr. Alfred Tulk (London: The Ray Society, 1847), pp. v-vii (p. vi). As early as 1842, Wilkinson had told J F I Tafel that he was 'curious to know something of the merits of Schelling's new system; and to hear whether it approximates to the Heavenly Doctrines of the New Jerusalem', but there is no evidence that he had followed this up prior to the publication of Oken's work: J J G Wilkinson, letter to J F I Tafel, 5 January 1842, in Swedenborg Society Archive K/126 (e).

92 Reill, *Vitalizing Nature*, p. 314 n. 16.

93 J J G Wilkinson, *Remarks on Swedenborg's Economy of the Animal Kingdom*, p. 22 n. Wilkinson's admiration for Oken's work was not unbridled; in a letter to Henry James, Sr, he observed that Oken's views 'have a certain order of truth' but ultimately are flawed because he has no concept of the Divine Human: J J G Wilkinson, letter to Henry James, Sr, 28 February 1847, in Swedenborg Society Archive, K/123.

94 Oken, *Elements of Physiophilosophy*, p. 2

95 Peabody, *Lectures in the Training Schools for Kindergartners*, p. 157.

96 Kant, *Kant on Swedenborg: Dreams of a Spirit-Seer and Other Writings*, p. 52.

97 Olaf Breidbach and Michael T Ghiselin have noted alchemical and cabalistic influences on Oken's system of nature, which they propose were transmitted through Paracelsus and Fludd: Olaf Breidbach and Michael T Ghiselin, 'Lorenz Oken and *Naturphilosophie* in Jena, Paris and London', in *History and Philosophy of the Life Sciences*, vol. 24, no. 2 (2002), pp. 219-47 (p. 233).

98 Philip F Rehbock, *The Philosophical Naturalists* (Madison, WI: University of Wisconsin, 1983), p. 39.

[99]   Breidbach and Ghiselin, 'Lorenz Oken', pp. 219-47.

[100] Ibid., pp. 229-31.

[101] For example, insects, which are skin animals, correspond to birds, which are nerve animals. These correspondences produce a complex network of interdependent relationships.

[102] Philip F Rehbock, 'Transcendental Anatomy', in *Romanticism and the Sciences*, ed. Andrew Cunningham and Nicholas Jardine (Cambridge: Cambridge University Press, 1990), pp. 144-60.

[103] Rehbock, *The Philosophical Naturalists*, p. 98.

[104] Ibid., p. 46.

[105] Ibid., p. 36. John Abernethy (1764-1831) was a student and follower of the vitalist physician John Hunter (1728-93), who also taught medicine to mesmerist John Benoit de Mainauduc (*c.* 1750-97), discussed in Chapter 2. Abernethy and his influence is discussed in more detail in Chapter 6. Cuvier (1769-1832) and Geoffroy (1772-1844) were influenced by the comparative anatomy of Johann Wolfgang von Goethe (1749-1832), whose works were informed by Swedenborg's scientific and theological works: Alice B Skinner, 'Poets with Swedenborgian Connections', in Robin Larsen, Stephen Larsen, James F Lawrence and William Ross Woofenden (eds.), *Emanuel Swedenborg: A Continuing Vision* (New York: Swedenborg Foundation, 1988), pp. 53-60 (p. 59).

[106] Robert Knox, *Great Artists and Great Anatomists; A Biographical and Philosophical Study* (London: John van Voorst, 1852; repr. New York: AMS, 1977), p. 63.

[107] Rehbock, *The Philosophical Naturalists*, p. 80. Stripped of its transcendentalism, this discipline is known today as comparative anatomy.

[108] These issues are discussed by Adrian Desmond, *The Politics of Evolution: Morphology, Medicine, and Reform in Radical London* (Chicago and London: University of Chicago Press, 1992).

[109] William Mac Cormac, *An Address of Welcome Delivered on the Occasion of the Centenary Festival of the Royal College of Surgeons of England* (London: Ballantyne, Hanson & Co. 1900), p. 115.

[110] According to Desmond's analysis, Green's Professorship at the Royal College of Surgeons reflected the conservative outlook of this institution: Desmond, *The Politics of Evolution*, pp. 260 ff.

[111] J H Green, quoted in Desmond, *The Politics of Evolution*, p. 268.

[112] William B Carpenter, *Nature and Man. Essays Scientific and Philosophical*, ed. J Estlin Carpenter (New York: D Appleton and Company, 1889), p. 158.

113 Desmond, *The Politics of Evolution*, pp. 210-22. William Benjamin Carpenter (1813-85) was a Unitarian and a Deist. Deists, who believed in the evolution of animals from below upwards, even if this was determined by laws that were originally infused by God, were often regarded as materialists at that time: ibid., pp. 5-6 n. The accusation of materialism was levelled at, but refuted by, Carpenter: ibid., p. 221.

114 The London University (now University College London) was founded in 1826 as a secular alternative to the Anglican Universities of Oxford and Cambridge. Popular with religious dissenters, London University promoted radical social causes and introduced transcendental anatomy into its medical curriculum. Robert Edmond Grant (1793-1874) was a Deist and Lamarckian. For Tulk's patronage of London University, see Richard Lines, 'The Swedenborg Society: A Very Short History', at <http://www.ucl.ac.uk/bloomsbury-project/articles/articles/lines_swedenborg.pdf>, accessed 08/10/2012. Tulk's attendance at Grant's lectures is mentioned by Desmond, *The Politics of Evolution*, p. 84 n.

115 James John Garth Wilkinson, *The Greater Origins and Issues of Life and Death* (London: James Speirs, 1885), p. 120.

116 Ibid., p. 117.

117 James John Garth Wilkinson, *The Grouping of Animals: A Paper read before the Veterinary Medical Association, Thursday, May 16, 1845* (London: Compton and Ritchie, 1845).

118 Ibid., pp. 6, 10.

119 After delivering this lecture, Wilkinson wrote to Henry James, Sr that 'I flung out the beastly hypothesis connecting [monkeys] with man': J J G Wilkinson, letter to Henry James, Sr, 18 November 1847, in Swedenborg Society Archive K/123.

120 Although Wilkinson did not acknowledge any prior source for this idea, the French naturalist Georges-Louis Leclerc, comte de Buffon (1707-88) had also proposed that domestic animals, with the horse at their head, should be classified next to man; he commented that 'scientific arrangements serve rather to confuse than to instruct': Georges-Louis Leclerc, comte de Buffon, *Buffon's Natural History, abridged*, 2 vols. (London: C & G Kearsley, 1792), vol. 2, p. 87. Buffon's *Natural History* was read 'by every educated person in Europe', so it is likely that Wilkinson was familiar with it: Ernst Mayr, *The Growth of Biological Thought* (Cambridge, MA: Harvard University, 1981), p. 330. In answer to the objection that domesticated animals were once wild, and that some (such as horses) can still be found in the wild as well as in the service of man, Wilkinson responded that these animals were created in a domesticated

condition originally, and the wild ones have degenerated. This idea too had been advanced previously by Buffon.

[121] Suzanne R Hoover, 'William Blake in the Wilderness. A Closer Look at his Reputation, 1827-1863', in *William Blake. Essays in honour of Sir Geoffrey Keynes*, ed. Morton D Paley and Michael Phillips (Oxford: Clarendon Press, 1973), pp. 310-48 (p. 311).

[122] Allan Cunningham, 'William Blake', in his *Lives of the Most Eminent British Painters, Sculptors, and Architects*, 6 vols. (London: John Murray, 1829-33), vol. II, pp. 142-79.

[123] G E Bentley, Jr and Martin K Nurmi, *A Blake Bibliography: Annotated Lists of Works, Studies, and Blakeana* (Minneapolis: University of Minnesota Press, 1964), p. 11 n. 8.

[124] J J G Wilkinson, letter to his fiancée Emma Marsh, 5 March 1838, in Swedenborg Society Archive K/124 (e). The copy of Blake's *Songs* that Tulk lent to Wilkinson is the same one that he had previously lent to Coleridge: see Geoffrey Keynes, 'Blake, Tulk, and Garth Wilkinson', in *Library* 4th Series, vol. 26 (1945), pp. 190-2 (p. 191).

[125] Clement Wilkinson, *James John Garth Wilkinson*, p. 35; Hoover, 'William Blake in the Wilderness', p. 332. Wilkinson met Peabody when she made a trip to London: Perry, *The Thought and Character of William James*, vol. I, p. 1332. Raymond Deck suggests that Wilkinson may also have introduced Blake's poems to Robert Browning: Raymond H Deck, Jr, 'Blake's *Poetical Sketches* finally arrive in America', in *The Review of English Studies*, New Series, vol. XXXI, no. 122 (May 1980), pp. 183-92 (p. 185). In the mid-1840s (the work is undated) Tulk himself published a limited edition of Blake's *Songs* in which the poems were arranged with spaces between them with the purpose, according to Wilkinson, 'that any who choose, might copy in the paintings with which the original is adorned': Keynes, 'Blake, Tulk, and Garth Wilkinson', p. 191.

[126] J J G Wilkinson, letter to his fiancée Emma Marsh, 6 November 1838, in Swedenborg Society Archive K/124 (e).

[127] J J G Wilkinson, letter to his fiancée Emma Marsh, 17 June 1839, in Swedenborg Society Archive K/124 (e). Wilkinson was shown the illuminations by artist Frederick Tatham (1805-78), who had inherited them from Blake's widow, whom he had helped after her husband's death: Hoover, 'William Blake in the Wilderness', pp. 325-6. Tatham and Wilkinson had been introduced by a mutual friend: Clement Wilkinson, *James John Garth Wilkinson*, p. 29.

[128] Keynes, 'Blake, Tulk, and Garth Wilkinson', p. 191.

[129] Henry Crabb Robinson's diary, 16 April 1848, quoted in Deck, 'Blake's *Poetical Sketches*', pp. 188-9.

130 Henry Crabb Robinson's diary, 9 May 1848, quoted in Deck, 'Blake's *Poetical Sketches*', p. 189.

131 Deck, 'Blake's *Poetical Sketches*', p. 190.

132 Ibid., p. 190; J J G Wilkinson, letter to Henry James, Sr, 28 April 1848, in Swedenborg Society Archive K/123.

133 Deck, 'Blake's *Poetical Sketches*', p. 186.

134 James John Garth Wilkinson, 'Preface' to William Blake, *Songs of Innocence and Experience. Shewing the Two Contrary States of the Human Soul* (London: Pickering, 1839), pp. iii-xxiii (p. xiv).

135 Ibid., pp. xvi-xvii. Blake believed that he was in almost constant contact with spirits. His friend Henry Crabb Robinson (1775-1867), describing a visit to Blake in 1825, remarked that 'He was as wild as ever. . .he talked, as usual, of the spirits, asserted that he had committed many murders'. Blake told Robinson that he had conversed with Socrates and Jesus Christ: Henry Crabb Robinson, *Diary, Reminiscences, and Correspondence*, vol. II, pp. 8, 22.

136 J J G Wilkinson, 'Preface' to the *Songs*, p. xxi.

137 Ibid., p. xx.

138 Ibid., pp. xxii-xxiii.

139 Rather ungraciously, Wilkinson complained about this, saying that he was against naming babies after other people, though he accepted James's proposal 'in the most grateful spirit': J J G Wilkinson, letter to Henry James, Sr, 2 September 1845, in Swedenborg Society Archive K/123. Garth Wilkinson James (1845-83), who became known as 'Wilkie', was the least successful of James's sons. He was seriously injured in the American Civil War, and founded several unsuccessful businesses before dying of kidney disease at the age of 38.

140 Henry James, Jr, letter to Howard Sturgis, 24 August 1912, in *The Letters of Henry James*, ed. Leon Edel, 4 vols. (Cambridge, MA: Belknap Press of Harvard University Press, 1974-84), vol. IV (1895-1916), pp. 624-5.

141 Raymond H Deck, Jr, 'The "Vastation" of Henry James, Sr.: New Light on James's Theological Career', in *Bulletin of Research in the Humanities*, vol. 83, no. 2 (Summer 1980), pp. 216-47 (pp. 225-6).

142 Henry James, Sr, *Society the Redeemed Form of Man, and the Earnest of God's Omnipotence in Human Nature: Affirmed in Letters to a Friend* (Boston: Houghton, Osgood and Company, 1879), p. 45. From the description, it is likely that James was suffering from what would now be regarded as a depressive illness with panic attacks.

[143] Vincenz Priessnitz (1799-1851), whose method included cold baths, the consumption of large amounts of water, avoidance of alcohol, a plain diet, exercise and fresh air: see R T Claridge, *Hydropathy; or, The Cold Water Cure, as practised by Vincent Priessnitz*, 3rd edn. (London: James Madden and Co., 1842).

[144] Deck, 'The "Vastation" of Henry James, Sr.', p. 227. Sophia Chichester (1795-1847) and her sister Georgiana Welch (1792-1879) were unusual in that they were upper-class female political radicals. Sophia, a young widow, and Georgiana, who was separated from her husband, lived on their estate in Gloucestershire and used their wealth to support religious and political radicals including James Pierrepoint Greaves (1777-1842), a follower of Jacob Boehme who described himself as a 'sacred socialist'; John ('Zion') Ward (1781-1837), who claimed to be Shiloh, whose coming was predicted in Genesis; and James ('Shepherd') Smith (1801-57), a friend of Fourierist Hugh Doherty (d. 1891) whom Garth Wilkinson met in Doherty's office. The sisters also supported an Owenite community. See Jackie Latham, 'The Political and the Personal: the radicalism of Sophia Chichester and Georgiana Fletcher Welch', in *Women's History Review*, vol. 8, no. 3 (1999), pp. 469-87.

[145] Deck, 'The "Vastation" of Henry James, Sr.', p. 227. Vastation, according to Swedenborg, is an important stage of spiritual development in which the internal man, with all its unwholesome impulses and memories, is fully opened and thus laid bare before the ego. This has interesting parallels with the process of psychoanalysis.

[146] Henry James, Sr, quoted in Perry, *The Thought and Character of William James*, vol. I, p. 21.

[147] This section is informed particularly by James's essays in Henry James, Sr, *Lectures and Miscellanies* (New York: Redfield, 1852), and Frederic Harold Young, *The Philosophy of Henry James, Sr.* (New York: Bookman Associates, 1951).

[148] Young, *The Philosophy of Henry James, Sr.*, p. 149.

[149] Henry James, Sr, quoted in ibid., p. 106.

[150] Henry James, Sr, quoted in ibid.

[151] Henry James, Sr, quoted in ibid., pp. 324-5.

[152] Although Henry James, Sr does not refer to it, this philosophy is derived directly from Swedenborg, particularly his *Divine Love and Wisdom*, which was James's favourite book. Swedenborg asserts that everything in creation is a triune of end, cause and effect. The end of creation as a whole is a heaven of immortal spirits derived from the human race. The end of the created universe is the spiritual Sun ('the first proceeding of Divine Love and Wisdom'), the cause is the spiritual world, and the effect

is the material world. The effect has no existence of itself, but comes into being only because of the end working through the cause. Everything in the universe is of use to serve the ultimate end. See Swedenborg, *Divine Love and Wisdom*, §§151-6, pp. 57-9; and Hugo Lj. Odhner, *Principles of the New Philosophy*, pp. 11-12.

153 Henry James, Sr, *Lectures*, p. 328.

154 Swedenborg argued that creation cannot be comprehended in its reality 'unless space and time are removed from thought': Swedenborg, *Divine Love and Wisdom*, §155, p. 58.

155 Nobel Laureate Erwin Schrödinger (1887-1961) addressed this question in his lecture on 'Mind and Matter' (1958). He observed that the relationship between sensual information and 'reality' was a puzzle even in the time of Democritus (5th century BC). Democritus described a debate between intellect and senses on the nature of reality: 'Intellect: 'Ostensibly there is colour, ostensibly sweetness, ostensibly bitterness, actually only atoms and the void'. Senses: 'Poor intellect, do you hope to defeat us while from us you borrow your evidence? Your victory is our defeat'.' The paradox here is that reason attempts to understand the world by negating the sense impressions upon which all scientific knowledge depends; the existence of atoms can be inferred only from our sensual experience of them: Erwin Schrödinger, *Mind and Matter* (Cambridge: Cambridge University Press, 1958), pp. 88-104 (p. 103).

156 Young, *The Philosophy of Henry James, Sr.*, p. 151. This brings to mind the analogy used in the Hermetic *Poimandres* of the 'man' (that is, the son of 'Mind, the father of all'), who 'saw in the water the form like himself as it was in nature', following which he descended into it and was captivated by it: Copenhaver, *Hermetica*, p. 3. In other words, man sees his own reflection in nature (as a finite being, he cannot do otherwise), and, believing it to be objective reality, becomes trapped in his own delusion.

157 See, for example, Plotinus, *Enneads*, vol. VI, pp. 11-53.

158 Henry James, Sr, quoted in Young, *The Philosophy of Henry James, Sr.*, p. 133.

159 Austin Warren, *The Elder Henry James* (New York: Macmillan, 1934), mentions Tulk only twice, in passing (pp. 72, 76), and Habegger, *The Father*, only mentions Tulk because James's wife Mary wrote that his ideas were 'unsatisfactory', although it appears that this was because she was not able to understand them (p. 240). Raymond H Deck, Jr, points to a possible influence of Tulk on James, but does not develop the idea: Deck, 'The "Vastation" of Henry James, Sr.', p. 241.

160 J J G Wilkinson, letter to Henry James, Sr, 2 September 1845, in Swedenborg Society Archive K/123. There is no recorded meeting between Tulk and James during his time

in London, but it would be very surprising if Wilkinson had not introduced James to his friend and early mentor.

[161] Charles Augustus Tulk, *Aphorisms*, p. 28.

[162] Henry James, Sr, quoted in Young, *The Philosophy of Henry James, Sr.*, p. 99.

[163] In dedicating his 1851 book, *The Human Body*, to James, Wilkinson said that 'It may remind you of happy hours that we have spent together': J J G Wilkinson, *The Human Body*, Dedication. James kept Wilkinson's letters, which are preserved in the Archive of the Swedenborg Society in London and in the library at Harvard University. Wilkinson also saved the letters from James, but these were lost during his lifetime: see Spilling, 'Dr. Wilkinson's Reminiscences of Carlyle', p. 107. The letters at the Swedenborg Society have been mined for information by several previous authors, firstly by his nephew and biographer Clement Wilkinson, who published extensive extracts that have been quoted by subsequent authors; the letters were explored more recently by Raymond H Deck, Jr (see Deck, 'The "Vastation" of Henry James, Sr.'). Letters referred to in this book as held at the Swedenborg Society Archive, have been transcribed by the author personally.

[164] Deck, 'The "Vastation" of Henry James, Sr.', p. 238.

[165] Ibid., p. 239.

[166] Ibid., p. 255.

[167] See Chapter 1.

[168] William James (ed.), *The Literary Remains of the Late Henry James* (Boston: James R Osgood and Co., 1885), pp. 376, 377. This belief can be found in contemporary assertions that Swedenborg lived in two worlds, the spiritual and the natural, a situation that would have rendered him dysfunctional; whereas, he lived in only one world that was both natural and spiritual.

[169] Habegger, *The Father*, pp. 295, 297.

[170] J J G Wilkinson, letter to Henry James, Sr, 28 June 1849, in Swedenborg Society Archive K/123.

[171] J J G Wilkinson, letter to Henry James, Sr, 27 December 1850, p. 3, in Houghton Library, Harvard University, at <http://nrs.harvard.edu/urn-3:FHCL.HOUGH:12249590>, accessed 11 June 2014.

[172] Habegger, *The Father*, p. 375.

[173] J J G Wilkinson, letter to Henry James, Sr, 27 December 1850, p. 2, in Houghton Library, Harvard University, at <http://nrs.harvard.edu/urn-3:FHCL.HOUGH:12249590>, accessed 11 June 2014.

[174] Henry James, Sr, letter to J J G Wilkinson, 6 September 1852, quoted in Perry, *The Thought and Character of William James*, vol. I, p. 23. James went on in the same letter to tell Wilkinson that he had heard also of a change in his friend's personal appearance: 'I left you a thin, scholarly, unobtrusive, somewhat shy manner of man, and now they tell me that you are become corpulent, florid, altogether potent and perhaps aggressive...Accordingly I must go over the water before two years are past, if only to be reintroduced to you'.

[175] J J G Wilkinson, letter to Henry James, Sr, 19 May 1853, in Swedenborg Society Archive K/123.

[176] Henry James, Sr, letter to Ralph Waldo Emerson, 1856, quoted in Habegger, *The Father*, p. 376.

[177] Habegger, *The Father*, p. 237.

[178] Henry James, Sr, *Christianity the Logic of Creation* (London: William White, 1857), pp. iii-iv.

[179] Henry James, Sr, letter to J J G Wilkinson, 9 September 1851, quoted by Clement Wilkinson, *James John Garth Wilkinson*, pp. 184-5.

[180] J J G Wilkinson, letter to Henry James, Sr, 20 May 1879, pp. 4, 2, in Houghton Library, Harvard University, at <http://nrs.harvard.edu/urn-3:FHCL.HOUGH:12249590>, accessed 11 June 2014.

[181] Henry James, Jr, letter to Howard Sturgis, 24 August 1912, in *The Henry James Letters*, vol. IV, pp. 624-5.

Chapter Four

[1] Baron Du Potet de Sennevoy, *Magnetism and Magic*, tr. and ed. A H E Lee (London: George Allen & Unwin Ltd., 1927), p. 84.

[2] J J G Wilkinson, letter to Henry James, Sr, 1 June 1849, in Swedenborg Society Archive K/123.

[3] Roger Cooter, *The Cultural Meaning of Popular Science. Phrenology and the Organization of Consent in Nineteenth-Century Britain* (Cambridge: Cambridge University Press, 1984), pp. 42-8.

[4] For a detailed discussion of mesmerism within the Victorian social and political context, see Alison Winter, *Mesmerized: Powers of Mind in Victorian Britain* (Chicago and London: University of Chicago Press, 1998).

[5] The earliest report of a technique that would now be recognized as hypnosis is recorded in a scroll from Egypt in the third century AD. This describes the induction of

a trance in a youth by fixation on a luminous object, giving rise to visions that were apparently sought for religious purposes: see Henri F Ellenberger, *The Discovery of the Unconscious: The History and Evolution of Dynamic Psychiatry* (London: Allen Lane, Penguin Press, 1970), p. 34.

6   A detailed account of Mesmer and his work is given by Vincent Buranelli, *The Wizard from Vienna: Franz Anton Mesmer and the Origins of Hypnotism* (London: Peter Owen, 1975).

7   Those who believed in the reality of a magnetic fluid were later dubbed 'fluidists'.

8   Buranelli, *The Wizard from Vienna*, pp.177-9.

9   These societies and their links with Swedenborgians are discussed in Chapter 2.

10   For a discussion of mesmerism in England in the late eighteenth century, see Chapter 2.

11   Adam Crabtree, *From Mesmer to Freud: Magnetic Sleep and the Roots of Psychological Healing* (New Haven: Yale University Press, 1993), p. 194.

12   Winter, *Mesmerized*, pp. 42-3. An earlier Royal Commission, ordered by Louis XVI, had concluded in 1784 that animal magnetism was a fiction and the phenomena were based purely on the effects of imagination: see Buranelli, *The Wizard From Vienna*, pp. 161-4.

13   Du Potet, *Magnetism and Magic*, p. 53.

14   Ibid., p. 80. White powder 'taken from a Druidic tomb', sprinkled on the charcoal circle, gave rise to visions of the dead: ibid., p. 82.

15   Ibid., p. 84. French magician Eliphas Levi (pseud. Alphonse Louis Constant, 1810-75) admired Du Potet, saying that magnetism had 'revealed to him the science of magic'. However, said Levi, Du Potet had taken care not to reveal too much about these powers, and therefore his books are not dangerous: Eliphas Levi, *Magic: A History of Its Rites, Rituals, and Mysteries*, tr. Arthur Edward Waite (Mineola, NY: Dover Publications, 2006), p. 339.

16   Du Potet, *Magnetism and Magic*, pp. 98-9.

17   Ibid., p. 102.

18   Ibid., p. 103.

19   J J G Wilkinson, letter to his fiancée Emma Marsh, 23 May 1837, in Swedenborg Society Archive K/124 (e).

20   Ibid.

21   J J G Wilkinson, letter to his fiancée Emma Marsh, 2 October 1837, in Swedenborg Society Archive K/124 (e).

22   J J G Wilkinson, letter to his fiancée Emma Marsh, 9 October 1837, in Swedenborg

Society Archive K/124 (e). The 'Henry' referred to here is possibly one of the household servants. The identity of 'Mr. Hewitt' is uncertain, but as the handwriting here is unclear this may be an early reference to Wilkinson's friend William Howitt (1792-1879).

23 J J G Wilkinson, letter to his fiancée Emma Marsh, 15 October 1837, in Swedenborg Society Archive K/124 (e). This telling letter illustrates that Wilkinson regarded mesmerism as the subjugation of will to that of the mesmerist, and indicates that he accepted Du Potet's assertion that the process is based on magic. In the same letter, he describes further experiments on the unfortunate Henry, who left the household soon afterwards.

24 John Elliotson, 'Utility of Mesmerism in various Diseases treated by different Gentlemen', in *The Zoist: A Journal of Cerebral Physiology & Mesmerism*, vol. II, no. VII (October 1844), pp. 376-88.

25 There is little doubt that Wilkinson's papers were 'cleansed' by his family of references to occult activities, including mesmerism and spiritualism, before they were deposited in archives that are available to the public. His wife is on record as being particularly anxious to erase references to Wilkinson's involvement with spiritualism (see Chapter 5). Because of this, research into Wilkinson's views on mesmerism and spiritualism is limited to his published articles, as well as archival snippets that were apparently overlooked before archiving, probably because interpretation of them is obscure.

26 Biographical information about Elliotson is given in Elizabeth S Ridgway, 'John Elliotson (1791-1868): a bitter enemy of legitimate medicine? Part I: Earlier years and the introduction to mesmerism', in *Journal of Medical Biography*, vol. 1 (1993), pp. 191-8.

27 Elliotson's notes on this demonstration were published as one of a series of five articles on mesmerism by Chenevix: Richard Chenevix, 'Experiments and Observations on Mesmerism', in *The London Medical and Physical Journal*, vol. 62 (1829), pp. 315-24. It is an indication of opposition to mesmerism within the establishment that Chenevix's involvement with mesmerism was omitted from his major obituaries: see, for example, 'Richard Chenevix, Esq. F.R.S.', in *The Gentleman's Magazine and Historical Chronicle*, vol. C (June 1830), pp. 562-3.

28 John Elliotson, 'Animal Magnetism. Experiments of Baron Dupotet', in *The Lancet*, vol. II (2 September 1837), pp. 836-40.

29 [Thomas Wakley], 'Animal Magnetism. Second report of facts and experiments', in *The Lancet*, vol. II (9 June 1838), pp. 377-83 (p. 379).

30 [Thomas Wakley], 'Animal Magnetism', in *The Lancet*, vol. II (26 May 1838), pp. 282-8; 'Animal Magnetism. Second report of facts and experiments', in *The Lancet*,

vol. II (9 June 1838), pp. 377-83; 'Animal Magnetism. Conclusion of second report of facts and experiments', in *The Lancet*, vol. II (16 June 1838), pp. 400-3; 'Animal Magnetism. Third report of facts and experiments', in *The Lancet*, vol. II (23 June 1838), pp. 441-6; 'Animal Magnetism. Fourth report.——Remarks and experiments', in *The Lancet*, vol. II (7 July 1838), pp. 516-9; 'Animal Magnetism. Fifth report of experiments and facts', in *The Lancet*, vol. 2 (14 July 1838), pp. 546-9; 'Animal Magnetism. Sixth report of experiments and facts', in *The Lancet*, vol. II (21 July 1838), pp. 585-90; 'Animal Magnetism. Seventh report of experiments and facts', in *The Lancet*, vol. II (28 July 1838), pp. 615-20.

[31] For example, Elliotson concluded that the potency of a magnetic pass depends upon the surface area of the hand that was used, so that two fingers are more potent than one, and the whole hand is the most potent: see [Wakley], 'Animal Magnetism. Third report of facts and experiments', in *The Lancet*, vol. II (23 June 1838), pp. 441-6.

[32] [Wakley], 'Animal Magnetism. Fourth report.——Remarks and experiments', in *The Lancet*, vol. II (7 July 1838), pp. 516-9. Elliotson here showed the same precision that had characterized his previous observations; he maintained that the operator's finger must be immersed in water up to the middle joint in order to magnetize water.

[33] John Elliotson, 'Cure of a true Cancer of the Female Breast with Mesmerism', in *The Zoist*, vol. VI, no. XXIII (October 1848), pp. 213-37.

[34] [Thomas Wakley], Editorials, in *The Lancet*, vol. II (8 September 1838), pp. 834-6 and vol. II (15 September 1838), pp. 873-7. Wakley recognized that the phenomena of mesmerism actually occur, but he dismissed the proposed mechanism. Rather that following the logical path of seeking an alternative explanation for these striking phenomena, Wakley chose to dismiss the whole process.

[35] [Thomas Wakley], 'Expulsion of Elizabeth O'Key—Resignation of Dr. Elliotson.——Meeting of Students', in *The Lancet*, vol. I (5 January 1839), pp. 561-2. Elliotson wrote a 36-page farewell letter to his students, but they declined to read it in public because it included derogatory references to other professors. It is an indication of Wakley's venom against Elliotson that he published a report about this in the *The Lancet*: [Thomas Wakley], 'Rejection of a farewell letter from ex-Professor Elliotson', in *The Lancet*, vol. I (9 March 1839), p. 888. Elliotson believed that his erstwhile friend had changed sides simply in order to keep in step with the changing tide of professional opinion about mesmerism.

[36] Elliotson, 'Animal Magnetism. Experiments of Baron Dupotet', p. 836. Elliotson does not name 'the necromancer of Grand Cairo', but implies that he was well known at that

time. We do not know the exact date of Elliotson's visit, but in 1850 Helena Blavatsky, founder of the Theosophical Society, visited Cairo where she is said to have met a Coptic magician called Paolos Metamon who became her teacher: see Jean Overton Fuller, *Blavatsky and Her Teachers* (London: East-West Publications, 1988), pp. 5-6. Metamon was described at that time as 'celebrated': see Mary K Neff (ed.), *Personal Memoirs of H. P. Blavatsky* (Wheaton, IL: Quest / Theosophical Publishing House, 1971), p. 165. So Metamon, or at least one of his circle, may have been the 'so often described' necromancer visited by Elliotson.

37 Elliotson quoted from Agrippa's *De Occulta Philosophia* regarding the phenomenon of thought transmission: John Elliotson, *Human Physiology* (London: Longman, Orme, Brown, Green & Longmans, 1840), p. 664. Amongst other references, Elliotson cited the Italian physician Petrus Pomponatius (1462-1525) who believed that the power of the imagination or will of one person can influence another, and can even extend to inanimate matter: ibid., p. 664. He also quoted from Joaannes Stobaeus (5th century AD) a passage attributed to Solon (*c.* 638-558 BC): 'Sometimes the fury of the worst disease,/ The hand by gentle stroking will appease': ibid., p. 665. It is plain that Elliotson had a wide-ranging knowledge of classical, medieval and contemporary literature on phenomena related to mesmerism.

38 Elliotson was especially interested in the alleged phenomenon of seeing with the fingers, remarking that he knew of 'no reason why one nerve of sense should not be able to perform the office of another': Elliotson, *Human Physiology*, p. 1184. Today, the phenomenon of synaesthesia, in which, for example, the sensation of touch is experienced in colour, is well established. However, this falls short of the phenomena described during mesmerism, in which, for example, it was alleged that printed words could be read by using the fingers. The possibility of 'finger-seeing' is still under active investigation today, mainly in relation to the perception of printed words and of colours through the fingers. The evidence for this is regarded as inconclusive: see Yung-Jong Shiah and Wai-Cheong Carl Tam, 'Do Human Fingers "See"?—"Finger-Reading" Studies in the East and West', in *European Journal of Parapsychology*, vol. 20, no. 2 (2005), pp. 117-34. Elliotson referred to the satirical poem 'Hudibras' which was written in the seventeenth century by Samuel Butler (1612-80). This included the lines 'Of Rosicrucian virtuosis,/ Who see with ears and hear with noses': Elliotson, *Human Physiology*, p. 661 n.

39 [Wakley], 'Animal Magnetism. Second report of facts and experiments', in *The Lancet*, vol. II (9 June 1838), p. 377; Elliotson, *Human Physiology*, p. 685.

40 John Elliotson, *John Elliotson on Mesmerism*, ed. Fred Kaplan (New York: Da Capo Press, 1982), p. 1169.

41 Ibid., p. 690 n.

42 Elliotson referred to his friend Dr Alderson of Hull, who had 'exploded the existence of apparitions, by demonstrating that the seeing of apparitions is symptomatic of certain states of disease': Elliotson, 'Animal Magnetism. Experiments of Baron Dupotet', p. 836.

43 Godwin, *The Theosophical Enlightenment*, pp. 190-1. It is claimed that Elliotson, after his conversion, 'said he had been living all his life in darkness, and had thought that there was nothing in existence but the material': Epes Sargent, *Planchette; or, The Despair of Science* (Boston: Roberts Brothers, 1869), p. 21.

44 Elliotson, 'Utility of Mesmerism', pp. 379-80. Elliotson used conventional treatment, but Wilkinson was also attended by his friend, homoeopath Decimus Hands (1805-72), who mesmerized him with beneficial effect. Hands and Wilkinson had attended Du Potet's demonstrations together. Wilkinson's illness was so severe that his brother William wrote in alarm about it to their father: William Wilkinson, letter to his father James John Wilkinson, 26 February 1859, in Swedenborg Society Archive K/124 (b).

45 J J G Wilkinson, letter to his fiancée Emma Marsh, 8 April 1839, in Swedenborg Society Archive K/124 (e). This was the year after Elliotson had been forced to resign from his clinical and academic positions, and Wilkinson's report shows that Elliotson still enjoyed substantial popularity.

46 J J G Wilkinson, letter to Henry James, Sr, 1 February 1844, in Swedenborg Society Archive K/123. George Bush (1796-1859) was professor of Hebrew and oriental literature at New York University. He became interested in mesmerism in 1843, and this led him to join the Swedenborgian church: see *Memoirs and Reminiscences of the Late Prof. George Bush*, ed. Woodbury M Fernald (Boston: Otis Clapp, 1860), pp. 279-81. Bush later published a book, *Mesmer and Swedenborg; or, the Relation of the Developments of Mesmerism to the Doctrines and Disclosures of Swedenborg* (New York: Allen, 1847), in which he set out his ideas comprehensively.

47 J J G Wilkinson, *Epidemic Man and His Visitations*, p. 4.

48 J J G Wilkinson, 'Swedenborg on Trance', in *The Zoist*, vol. V, no. XX (January 1848), pp. 345-7 (p. 345).

49 J J G Wilkinson, letter to Henry James, Sr, 2 July 1846, in Swedenborg Society Archive K/123. Wilkinson was not alone in believing that this story was possibly true, it was taken seriously by many people when it was published in England: see Winter, *Mesmerized*, p. 121.

50 For Wilkinson's friendship with Chauncey Hare Townshend (1798-1868), see J J G Wilkinson, letter to J F I Tafel, 9 July 1841, in Swedenborg Society Archive K/126 (e).

51 J J G Wilkinson, 'Mesmerism', in *The Monthly Magazine*, vol. IV (1840), pp. 443-58.

52 Ibid., p. 456.

53 Ibid., p. 458. The difference in perception between spirits and people who are still in the natural world is discussed by Swedenborg, *Heaven and Hell*, §§461-2, pp. 336-8.

54 J J G Wilkinson, 'Mesmerism', p. 456.

55 J J G Wilkinson, *The Human Body*, p. 392.

56 James John Garth Wilkinson, 'Sleep II. Mesmerism and Hypnotism', handwritten lecture notes, in Swedenborg Society Archive A/56 (i), p. 3. The social significance of the relationship between the 'active' mesmerist (usually male) and the 'passive' subject (usually female) is clear. Wilkinson likened this to the relationship of 'Father and Mother with child, of husband and wife, of sovereign and subject': ibid., p. 31.

57 Mesmerized subjects can develop supernormal powers because 'the subjugation of the body always sets free the mind': ibid., p. 34.

58 J J G Wilkinson, *The Human Body*, p. 392.

59 Ibid., p. 393.

60 Bush, *Mesmer and Swedenborg*, p. 71.

61 Swedenborg, *Divine Love and Wisdom*, §291, p. 123. According to Swedenborg, this 'sphere', which everybody has both in the material and in the spiritual world, carries information about the 'loves' of a person; thus, the sphere carries information about a person's (or, after death, the spirit's) inclination towards the material or the spiritual. This sphere is very obvious in the spiritual world where like spirits automatically congregate (in heaven or in hell), but in life it gives rise to feelings of attraction to or repulsion from another person.

62 Bush, *Mesmer and Swedenborg*, p. 29.

63 J J G Wilkinson, *Greater Origins*, pp. 372-96.

64 Ibid., pp. 372-3.

65 Ibid., p. 391.

66 Ibid., p. 373.

67 Ibid., p. 380.

68 Ibid., p. 379.

69 J J G Wilkinson, *The Human Body*, p. 263.

70 Ibid., pp. 264, 263.

71 Ibid., p. 263.

72 Ibid., p. 264.

73 Ibid., pp. 393-4.

74 Ibid., pp. 394-5.

75 The Philosophy of Paracelsus is usefully discussed by Andrew Weeks, *Paracelsus: Speculative Theory and the Crisis of the Early Reformation* (Albany, NY: State University of New York Press, 1997). The correspondence between the macrocosm and the microcosm is of course a core theme of Western esotericism. Paracelsus, unlike Swedenborg, emphasized correspondences between humans and the planets and stars. Paracelsus regarded epidemics—particularly the plague—as being the result of human wickedness which emanates from humans into the cosmos and is transmitted back to them (Weeks, *Paracelsus*, pp.70-1). However, Paracelsus stopped short of suggesting (as Wilkinson proposed, following Swedenborg) that all noxious plants and animals are thus created. Wilkinson's concept of 'sphere-perception', which he says is 'high ground' that is 'not important for many at present' (J J G Wilkinson, *Greater Origins*, p. 373), is plainly analogous to Paracelsus's concept of seeing by the 'light of nature': see Nicholas Goodrick-Clarke (tr. and ed.), *Paracelsus: Essential Readings* (Berkeley, CA: North Atlantic Books, 1999), p. 96. The most striking similarity between Wilkinson and Paracelsus is their desire to use this occult knowledge to inform the treatment of disease. Swedenborg did not regard the study of medicine as the path to higher knowledge; he made a particular note of Plato's comment that 'Not one of these arts, such as medicine, is of any moment for the acquiring of the truest wisdom': Swedenborg, *A Philosopher's Notebook*, p. 339. The original quotation does not include the phrase 'such as medicine' which apparently was interpolated by Swedenborg: see Plato, *Epinomis*, 976a, tr. Richard D McKirahan, Jr, in Plato, *Complete Works*, ed. John M Cooper (Indianapolis: Hackett Publishing, 1997), pp. 1617-33 (p. 1620).

76 Wilkinson sets out his theory of epidemics in *Epidemic Man and his Visitations*. This is considered further in Chapter 7.

77 Wilkinson mentioned that he was reading Paracelsus in a letter to his fiancée Emma Marsh, undated (1837/8), in Swedenborg Society Archive K/124 (e). We do not know whether Wilkinson read the primary works of Paracelsus, which were available although difficult to access, or whether he had read only Robert Browning's drama *Paracelsus* (1835), which was widely known at the time, and which was regarded as 'the best picture of Paracelsus in the English language': Charles Webster, 'The Nineteenth-Century Afterlife of Paracelsus', in Roger Cooter (ed.), *Studies in the*

History of Alternative Medicine (London: Macmillan Press, 1988), pp. 79-88 (pp. 82-3).

[78] Swedenborg, *The Animal Kingdom*, quoted in J J G Wilkinson, *Emanuel Swedenborg*, p. 123. Swedenborg discussed the mechanism of telepathy in his early work *On Tremulation*: see John S Haller, Jr, *Swedenborg, Mesmer, and the Mind/Body Connection. The Roots of Complementary Medicine* (West Chester, PA: Swedenborg Foundation, 2010), p. 13.

[79] J J G Wilkinson, *Emanuel Swedenborg*, pp. 121-7.

[80] Ibid., p. 123.

[81] J J G Wilkinson, 'Swedenborg on Trance', pp. 345-6.

[82] Ibid. Wilkinson quotes from the posthumously published third part of *The Economy of the Animal Kingdom*, known in English translation as *The Fibre*. Wilkinson admitted that Swedenborg might also have learned of the shamanic activities of the Lapps from John Scheffer, *The History of Lapland* (Oxford: George West and Amos Curtein, 1674). Wilkinson had been told about this book but had not read it; had he done so, he would have found a description of trance induction by drumming, with results similar to those described by Swedenborg: Scheffer, *The History of Lapland*, pp. 45-60. There is no evidence that Swedenborg did in fact travel to Lapland.

[83] Emanuel Swedenborg, quoted in Alfred Acton, *Swedenborg's Preparation* (London: Swedenborg Society, 1951), p. 20.

[84] The physiological responses to self-hypnosis and to meditation, which include a significant diminution or even cessation of respiration, are discussed by Leona VandeVusse, Lisa Hanson, Margaret A Berner and Jill M White Winters, 'Impact of Self-Hypnosis in Women on Select Physiological and Psychological Parameters', in *Journal of Obstetric, Gynecologic and Neonatal Nursing*, vol. 39, no. 2 (March/April 2010), pp. 159-68, and J Kesterson and N F Clinch, 'Metabolic rate, respiratory exchange ratio, and apneas during meditation', in *American Journal of Physiology*, vol. 256 (1989), pp. 632-8.

[85] For example, the *Bhagavad Gita* refers to yogis who offer 'the movement of the outgoing breath into the incoming, and the incoming breath into the outgoing, and thus at last remain in trance, stopping all breathing': *Bhagavad-Gita as it is*, tr. A C Bhaktivedanta Swami Prabhupada, 2nd edn. (Watford: The Bhaktivedanta Book Trust, 2006), p. 212. The use of breathing techniques by Christians, including Hesychasts, is discussed in Elémire Zolla, 'The Art of Breathing in the West', in *Studies in Comparative Religion*, vol. 2 , no. 3 (Summer 1968), at <http://www.

studiesincomparativereligion.com/Public/articles/The_Art_of_Breathing_in_the_
West-by_Elemire_Zolla.aspx>, accessed 5 May 2012.

86 Winter, *Mesmerized*, pp. 246-75.

87 For example, the Anglican evangelical preacher and former Arctic explorer William
Scoresby (1789-1857) had made a scientific study of terrestrial magnetism and
regarded mesmerism, or 'Zoistic magnetism' as he called it, as a phenomenon akin
to terrestrial magnetism, in which the magnetic fluid could be used to promote moral
regeneration by exerting the will of the morally strong over that of the weak (Winter,
Mesmerized, pp. 254-60). The accusation that mesmerism was demonic was made
most influentially by Hugh M'Neile (1795-1879), an Anglican clergyman in Liverpool
who published his sermon on 'Satanic agency and mesmerism' in 1842 (Winter,
Mesmerized, pp. 260-1). M'Neile's thesis was subsequently refuted by James Braid.

88 J. S., 'Remarks on Mesmerism', in *The Intellectual Repository*, New Series, vol. V, no.
58 (October 1844), pp. 389-92.

89 X., 'Mesmerism', in *The Intellectual Repository*, New Series, vol. V, no. 59 (November
1844), pp. 424-5.

90 Editorial, 'Remarks of the Editor on the same subject [mesmerism]', in *The Intellectual
Repository*, New Series, vol. V, no. 59 (November 1844), pp. 425-34 (p. 426).

91 Ibid., p. 428. Swedenborg's 'atmospheres', which arise from the sun, include three
'natural' atmospheres: the first, 'aerial' atmosphere provides the medium of hearing;
a second purer atmosphere is the medium of sight; and the third, still purer atmosphere produces magnetic forces. Since man is a microcosm, this finest, magnetic
atmosphere has a corresponding mental function, which is reasoning: Swedenborg,
Spiritual Diary, vol. I, §222, pp. 49-50.

92 Editorial, 'Remarks of the Editor', in *The Intellectual Repository*, New Series, vol. V,
no. 59 (November 1844), p. 431.

93 George Combe (1788-1858) was a friend of Charles Augustus Tulk, who, together
with Elliotson, was a senior member of the British Phrenological Association: Edward
Sheppard Symes, Report to the Phrenological Society, *The Zoist*, vol. I, no. III (October
1843), pp. 224-7.

94 Winter, *Mesmerized*, pp. 117-19.

95 The localization of cerebral function is discussed by Swedenborg in his work *The Brain,
Considered Anatomically, Physiologically and Philosophically*, tr. R L Tafel, 2 vols.
(London: James Speirs, 1882-7; repr. Bryn Athyn, PA: Swedenborg Scientific Association,
2010). Wilkinson assisted in this translation, which Tafel dedicated to him for his

'scholarship and genius' in translating Swedenborg's scientific works. Wilkinson was concerned that the work would appear to endorse vivisection, which he vehemently opposed, and requested that Tafel should dissociate Swedenborg's method of investigation from the crudity of vivisection, which Tafel duly did in his preface: J J G Wilkinson, letter to R L Tafel, 11 April 1882, in Swedenborg Society Archive K/125 (1).

[96] This was pointed out in several leading medical journals of the day: for example, see T Abell, 'The Phrenology of Swedenborg', in *Boston Medical and Surgical Journal*, vol. IX, no. 18 (11 December 1833), pp. 277-80. For an assessment of Swedenborg's theory of cerebral localization from today's perspective, see Konrad Akert and Michael P Hammond, 'Emanuel Swedenborg (1688-1772) and his contributions to neurology', in *Medical History*, vol. 6 (July 1962), pp. 254-62.

[97] J J G Wilkinson, *The Human Body*, p. 46.

[98] Ibid., p. 45. Wilkinson proposed that this was 'a comparative phrenology of the human race itself' (ibid., p. 46) but again characteristically he fails to develop this idea, which from a Swedenborgian perspective might relate to the correspondence between the Divine Human, the heavens and humanity.

[99] Biographical information on James Braid is taken from Arthur Edward Waite, 'Biographical Introduction', in James Braid, *Braid on Hypnotism: Neurypnology*, ed. Arthur Edward Waite (London: George Redway, 1899), pp. 1-66; and Donald Robertson, 'James Braid's Life & Work', in James Braid, *The Discovery of Hypnosis. The Complete Writings of James Braid, the Father of Hypnotherapy*, ed. Donald Robertson ([n.p.]: National Council for Hypnotherapy, 2008), pp. 8-16.

[100] Robertson, 'James Braid's Life & Work', p. 8. The Wernerian Society was named after German geologist Abraham Gottlob Werner (1749-1817). Its proceedings were published in the *Edinburgh New Philosophical Journal* which was edited by Robert Jameson (1774-1854), Regius Professor of Natural History at Edinburgh University who founded the Society. The value of Swedenborg's scientific work was still recognized and referred to at that time by members of the Society; see, for example, George Bellas Greenough, 'Remarks on the Theory of the Elevation of Mountains', in *Edinburgh New Philosophical Journal*, vol. 17 (1834), pp. 205-27 (p. 211).

[101] For example, Braid responded to the to the proposition that his cures were nothing new and were simply the effects of imagination by saying 'can anyone who has attended to what I have given as my opinion, say that this either *was*, or *is* my opinion?': James Braid, *Neurypnology; or, The Rationale of Nervous Sleep, Considered in Relation with Animal Magnetism. Illustrated by Numerous Cases of its Successful Application*

in the Relief and Cure of Disease (London: John Churchill, 1843), p. 8. After describing his cure by hypnosis of three cases of visual impairment, he concluded that 'the improvement could not at all be attributable to imagination, but to the altered condition in the capillary circulation and distribution of the *vis nervosa*' (ibid., p. 176).

102 Braid, *Neurypnology*, p. 17. In a footnote, Braid again emphasized that this effect is not due to the imagination, but is a physical effect.

103 Ibid., p. 16.

104 Waite, 'Biographical Introduction', p. 33. A better-known translation of Reichenbach's work, by John Ashburner, is Baron Charles von Reichenbach, *Physico-Physiological Researches on the Dynamics of Magnetism, Electricity, Heat, Light, Crystallization, and Chemism, in their relations to Vital Force*, tr. John Ashburner (London: Hippolyte Baillière, 1850). Ashburner dedicated this book to his friend Elliotson.

105 Karl von Reichenbach (1788-1869) believed that the aurora borealis is an Odic flame that can be seen by everybody: see Reichenbach, *Physico-Physiological Researches*, pp. 5-36.

106 James Braid, *The Power of the Mind over the Body: An Experimental Inquiry into the Nature and Cause of the Phenomena Attributed by Baron Reichenbach and others to a New Imponderable*; repr. in *The Discovery of Hypnosis*, pp. 236-50.

107 The history of this concept within Western esotericism has been traced from classical times through to the twentieth century by Marieke J E van den Doel and Wouter J Hanegraaff, 'Imagination', in *DGWE*, pp. 606-16.

108 Coleridge discusses this in his *Biographia Literaria* (London: J M Dent, 1930), pp. 159-60.

109 Henry Corbin, *Alone with the Alone. Creative Imagination in the Sūfism of Ibn 'Arabī*, tr. Ralph Manheim (New Jersey: Princeton University Press, 1997), p. 189. The belief that mesmeric somnambulists were able to gain access to the spiritual world, and that they developed the kind of supernatural abilities such as clairvoyance begs the question of the relationship, if any, between the 'imagination' that was believed to underpin mesmerism, and the 'creative imagination' of Western esotericism. Corbin outlines the varieties of imagination that were described by the Sufi mystic Ibn 'Arabī (1165-1240). 'Arabī distinguished between 'conjoined' imagination that lives and dies with the imagining subject, and imagination that is self-subsisting and survives death to become the organ of 'perception' of the soul. Both of these forms of imagination were regarded as real, as they are both expressions of the 'absolute Imagination': Corbin, *Alone with the Alone*, pp. 219-20. Ibn 'Arabī's self-subsisting imagination is analogous to Wilkinson's mesmeric

medium, which Wilkinson regarded as identical with Swedenborg's soul-substance that survives after death and provides the organ of (spiritual) perception for spirits.

[110] Paracelsus described, for example, a *'magica imaginato'*, by means of which emotions such as envy, hatred and deceit go to the heavens and come back as 'supernatural diseases' such as the plague: Weeks, *Paracelsus*, p.71. He believed that remedies for disease could be discerned by knowing the 'virtues' of natural agents such as plants, in relation to the heavens and to the human condition, a process that depends upon exercising the active imagination as an intermediary between the macrocosm and the microcosm: Walter Pagel, *Paracelsus. An Introduction to Philosophical Medicine in the Era of the Renaissance*, 2nd edn. (Basel; New York: Karger, 1982), pp. 126-202. Paracelsus regarded fancy, in contrast to true imagination, as the 'madman's cornerstone': Corbin, *Alone with the Alone*, p. 179.

[111] Swedenborg's concept is not mentioned in van den Doel and Hanegraaff's essay on 'Imagination'.

[112] Swedenborg, *Spiritual Diary*, vol. I, §192, pp. 29-30.

[113] J J G Wilkinson, letter to Henry James, Sr, 23 January 1848, in Swedenborg Society Archive K/123.

[114] J J G Wilkinson, *The Human Body*, p. 402 n. Warren Felt Evans (1817-89), a Swedenborgian minister who was the first published author of the 'New Thought' movement, had read Wilkinson's work: Warren Felt Evans, *Esoteric Christianity and Mental Therapeutics* (Boston: H H Carter & Karrick, 1886), p. 95.

[115] J J G Wilkinson, *War, Cholera, and the Ministry of Health*, p. 14.

[116] J J G Wilkinson, letter to his wife Emma Wilkinson, 13 October, 1848, in Swedenborg Society Archive K/124 (a). Wilkinson had recently returned from France, where he had witnessed many horrors during the Paris uprising. He would undoubtedly have taken the subject's reaction as confirmation of his belief in the more controversial claims for mesmerism, including thought transference.

[117] J J G Wilkinson, letter to his wife Emma Wilkinson, 19 October 1848, in Swedenborg Society Archive K/124 (a). Wilkinson's emphasis on respiration as the key to the hypnotic state plainly refers to Swedenborg's spiritual practice.

[118] J J G Wilkinson, 'Sleep II. Mesmerism and Hypnotism'. Wilkinson did admit of some overlap between the two, such that sleep could be induced by either method, and psychological mechanisms came into play in mesmerism, in addition to the effect of the mesmerizer's sphere.

[119] J J G Wilkinson, *The Human Body*, pp. 399-400.

120 Ibid., p. 401 n. Today this is referred to as the placebo effect: see, for example, Arthur K Shapiro and Elaine Shapiro, *The Powerful Placebo. From Ancient Priest to Modern Physician* (Baltimore: Johns Hopkins University Press, 1997).

121 Donald Robertson, 'James Braid's Life & Work', p. 13.

122 James Braid, *Magic, Witchcraft, Animal Magnetism, Hypnotism, and Electrobiology; Being a Digest of the Latest Views of the Author on These Subjects*, 3rd edn. (London: John Churchill, 1852); repr. in *The Discovery of Hypnosis*, pp. 131-67 (p. 148).

123 The quote is taken from Dugald Stewart, *Elements of the Philosophy of the Human Mind*, in Dugald Stewart, *The Works of Dugald Stewart*, 7 vols. (Cambridge: Hilliard and Brown, 1829), vol. III, p. 157.

124 The term 'dynamic psychology' is taken here to mean the branch of psychology that relies on a priori assumptions concerning the importance of emotions, usually relating to past experiences, and internal mental mechanisms in the production of mental and behavioural phenomena, either normal or abnormal. The stereotypical example is the psychology of Sigmund Freud. This contrasts with descriptive psychology which relies on the experimental observation of thought processes and behaviour, from which hypotheses are generated and empirically tested. Today, dynamic psychology is marginalized within the disciplines of psychology and psychiatry, but it still has considerable influence in the humanities.

Braid's work was translated into French and German, and was much better known in Germany than in England: Arthur Edward Waite, 'Preface', in *Braid on Hypnotism*, pp. v-viii (pp. vii-viii). Braid's last thoughts on hypnotism were written in 1860, the final year of his life, and sent as evidence to the French Academy of Sciences which had commissioned the investigation of hypnotism: Braid, *The Discovery of Hypnosis*, p. 64. The central importance of James Braid's discovery of hypnosis, and the introduction of Braid's system, by means of his published works, into medical practice in France and Germany, is given little attention in the standard 'story' of psychoanalysis. The evidence that Garth Wilkinson was a key figure in guiding Braid towards his psychological formulation of hypnosis places Wilkinson on the pathway towards the development of psychodynamic theory.

125 Carter's biographical details are taken from J Estlin Carpenter, 'William Benjamin Carpenter. A Memorial Sketch', in William B Carpenter, *Nature and Man*, pp. 3-152.

126 Whilst at Edinburgh, the young Carpenter was gratified to find that he could hold his own with his professors in conversations about Goethe's philosophy. He also developed his interest in the ubiquity of the vital force at that time.

127 William Robert Grove (1811-96) published his ideas in *The Correlation of Physical Forces* (1846).

128 William B Carpenter, 'On the Mutual Relations of the Vital and Physical Forces', in *Philosophical Transactions of the Royal Society of London*, vol. 140 (1850), pp. 727-57.

129 William B Carpenter, 'On the Influence of Suggestion in Modifying and directing Muscular Movement, independently of Volition', in *Proceedings of the Royal Institution of Great Britain*, vol. 1 (12 March 1852), pp. 147-53. The concept of (although not the term) ideo-motor reflexes had been put forward in England by Thomas Laycock (1812-76) in 1840-5. Laycock based his ideas on the phenomenon of hydrophobia, a condition reported in people suffering from rabies, in which fear and the urge to run away is engendered by the idea of drinking water. Laycock traced this concept back to earlier authorities including Albrecht von Haller (1708-77). Carpenter denied that Laycock had introduced the idea before him, and said that Laycock had merely crystallized ideas that Carpenter had outlined tentatively in his own earlier works: see Vance M D Hall, 'The contribution of the physiologist, William Benjamin Carpenter (1813-1885), to the development of the principles of the correlation of forces and the conservation of energy', in *Medical History*, vol. 23, no. 2 (April 1979), pp. 129-55. A similar concept, with a wider application, was developed independently in Germany by such people as Johann Friedrich Herbart (1776-1841), Rudolf Hermann Lotze (1817-81), and Emil Harless (1820-62): see Armin Stock and Claudia Stock, 'A short history of ideo-motor action', in *Psychological Research*, vol. 68 (April 2004), pp. 176-88.

130 William B Carpenter, *Principles of Mental Physiology, with their applications to the training and discipline of the mind, and the study of its morbid conditions* (London: Henry S King, 1875), p. 515.

131 Carpenter's concepts plainly foreshadow those of Freud in his later development of psychoanalysis.

132 John S Haller, Jr, *Swedenborg, Mesmer, and the Mind/Body Connection*, p. 20.

133 For Wilkinson's friendship with William B Carpenter, see Clement Wilkinson, *James John Garth Wilkinson*, p. 51; and J J G Wilkinson, letter to his wife Emma Wilkinson, 12 April 1849, in Swedenborg Society Archive K/124 (a). For Carpenter's discussion of Swedenborg, see William B Carpenter, *Nature and Man*, pp. 246-7. Here, Carpenter expresses his regret that the achievements of Swedenborg the scientist had been overlooked because of the focus on his communication with the spirit world.

134 Swedenborg calls this single point the 'first simple' or 'Natural Point' which is the first manifestation of the infinite: see Emanuel Swedenborg, *The Principia; or, the First Principles of Natural Things*, tr. Augustus Clissold, 2 vols. (London: W Newbery, 1845-6), vol. I, pp. 46-71.

135 Emanuel Swedenborg, *A Compendium of the Theological and Spiritual Writings of Emanuel Swedenborg*, ed. W M Fernald (Boston: Crosby and Nichols, and Otis Clapp, 1854), p. 15. The source of the quotation is not given in this work, but elsewhere part of the same quotation is attributed to a letter from Patterson to a Dr Atlee, who had sent him a copy of the *Principia*: see Nathaniel Hobart, *Life of Emanuel Swedenborg; with some account of his Writings* (Boston: Allen and Goddard, 1831), p. 19. Hobart's book has been identified as a source text for Emerson's essay on Swedenborg: see Clarence Paul Hotson, 'Emerson's Biographical Sources for "Swedenborg"', in *Studies in Philology*, vol. 26, no. 1 (January 1929), pp. 23-46 (p. 37).

136 This is discussed in Lamm, *Swedenborg*, pp. 40-1.

137 J J G Wilkinson, *The Human Body*, p. 401 n.

138 Ibid.

139 Ibid., pp. 401-2 n. Wilkinson's concept of the mind being present throughout the body is derived from his Swedenborgian formulation of physiology.

140 Armin Stock and Claudia Stock, 'A short history of ideo-motor action', p. 176.

141 Other points of similarity between the thoughts of Carpenter and those of Wilkinson can be found, including their mutual rejection of idealist philosophies (for Carpenter's views see Carpenter, *Nature and Man*, pp. 184-210) and of Darwin's theory of evolution. However, my purpose here is to illustrate the congruence between Carpenter and Wilkinson regarding the ideas for which Carpenter is best known: the unity of forces and ideo-motor action.

142 Braid, *Magic, Witchcraft, Animal Magnetism*, in *The Discovery of Hypnosis*, p. 148.

143 Carpenter did not name Wilkinson, but Braid later identified Carpenter's 'intelligent friend' as Garth Wilkinson: see Braid, *Magic, Witchcraft, Animal Magnetism*, in *The Discovery of Hypnosis*, pp. 148-9.

144 Robert H Wozniak, *Classics in Psychology 1855-1914: Historical Essays* (Bristol: Thoemmes Press, 1999), p. 35.

145 J J G Wilkinson, letter to Emerson, 13 February 1848, in Swedenborg Society Archive K/125 (3). Prompted by Wilkinson, Morell included a section on Swedenborg in the second edition of his major survey of philosophy: J D Morell, *An Historical and Critical View of the Speculative Philosophy of Europe in the Nineteenth Century*

(New York: Carter and Brothers, 1853), pp. 202-6; see also Chapter 1.

146 J J G Wilkinson, letter to Henry James, Sr, 4 April 1848, cited in Clement Wilkinson, *James John Garth Wilkinson*, p. 51; see also Chapter 1. Wilkinson read his lecture on the Human Form to the Morells in 1848: J J G Wilkinson, letter to his wife Emma Wilkinson, 14 April 1848, in Swedenborg Society Archive K/124 (a). In 1853 Noble published his *Elements of Psychology*, which promotes a non-dualistic concept of body and soul similar to that of Wilkinson.

Chapter Five

1   J J G Wilkinson, letter to Henry James, Sr, 13 October 1855, p. 3, in Houghton Library, Harvard University, at <http://nrs.harvard.edu/urn-3:FHCL.HOUGH:12249590>, accessed 11 June 2014.

2   J J G Wilkinson, *Greater Origins*, p. 420. 'Spiritism' is a disparaging term adopted by followers of Swedenborg to refer to spiritualism, who believed that this practice was not a 'spiritual' one.

3   Frank Podmore, *Modern Spiritualism: A History and a criticism*, 2 vols. (London: Methuen & Co., 1902), vol. I, pp. 179-84.

4   William Howitt, *The History of the Supernatural*, 2 vols. (London: Longman, Green, Longman, Roberts & Green, 1863), vol. I, p. 17.

5   Ibid., p. 18.

6   Ibid., p. 19.

7   Mary Howitt, 'Appendix', in Joseph Ennemoser, *The History of Magic*, tr. William Howitt, 2 vols. (London: Henry G Bohn, 1854), vol. II, pp. 341-518 (pp. 388-96). Spiritualists made use of Wesley's opinion about spirits to support their cause, for example quoting him as saying, 'How much will it add to the happiness of those spirits which are already discharged from the body, that they are permitted to minister to those they have left behind?': 'Spiritualism and John Wesley', in *The Spiritual Magazine*, vol. 1 (1860), pp. 177-83 (p. 179).

8   Mary Howitt (1799-1888) remarked that, 'The power of supposed witchcraft and of spiritual manifestation seem to us identical . . . it possesses many features which seem to imply a close connection with the mysterious agency called Animal Magnetism': Mary Howitt, 'Appendix', p. 518.

9   James John Garth Wilkinson, *The Homoeopathic Principle Applied to Insanity. A Proposal to Treat Lunacy by Spiritualism* (Boston: Otis Clapp, 1857), pp. 6-7.

10 See *Conjuring Spirits: Texts and Traditions of Medieval Ritual Magic*, ed. Claire

Fanger (Pennsylvania: Pennsylvania State University Press, 1998).

[11] Robert A Gilbert and John Hamill (eds.), *The Rosicrucian Seer. Magical Writings of Frederick Hockley* (Wellingborough: Aquarian Press, 1986), pp. 11-25 (p. 21). For further information on Ebenezer Sibly, see Chapter 2.

[12] Gilbert and Hamill (eds.), *The Rosicrucian Seer*, pp. 149, 167.

[13] Garth Wilkinson's attitude towards magic hardened as he aged. As a young man, he had accepted the magical claims of Du Potet (see Chapter 4). In later life, he rejected magic, saying that it 'arises from the spiritual world, and from the abuse of correspondences. It is the fruit of an evil science in conjunction with a wicked will. Its creations are delusions': J J G Wilkinson, 'Magic'. Undated notebook, p. 1, in Swedenborg Society Archive A/245. Although undated, this note was written after 1887 as it refers to his book *Revelation, Mythology, Correspondences* (London: James Speirs, 1887).

[14] Geoffrey K Nelson, *Spiritualism and Society* (London: Routledge & Kegan Paul, 1969), p. 92.

[15] These letters are reproduced in Gilbert and Hamill (eds.), *The Rosicrucian Seer*, pp. 145-83. Owen's utopian socialism, and his conversion to spiritualism, are discussed in Chapter 8.

[16] J J G Wilkinson, letter to Henry James, Sr, 2 September 1847, in Swedenborg Society Archive K/123. Text from the body of Wilkinson's letter was published subsequently in the *New York Daily Tribune* in a letter on spiritualism signed 'H.J.', presumably Henry James, Sr. In this letter James refers to the information as having come from a respected friend 'with an intellect disciplined in the whole compass of knowledge', but published without permission! The article was kept by Wilkinson in a notebook, in which he refers to the publication as his own: Swedenborg Society Archive A/183 (p). This illustrates the complex relationship between James and Wilkinson at that time.

[17] J J G Wilkinson, letter to Henry James, Sr, 2 September 1847, in Swedenborg Society Archive K/123.

[18] Ibid.

[19] Ibid.

[20] In a comment on this, Wilkinson shows an awareness of the operation of unconscious mental mechanisms: 'Something similar to this has occurred with other things that have befallen her in the mesmeric state; as ideas, they are lost in the waking state, but as secret springs and forces they are not lost, and of some of them she avers that they will operate upon her as long as she lives, though she will always be unconscious of

them': J J G Wilkinson, letter to Henry James, Sr, 18 September 1847, in Swedenborg Society Archive K/123.

21 Ibid.

22 J J G Wilkinson, letter to Henry James, Sr, 19 May 1853, in Swedenborg Society Archive K/123.

23 The work of John Clowes in Lancashire has been discussed in Chapter 2.

24 See Janet Oppenheim, *The Other World: Spiritualism and Psychical Research in England, 1850-1914* (Cambridge: Cambridge University Press, 1985).

25 Frithjof Schuon describes the process by which new religions emerge when the old ones have become formulaic and no longer meet the needs of society at that time. This analysis can be applied generally, for example, to the emergence of Buddhism from Hinduism, and Christianity from Judaism: see Frithjof Schuon, *The Transcendent Unity of Religions* (Wheaton, IL: Theosophical Publishing House, 1993), pp. 95-6.

26 This issue is discussed in detail in Alex Owen, *The Darkened Room: Women, Power and Spiritualism in Late Nineteenth-Century England* (London: Virago Press, 1989).

27 Ibid., p. 143.

28 It was not until 1882 that the Married Women's Property Act gave women rights separate from their husbands. See Chapter 8 for a discussion of Wilkinson's support for the women's movement.

29 Logie Barrow, 'Socialism in Eternity: The Ideology of Plebeian Spiritualists, 1853-1913', in *History Workshop Journal*, no. 9 (Spring 1980), pp. 37-69.

30 Logie Barrow, *Independent Spirits: Spiritualism and English Plebeians 1850-1910* (London: Routledge and Kegan Paul, 1986), p. 41.

31 Elihu Rich (1819-75) is an obscure figure. A friend of Florence Theobald referred to him as a 'good Swedenborgian and Spiritualist, who passed on after a life of obscurity like so many others have done': F J Theobald, *More 'Forget-me-nots from God's Garden'* (London: Psychological Press Association, 1882), p. 121.

32 Carl Theophilus Odhner, *Annals of the New Church*, p. 443.

33 Edward Smedley, W Cooke Taylor, Henry Thompson and Elihu Rich, *The Occult Sciences: Sketches of the Traditions and Superstitions of Past Times, and the Marvels of the Present Day* (London and Glasgow: Richard Griffin and Company, 1855). This work was in the series of the *Encyclopaedia Metropolitana: or, System of Universal Knowledge*, which had been inspired by Samuel Taylor Coleridge. In his editorial preface to *The Occult Sciences*, Rich counters criticism of the uncritical

and 'affirmative' presentation in his book by saying that 'certain facts lose their significance...unless related with the air of a believer'.

34 Podmore, *Modern Spiritualism*, vol. II, p. 32.

35 E[lihu] R[ich], *Notes on Certain Forms of Spiritualism addressed to the Members of the "New Church", with remarks on a recent obituary* (London: William White, 1858).

36 Ibid., p. 9. James Knight (1790-1858), although a leader of the Swedenborgian community in Derby, was regarded with disapproval by the hierarchy of the sectarian New Church because of his other esoteric interests. His obituary in the *Monthly Observer and New Church Record* in November 1858, quoted by Rich, praised Knight's work for the New Church but condemned his other esoteric pursuits: 'he was strongly prone to astrological studies and pursuits, the love of which remained with him to the last...and advice was received from a "familiar spirit," with whom he professed to be in communication... With the weakness of mind produced by these pursuits, it is not to be wondered at that he drifted into the practice of mesmerism, clairvoyance, spiritualism, and other kindred fancies': E[lihu] R[ich], *Notes on Certain Forms of Spiritualism*, p. 4.

37 Ibid., p. 19. For more on Hartley's relationship with Swedenborg, see Chapter 2.

38 E[lihu] R[ich], *Notes on Certain Forms of Spiritualism*, p. 31. Presumably Clowes' amanuensis recorded, to his dictation, his spiritually inspired sermons and writings.

39 Ibid., p. 25.

40 Ibid., p. 10.

41 C. D. (pseud. Sophia De Morgan), *From Matter to Spirit. The Result of Ten Years' Experience in Spirit Manifestations. Intended as a Guide to Enquirers* (London: Longman, Green, Longman, Roberts & Green, 1863), pp. 302-3. On the anonymity of this publication, see Nelson, *Spiritualism and Society*, p. 90.

42 J J G Wilkinson, handwritten notes, undated but in a bundle from 1855-6, in Swedenborg Society Archive K/126 (b). Annie Milner was not the only medium to claim to have seen Wilkinson in the spirit world. Ethan Allen Hitchcock (1798-1870), an American writer on Hermetic topics including spiritual alchemy, claimed in the mid-nineteenth century that he was introduced to Swedenborg in the spirit world by 'his friend *Mr. Wilkinson*, whom I met in the spiritual world also': Ethan Allen Hitchcock, *Swedenborg, a Hermetic Philosopher. Being a sequel to Remarks on Alchemy and the Alchemists. Showing that Emanuel Swedenborg was a Hermetic Philosopher and that his writings may be interpreted from the point of view of*

Hermetic Philosophy. With a Chapter comparing Swedenborg and Spinoza (New York: D Appleton & Company, 1858), p. 119. Whilst this does not conclusively identify *Garth* Wilkinson as the subject, that interpretation is the most plausible; there were no other Wilkinsons associated with Swedenborg that would have been known to Hitchcock at that time.

43 J J G Wilkinson, handwritten notes, undated but in a bundle from 1855-6, in Swedenborg Society Archive K/126 (b). 'Spirit guides' were frequently identified as American Indians. See Rayna Green, 'The Tribe Called Wannabee: Playing Indian in America and Europe', in *Folklore*, vol. 99, no. 1 (1988), pp. 30-55 (p. 40).

44 Although several spiritualist 'groups' are considered separately, it seems that there was considerable overlap between membership as well as some commonality of mediums. Thus, Sophia De Morgan (1809-92), who had evidently attended seances at which Elihu Rich's medium Annie Milner was the medium, is recorded also as a member of Howitt's circle.

45 Ashburner, who wrote an account of a seance with Mrs Hayden (Podmore, *Modern Spiritualism*, vol. II, pp. 16-18) also wrote on animal magnetism and spiritualism, in a book dedicated to his friend, John Obadiah Newell Rutter (1799-1888), who had invented an instrument (the magnetoscope) by means of which it was claimed that magnetic forces in the human body could be demonstrated through the movement of a pendulum: John Ashburner, *Notes and Studies in the Philosophy of Animal Magnetism and Spiritualism* (London: H Baillière, 1867). It was believed that the same magnetic forces underpinned spiritualism. It was claimed that the pendular swing was modified by homoeopathic medicines placed on the hand of the operator, with the greatest effect produced by the highest dilutions. Another friend of Ashburner, Theodore Leger (1799-1853), claimed to have demonstrated differential effects on the pendulum from different phrenological areas: Ashburner, *Notes and Studies*, pp. 59-81. The magnetoscope provides a good demonstration of the perceived relationship between animal magnetism, spiritualism, phrenology and homoeopathy at that time, as well as the contemporary attempts to apply scientific method to the investigation of these phenomena.

46 Augustus De Morgan (1806-71) was Professor of Mathematics at University College London. His wife Sophia worked with Mrs Hayden, and Augustus became convinced of the validity of spiritualist manifestations, although he remained sceptical about their spiritual origin. He wrote the preface to his wife's book, *From Matter to Spirit*: see John Beloff, *Parapsychology: A Concise History* (London: Athlone Press, 1993), pp. 46-7.

47 Mrs Newton Crossland (1812-95) wrote mainly under the name of Camilla Toulmin, but published an account of her experiences with spiritualism under her own name: Mrs Newton Crossland, *Light in the Valley. My Experiences of Spiritualism* (London: Routledge, 1857). In this work, Mrs Crossland described Swedenborg as 'one of the most extraordinary mediums of whom the world has any record' (p. 106). She also quoted a letter from a medium calling herself 'Comfort', anticipating the time when Garth Wilkinson's proposals for the treatment of lunacy through spiritualism, when spiritualism would be regarded 'not as insanity, but as *a key whereby to unlock insanity*' (p. 124).

48 Benjamin Coleman had visited America where he attended a seance held by one of the Fox sisters, Kate: Benjamin Coleman, *Spiritualism in America* (London: F Pitman, 1861), pp. 12, 23.

49 Maurice Nenner was Professor of Hebrew at the Dissenters' College in St John's Wood.

50 See Oppenheim, *The Other World*, p. 37, and Alex Owen, *The Darkened Room*, p. 21.

51 Amice Lee, *Laurels and Rosemary. The Life of William and Mary Howitt* (London: Oxford University Press, 1955), p. 333; Joseph Ennemoser, *The History of Magic*, tr. William Howitt, 2 vols. (London: Henry G Bohn, 1854).

52 Howitt refers to Wilkinson's biography of Swedenborg and *The Human Body*, and uses quotes from Wilkinson to introduce two of the chapters in the second volume of his work: see William Howitt, *The History of the Supernatural*, vol. II, pp. 21, 311, 395, 433.

53 William Howitt, *The History of the Supernatural*, vol. I, p. 81.

54 Lee, *Laurels and Rosemary*, p. 333.

55 Ibid., p. 248.

56 Ibid., p. 300.

57 Philip Hoare, *England's Lost Eden: Adventures in a Victorian Utopia* (London: Harper Perennial, 2006), p. 198.

58 Ibid., p. 201.

59 Ibid., pp. 212-13.

60 Anne Taylor, *Laurence Oliphant 1829-1888* (Oxford: Oxford University Press, 1982), pp. 113-45; Clement Wilkinson, *James John Garth Wilkinson*, pp. 102-3.

61 For Rossetti's involvement with the Cowper-Temples, see Hoare, *England's Lost Eden*, pp. 205-9.

62 Wilkinson wrote of Ruskin that he 'hops along on one leg of criticism with a power and rapidity quite new; and sometimes moves so fast that his Hopping even mimics Progress': John Lone (pseud. J J G Wilkinson), *Painting with Both Hands*, p. 10. In

1878, Wilkinson wrote to Ruskin that 'you will rebuke the Circe of Art, instead of aiding and abetting her, and will teach artists to be men, when you traverse their Art with religious duties involving their care and attention to many unpleasant every-day disciplines, which are the only correctives of Art against worldliness, luxury and selfishness': J J G Wilkinson, letter to Ruskin, 1 July 1878, in Swedenborg Society Archive K/125 (4).

63 'Spiritualism in London', in *The British Spiritual Telegraph*, vol. 1 (1857), p. 14.

64 The following information on Ruskin's involvement with spiritualism is derived primarily from Hoare, *England's Lost Eden*, pp. 197-276, and Van Akin Burd (ed.), *Christmas Story: John Ruskin's Venetian Letters of 1876-1877* (Newark: University of Delaware Press, 1990), pp. 30-68.

65 For more on William Gregory see Chapter 6.

66 William Holman Hunt, *Pre-Raphaelitism and the Pre-Raphaelite Brotherhood*, 2 vols. (London: Macmillan, 1905), vol. II, p. 271. William Holman Hunt (1827-1910) was an artist and one of the founders of the Pre-Raphaelite Brotherhood.

67 James Gregory, *Reformers, Patrons and Philanthropists. The Cowper-Temples and High Politics in Victorian England* (London and New York: Tauris Academic Studies, 2010), p. 119. François-Louis Bugnion (1822-80), a little-known figure in Swedenborgian history, was a Swiss-born Unitarian missionary who travelled widely. He was involved with Thomas Lake Harris in forming the Brotherhood of New Life in America, and set up several utopian communities there which failed. In 1861 he became a naturalized British subject and was adopted by the New Church as a missionary, serving in Mauritius, India and elsewhere: see biography at <http://adb.anu.edu.au/biography/bugnion-francois-louis-3106>, accessed 24 April 2014.

68 Lord Mount-Temple, letter to J J G Wilkinson, 10 October 1888, in Swedenborg Society Archive K/125 (36).

69 William M Wilkinson, *Spirit Drawings: A Personal Narrative* (London: Chapman & Hall, 1858).

70 See Ronald Pearsall, *The Table-Rappers: The Victorians and the Occult* (Stroud: Sutton Publishing, 2004), pp. 102-17.

71 J J G Wilkinson, letter to his wife Emma Wilkinson, 13 September 1856, in Swedenborg Society Archive K/124 (a).

72 These developments are discussed in Chapters 1 and 7 respectively.

73 'Notice to Readers and Correspondents', in *The Newchurchman*, vol. 2, no. 14 (February 1856).

74 Ibid.

75 Podmore, *Modern Spiritualism*, vol. II, pp. 255-7.

76 Daniel Dunglas Home, *Incidents in My Life* (New York: Carleton, 1863), p. 95.

77 Early attendees at Home's seances in London were Lord Brougham (1778-1868) and scientist Sir David Brewster (1781-1868): see Mme Dunglas Home, *D. D. Home. His Life and Mission*, ed. Arthur Conan Doyle (London: Kegan Paul, Trench, Trubner, 1921), p. 24.

78 Ibid., p. 31.

79 J J G Wilkinson, letter to Mr Westwood, 11 May 1855, in Swedenborg Society Archive K/89. In this letter Wilkinson thanks Westwood for a poem about a cat; this may have been Thomas Westwood (1814-88), one of the lesser Victorian poets.

80 Home, *Incidents in My Life*, pp. 106-25. In 1856 Wilkinson republished this article, again under the pseudonym of 'Verax', in the first issue of the *Spiritual Herald*. This article was received positively by a reviewer in *The Newchurchman*, who declared that this piece on its own justified the price of the journal, 'alike for its incidents and the beauty and force of its style': 'Notice to Readers and Correspondents', in *The Newchurchman*, vol. 2, no. 14 (February 1856).

81 Home, *Incidents in My Life*, pp. 106-25.

82 Lee, *Laurels and Rosemary*, p. 249.

83 William Crookes, *Researches in the Phenomena of Spiritualism* (London: J Burns, 1874), pp. 9-19. Crookes's support for the phenomena produced by Home and other spiritualist mediums led to him being condemned by many of his fellow scientists, with the threat that he should be stripped of his FRS. He later became President of the Society for Psychical Research, and developed further his interest in the occult by joining the Theosophical Society and becoming initiated into the Hermetic Order of the Golden Dawn: see Oppenheim, *The Other World*, p. 347 and Alex Owen, *The Place of Enchantment: British Occultism and the Culture of the Modern* (Chicago and London: Univesity of Chicago Press, 2004), p. 70.

84 For a detailed discussion of Nathaniel Hawthorne in a Swedenborgian context, including his attitude towards spiritualism, see Devin P Zuber, 'Spiritualized science and the celestial artist: Nathaniel Hawthorne and Swedenborgian aesthetics', in *Philosophy, Literature, Mysticism: an anthology of essays on the thought and influence of Emanuel Swedenborg*, ed. Stephen McNeilly (London: Swedenborg Society, 2013), pp. 175-216.

85 Julian Hawthorne, *Nathaniel Hawthorne and His Wife: A Biography*, 2 vols. (Boston

and New York: Houghton Mifflin, 1884), vol. II, p. 150.

[86] Alex Owen, *The Darkened Room*, p. 79.

[87] The source for this account of Davis is Podmore, *Modern Spiritualism*, vol. I, pp. 158-76.

[88] The quote is from Andrew Jackson Davis, *The Great Harmonia*, 6 vols. (Boston: Benjamin B Mussey & Co, 1850-61), vol. III (1852), p. 210.

[89] J J G Wilkinson, letter to Henry James, Sr, 2 September 1847, in Swedenborg Society Archive K/123.

[90] J J G Wilkinson, letter to Henry James, Sr, 18 September 1847, in Swedenborg Society Archive K/123.

[91] J J G Wilkinson, letter to Henry James, Sr, 1 October 1847, in Swedenborg Society Archive K/123.

[92] J J G Wilkinson, 'From our London Correspondent' (letter dated 2 October 1847), in *The New Jerusalem Magazine* (Boston), vol. XXI, no. CCXLII (November 1847), p. 81.

[93] J J G Wilkinson, *The New Jerusalem and the Old Jerusalem*, p. xii.

[94] See J F C Harrison, *The Second Coming. Popular Millenarianism 1780-1850* (London: Routledge & Kegan Paul, 1979).

[95] Bryan R Wilson, *Magic and the Millennium. A Sociological Study of Religious Movements of Protest among Tribal and Third-World Peoples* (London: Heinemann, 1973), pp. 31-69.

[96] Harrison, *The Second Coming*, p. 5. See also Chapter 2.

[97] Garth Wilkinson's involvement with the radical politics of his time is discussed in detail in Chapter 8.

[98] See Chapter 8 for a detailed discussion of the relationship between Swedenborgianism and Fourierism.

[99] Harrison, *The Second Coming*, pp. 57-85.

[100] Ibid., pp. 86-134.

[101] Ibid., p. 142.

[102] Ibid., pp. 156-7.

[103] W Anderson Smith, *'Shepherd' Smith the Universalist: the Story of a Mind* (London: Sampson Low, Marston & Company, 1892), pp. 6-10.

[104] J J G Wilkinson, 'From our London Correspondent' (letter dated 2 October 1847), in *The New Jerusalem Magazine* (Boston), vol. XXI, no. CCXLII (November 1847), p. 80.

[105] George Bush, *Davis' Revelations Revealed* (1847), p. 7, cited in Podmore, *Modern Spiritualism*, vol. I, pp. 170-1 n. Although Davis claimed never to have read

Swedenborg before writing his *Principles of Nature*, he was widely accused of plagiarism, not only from Swedenborg but also from other writers: see Podmore, *Modern Spiritualism*, vol. I, pp. 165-8.

[106] J J G Wilkinson, letter to Henry James, Sr, 27 June 1850, in Swedenborg Society Archive K/123.

[107] Unless otherwise indicated, biographical information on Harris is taken from Gabay, *Covert Enlightenment*, pp. 233-7.

[108] Nelson, *Spiritualism and Society*, p. 18.

[109] Thomas L Harris, letter to J J G Wilkinson, 21 October 1859, in Swedenborg Society Archive K/125 (18).

[110] Thomas L Harris, *A Lyric of the Golden Age* (New York: Partridge and Brittan, 1856), p. xv.

[111] Thomas L Harris, letter to J J G Wilkinson, 2 February 1859, in Swedenborg Society Archive K/125 (18). At that time, Wilkinson was a highly valued contact in England for visiting spiritualists and Swedenborgians: see R M Theobald, *Passages from the Autobiography of a Shakespeare Student* (London: Robert Banks & Son, 1912), p. 63.

[112] J J G Wilkinson, letter to John Thomson, 1 September 1893, in Swedenborg Society Archive K/125 (15).

[113] James John Garth Wilkinson, *Our Social Health. A Discourse delivered before the London "Ladies' Sanitary Association," February 28, 1865* (Boston: S Welles Cone, 1865), p. 12 n. The need to progress from the spiritual to the celestial level of understanding was emphasized by the early Christian fathers: for example, Niketas Stethatos (1005-90) said that 'The mystical stage of perfection...is characterized by the spirit's passing through the sphere of the lesser aerial spirits and entering the ranks of the higher celestials...It engages us...in the unraveling of hidden mysteries, symbols, and obscure passages in holy Scripture...Whoever attains this stage...[will] share the company of the highest angelic powers, the cherubim and the seraphim': Niketas Stethatos, *Gnostic Chapters* 44, quoted in *The Book of Mystical Chapters: Meditations on the Soul's Ascent From the Desert Fathers and Other early Christian Contemplatives*, tr. and ed. John Anthony McGuckin (Boston: Shambhala, 2002), pp. 174-6.

[114] Elihu Rich noted that 'The mediumship of Mr. Thomas L. Harris marks an epoch in the New Church, and I rejoice to observe...that his mission is distinctly recognised by a large body of our American brethren': E[lihu] R[ich], *Notes on Certain Forms of Spiritualism*, p. 26.

[115] See Lines, *A History of the Swedenborg Society 1810-2010*, pp.56-9.

[116] Thomas L Harris, letter to J J G Wilkinson, 27 October 1860, in Swedenborg Society Archive K/125 (18). Earlier in the year, Harris had written from Norway to Wilkinson requesting some fishing tackle: Thomas L Harris, letter to J J G Wilkinson, 13 July 1860, in Swedenborg Society Archive K/125 (18).

[117] Thomas L Harris, letter to J F Glasgow, 28 March 1861, in Swedenborg Society Archive K/125 (18). Harris's return to America coincided with the outbreak of the American Civil War, which he probably regarded as the earthly correspondence of the crisis in the spiritual world.

[118] In 1860 Laurence Oliphant (1829-88) asked Garth Wilkinson for an introduction to Harris, but Wilkinson refused, advising Oliphant that it would be in his best interest to avoid Harris: Clement Wilkinson, *James John Garth Wilkinson*, p. 103. Oliphant and his mother later went to America to join Harris's community, the Brotherhood of the New Life, where Harris demanded total subjugation and manual labour from them: Anne Taylor, *Laurence Oliphant*, pp. 113-45. Harris was also an honoured guest at the home of the Cowper-Temples at Broadlands, and he was intent on persuading William Cowper-Temple to join his utopian community, the Brotherhood of New Life, at Brocton in New York State: Hoare, *England's Lost Eden*, pp. 212-13. The Cowper-Temples helped to fund this community, but did not make the same mistake as Oliphant by joining it.

[119] J J G Wilkinson, letter to John Thomson, 1 September 1893, in Swedenborg Society Archive K/125 (15).

[120] See Nelson, *Spiritualism and Society*.

[121] Barrow, *Independent Spirits*, p. 105.

[122] For a full discussion of Emerson's views on spiritualism, see John B Wilson, 'Emerson and the "Rochester Rappings"', in *The New England Quarterly*, vol. 41, no. 2 (June 1968), pp. 248-58. Wilson quotes Emerson as describing spiritualism as 'the Rat-revelation' (p. 248) and Henry Thoreau similarly saying that 'The hooting of owls, the croaking of frogs, is celestial wisdom in comparison' (p. 249).

[123] Thomas Carlyle, letter to John A Carlyle, 26 March 1858, in *Carlyle Letters Online*, at <http://carlyleletters.dukejournals.org/cgi/content/full/33/1/lt-18580326-TC-JAC-01>, accessed 5 February 2013: 'Wilk*n* I believe is quite given up to *rapping*, to—in fact to quacking & being quacked, I believe, for Homeopathy &c &c accompany all that of the spirits'. For the view of Henry James, Sr, see his letter to Ralph Waldo Emerson, 1856, quoted in Habegger, *The Father*, p. 376.

124 James Thomson, *The Speedy Extinction of Evil and Misery: Selected Prose of James Thomson*, ed. William David Schaefer (Berkeley: University of California Press, 1967), p. 288.

125 J J G Wilkinson, letter to William James, 17 March 1883, pp. 3-4, in Houghton Library, Harvard University, at <http://nrs.harvard.edu/urn-3:FHCL.HOUGH:12249589>, accessed 11 June 2014. In the same letter, Wilkinson enclosed a manuscript of *The Welsh Fasting Girl*, written by his brother William with a commentary by Garth himself. This came to be one of William James's most prized possessions: Robert D Richardson, *William James: In the Maelstrom of American Modernism* (New York: Houghton-Mifflin, 2006), p. 265. It concerned the case (now regarded as an early description of anorexia nervosa) of a young girl who allegedly survived for two years without food, but who died after eight days without food when under observation by nurses. Her father was found guilty of manslaughter by not forcing her to take food. In his commentary, Wilkinson was sympathetic to the idea that prolonged life with minimal or no food is possible, and said that the girl's death had been due to the 'adverse magnetic influences of a posse of doctors and nurses' who had in essence murdered her: W M Wilkinson, *The Cases of the Welsh Fasting Girl and her Father. On the Possibility of Long-Continued Abstinence from Food; with Supplementary Remarks by J.J. Garth Wilkinson*, 3rd edn. (London: J Burns, 1870), p. 49.

126 James John Garth Wilkinson, *On Human Science, Good and Evil, and its Works; and on Divine Revelation and its Works and Sciences* (London: James Spiers, 1876), p. 262.

127 J J G Wilkinson, letter to the London Dialectical Society, 12 February 1869, in *Report on Spiritualism, of the Committee of the London Dialectical Society, together with the Evidence, Oral and Written, and a Selection from the Correspondence* (London: Longmans, Green, Reader and Dyer, 1871), pp. 234-5 (p. 235).

128 Sigstedt, *Swedenborg Epic*, p. 345.

129 Arthur Conan Doyle, in his book on spiritualism, cited this opinion of Garth Wilkinson, but objected strongly to it, on the grounds that, in his view, people are not intrinsically evil: see Arthur Conan Doyle, *The History of Spiritualism*, 2 vols. (London: Cassell, 1926), vol. I, p. 14. Wilkinson also recognized that much of what passes as spiritualism was in fact fraudulent; he said of spiritualism, that 'where it is not a mortal imposture [it] is a power, though often an infernal one': J J G Wilkinson, *Revelation, Mythology, Correspondences*, pp. 142-3.

[130] 'Contemporary Portraits: J. J. Garth Wilkinson', in *The University Magazine*, vol. 3 (June 1879), pp. 673-92.

[131] J J G Wilkinson, *Epidemic Man and His Visitations*, pp. 113-14.

[132] Emma Wilkinson, letter to Julian Hawthorne, 19 June 1885, in Julian Hawthorne, *Hawthorne and His Circle* (New York and London: Harper & Brothers, 1903), pp. 236-7.

[133] Clement Wilkinson, *James John Garth Wilkinson*, pp. 89-90.

[134] Obituary, in *Light*, 28 October 1899, in Swedenborg Society Archive A/183 (i).

[135] 'James John Garth Wilkinson', in *Light*, 24 June 1911, pp. 294-5 (p. 294).

Chapter Six

[1] al-Ghazālī, *The Alchemy of Happiness*, tr. Claud Field (London: John Murray, 1910), pp. 28-9.

[2] This is an expression of the 'incompatibility' position, in which free will is impossible if determinism is true. It should be noted though, that there are also philosophers who take the approach that the two are compatible. This debate, which is beyond the scope of the present work, is outlined from the perspective of modern neuropsychology by Dirk De Ridder, Jan Verplaetse and Sven Vanneste, 'The predictive brain and the "free will" illusion', in *Frontiers in Psychology*, vol. 4 (April 2013), p. 131.

[3] Elizabeth L Haigh, 'The Vital Principle of Paul Joseph Barthez: The Clash Between Monism and Dualism', in *Medical History*, vol. 21 (1977), pp. 1-14 (p. 1).

[4] Vitalist approaches to medical treatment are discussed by Matthew Wood, *The Magical Staff: The Vitalist Tradition in Western Medicine* (Berkeley, CA: North Atlantic Books, 1992). Some of the 'complementary' approaches have also been given rationales that aim for consistency with today's mechanistic principles.

[5] This differs from deism, which accepts that God created the world and its laws but then played no further active role. Wilkinson roundly rejected deism, which has no place for revelation and divine inspiration.

[6] This formulation of Wilkinson's approach to science was informed by the current discussion regarding the reception of Western science by Islamic nations which is set out in Seyyed Hossein Nasr, *The Need for a Sacred Science* (Albany: State University of New York Press, 1993). Nasr contrasts Islamic 'traditional science', which is based on a philosophy that emphasizes 'the hierarchic nature of reality, the predominance of the spiritual over the material, the sacred nature of the cosmos, the inseparability of man's destiny from that of the natural and cosmic environment, and the unity of

knowledge and the interrelatedness of all things', with modern Western science that is based upon reasoning from empirical observation, without guidance from any a priori metaphysical constructs: ibid., p. 73. Esoteric Islam also holds the doctrine of the universal man (*al-insān al-kāmil*): ibid., p. 90. The similarity between the concepts of Swedenborg and those of esoteric Islam have been discussed by Henry Corbin, *Swedenborg and Esoteric Islam*. For Nasr, traditional science can be expressed in ways that would not be recognized by modern science, including mythology, sacred music (which, like mathematics, echoes the harmony of the universe) and sacred art, which depicts divine archetypes.

7   J J G Wilkinson, *Greater Origins*, p. 125. Swedenborg, who like other scholars of his time generally wrote in Latin, used the word *scientia*, which is properly translated as 'knowledge'. However, *scientia* has commonly been translated as 'science' in English versions of his work, including the translations by Garth Wilkinson.

8   The characteristics of scientism have been identified as: '(1) the assumption that the mathematized science of natural phenomena is a model science to which all other sciences ought to conform; (2) that all realms of being are accessible to the methods of the sciences of phenomena; and (3) that all reality which is not accessible to sciences of phenomena is either irrelevant or, in the more radical form of the dogma, illusionary': Eric Voegelin, 'The Origins of Scientism', in *Social Research*, vol. 15, no. 4 (December 1948), pp. 462-94 (p. 462). Friedrich August von Hayek (1899-1992) is credited with popularizing of the term 'scientism'. He claimed that the term was borrowed from the French, who wrote of *Scientisme* in the early twentieth century: F A Hayek, 'Scientism and the Study of Society', in *Economica*, New Series, vol. 9, no. 35 (August 1942), pp. 267-91. It is apparently unrecognized that Garth Wilkinson wrote extensively on the subject of scientism in the second half of the nineteenth century, using the term in exactly the same way as Hayek. Wilkinson's embracing of heterodox medical approaches, although initially precipitated by his repulsion from orthodox medical treatment methods, was firmly grounded in his acceptance of Swedenborgian principles and rejection of scientism. According to Roger Cooter, it was unusual for heterodox practitioners to be so explicit: 'Most Victorians did not see alternative medical theories and practices as offering *explicitly* some kind of bulwark against the metaphysics of the scientising medicine; what stuck in their craw, more often than not, was simply the naked arrogance and elitist aspirations of the orthodox practitioners'. Rather dismissively—and certainly not in a manner applicable to Wilkinson—Cooter claimed that 'the heterodox in medicine were

most often enthusiasts whose thinking was muddled and eclectic': see Roger Cooter, 'Alternative Medicine, Alternative Cosmology', in Cooter (ed.), *Studies in the History of Alternative Medicine*, pp. 63-78 (pp. 65, 70).

9   J J G Wilkinson, *On Human Science*, p. 7.

10   J J G Wilkinson, *The New Jerusalem and the Old Jerusalem*, p. 293.

11   As a young man, Wilkinson regarded Swedenborg and Fourier as 'the arms and legs of spiritual science': James John Garth Wilkinson, 'Correspondence', in *Aesthetic Papers*, ed. Elizabeth Palmer Peabody (Boston: The Editor, 1849), pp. 112-45 (p. 134). Wilkinson regarded the 'illicit connexion of medicine with the State' as being 'fed by the scientism that underlies it': J J G Wilkinson, *On Human Science*, p. 51.

12   Cyril Bailey, *The Greek Atomists and Epicurus* (Oxford: Clarendon Press, 1928); Friedrich Solmsen, 'Epicurus on Void, Matter and Genesis: Some Historical Observations', in *Phronesis*, vol. 22 (1977), pp. 263-81.

13   James John Garth Wilkinson, *The Soul is Form and doth the Body make: The Heart and the Lungs, the Will and the Understanding. Chapters in Psychology* (London: James Speirs, 1890), p. 239.

14   Charles S Myers, 'Vitalism: A Brief Historical and Critical Review', in *Mind*, New Series, vol. 9, no. 34 (April 1900), pp. 218-33, and no. 35 (July 1900), pp. 319-31; Max Neuburger, 'An Historical Survey of the Concept of Nature from a Medical Viewpoint', in *Isis*, vol. 35, no. 1 (Winter 1944), pp. 16-28; Hans Driesch, *The History and Theory of Vitalism*, tr. C K Ogden (London: Macmillan, 1914).

15   Richard Sorabji, 'Body and Soul in Aristotle', in *Philosophy*, vol. 49, no. 187 (January 1974), pp. 63-89.

16   J J G Wilkinson, *The Soul is Form*, p. 9.

17   Ibid., p. 94.

18   W K C Guthrie, 'Plato's Views on the Nature of the Soul', in Gregory Vlastos (ed.), *Plato. A Selection of Critical Essays*, 2 vols. (New York: Doubleday, 1971), vol. II, pp. 230-43; Sarah Broadie, 'Soul and Body in Plato and Descartes', in *Proceedings of the Aristotelian Society*, vol. 101 (2001), pp. 295-308; Eric J Roberts, 'Plato's View of the Soul', in *Mind*, vol. 14, no. 55 (July 1905), pp. 371-89.

19   J J G Wilkinson, *Emanuel Swedenborg*, p. 115.

20   J J G Wilkinson, *Remarks on Swedenborg's Economy of the Animal Kingdom*, p. 7.

21   This is discussed by Edward Grant, *A History of Natural Philosophy: From the Ancient World to the Nineteenth Century* (Cambridge: Cambridge University Press, 2007).

22   For a detailed discussion of this topic see Allen G Debus, *Man and Nature in the*

Renaissance (Cambridge: Cambridge University Press, 1978).

23 There were of course many transitional positions. An example of this is the discovery of the circulation of the blood by William Harvey (1578-1657), which was driven by his awareness of the Aristotelian principle of the archetypal supremacy of the circle. This aspect of Harvey's belief system has been written out of the standard medical histories: see Walter Pagel, 'William Harvey: Some Neglected Aspects of Medical History', in *Journal of the Warburg and Courtauld Institutes*, vol. 7 (1944), pp. 144-53. The circulation of the blood had previously been postulated for the same metaphysical reason by other philosophers, such as Giordano Bruno (1548-1600): Walter Pagel, 'Giordano Bruno: the Philosophy of Circles and the Circular Movement of the Blood', in *Journal of the History of Medicine and Allied Sciences*, vol. 6 (Winter 1951), pp. 116-24. However, unlike Bruno who saw no need for empirical verification of this idea, Harvey investigated the hypothesis by means of observation and experiment of the kind that would eventually define modern science, which has no place for esoteric concepts.

24 Philip R Sloan, 'Descartes, the sceptics, and the rejection of vitalism in seventeenth-century physiology', in *Studies in the History and Philosophy of Science*, vol. 8 (1977), pp. 1-28.

25 Walter Pagel, *Joan Baptista Van Helmont. Reformer of Science and Medicine* (Cambridge: Cambridge University Press, 1982).

26 One of the more extreme expressions of this is found in *L'Homme machine* (*Man a Machine*) by Julien Offray de La Mettrie (1709-51), which was published anonymously in 1748. La Mettrie regarded humans simply as mechanistic products of natural laws, like other animals: Julien Offray de La Mettrie, *Man a Machine and Man a Plant*, tr. Richard A Watson and Maya Rybalka (Indianapolis: Hackett, 1994).

27 Harold J Cook, 'Boerhaave and the Flight from Reason in Medicine', in *Bulletin of the History of Medicine*, vol. 74, no. 2 (2000), pp. 221-40; Andrew Cunningham, 'Medicine to Calm the Mind: Boerhaave's Medical System and Why It Was Adopted in Edinburgh', in Andrew Cunningham and Roger French (eds.), *The Medical Enlightenment of the Eighteenth Century* (Cambridge: Cambridge University Press, 1990), pp. 40-66.

28 Reill, *Vitalizing Nature*, pp. 33 ff. credits Georges-Louis Leclerc, comte de Buffon (1707-88) with popularizing the vitalist reaction against mechanism in the mid-eighteenth century. In his popular *Histoire Naturelle*, published in 1749, Buffon proposed that life is animated by an occult force that cannot be reduced to mathematical laws.

29 Thomas Thomson, *History of the Royal Society* (London: Robert Baldwin, 1812), p. 120.

30 Albrecht von Haller (1708-77) was held in high regard by Garth Wilkinson. In the context of discussing great anatomists who accepted the reality of animal spirits, Wilkinson said that 'Boerhaave's pupil, Haller...stands as a mountain between the present and the past, and reflects from his summit the departed learning of seventeen centuries': J J G Wilkinson, *The Human Body*, pp. 57-8.

31 The concept of irritability had been first developed by the Paracelsian physician Joan Baptista van Helmont (1579-1644) and then promoted by English physician Francis Glisson (1598-1677): Owsei Temkin, 'The Classical Roots of Glisson's Doctrine of Irritation', in *Bulletin of the History of Medicine*, vol. 38 (1964), pp. 297-328 (p. 297).

32 Oswei Temkin, 'Albrecht von Haller, "A Dissertation on the Sensible and Irritable Parts of Animals" ', in *Bulletin of the Institute of the History of Medicine*, vol. IV, no. 8 (October 1936), pp. 651-99 (p. 659).

33 Albrecht von Haller, quoted in Guido Giglioni, 'What Ever Happened to Francis Glisson? Albrecht Haller and the Fate of Eighteenth-Century Irritability', in *Science in Context*, vol. 21, no. 4 (2008), pp. 465-93 (p. 478). Here, von Haller is expressing the esoteric concept that the human is a microcosm of the universe, with the soul as intermediary. Haller's theories of irritability and sensibility have been characterized as a residual form of vitalism: William Coleman, *Biology in the Nineteenth Century* (Cambridge: Cambridge University Press, 1971), pp. 146-50.

34 Ebenezer Sibly's interest in astrology and the invocation of spirits has been discussed in Chapter 2, where it was noted that, even though his *Key to Physic* ran into five editions which spanned the late eighteenth and early nineteenth centuries, he has been largely ignored by historians of esoteric medicine: see Debus, 'Scientific Truth and Occult Tradition'.

35 Ebenezer Sibly, *A Key to Physic, and the Occult Sciences. Opening to mental view, The SYSTEM and ORDER of the Interior and Exterior HEAVENS; The analogy betwixt ANGELS, and SPIRITS of MEN...* (London: Champante and Whitrow, 1795), p. 5.

36 Sibly, *A Key to Physic*, p. 287.

37 This reflects the Aristotelian view of the leading theoretician of Montpellier vitalism, Paul Joseph Barthez (1734-1806), who said that the thinking soul could not 'explain bodily functions such as the beating of the heart or digestion, functions of which it was unaware and over which it exercised no control': Elizabeth A Williams, *A Cultural History of Medical Vitalism in Enlightenment Montpellier*, p. 263. Barthez regarded the vital principle as different from both soul and material body. It is the vital principle that organizes and controls the bodily vital functions. For this

reason, Barthez attacked the animist medical concepts of Georg Ernst Stahl (1659-1734), who followed Plato in regarding the soul as the controller of vital functions; in Barthez's view, no medical intervention can affect the soul, and the soul cannot affect the body. See ibid., p. 265.

[38] L S Jacyna, 'Immanence or Transcendence: Theories of Life and Organization in Britain, 1790-1835', in *Isis*, vol. 74, no. 3 (September 1983), pp. 310-29 (p. 315).

[39] Roy Porter (ed.), *Cambridge Illustrated History of Medicine* (Cambridge: Cambridge University Press, 1996), p. 166; William F Bynum and Roy Porter (eds.), *Companion Encyclopedia of the History of Medicine*, 2 vols. (London: Routledge, 1993), vol. 2, p. 974.

[40] See Chapter 2.

[41] Roy R Male, Jr, 'The Background of Coleridge's Theory of Life', in *The University of Texas Studies in English*, vol. 33 (1954), pp. 60-8.

[42] John Abernethy, *Introductory Lectures, Exhibiting Some of Mr. Hunter's Opinions Respecting Life and Diseases* (London: Longman, Hurst, Rees, Orme and Brown, 1819), pp. 32, 78-9.

[43] Richard Saumarez, *A New System of Physiology*, 2 vols. (London: T Cox, 1798); Jacyna, 'Immanence or Transcendence', p. 315.

[44] Saumarez, *A New System of Physiology*, vol. I, p. 49.

[45] Ibid., p. 158. Coleridge, obviously unaware of Sibly's earlier book, met Saumarez in 1812 and observed that he had 'subverted the tyranny of the mechanic system in physiology' and that by 'substituting life and progressive power, for the contradictory *inert force*, [he] has a right to be known and remembered as the first instaurator of the dynamic philosophy in England': Coleridge, *Biographia Literaria*, p. 80 n.

[46] Henry Power, 'Physiology in 1800', in *The British Medical Journal*, vol. 2, no. 2087 (29 December 1900), pp. 1841-5 (p. 1841).

[47] William Coleman, *Biology in the Nineteenth Century*, pp. 146-50.

[48] Power, 'Physiology in 1800', p. 1841.

[49] Myers, 'Vitalism', p. 231.

[50] John Abernethy, *An Enquiry into the Probability and Rationality of Mr. Hunter's Theory of Life* (London: Longman, Hurst, Rees, Orme and Brown, 1814). Garth Wilkinson was evidently aware of Abernethy's work, but quoted him only with reference to his anatomical work, which supported Swedenborg's view about the blood supply to the heart muscle: J J G Wilkinson, *The Human Body*, p. 190.

[51] Male, 'The Background of Coleridge's Theory of Life', p. 62.

52 Abernethy, *An Enquiry into the Probability and Rationality of Mr. Hunter's Theory of Life*, p. 88.
53 Carpenter's association with Garth Wilkinson has been discussed in Chapter 4.
54 Carpenter, 'On the Mutual Relations of the Vital and Physical Forces', p. 752.
55 'Mechanism of Vital Actions', in *The North American Review*, vol. LXXXV, no. 176 (July 1857), pp. 39-77.
56 Gregory's wife was also an active spiritualist: see Chapter 5.
57 Timothy O Lipman, 'Vitalism and Reductionism in Liebig's Physiological Thought', in *Isis*, vol. 58, no. 2 (Summer 1967), pp. 167-85.
58 William Gregory, 'Editor's Preface', in Justus von Liebig, *Researches on the Motion of the Juices of the Animal Body*, tr. William Gregory (Philadelphia: T B Peterson, 1850), p. 3.
59 Matthew H Kaufman, 'William Gregory (1803-58): Professor of Chemistry at the University of Edinburgh and Enthusiast for Phrenology and Mesmerism', in *Journal of Medical Biography*, vol. 16, no. 3 (2008), pp. 128-33.
60 William Gregory, *Letters to a Candid Inquirer, on Animal Magnetism* (Philadelphia: Blanchard and Lee, 1851).
61 Ibid., p. 179.
62 Ibid., p. 211.
63 Lionel S Beale, *Protoplasm; or, Life, Force, and Matter* (London: J Churchill, 1870), p. 1.
64 Ibid., p. 77.
65 Thomas Henry Huxley, *On the Physical Basis of Life* (Yale College, New Haven, CT: The College Courant, 1869), p. 11.
66 Ibid., p. 16.
67 J J G Wilkinson, *Greater Origins*, p. 218.
68 J J G Wilkinson, *On Human Science*, p. 98.
69 J J G Wilkinson, *Epidemic Man and His Visitations*, p. 7.
70 J J G Wilkinson, *On Human Science*, p. 98.
71 Ibid., pp. 99, 100.
72 Ibid., p. 168.
73 Ibid., p. 98.
74 Ibid., p. 100.
75 Editorial, 'Carl Ludwig and Vitalism', in *British Medical Journal*, vol. 1, no. 1832 (8 February 1896), pp. 354-5.

[76] Gustav von Bunge, 'Introduction—Vitalism and Mechanism', in *Text-Book of Physiological and Pathological Chemistry*, tr. Florence A Starling, ed. Ernest H Starling (Philadelphia: P Blakiston's Son & Co., 1902), pp. 1-12 (p. 12).

[77] Antoine Faivre, *Access to Western Esotericism* (Albany, NY: State University of New York, 1994), pp. 3-47. The quotation is from Nicholas Goodrick-Clarke, *The Western Esoteric Traditions*, p. 8.

[78] Jane Williams-Hogan, 'The Place of Emanuel Swedenborg in Modern Western Esotericism', in Antoine Faivre and Wouter J Hanegraaff (eds.), *Western Esotericism and the Science of Religion* (Leuven: Peeters, 1998), pp. 201-52.

[79] J J G Wilkinson, *Greater Origins*, p. 274.

[80] Animism, the belief that everything in the natural world has its own soul and volition, is discussed in Graham Harvey, *Animism: Respecting the Living World* (London: C Hurst & Co., 2005).

[81] J J G Wilkinson, *Greater Origins*, p. 307.

[82] J J G Wilkinson, *Emanuel Swedenborg*, p. 186.

[83] J J G Wilkinson, *Remarks on Swedenborg's Economy of the Animal Kingdom*, p. 55. The concept of intelligence at the molecular level had also been promoted by the English physician Francis Glisson (1599-1677), who believed that intelligent molecules have knowledge of their ultimate form, and so are able to aggregate themselves into forms that reach higher and higher planes of awareness: Giglioni, 'What Ever Happened to Francis Glisson?', p. 478. Garth Wilkinson was aware of Glisson's work, describing him as 'the illustrious Glisson, our countryman': J J G Wilkinson, *The Human Body*, p. 58. In his physiological works, Swedenborg made much use of Glisson's anatomical findings, particularly those relating to the liver and the lymphatic system.

[84] J J G Wilkinson, *Remarks on Swedenborg's Economy of the Animal Kingdom*, p. 56 (emphasis added).

[85] Emanuel Swedenborg, *Apocalypse Explained*, tr. John C Ager, rev. John Whitehead, 6 vols. (West Chester, PA: Swedenborg Foundation, 1995-7), vol. VI, §1196.3-4, pp. 345-6.

[86] Oken, *Elements of Physiophilosophy*, p. 23.

[87] Wouter Hanegraaff points out that 'it is the force of divinity that "enlivens" nature', and therefore 'the concept [of living nature] is most properly described as a form of panentheism'. Panentheism, the concept that God permeates the whole cosmos yet remains ontologically distinct from it, is a term that was introduced by German

philosopher Karl Christian Friedrich Krause (1781-1832), who was a Swedenborgian. See Hanegraaff, *New Age Religion and Western Culture*, p. 398. For useful essays on panentheism see Philip Clayton and Arthur Peacocke (eds.), *In Whom We Live and Move and Have Our Being: Panentheistic Reflections on God's Presence in a Scientific World* (Grand Rapids, MI: William B Eerdmans, 2004). Swedenborg made it clear that this dependence works both ways, when he said that the whole 'spiritual universe could not come into being without a natural universe, in which the spiritual one might produce its effects and perform its services': Swedenborg, *The True Christian Religion*, vol. 1, §76, p. 96.

88   Wilkinson spent most of his adult life railing against the illogicality and cruelty of vivisection. This is discussed in detail in Chapter 8.

89   Deck, 'The "Vastation" of Henry James, Sr.', pp. 230-1.

90   J J G Wilkinson, letter to his fiancée Emma Marsh, 8 October 1839, in Swedenborg Society Archive K/124 (e).

91   J J G Wilkinson, *The New Jerusalem and the Old Jerusalem*, p. 205. Augustus Clissold appears as the translator named on the title page of the English translation of Swedenborg's *Economy*. In the preface to the first volume Wilkinson is named as the editor of the entire work and as the translator of Part 2.

92   Swedenborg, *Economy*, vol. I, §19, p. 10. Swedenborg developed this theme in his subsequent work *The Animal Kingdom*, pointing out that reasoning from a priori principles leads to false conclusions and ignorance. He asked 'Can you tell me by synthesis or *a priori*, before seeing the viscera or examining the interior parts, what is contained within the animal body?': Swedenborg, *The Animal Kingdom*, vol. I, §10, p. 7.

93   Swedenborg, *Economy*, vol. I, §3, pp. 1-2.

94   Garth Wilkinson characteristically expands on this theme, saying that we assimilate from the air the 'scented and tinted winds' from around the world, so that we 'drink the atmosphere with the planet dissolved in it', making us 'the builded aroma of the world': J J G Wilkinson, *The Human Body*, p. 94.

95   Swedenborg, *Economy*, vol. I, §270, p. 239.

96   Ibid., vol. II, §579, p. 5

97   Swedenborg was by no means the first person to observe human anatomy in order to clarify theology. Perhaps the most famous earlier example was Michael Servetus (1511-53), a contemporary of the great anatomist Andreas Vesalius (1514-64). Servetus believed that the Holy Spirit can be understood properly only through the study of

anatomy. He is credited with the first description of the pulmonary circulation, and he made that discovery as a direct result of his theology. He described this in a chapter of his major theological work *Christianismi Restitutio* (1553). Servetus believed that the divine spirit—the breath of God—is introduced into the body through the air breathed into the lungs; blood moves from the heart to the lungs where it absorbs the divine spirit, which is taken in the blood back to the heart: Michael Servetus, 'The Description of the Lesser Circulation', from *Christianismi Restitutio* (1553), in *Michael Servetus: A Translation of His Geographical, Medical and Astrological Writings with Introductions and Notes*, ed. Charles Donald O'Malley (Philadelphia: American Philosophical Society, 1953), p. 202. A striking similarity between the theology of Servetus and that of Swedenborg has been noted by several authors: Andrew M T Dibb, *Servetus, Swedenborg and the Nature of God* (Lanham, MD: University Press of America, 2005); and Carl Theophilus Odhner, *Michael Servetus: His Life and Teachings* (Philadelphia: J B Lippincott, 1910). Most of these similarities relate to concepts drawn from the Western esoteric tradition. Servetus was burned at the stake for his beliefs, which included rejection of the Trinitarian dogma of three persons.

[98] Lamm, *Swedenborg*, p. 74. This is an expression of the esoteric concept of 'living nature'.

[99] Swedenborg, *Economy*, vol. II, §591, p. 14.

[100] Ibid., vol. I, §270, p. 240

[101] Hugo Lj. Odhner, *The Human Mind*, pp. 21-2, 53. Swedenborg also refers to this spirituous fluid as 'the animal spirit'; he wrote an essay with this title which was translated and published by Garth Wilkinson in a collection of Swedenborg's previously unpublished works: Swedenborg, *Posthumous Tracts*, pp. 41-57.

[102] Swedenborg, *Economy*, vol. II, §237, p. 227. This plainly resonates with the concepts of Haller.

[103] Ibid., §251, p. 236.

[104] Swedenborg, *The Animal Kingdom*, vol. I, §16, p. 11.

[105] Ibid., §12, p. 8.

[106] Ibid., §12, p. 9.

[107] Ibid.

[108] Swedenborg's meditative practices are discussed in detail in Chapter 5.

[109] These ways of attaining spiritual insights have a more general relevance. The authority on comparative religions, Frithjof Schuon, describes three universally recognized ways of gaining sacred knowledge. The first is by the use of human reason, for example

developing philosophical arguments to 'prove' the existence of God. This can lead to the construction of a metaphysics based upon human reason alone: such constructs were dismissed by Swedenborg and Wilkinson alike. The second approach is theological and based on faith, so that, for example, the existence of God is accepted as a given, based upon scriptural authority and religious dogma. The third and highest approach is through the intellect. In this context, intellect is not reason, but a manifestation of the absolute in the human soul, by means of which direct insight into spiritual reality can be gained. Sacred knowledge of this kind carries an absolute certainty that no longer depends upon reason or faith: see Schuon, *The Transcendent Unity of Religions*, pp. xxix-xxxiv. It is evident that Swedenborg described the highest process for gaining sacred knowledge even before he developed his spiritual visions.

[110] Inge Jonsson has highlighted a notable exception, which is Swedenborg's first statement in its developed form about the concept of correspondence, although this is only made in a footnote to a section on the kidney: see Jonsson, *Visionary Scientist*, pp. 109-10. Swedenborg says that 'In our Doctrine of Representations and Correspondences, we shall treat of both these symbolical and typical representations, and of the astonishing things which occur, I will not say in the living body only, but throughout nature, and which correspond so entirely to supreme and spiritual things, that one would swear that the physical world was purely symbolical of the spiritual world...I intend hereafter to communicate a number of examples of such correspondences, together with a vocabulary containing the terms of spiritual things': Swedenborg, *The Animal Kingdom*, vol. I, §293, p. 451 n. (u).

[111] He did, however, make use of the esoteric microcosm-macrocosm concept; for example, in *The Animal Kingdom*, he says that 'the animal microcosm imitates the macrocosm in all its properties', commenting in a footnote that 'Thus we are instructed by the one respecting the other; by the organic animal body respecting the phenomena of the world, and *vice versa*. If each were not modelled to the other, there would be no agreement between them, nor would the animal world live in harmony with the order and laws of the universe': Swedenborg, *The Animal Kingdom*, vol. I, §133, pp. 172-3 & n. (i).

[112] Swedenborg, *Spiritual Diary*, vol. I, §1145 $^1/_2$, p. 364.

[113] Swedenborg, *Heaven and Hell*, §95, p. 62.

[114] Emanuel Swedenborg, *On the Divine Love. On the Divine Wisdom*, tr. E C Mongredien (London: Swedenborg Society, 1986), §92, pp. 98-9.

[115] Swedenborg, *Divine Love and Wisdom*, §420, pp. 195-6.

[116] John Clowes, *Letters on the Human Body* (London: Hodson & Son, 1862), p. 3.

[117] Ibid., p. 26. The nature of the relationship between the 'easy problems' of consciousness which relate to basic abilities to discriminate stimuli, report information, etc., and the 'hard problems' which relate to phenomenal consciousness (knowing subjectively what it is like to be conscious) still exercises philosophers today: see David J Chalmers, 'Consciousness and its Place in Nature', in Stephen P Stich and Ted A Warfield (eds.), *The Blackwell Guide to the Philosophy of Mind* (Oxford: Blackwell, 2003), pp. 102-42.

[118] Clowes, *Human Body*, pp. 30-1. Clowes no doubt believed that the opening of his 'intellectual eye' explained his own experiences of spirit manifestations.

[119] Ibid., p. 33.

[120] Ibid., p. 26. Carl Gustav Jung (1875-1961) later reached a very similar conclusion when he observed that 'man is indispensable for the completion of creation...in fact, he himself is the second creator of the world, who alone has given to the world its objective existence—without which, unheard, unseen, silently eating, giving birth, dying, heads nodding through the millions of years, it would have gone on in the profoundest night of non-being down to its unknown end': C G Jung, *Memories, Dreams, Reflections*, ed. Aniela Jaffé, tr. Richard and Clara Winston (London: Collins and Routledge & Kegan Paul, 1964), p. 240. A present-day philosopher of consciousness, Max Velmans, has also concluded that the function of human consciousness is to 'real-ize' the natural world: Max Velmans, *Understanding Consciousness* (London: Routledge, 2000), pp. 280-1.

[121] J J G Wilkinson, *The Soul is Form*, p. 12. Others had also used the term 'psychological physiology', but quite differently, to mean the relationship between the physical stimulation of sensation and its nerve pathways, and the subjective experience of that sensation; for example, John Cockle, 'A Supplementary Address on Psychological Physiology', in *British Medical Journal*, vol. 2, no. 984 (8 November 1879), pp. 723-4.

[122] J J G Wilkinson, *The Human Body*, p. xvii

[123] Ibid., p. xviii

[124] Ibid., p. xxii

[125] Ibid., pp. 289-90.

[126] Ibid., p. 299.

[127] Ibid., p. 68. Here Wilkinson is following Swedenborg's concept of a 'spirituous fluid' that is produced in the 'glands' (cells) of the cerebral hemispheres and which is at the boundary of the natural and the spiritual, forming a point of contact between the two. This is discussed by Hugo Lj. Odhner, *Principles of the New Philosophy*, p. 31.

[128] J J G Wilkinson, *The Human Body*, p. 295.

[129] Ibid., p. 300.

[130] This notion of a cosmic circuit in which the human body is the outer limit reflects the Neoplatonist view, as expressed by Jean Trouillard: 'The body that the soul animates and through which it is placed in the cosmos is not an extrinsic addition but the circuit that it travels in order to be reunited with itself': J Trouillard, *La Mystagogie de Proclos* (Paris: Les Nelles Lettres, 1982), p. 251, translated in Gregory Shaw, *Theurgy and the Soul. The Neoplatonism of Iamblicus* (University Park, PA: The Pennsylvania State University Press, 1995), p. 46.

[131] J J G Wilkinson, *The Human Body*, p. 298.

[132] J J G Wilkinson, *Greater Origins*, pp. 114-15.

[133] Ibid., p. 277.

[134] Ibid.

[135] J J G Wilkinson, *The Human Body*, p. 189.

[136] Ibid., p. 251.

[137] Ibid., p. 114.

[138] Ibid., p. 115. Wilkinson does not write about achieving trance states himself, but this theme will recur when discussing his approach to medical practice.

[139] J J G Wilkinson, *The Soul is Form*, p. 97.

[140] Ibid., p. 101.

[141] Ibid., p. 112.

[142] J J G Wilkinson, *The New Jerusalem and the Old Jerusalem*, p. 201.

[143] J J G Wilkinson, *The Human Body*, p. 291. In the 1830s and 1840s, the likeness between human anatomy and the 'social body' was a widely used metaphor, in which society was regarded as an integrated system of interdependent organic units, which was lacking an overall regulatory mechanism like the human nervous system. The social body could be 'dissected', which involved increasing intrusion into people's lives, to the extent of inspecting their homes: see Mary Poovey, *Making a Social Body: British Cultural Formation 1830-1864* (Chicago: University of Chicage Press, 1995), pp. 73-97. Any social 'diseases' such as squalor and prostitution could be addressed by statutory interventions such as public sanitation measures and the compulsory examination of prostitutes. Garth Wilkinson, who regarded such social diseases as spiritual in origin, was against compulsory state intervention: see Chapter 8.

[144] This is discussed in detail in Chapter 8.

[145] J J G Wilkinson, *The Human Body*, p. 305.

[146] See Chapter 4.

[147] J J G Wilkinson, 'Correspondence', p. 123.

Chapter Seven

[1] Paracelsus, *Paracelsus: Selected Writings*, ed. Jolande Jacobi, tr. Norbert Guterman (Princeton, NJ: Princeton University Press, 1979), p. 64.

[2] Bruce Haley, *The Healthy Body and Victorian Culture* (Cambridge, MA: Harvard University Press, 1978), pp. 1-22.

[3] Roger Cooter, 'Introduction: The Alternations of Past and Present', in Cooter (ed.), *Studies in the History of Alternative Medicine*, pp. x-xx. The close relationship between religious Nonconformism and medical heterodoxy is discussed by John V Pickstone, 'Establishment and Dissent in Nineteenth-Century Medicine: An Exploration of some Correspondence and Connections between Religious and Medical Belief-Systems in Early Industrial England', in W J Shiels (ed.), *The Church and Healing* (Oxford: Blackwell, 1982), pp. 165-89. Heterodox medical systems were favoured not only by followers of Swedenborg, but also by other Nonconformists such as Methodists. John Wesley's *Primitive Physick* (1747) was anti-professional and deplored medical obscurantism; he advocated a return to traditional medical approaches using herbs and other simple remedies: Pickstone, 'Establishment and Dissent', p. 171.

[4] Emanuel Swedenborg, *The Fibre*, §§380-94, pp. 261-8. Swedenborg wrote about the absorption of toxins from the air in an essay on 'Animal Spirits' that was published posthumously in translation by Garth Wilkinson: see Swedenborg, *Posthumous Tracts*, pp. 49-50. Here, Swedenborg describes the absorption through the pores of the skin of either beneficial elements (from 'spring breezes and exhalations') or of 'morbid, pestilential and poisonous contagions'. In an echo of Paracelsus, who believed that all matter derives from mercury, sulphur and salt, Swedenborg declared that a 'sulphureo-saline principle' imbibed from the ether is transmitted to the cortex of the brain. He said that he had written an entire treatise on this topic, though this does not appear in the known corpus of his writings.

[5] Swedenborg, *The Fibre*, §374, p. 257.

[6] Ibid., §389, p. 266.

[7] A useful account of Swedenborg's views on illness in his theological period can be found in Clyde W Broomwell (ed.), *Divine Healing: The Origin and Cure of Disease As Taught in the Bible and Explained by Emanuel Swedenborg* (Boston: Geo. H Ellis, 1907).

8   Swedenborg, *The True Christian Religion*, vol. 1, §103, p. 129; Swedenborg, *Divine Love and Wisdom*, §432, p. 203. The notion that the soul is derived paternally is of course very ancient: see, for example, Abraham P Bos, 'Aristotle on Soul and Soul-"Parts" in Semen (*GA* 2.1, 735a4-22)', in *Mnemosyne*, vol. 62, no. 3 (2009), pp. 378-400.

9   Swedenborg proposed that the reasoning mind is dependent on the body to function but is intermediate between the soul and the body. Spirits that enter man do not give rise directly to thoughts in the reasoning mind, but rather have their effects on the will and understanding at a level that we would now call unconscious.

10   It is of interest to relate Swedenborg's concepts to the debate on the issue of free will that continues today. A distinction has been made between the so-called 'easy problem' of free will, which questions how the subjective experience of free will relates to neurophysiological measurements, and the 'hard problem' which questions the mechanism by which a mental choice can influence bodily behaviour: see Azim F Shariff, Jonathan Schooler and Kathleen D Vohs, 'The Hazards of Claiming to Have Solved the Hard Problem of Free Will', in John Baer, James C Kaufman and Roy Baumeister (eds.), *Are we Free? Psychology and Free Will* (New York: Oxford University Press, 2008), pp. 181-204. Evidence that the neurophysiological impulses initiating an action can be recorded in the brain *before* the conscious experience of choice has led materialists to dismiss free will as illusory. More sophisticated commentators have suggested that the initial *impulse* to act is generated unconsciously and so outside our control, but we exercise lower-order control over whether or not the action comes to fruition. An analogy is with sailors who cannot control the wind and waves, but who can nevertheless use their sails and rudder to move in their chosen direction. Carrying the analogy into Swedenborg's theory, the spirits causing unconscious impulses are like the wind and waves of the sailors, and the conscious exercise of choice is like their use of sails and rudder. The 'hard problem' of free will is readily accounted for if Swedenborg's concept of the extension of the mind throughout the body by correspondence is accepted.

11   Swedenborg, *Arcana Caelestia*, vol. VII, §5712, p. 429.

12   For example, the spirits of hypocrites who preached holiness but did not live holy lives give rise to pain of the teeth and gums, whereas the spirits of those who overindulged in bodily pleasure give rise to stomach ailments in people who have the same inclination: Swedenborg, *Arcana Caelestia*, vol. VII, §5720, pp. 432-3 and §5723, p. 434.

13   See ibid., §§5711-26, pp. 428-35.

[14] Swedenborg believed that in the absence of evil, a person will still die in old age, but free from disease: ibid., §5726, p. 435.

[15] See ibid., §5713, p. 430, where Swedenborg points out that the spiritual origin of diseases 'does not make it impossible for a person to be healed by natural remedies, for the Lord's providence works in co-operation with means such as these'.

[16] See ibid., §5725, p. 435.

[17] When the finest tubules of the inner man are opened to the Lord and hence to God, the infernal spirits can have no effect: ibid., §§5711-26, pp. 428-35. Illness cannot occur, and any infernal spirits already present are cast out by angels, so that healing occurs. According to Swedenborg, this is why healing was emphasized so much in Christ's ministry: ibid., vol. X, §8364, pp. 149-51. According to Swedenborg, Christ's healing of the blind, dumb, deaf, lame, etc., corresponds with spiritual awakening, both of individuals and of nations. He pointed out that there is a complete contrast between divine miracles, which are of heaven, and magical miracles, which may appear outwardly similar to divine miracles, but are brought about so that the magician can dominate others, and are therefore of hell: ibid., vol. IX, §7337, pp. 311-12. In other words, he believed that physical healing was not Christ's primary goal, but is rather an automatic accompaniment, or outward sign, of the inner man being turned to God.

[18] Some similarities between Paracelsian and Swedenborgian concepts are inevitable, given that they were both writing within the broad paradigm of Western esotericism. An influence of Paracelsus on Swedenborg has been proposed, for example, by James Wilson, 'Swedenborg, Paracelsus, and the Dilute Traces: A Lyrical and Critical Reflection on Mysticism, Reform, and the Nature of Influence', in *The New Philosophy*, vol. CXIV, nos. 3-4 (July-December 2011), pp. 175-206. Martin Lamm concludes that 'Swedenborg could not have avoided acquaintance with the medical systems of the Renaissance, such as those of Paracelsus and van Helmont. . . It is probable that he had read these two masters in the original': Lamm, *Swedenborg*, p. 56.

[19] J J G Wilkinson, letter to his fiancée Emma Marsh, undated (1837/8?), in Swedenborg Society Archive K/124 (e).

[20] J J G Wilkinson, *The Human Body*, p. 344.

[21] J J G Wilkinson, *Epidemic Man and His Visitations*, p. 16. The concept of correspondence between diseases and the phenomena of nature is an ancient one. For example, it was believed that epilepsy corresponds to earthquakes. Paracelsus said that 'Earthquakes and falling sickness [epilepsy] have the same causes': see Paracelsus, *The Diseases that Deprive Man of his Reason, such as St. Vitus' Dance, Falling*

Sickness, Melancholy, and Insanity, and their Correct Treatment, tr. Gregory Zilboorg, in *Four Treatises of Theophrastus von Hohenheim called Paracelsus*, ed. Henry E Sigerist (Baltimore: The John Hopkins University Press, 1941), pp. 127-212 (p. 144). Today, a correspondence between epilepsy and earthquakes is still recognized, although within the scientific paradigm that both phenomena are governed by the same 'power laws': see Ivan Osorio, Mark G Frei, Didier Sornette, John Milton and Ying-Cheng Lai, 'Epileptic Seizures: Quakes of the Brain?', in *Physical Review E*, vol. 82, no. 2 (20 August 2010), article no. 21919.

22 The early microscopist Antonie Philips van Leeuwenhoek (1632-1723) was the first to describe single-celled organisms which he called 'animalcules' and which include what we would now call bacteria, although their role in disease was not recognized at that time. In *The Animal Kingdom*, Swedenborg wrote that Leeuwenhoek's animalcules were ephemeral bodies that were put on by fragments of the animal spirit; Swedenborg believed that spermatozoa were the same type of entity: Swedenborg, *The Animal Kingdom*, vol. I, §81, pp. 99-100 n. (m) and pp. 102-3 n. (o). Wilkinson extended this idea to accommodate the association between bacteria and disease which was well known in his day.

23 J J G Wilkinson, *Epidemic Man and His Visitations*, p. 38. In Wilkinson's view, 'The Godless cravings of the rich for what they cannot get, and do not deserve, corresponds in them to the unsatisfied appetites and hungers of the poor, which also are for things beyond their reach, often as a consequence of ill-desert on their own part or that of their ancestors': ibid.

24 Ibid., pp. 57, 55.

25 Ibid., p. 47.

26 The concept of diseased spheres comes from Swedenborg, who said that 'When a person falls sick in this way he has contracted his sickness from the life that is his; in his case an unclean sphere corresponding to the sickness attaches itself and is present as the cause from which the sickness springs': *Arcana Caelestia*, vol. VII, §5715, p. 430. It is typical of Wilkinson's thinking that he extends this concept into an argument against moving patients from their homes into hospitals, and combines it with his antipathy to the orthodox medical treatment of his day. Surprisingly given his views on hospital treatment, Wilkinson was an attending physician at the short-lived Hahnemann Hospital in London, which lasted only from 1850-2: *The British and Foreign Homoeopathic Medical Directory*, ed. George Atkin (London: Aylott & Co., 1853), p. 34.

27 J J G Wilkinson, *Epidemic Man and His Visitations*, p. 81. Paracelsus also made extensive

use of the light analogy, emphasizing that seeing by the 'light of nature' was essential for a physician to be effective: see Charles Webster, *Paracelsus: Medicine, Magic and Mission at the End of Time* (New Haven: Yale University Press, 2008), pp. 153-6.

[28] James John Garth Wilkinson, 'Medical Specialism', in *The Homoeopathic World*, vol. 24 (September 1889), p. 392.

[29] Ibid., p. 390.

[30] Ibid., p. 395.

[31] See Chapter 4.

[32] See R T Claridge, *Hydropathy*.

[33] J J G Wilkinson, *The Human Body*, p. 386

[34] J J G Wilkinson, letter to Henry James, Sr, 13 July 1849, in Swedenborg Society Archive K/123.

[35] J J G Wilkinson, 'Flexible Magnetine Appliances. Testimonials', in *Englishwoman's Domestic Magazine* (1 November 1877), p. 8.

[36] *Dynamis* was an ancient Greek term used by such philosophers as Plato and Aristotle to mean potential, power and potency, in contrast to *energeia* which refers to actuality.

[37] Samuel Hahnemann, *Organon of Medicine*, tr. R E Dudgeon (London: W Headland, 1849), §§9-11, pp. 115-16.

[38] Ibid., §29, pp. 127-8. As discussed later, Wilkinson found this explanation unsatisfactory. Dudgeon adds a footnote (p. 128) commenting that Hahnemann had later modified his view about the mode of action of homoeopathic remedies, but the revised ideas were not published in full until a 6th edition of Hahnemann's *Organon* was published posthumously in 1921 (in English translation by William Boericke).

[39] Hahnemann, *Organon*, §16, p. 118.

[40] Swedenborg, *Divine Love and Wisdom*, §336, p. 141.

[41] Emanuel Swedenborg, *Adversaria*, §7484, quoted in 'Hahnemann and His Discovery', in *New Church Life*, vol. III, no. 1 (January 1883), pp. 2-4 (p. 4).

[42] Swedenborg, *Apocalypse Explained*, vol. VI, §1214.2, p. 376.

[43] A B G, 'Honor to the Late Dr. Gram', in *New Jerusalem Messenger*, vol. 39, no. 12 (22 September 1880), p. 168.

[44] Marguerite Beck Block, *The New Church in the New World. A Study of Swedenborgianism in America* (New York: Henry Holt, 1932), pp. 161-5.

[45] William E Payne, 'Homoeopathy. Or the Science of Medicine considered in its Relation to the Doctrines of the Church', in *The Newchurchman*, vol. 2, no. 6 (April 1844), pp. 509-64.

46 Richard DeCharms, 'Have the Principles of Homoeopathy an Affinity with the Doctrines of the New Church?', in *New Church Repository*, vol. 3, no. 11 (November 1850), pp. 501-8.

47 Ibid., p. 504.

48 William H Holcombe, 'Homoeopathy and Its New Church Affinities', in *New Church Repository*, vol. 3, no. 12 (December 1850), pp. 540-5. In this article, Holcombe declared that 'although an ardent receiver of Swedenborg's philosophy, I have been for several years, and expect to continue, a practitioner of the so-called Allopathic medicine' (p. 540). Holcombe was converted to homoeopathy shortly afterwards, after observing the benefits of homoeopathic remedies in cholera: see the posthumous publication William Henry Holcombe, *The Truth about Homoeopathy...also a Sketch of the Life of Dr. Holcombe* (Philadelphia: Boericke and Tafel, 1894), p. 40.

49 William M Murdoch, 'Homoeopathy Again', in *The New Church Messenger* (Cincinnati), vol.II, no. VII (1 June 1854), p. 112.

50 J J G Wilkinson, letter to Henry James, Sr, 8 February 1855, in Swedenborg Society Archive K/123.

51 J J G Wilkinson, *War, Cholera, and the Ministry of Health*, p. 37.

52 J J G Wilkinson, letter to his father James John Wilkinson, 28 December 1852, in Swedenborg Society Archive K/124 (b).

53 The original certificate is held in Swedenborg Society Archive A/183 (k).

54 Peter Morrell, 'British Homeopathy during two centuries', at <http://www.homeoint.org/morrell/british/swedenborg.htm>, accessed 5 June 2009.

55 John S Haller, Jr, *The History of American Homeopathy: The Academic Years, 1820-1935* (New York: Haworth Press, 2005), p. 161. Wilkinson wrote to Henry James asking for his help to obtain this MD certificate: 'There is a service that you might do me in this wise: Can you find out for me whether, for what I am, I can, without trouble, take the degree of M.D. from the Homeopathic College in Philadelphia? It is rather important that I should have that degree; viz. of M.D.; and I cannot get it in England. Pray, at your leisure, attend to this little mission for me'. J J G Wilkinson, letter to Henry James, Sr, 30 December 1852, in Swedenborg Society Archive K/123.

56 George Wyld, *Notes of My Life*, p. 34.

57 J J G Wilkinson, *The Human Body*, p. 374.

58 Ibid., p. 372.

59 Ibid., p. 371.

60 Ibid., p. 372.

61   Wilkinson compares this to the spread of contagious diseases, which can begin with a small lesion in one person, then spread to the whole body and ultimately to a whole society.

62   J J G Wilkinson, *The Human Body*, p. 375.

63   Ibid., p. 379.

64   Ibid., p. 381.

65   Ibid.

66   Ibid., pp. 167-8.

67   Ibid., p. 168.

68   Ibid., p. 375.

69   J J G Wilkinson, handwritten notes and drawings, in Swedenborg Society Archive A/150 (a).

70   Ibid. See in particular the drawing and notes for 'the Uses of phosphorus' (attributed to 'Hahnemann') and 'Allium Sativum' (attributed to '† Hahnemann').

71   J J G Wilkinson, notes and drawing on 'Miss Taylor's case', in Swedenborg Society Archive A/150 (a).

72   J J G Wilkinson, notebook, in Swedenborg Society Archive A/150 (a). Mother tinctures are the first extraction of a medicine in alcohol or water, before further homoeopathic dilution.

73   It has been suggested that Wilkinson personally observed the harmful effects of Hekla lava on animals, and there collected some of the ash: see James Compton Burnett, *Fifty Reasons for Being a Homoeopath* (London: The Homoeopathic Publishing Co. 1888), p. 66. This assertion has been repeated in a more recent publication: Treuherz, 'The Origins of Kent's Homeopathy', p. 130. This account appears to be fanciful: there is no such account in Wilkinson's notebooks relating to his trips to Iceland.

74   Wilkinson described his findings with Hekla Lava in a letter to William Holcolmbe. The letter, together with a favourable account of Holcombe's own experience of using the remedy, is reproduced in full in William H Holcombe, 'Hekla-lava', in *Transactions of the Twenty-Third Session of the American Institute of Homoeopathy*, New Series (Chicago: Lakeside Press, 1871), pp. 441-4.

75   George Herbert, 'Man', quoted in J J G Wilkinson, *Epidemic Man and His Visitations*, p. 127.

76   J J G Wilkinson, letter to Henry James, Sr, 14 November 1852, in Swedenborg Society Archive K/123.

77   J J G Wilkinson, letter to his father James John Wilkinson, 28 December 1852, in Swedenborg Society Archive K/124 (b). Paracelsus was also an advocate of using the

insights of folk medicine; he travelled widely in search of cures, and said that 'The physician does not learn everything he must know and master at high colleges alone; from time to time he must consult old women, gypsies, magicians, wayfarers, and all manner of peasant folk and random people, and learn from them': Paracelsus, *Selected Writings*, p. 57.

[78] J J G Wilkinson, letter to Henry James, Sr, 30 December 1852, in Swedenborg Society Archive K/123.

[79] James John Garth Wilkinson, 'Some Deductions from the Principle involved in Vaccination. A Paper read before the Hahnemann Medical Society, Feb. 7, 1854', in *The British Journal of Homoeopathy*, vol. XII (1854), pp. 250-60. At this time Wilkinson was still a supporter of vaccination. In 1839, when his sister contracted smallpox when staying at his house, he vaccinated the whole household, including himself: see Clement Wilkinson, *James John Garth Wilkinson*, p. 264. He would later become a leader of the anti-vaccination movement. This is discussed in Chapter 8.

[80] J J G Wilkinson, 'Some Deductions from the Principle involved in Vaccination', p. 252.

[81] Ibid., p. 258.

[82] John James Drysdale, 'A Few Remarks on Animal Poisons as Remedies', in *The British Journal of Homoeopathy*, vol. XII (1854), pp. 260-6.

[83] Ibid., p. 261.

[84] Ibid., p. 266.

[85] See National Center for Homeopathy, at <http://www.homeopathycenter.org/remedy/hippozeninum>, accessed 10 May 2016.

[86] J J G Wilkinson, *The Homoeopathic Principle Applied to Insanity. A Proposal to Treat Lunacy by Spiritualism* (Boston: Otis Clapp, 1857).

[87] See Alex Owen, *The Darkened Room*, pp. 139-67.

[88] J J G Wilkinson, *The Homoeopathic Principle Applied to Insanity*, p. 5.

[89] Ibid., p. 8.

[90] Ibid., p. 11.

[91] Ibid., p. 14.

[92] Ibid., p. 15.

[93] J J G Wilkinson, Address Book, 1892, in Swedenborg Society Archive A/183 (r). Wilkinson's proposal plainly resonates with today's art therapy. In Wilkinson's time, the arts were used in the more progressive asylums such as the Bethlem Hospital, but this was recreational rather than therapeutic: see John M MacGregor, *The Discovery of the Art of the Insane* (Princeton, NJ: Princeton University Press, 1989), pp. 124-5.

94 The most famous English asylum doctor of that era was Henry Maudsley (1835-1918), who wrote an essay explaining that Emanuel Swedenborg was a madman: Henry Maudsley, 'Emanuel Swedenborg', in his *Body and Mind: An Inquiry into their Connection and Mutual Influence, Specially in Reference to Mental Disorders: An Enlarged and Revised Edition* (New York: D Appleton, 1890), pp. 163-217.

95 C Lockhart Robertson, 'The Homoeopathic Principle applied to Insanity: a Proposal to treat Lunacy by Spiritualism: By JAMES JOHN GARTH WILKINSON, M.D.', in *The Asylum Journal of Mental Science*, vol. IV, no. 25 (April 1858), pp. 360-96. In this article, homoeopathy is referred to as a 'strange mental delusion', that is an 'odd Chinese-like imitation of science' (p. 366), and spirit writing and drawing is dismissed as the effect of imagination acting without volition: an example, thought the author, of Carpeneter's 'unconscious cerebration', a concept that Wilkinson was very well aware of.

96 Ibid., p. 368.

97 James John Garth Wilkinson, *The Affections of Armed Powers: a Plea for a School of Little Nations* (London: James Speirs, 1897), p. 139.

98 Wilkinson's friend Robert Masters Theobald (1835-1908) was struck off the Medical Register for publishing an account of this treatment: see Count Cesare Mattei, *Electro-Homoeopathic Medicine: A New Medical System being a Popular and Domestic Guide Founded on Experience*, tr. R M Theobald, 2nd edn. (London: David Stott, 1891).

99 J J G Wilkinson, in Swedenborg Society Archive A/150 (a). Belief in fairies was widely prevalent during the nineteenth century: see Nicola Brown, *Fairies in Nineteenth-Century Art and Literature* (Cambridge: Cambridge University Press, 2001), pp. 12-18.

100 Swedenborg differentiated between the spiritual and the higher celestial realms, so Wilkinson evidently thought that it was necessary to produce 'celestial medicines' that would operate on a higher level than the usual homoeopathic remedies. He gives no indication of how this might be applied in practice.

101 Peter Morrell, 'Triumph of the light—isopathy and the rise of transcendental home-opathy, 1830-1920', in *Medical Humanities*, vol. 29, no. 1 (2003), pp. 22-32.

102 J J G Wilkinson, *The Human Body*, p. 372.

103 R E Dudgeon, 'Lecture on the History of Homoeopathy', in *Annals and Transactions of the British Homoeopathic Society and of the London Homoeopathic Hospital*, vol. VII (1876), p. 317, cited by Philip A Nicholls, *Homoeopathy and the Medical Profession* (London: Croom Helm, 1988), p. 184

[104] R E Dudgeon, *Lectures on the Theory and Practice of Homoeopathy* (New Delhi: B Jain Publishers, 2007), p. 345. Constantine Hering (1800-80) devoted half a century to amassing a collection of the works of Paracelsus. His library is now housed at the Hahnemann University in Philadelphia: see <https://www.nlm.nih.gov/exhibition/paracelsus/collections.html>, accessed 22 July 2016.

[105] Dudgeon, *Lectures*, pp. 143, 160.

[106] [Samuel Brown], 'Physical Puritanism', in *The Westminster and Foreign Quarterly Review*, vol. 57, no. 112 (=New Series vol. 1, no. 2) (1 April 1852), pp. 405-42.

[107] J F C Harrison, 'Early Victorian Radicals and the Medical Fringe', in W F Bynum and Roy Porter (eds.), *Medical Fringe and Medical Orthodoxy* (London: Croom Helm, 1987), pp. 198-215.

[108] Wilkinson's politics are discussed in Chapter 8.

[109] Alex Owen, *The Darkened Room*, p. 79; Ellic Howe, *The Magicians of the Golden Dawn. A Documentary History of a Magical Order 1887-1923* (London: Routledge & Kegan Paul, 1972), p. 51.

[110] J J G Wilkinson, letter to William Boericke, 19 October 1893, in Swedenborg Society Archive K/125 (2).

[111] J J G Wilkinson, *Swedenborg Among the Doctors*, p. 19.

[112] Treuherz, 'The Origins of Kent's Homeopathy', p. 132.

[113] J J G Wilkinson, letters to William Boericke, 2 November 1894 and 29 January 1896, in Swedenborg Society Archive, K/125 (2).

[114] William Henry Holcombe, *How I became a Homoeopath* (New York: Boericke & Tafel, 1877), p. 17.

[115] Morrell, 'Triumph of the Light', p. 26.

[116] Philip A Nicholls, *Homoeopathy and the Medical Profession*, pp. 259-77.

[117] Wood, *The Magical Staff*, pp. 135-65.

[118] Samuel Hahnemann noted that disease is accompanied by 'changes in the state of the mind and disposition', but he did not emphasize the primacy of mental symptoms: Hahnemann, *Organon*, §213, p. 266. Even in his later years, he did not take the detailed history of character, psychological traits and constitution that would become regarded as mandatory for Kent and his followers: see Hahnemann's casebooks, researched by Rima Handley, *In Search of the Later Hahnemann* (Beaconsfield: Beaconsfield Publishers, 1997), p. 25. The similarities between the thinking of Wilkinson and Kent have been remarked upon in Treuherz, 'The Origins of Kent's Homeopathy'.

[119] James Tyler Kent, 'Use of the Repertory', in *New Remedies, Clinical Cases, Lesser Writings, Aphorisms and Precepts* (Calcutta: Sett Dey, 1963), pp. 199-201 (p. 201).

[120] Ibid., p. 200. Before this, homoeopaths made use of complex repertories based on symptoms in order to choose their remedies.

[121] Colin Griffith, *The New Materia Medica. Key Remedies for the Future of Homoeopathy* (London: Watkins Publishing, 2007).

[122] George Vithoulkas, 'British Media Attacks on Homeopathy: Are they Justified?', in *Homeopathy*, vol. 97 no. 2 (April 2008), pp. 103-6.

[123] J J G Wilkinson, handwritten notes and drawings, in Swedenborg Society Archive A/150 (a); Griffith, *The New Materia Medica*, pp. 13-40.

[124] Ibid., pp. 544-6.

Chapter Eight

[1] Jeremy Bentham, *An Introduction to the Principles of Morals and Legislation*, 2 vols. (London: W Pickering, 1823), vol. I, p. 1.

[2] Swedenborg, *The True Christian Religion*, vol. 2, §490, p. 549.

[3] See Swedenborg, *Divine Love and Wisdom*, §§331-5, pp. 138-40.

[4] Bentham, *Principles of Morals and Legislation*, vol. I, pp. 3-4.

[5] H S Jones, *Victorian Political Thought* (Basingstoke: Macmillan, 2000), pp. 5, 44-52.

[6] J J G Wilkinson, *On Human Science*, pp. 167-8.

[7] Hugo Lj. Odhner, *Principles of the New Philosophy*, pp. 32-3.

[8] For a detailed discussion of Swedenborgians and homoeopathy, see Chapter 7.

[9] It was entirely possible to accept the notion of an organic society whilst rejecting Darwinism; this was the position taken by Gladstone (as well as Garth Wilkinson): see H S Jones, *Victorian Political Thought*, p. 76.

[10] Ibid., p. 89.

[11] W J Mander, 'Hegel and British Idealism', in Lisa Herzog (ed.), *Hegel's Thought in Europe: Currents, Crosscurrents and Countercurrents* (Basingstoke: Palgrave Macmillan, 2013), pp. 165-76 (p. 174).

[12] Richard Brent, *Liberal Anglican Politics: Whiggery, Religion, and Reform 1830-1841* (Oxford: Clarendon Press, 1987). It was because of this liberalizing tendency in the Anglican Church that Garth Wilkinson felt able to remain a member of it; see Chapter 1.

[13] Carl Schmitt, quoted in David Nicholls, *Deity and Domination: Images of God and the State in the Nineteenth and Twentieth Centuries* (London and New York: Routledge, 1994), p. 13.

14   See J J G Wilkinson, *On Human Science*, p. 533; J J G Wilkinson, *Revelation, Mythology, Correspondences*, p. 17.

15   H S Jones, *Victorian Political Thought*, p. 77.

16   See, for example, J J G Wilkinson, *On Human Science*, pp. 271-6.

17   James John Garth Wilkinson, *Swedenborg's Doctrines and the Translation of his Works* (London: James Spiers, 1882), pp. 6-7.

18   J J G Wilkinson, *Swedenborg Among the Doctors*, pp. 43-4.

19   J J G Wilkinson, letter to his daughter Emma Pertz, 30 May 1889, in Swedenborg Society Archive K/124 (c).

20   J J G Wilkinson, *On Human Science*, pp. 532-3.

21   Ibid., p. 536.

22   The circumstances leading to the June uprising in Paris were complex, but it was fomented by republican and socialist groups and became a full-scale uprising when government troops responded to their initial protests by killing some of the workers: see Jeremy D Popkin, *A History of Modern France*, 3rd edn. (Upper Saddle River, NJ: Pearson Prentice Hall, 2005), pp. 115-24.

23   Wilkinson's wife was very much against him going to Paris; as he said to James, 'The poor wife is a little quiet with me for going': J J G Wilkinson, letter to Henry James, Sr, 23 June 1848, p. 1, in Houghton Library, Harvard University, at <http://nrs.harvard.edu/urn-3:FHCL.HOUGH:12249590>, accessed 11 June 2014.

24   John Cunningham, 'Lord Wallscourt of Ardfry (1797-1849): An Early Irish Socialist', in *Journal of the Galway Archaeological and Historical Society*, vol. 57 (2005), pp. 90-112. In the period leading up to the Paris uprising, Wallscourt wrote to Wilkinson that 'The news from Paris is indeed glorious, the dawn of light and real liberty is about to break forth': Wallscourt, letter to J J G Wilkinson, 1 March 1848, in Swedenborg Society Archive K/125 (24).

25   J J G Wilkinson, letter to his wife Emma Wilkinson, 27 June 1848, in Swedenborg Society Archive K/124 (a).

26   Ibid. Despite these socialist sentiments, Wilkinson enjoyed the hospitality of the upper classes whilst in Paris. He wrote of a dinner hosted by Wallscourt at which he was served with truffles, cock's combs and other 'rare and odd things': J J G Wilkinson, letter to his wife Emma Wilkinson, 30 June 1848 in Swedenborg Society Archive K/124 (a). He also attended the funeral of two French officers: J J G Wilkinson, letter to his wife Emma Wilkinson, 29 June 1848 in Swedenborg Society Archive K/124 (a).

27   Dorothy Thompson, *The Chartists* (London: Temple Smith, 1984), p. 321.

28 J J G Wilkinson, letter to Henry James, Sr, 11 April 1848, pp. 4-5, in Houghton Library, Harvard University, at <http://nrs.harvard.edu/urn-3:FHCL.HOUGH:12249590>, accessed 11 June 2014.

29 J J G Wilkinson, letter to his wife Emma Wilkinson, 10 April 1848, in Swedenborg Society Archive K/124 (a).

30 Dorothy Thompson, *The Chartists*, p. 321.

31 J J G Wilkinson, letter to his wife Emma Wilkinson, 7 April 1848, in Swedenborg Society Archive K/124 (a).

32 J J G Wilkinson, letter to Henry James, Sr, 21 April 1848, in Swedenborg Society Archive K/123.

33 The origins of the term 'utopian socialism' have been discussed by Arthur E Bestor, Jr, 'The Evolution of the Socialist Vocabulary', in *Journal of the History of Ideas*, vol. 9, no. 8 (June 1948), pp. 259-302. The term 'socialism' was first coined by Owen and became synonymous with Owenism. The term 'utopian' was first coined by Sir Thomas More in the sixteenth century, and came to mean 'not merely ideally perfect, but impossibly and extravagantly ideal': ibid., p. 287. Owen and Fourier did not use this term about themselves. Marx and Engels in the *Communist Manifesto* used the term 'communist' in preference to 'socialist', because of the Owenite association of socialism. They used the word 'utopian' disparagingly in relation to Owenism and Fourierism, and the term 'utopian socialism' has since been adopted to refer to all pre-Marxist socialism.

34 Robert Owen summarized his thesis in the answers to two questions in his *The Life of Robert Owen. Written by Himself*, 2 vols. (London: Effingham Wilson, 1857-8), vol. I, p. xx: '*First*. Who or what created the material from which man's character is formed? The obvious reply is—the Great Creating Power of the Universe. *Second*. Who places each individual within the surroundings which form his language, religion, habits, manners. . .Answer—Society'.

35 George Rapp (1757-1847) was a German immigrant to America who established a community founded upon esoteric millennialist principles that were developed from Behmenist theosophy, Rosicrucianism, Freemasonry and alchemy: see Arthur Versluis, 'Western Esotericism and the Harmony Society', at <http://www.esoteric.msu.edu/Versluis.html>, accessed 27 April 2013.

36 Owen believed that putting his theories into practice would 'harmonise man to nature [and so also to the Creator] by consistent obedience to all her laws', and thus 'unite mankind through future ages as one man'. This 'will make the earth a

paradise and its inhabitants angels': Robert Owen, *Life*, vol. I, p. xliii. The idea that humankind will be transmuted into the united angelic body of a single human is distinctly Swedenborgian. There were many Swedenborgians in the New Harmony community, and a Swedenborgian minister, Daniel Roe, formed the short-lived Yellow Springs Owenite community in Ohio: J F C Harrison, *Robert Owen and the Owenites in Britain and America: The Quest for the New Moral World* (London: Routledge and Kegan Paul, 1969), p. 107.

37 In his autobiography, Owen observed that 'In taking a calm retrospect of my life from the earliest remembered period of it to the present hour, there appears to me to have been a succession of extraordinary or out-of-the-usual-way events, forming connected links of a chain, to compel me to proceed onward to complete a mission, of which I have been an impelled agent, without merit or demerit of any kind on my part': Robert Owen, *Life*, vol. I, p. xliii. His later followers took this a step further, by regarding Owen as a prophet greater than John the Baptist and asking for scraps of his handwriting that could be kept as relics like those of a saint: see Frank Podmore, *Robert Owen A Biography*, 2 vols. (London: Hutchinson & Co., 1906), vol. II, p. 636.

38 Hockley's correspondence with Owen is reproduced in Gilbert and Hamill (eds.), *The Rosicrucian Seer*, pp. 145-83. Hockley had worked in the occult bookshop of John Denley (see Chapter 2) where he had copied many esoteric manuscripts. He came to be regarded as an esoteric 'Master' and had several disciples. Later he was centrally involved with spiritualism. It is claimed that he knew Daniel Dunglas Home and 'the editors of all the main Spiritualist journals', which would include Garth's brother William, but there is no record of him being acquainted with Garth Wilkinson: see Gilbert and Hamill (eds.), *The Rosicrucian Seer*, pp. 11-13.

39 See Robert Owen, *Life*, vol. I, p. xxxiv.

40 J J G Wilkinson, letter to his wife Emma Wilkinson, 4 July 1848, in Swedenborg Society Archive K/124 (a).

41 Harrison, *Robert Owen*, p. 32.

42 This account of Fourier's beliefs is informed by Carl J Guarneri, *The Utopian Alternative: Fourierism in Nineteenth-Century America* (Ithaca: Cornell University Press, 1991).

43 'By the way, the Fourierist gents become daily more tedious. The *Phalange* [the Fourierist journal] is nothing but nonsense. The information contained in Fourier's posthumous work is confined entirely to the *mouvement aromal* and the mating of the planets which would appear to take place *plus ou moins* from behind. The mating

of Saturn and Uranus engenders dung-beetles——which in any case the Fourierists themselves are': Engels, letter to Marx, 19 August 1846, at <http://marxists.anu.edu.au/archive/marx/works/1846/letters/46_08_19.htm>, accessed 22 July 2016.

[44] Charles Julius Hempel, *The True Organization of the New Church, as indicated in the Writings of Emanuel Swedenborg, and demonstrated by Charles Fourier* (New York: William Radde and London: H Ballière, 1848).

[45] Ibid., p. 232.

[46] Parke Godwin, *A Popular View of the Doctrines of Charles Fourier* (New York: J S Redfield, Clinton Hall, 1844), p. 106.

[47] Block, *The New Church in the New World*, pp. 155-6.

[48] Philip F Gura, *American Transcendentalism: A History* (New York: Hill and Wang, 2007), p. 156.

[49] John Humphrey Noyes, *History of American Socialisms* (Philadelphia: J B Lippincott & Co., 1870), p. 546.

[50] Ibid., p. 548.

[51] Block, *The New Church in the New World*, pp. 149-50. The contrast between the socially active non-sectarian followers of Swedenborg and the inward-looking sectarian members of the New Church in England has been discussed in Chapter 2.

[52] Block, *The New Church in the New World*, p. 150.

[53] Habegger, *The Father*, p. 248.

[54] J J G Wilkinson, letter to Henry James, Sr, 29 November 1845, p. 8, in Houghton Library, Harvard University, at <http://nrs.harvard.edu/urn-3:FHCL.HOUGH:12249590>, accessed 11 June 2014. After his visit, Tweedy began regularly sending Wilkinson copies of the Fourierist journal the *Harbinger*.

[55] Henry James, Sr, *Moralism and Christianity; or Man's Experience and Destiny. In Three Lectures* (New York: J S Redfield, 1850), p. 92.

[56] William Hall Brock, 'The Swedenborgianized Fourierism of Henry James: A Study in Pathology', at <http://leavesofgrass.org/billbrock/fch06.htm>, accessed 29 April 2013.

[57] Charles Augustus Tulk, letter to his sister, 8 June 1842, copied in a handwritten bound volume, 'Tulk on the Lord's Prayer and Correspondence', Swedenborg Society Archive A/8.

[58] J J G Wilkinson, letter to J F I Tafel, 26 March 1842, in Swedenborg Society Archive K/126 (e). Joseph Friedrich Immanuel Tafel (1796-1863) was a follower of Swedenborg and was at that time the librarian at the Royal University of Tubingen. Wilkinson corresponded with him regarding the publication of Swedenborg's manuscripts.

59 J J G Wilkinson, letter to Henry James, Sr, 3 February 1846, in Swedenborg Society Archive K/123.

60 J J G Wilkinson, letter to Henry James, Sr, 17 June 1846, in Swedenborg Society Archive K/123.

61 J J G Wilkinson, letter to Henry James, Sr, 18 October 1847, in Swedenborg Society Archive K/123.

62 J J G Wilkinson, letter to Henry James, Sr, 17 July 1847, in Swedenborg Society Archive K/123.

63 Ralph Waldo Emerson, letter to Lidian Emerson, 20 April 1848, in *The Letters of Ralph Waldo Emerson*, vol. IV (1848-55), p. 58.

64 J J G Wilkinson, letter to Henry James, Sr, 25 February 1848, p. 2, in Houghton Library, Harvard University, at <http://nrs.harvard.edu/urn-3:FHCL.HOUGH:12249590>, accessed 11 June 2014.

65 J J G Wilkinson, letter to Henry James, Sr, 2 August 1847, p. 4, in Houghton Library, Harvard University, at <http://nrs.harvard.edu/urn-3:FHCL.HOUGH:12249590>, accessed 11 July 2014.

66 J J G Wilkinson, letter to Henry James, Sr, 17 May 1850, p. 1, in Houghton Library, Harvard University, at <http://nrs.harvard.edu/urn-3:FHCL.HOUGH:12249590>, accessed 11 July 2014.

67 J J G Wilkinson, letter to Henry James, Sr, 5 April 1850, pp. 9, 12, in Houghton Library, Harvard University, at <http://nrs.harvard.edu/urn-3:FHCL.HOUGH:12249590>, accessed 11 June 2014.

68 J J G Wilkinson, *On Human Science*, p. 354.

69 Rudolph Leonard Tafel, *Socialism and Reform in the Light of the New Church* (London: James Speirs, 1891).

70 J J G Wilkinson, *On Human Science*, p. 469.

71 Ibid., p. 472

72 Ibid., p. 551. Wilkinson would have seen the Derbyshire moors first-hand during his lecture tour of 1849, during which he visited Manchester, Sheffield and Derby, a trip that would have required him to travel across the Pennines. The campaign for greater public access to the Derbyshire moors was in its infancy when Wilkinson was writing. This was mainly a working-class campaign, with close links to socialism and the co-operative movement. It was not until 1932 that this came to fruition, with the famous trespass on Kinder Scout. See Howard Hill, *Freedom to Roam. The Struggle for Access to Britain's Moors and Mountains* (Ashbourne: Moorland Publishing, 1980).

73 J J G Wilkinson, *On Human Science*, pp. 435, 436, 463.

[74] Wilkinson's liberalizing campaigns are discussed by Barrow, 'An Imponderable Liberator', pp. 29-31.

[75] This section is informed by W L Burn, *The Age of Equipoise: A Study of the Mid-Victorian Generation* (New York: W W Norton, 1964), pp. 202-11.

[76] Ibid., p. 205, quoting William Carmichael, former registrar of the Royal College of Physicians.

[77] The relationship between homoeopathy and Swedenborgianism (and Wilkinson's practice of homoeopathy) are discussed in Chapter 7.

[78] James John Garth Wilkinson, *Unlicensed Medicine; with a Plan for Extending Homoeopathy* (London: R Theobald and Manchester: H Turner, 1855).

[79] Ibid., p. 15.

[80] Ibid., p. 19.

[81] Clement Wilkinson, *James John Garth Wilkinson*, p. 264.

[82] J J G Wilkinson, 'Some Deductions from the Principle involved in Vaccination', p. 252.

[83] James John Garth Wilkinson, *Small-Pox and Vaccination* (London: F Pitman, 1871), pp. 43-4.

[84] Helena Wojtczak, '[Anna Maria] Helena, Comtesse de Noailles (c.1826-1908)', at <http://www.historyofwomen.org/biogs.html>, accessed 16 April 2013. According to George F Chambers, *East Bourne Memories of the Victorian Period 1845 to 1901 and Some Other Things of Interest, Divers and Sundry* (Eastbourne: V T Sumfield, 1910), p. 21, the Countess was regarded as eccentric in her day: 'the Comtesse De Noailles...was somewhat of a "crank," especially in her dress. She used to go about in flowing garments like a Bedouin Arab and with only sandals on her feet, but she was kind to the poor, and liberal in the distribution of her money, though it was distributed on somewhat fanciful lines. For instance she gave £1000 to the Anti-Vaccinationists'.

[85] This account is based on information in William White, *The Story of a Great Delusion* (London: E W Allen, 1885); the quote in from p. 550. When the Countess de Noailles first approached Wilkinson, anti-vaccinationism was already a national movement: see Nadja Durbach, *Bodily Matters: The Anti-Vaccination Movement in England, 1835-1907* (Durham, NC: Duke University Press, 2005), p. 38.

[86] White, *Great Delusion*, p. 548.

[87] Clement Wilkinson, *James John Garth Wilkinson*, p. 131.

[88] James John Garth Wilkinson, *Vaccination as a Source of Small-Pox* (London: London Society for the Abolition of Compulsory Vaccination, 1884), p. 6.

[89] James John Garth Wilkinson, *The Infectious Nature of the Vaccine Disease, and the*

necessity of excluding the vaccinated and re-vaccinated, during that disease, from intercourse with healthy persons (London: The Mothers' Anti-Compulsory Vaccination League, 1877).

90   J J G Wilkinson, *Small-Pox and Vaccination*, p. 22.

91   This section is informed largely by Durbach, *Bodily Matters*.

92   The first published protest against compulsory vaccination, *Our Medical Liberties* (1854) was that of John Gibbs, a hydropath: see Durbach, *Bodily Matters*, pp. 32-3.

93   Wilkinson did flirt with teetotalism as a young man, writing to Henry James, Sr in 1850 that 'my teetotalism has thawed for the nonce…My experience of it is, that at first, for some months, it seemed to lighten the Spiritual part of me…By degrees, however, body was heard clamoring below': J J G Wilkinson, letter to Henry James, Sr, 11 January 1850, p. 1, in Houghton Library, Harvard University, at <http://nrs. harvard.edu/urn-3:FHCL.HOUGH:12249590>, accessed 11 June 2014.

94   James John Garth Wilkinson, 'Preface and Supplement', in J J G Wilkinson and William Young (eds.), *Vaccination Tracts* (Providence: Snow & Farnham, 1892), pp. 3-31 (p. 22). William Young had begun the editing of these tracts, and Garth Wilkinson completed the task.

95   Ibid., pp. 11-12.

96   Ibid., p. 22.

97   J J G Wilkinson, *On Human Science*, p. 48.

98   Wilkinson's view was echoed by other 'high potency' homoeopaths: Constantine Hering, a pioneer of homoeopathy in America who had trained under Samuel Hahnemann, referred to vaccination as 'poisoning the blood' in an English newspaper: J J G Wilkinson, 'Preface and Supplement', in Wilkinson and Young (eds.), *Vaccination Tracts*, p. 11.

99   James John Garth Wilkinson, *A Safe and Easy Way in which Poor and Rich alike can Isolate Themselves, and Treat Themselves, if they take the Smallpox* (London: William Young, 1878), in Swedenborg Society Archive L/452.

100   Ibid., p. 10.

101   This discussion is informed by Richard D French, *Antivivisection and Medical Science in Victorian Society* (Princeton: Princeton University Press, 1975).

102   Rod Preece, 'Darwinism, Christianity, and the Great Vivisection Debate', in *Journal of the History of Ideas*, vol. 64, no. 3 (July 2003), pp. 399-419.

103   French, *Antivivisection*, p. 358.

104   J J G Wilkinson, *On Human Science*, p. 94.

105   Ibid., pp. 9-10.

[106]   Ibid., p. 12.

[107]   Ibid., p. 88.

[108]   For example, Francis William Newman (1805-97) was Chairman of the Vegetarian Society from 1873 to 1884.

[109]   This section has been informed by the work of Judith R Walkowitz, *Prostitution and Victorian Society. Women, Class, and the State* (Cambridge: Cambridge University Press, 1980).

[110]   Ibid., pp. 57-63.

[111]   Ibid., p. 1.

[112]   The LNA is discussed in detail in ibid., pp. 113-36.

[113]   James John Garth Wilkinson, *The Forcible Introspection of Women for the Army and Navy by the Oligarchy, Considered Physically* (London: F Pitman, 1870).

[114]   Ibid., p. 9.

[115]   Ibid., p. 15.

[116]   Ibid., p. 23.

[117]   Ibid., p. 27.

[118]   Josephine Butler, letter to J J G Wilkinson, 14 April 1873, in Swedenborg Society Archive K/125 (39).

[119]   Josephine Butler, letter to J J G Wilkinson, 11 July (no year given), in Swedenborg Society Archive K/125 (39).

[120]   J J G Wilkinson, letter to Mrs Jacob Bright, 21 March 1870, in Swedenborg Society Archive K/125 (8).

[121]   J J G Wilkinson, letter to Mrs Jacob Bright, 17 December 1877, in Swedenborg Society Archive K/125 (8).

[122]   Clement Wilkinson, *James John Garth Wilkinson*, p. 93.

[123]   J J G Wilkinson, letter to Henry James, Sr, 2 May 1845, in Swedenborg Society Archive K/123.

[124]   Harriet Martineau, *A History of the Thirty Years' Peace, A.D. 1816-1846*, 4 vols. (London: George Bell, 1877), vol. II, p. 308.

[125]   Thomas Carlyle, *Chartism* (London: James Fraser, 1840), p. 5.

[126]   For Wilkinson's support for Peel, see J J G Wilkinson, letter to Henry James, Sr, 4 July 1850, in Swedenborg Society Archive K/123.

[127]   J J G Wilkinson, letter to Samuel Hoare, 20 November 1885, in Swedenborg Society Archive K/125 (14).

[128]   The Battle of Majuba Hill (1881) was a decisive defeat for the British in the first Boer

War. A few years later it was said that 'Englishmen have always resented the weakness and inconstancy displayed by the Government of Mr Gladstone in 1881. It is, indeed, a bitter recollection that the lives lost in the earlier Boer war were sacrificed for a cause which the Government at the first check were ready to desert': 'The Policy of Majuba Hill', in *Grey River Argus*, 28 May 1904, p.1. In his policy on Ireland, Gladstone remained publicly opposed to Home Rule for reasons of political expediency, even after he had changed his mind and become a supporter; his support was made public against his wishes by his son, Herbert Gladstone: Paul Adelman, *Gladstone, Disraeli and Later Victorian Politics* (London: Longman, 1970), pp. 44-50. After General Gordon, who was something of a popular hero, was killed in 1885 at the Siege of Khartoum, the British public blamed Gladstone for having failed to send relief: Roy Jenkins, *Gladstone* (London: Papermac, 1996), pp. 500-16. These and other events led many to conclude that Gladstone's Liberal Party was weak and not to be trusted.

[129] Clement Wilkinson, *James John Garth Wilkinson*, p. 93.

Chapter Nine

[1] F W J Schelling, *Historical-Critical Introduction to the Philosophy of Mythology*, tr. Mason Richey and Markus Zisselsberger (Albany, NY: State University of New York Press, 2007), p. 144.

[2] J J G Wilkinson, *The Book of Edda Called Voluspa*, p. 8.

[3] J J G Wilkinson, *The Human Body*, pp. 169-251.

[4] Ibid., p. 172. I have been unable to trace the origin of this quote.

[5] David Boyd Hancock, 'Ancient Egypt in 17th and 18th Century England', in Ucko and Champion (eds.), *The Wisdom of Ancient Egypt*, pp. 133-60.

[6] For more on Newton and Stukeley, see Chapter 2.

[7] Robert A Segal, 'Myth and Science: Their Varying Relationships', in *Religion Compass*, vol. 3, no. 2 (March 2009), pp. 337-58.

[8] Edward B Tylor, *Primitive Culture: Researches into the Development of Mythology, Philosophy, Religion, Art, and Custom*, 2 vols. (London: John Murray, 1871), vol. I, p. 15.

[9] For this discussion of the political implications of Frazer's thesis I am indebted to Eric Csapo, *Theories of Mythology* (Oxford: Blackwell Publishing, 2005), pp. 44-57.

[10] James Kissane, 'Victorian Mythology', in *Victorian Studies*, vol. 6 (September 1962), pp. 5-28.

[11] George Grote, *History of Greece*, 12 vols. (New York: Harper & Brothers, 1867), vol. I, p. 450.

12 The major textbook on the history of Greece before that of George Grote (1794-1871) was that by Connop Thirlwall (1797-1875), who took a historicist view of Greek mythology: see Frank M Turner, *Contesting Cultural Authority: Essays in Victorian Intellectual Life* (Cambridge: Cambridge University Press, 1993), pp. 322-61.

13 Harriet Grote, *The Personal Life of George Grote* (London: J Murray, 1873); M L Clarke, *George Grote: A Biography* (London: Athlone Press, 1962); Frank M Turner, *The Greek Heritage in Victorian Britain* (New Haven: Yale University Press, 1981), pp. 83-94.

14 In his electoral address Grote declared that his aim was 'to advance the well-being and improve the character of the LABOURING CLASSES', which he thought could be achieved 'by diffusing wholesome instruction on social and economic subjects, as well as by keeping the necessities of life untaxed, and favouring, instead of disturbing, the natural distribution of capital': Clarke, *George Grote*, p. 49.

15 Grote's model was August Comte's Law of Three Stages: new-found religion; followed by metaphysics; and finally science. Grote believed that science and religion were incompatible, saying that 'in every particular case the admission of one involved the rejection of the other': Grote, *History of Greece*, vol. I, p. 359. Comte's model had been popularized in England by Harriet Martineau, who had published in 1853 a two-volume abridged translation of *The Positive Philosophy of August Comte*.

16 Walter Pater (1839-94) likened the 'virtues' of art works to those of herbs and gems: see the preface to Walter Pater, *Studies in the History of the Renaissance* (London: Macmillan, 1873), p. ix.

17 Jeffrey Wallen, 'Physiology, Mesmerism and Walter Pater's "Susceptibilities to Influence"', in *Walter Pater: Transparencies of Desire*, ed. Laurel Brake, Leslie Higgins and Carolyn Williams (Greensboro, NC: ELT Press, 2002), pp. 73-93.

18 Walter Pater, *Greek Studies: A Series of Essays* (London: Macmillan, 1897), p. 22. This essay was first published in 1876.

19 Gowan Dawson, 'X-Club not X-Files: Walter Pater, Spiritualism and Victorian Scientific Naturalism', in Julie Scanlon and Amy Waste (eds.), *Crossing Boundaries: Thinking Through Literature* (Sheffield: Sheffield Academic Press, 2001), pp. 56-71.

20 Frank M Turner, *Between Science and Religion: The Reaction to Scientific Naturalism in Late Victorian England* (New Haven and London: Yale University Press, 1974), p. 54.

21 Dawson, 'X-Club'.

22 Tylor, *Primitive Culture*, vol. I, p. 129.

23 George W Stocking, 'Animism in Theory and Practice: E.B. Tylor's Unpublished "Notes on Spiritualism" ', in *Man*, vol. 6 no. 1 (March 1971), pp. 88-104.

24 Tylor, Diary, 19 and 27 November 1872, in Stocking, 'Animism', pp. 99, 101.

25 Tylor, Diary, 28 November 1872, in Stocking, 'Animism', p. 100.

26 Tylor, Diary, 23 November 1872, in Stocking, 'Animism', p. 99.

27 Stocking, 'Animism', p. 95.

28 James George Frazer, *The Golden Bough: A Study in Magic and Religion*, 3rd edn., Part I, *The Magic Art and the Evolution of Kings*, 2 vols. (London: MacMillan, 1920), vol. I, pp. 55-174.

29 Ibid., p. 54.

30 Ibid., p. 119.

31 John Stuart Mill, letter to William Thomas Thornton, 14 June 1862, in *The Collected Works of John Stuart Mill*, ed. Francis E Mineka and Dwight N Lindley, 33 vols. (Toronto: University of Toronto Press, London: Routledge and Kegan Paul, 1972), vol. XV, *The Later Letters of John Stuart Mill 1849-1873 Part II*, p. 539.

32 Stephanie L Barczewski, *Myth and National Identity in Nineteenth-Century Britain: The Legends of King Arthur and Robin Hood* (Oxford: Oxford University Press, 2000).

33 Antoine Faivre, *Theosophy, Imagination, Tradition*, tr. Christine Rhone (Albany: State University of New York, 2000), pp. 99-136; Faivre, *Access to Western Esotericism*, pp. 66-70, 128-33.

34 Robert Lamberton, 'Language, Text and Truth in Ancient Polytheistic Exegesis', in Jon Whitman (ed.), *Interpretation and Allegory: Antiquity to the Modern Period* (Boston: Brill Academic Publishers, 2003), pp. 73-88.

35 Jean Leclercq, *The Love of Learning and the Desire for God: A Study of Monastic Culture*, tr. Catharine Misrahi, 3rd edn. (New York: Fordham University Press, 2003), p. 119.

36 D P Walker, *The Ancient Theology* (London: Duckworth, 1972), pp. 1-21; James Hankins, *Plato in the Italian Renaissance* (Leiden: Brill, 1990), pp. 282-7.

37 David A Pailin, *Attitudes to Other Religions: Comparative Religion in Seventeenth- and Eighteenth-Century Britain* (Manchester: Manchester University Press, 1984), pp. 23-44.

38 Richard Heinberg, *Memories and Visions of Paradise: Exploring the Universal Myth of a Lost Golden Age* (Los Angeles: Tarcher, 1989).

39 Ibid., p. 11.

40 Mircea Eliade, *Myths, Dreams and Mysteries*, tr. Philip Mairet (London: Harvill Press, 1960).

41 Hesiod (*c.* 700 BC) recorded the myth of a Golden Age followed by a gradual deterioration through ages of Silver, Brass, Heroes and Iron which he regarded as his own age. Porphyry (*c.* 232-303 AD) described the Age of Cronus, a pre-agricultural age in which men lived a life of leisure, food was abundant, they had no worries, and there was no disease and no war. Similar Golden Age mythology exists throughout the Western world in separate traditions including the Hebraic Garden of Eden, the Sumerian Dilmun, the Iranian Garden of Yima, the Egyptian Tep Zepi, and the Greek Golden Age. The same Paradise myth can also be found throughout the Orient. The Hebrew and the Greek myths have been the most influential in the West. See Heinberg, *Memories and Visions of Paradise*.

42 Swedenborg's writings on the five spiritual ages of man are discussed in detail in P L Johnson, *The Five Ages*.

43 Swedenborg said explicitly that 'The golden age was the time of the Most Ancient Church': *Arcana Caelestia*, vol. II, §1551, p. 178.

44 Swedenborg, *Arcana Caelestia*, vol. I, §920, pp. 362-3.

45 Emanuel Swedenborg, *On the Sacred Scripture or the Word of the Lord from Experience*, tr. John Chadwick (London: Swedenborg Society, 1997), §18, pp. 19-20.

46 Swedenborg, *The True Christian Religion*, vol. 1, §205, p. 266. As discussed above, this concept of the origin of idolatry was commonly held in Swedenborg's time.

47 Swedenborg, *Arcana Caelestia*, vol. V, §3667, p. 15.

48 Swedenborg, *The True Christian Religion*, vol. 2, §§753-91, pp. 809-42. Swedenborg's New Church can be related to other concepts of a 'New Age' or 'Age of Aquarius'. For a discussion of the relationship between Swedenborg's ages of man and those of other systems, see P L Johnson, *The Five Ages*, pp. 223-6.

49 Schelling, *Historical-Critical Introduction to the Philosophy of Mythology*.

50 Ibid., p. 170.

51 Horn, *Schelling and Swedenborg*.

52 Max Müller, *My Autobiography: A Fragment* (London: Longmans, Green & Co, 1901), p. 152.

53 *The Life and Letters of the Right Honourable Friedrich Max Müller*, ed. Georgina Adelaide Müller, 2 vols. (London: Longmans, Green & Co., 1902), vol. I, pp. 23, 56.

54 Max Müller, *Three Introductory Lectures on the Science of Thought* (Chicago: Open Court Publishing, 1888), p. 87.

55   Max Müller, 'Comparative Mythology' (1856), in *Chips from a German Workshop*, 2nd edn., 5 vols. (London: Longmans, Green & Co., 1867-75), vol. II, pp. 1-146 (p. 109).

56   This aspect of Müller's work is discussed by Csapo, *Theories of Mythology*.

57   This is discussed by Stefan Arvidsson, *Aryan Idols: Indo-European Mythology as Ideology and Science* (Chicago: University of Chicago Press, 2006).

58   J J G Wilkinson, letter to Viktor Rydberg, 1890, in Clement Wilkinson, *James John Garth Wilkinson*, p. 173. Viktor Rydberg (1828-95) was a Swedish scholar who published *Teutonic Mythology* in 1886.

59   *The Life and Letters of the Right Honourable Friedrich Max Müller*, vol. I, p. 136, vol. II, p. 166.

60   William E Gladstone, *Studies on Homer and the Homeric Age*, 3 vols. (Oxford: Oxford University Press, 1858), vol. II, p. 3.

61   For example, Schelling wrote that 'That divine power, integrating the whole, embraces not merely nature, but also the spirit world, and the soul dwelling above both. Therefore these also receive a spatial reference by that integration; the old belief in a place, an abode of spirits, again receives meaning and truth': F W J Schelling, *The Ages of the World*, tr. Frederick de Wolfe Bolman, Jr (New York: Colombia University Press, 1942), p. 214.

62   William E Gladstone, *The Gladstone Diaries with Cabinet Minutes and Prime-Ministerial Correspondence*, ed. M R D Foot and H C G Matthew, 14 vols. (Oxford: Clarendon Press, 1968-94), vol. IX (1986), p. 354, entry for 16 October 1878.

63   Gladstone, *Gladstone Diaries*, vol. XI (1990), p. 231 n.

64   David W Bebbington, *William Ewart Gladstone: Faith and Politics in Victorian Britain* (Grand Rapids, MI: Eerdmans Publishing Co., 1993), pp. 47-8.

65   Chevalier Ramsay, *The Philosophical Principles of Natural and Revealed Religion. Unfolded in a Geometrical Order* (Glasgow: Robert Foulis, 1748).

66   Isaac Newton, MS in Bodleian Library, cited in Ucko and Champion (eds.), *The Wisdom of Ancient Egypt*, pp. 139-40. Newton also shared Swedenborg's anti-Trinitarian views.

67   Carl Theophilus Odhner, 'An Autobiography', in *New Church Life*, vol. XL, no. 6 (June 1920), pp. 343-8 (p. 343).

68   Alice E Grant, 'A New Church Work on Mythology', in *New Church Life*, vol. XLVII, no. 10 (October 1927), pp. 604-5.

69   Carl Theophilus Odhner, *The Golden Age: The Story of the Most Ancient Church* (Bryn Athyn, PA: The Academy Book Room, 1913; repr. 1975).

70 It is important to recognize that within Wilkinson's Swedenborgian conceptual frame-
    work, Adam was not the first individual person, but the first and highest 'Church' or
    epoch of human spirituality. This is based upon a spiritual interpretation of the book
    of Genesis, as outlined by Swedenborg in his *Arcana Caelestia*.

71 J J G Wilkinson, *Revelation, Mythology, Correspondences*, p. 36. Here Wilkinson
    uses the term imagination in relation to fancy rather than active imagination: see
    Chapter 4.

72 J J G Wilkinson, *Revelation, Mythology, Correspondences*, p. 163.

73 Ibid.

74 Ibid., p. 17.

75 Wilkinson reveals his ambivalence about the place in the world of Africans, who he
    thought might be 'taken for granted' as savages, but for the fact that their line does
    not die out, and they are useful in the world, for example in the West Indies and the
    United States; but he goes on to denounce slavery. He cites Swedenborg, who held black
    Africans in very high esteem, as saying that black people have in them 'a celestial
    genius'. He concluded that black people are 'probably incapable of any but compulsory
    civilization', that they need 'good masters, or a law-abiding society around them',
    and that they require 'white guidance': see J J G Wilkinson, *Revelation, Mythology,
    Correspondences*, pp. 184-91.

76 Ibid., pp. 149-50.

77 Ibid., p. 198.

78 Kennings are figurative terms used to denote concrete objects, particularly in Old
    Norse poetry: examples are 'wave's steed' for ship, or 'wound-hoe' for spear. This is
    similar to Müller's concept of phrases used instead of proper nouns, but the Norse
    people used these for poetic reasons rather than because of any lack of proper nouns.

79 The life and work of Berossos is discussed by Gerald P Verbrugghe and John M
    Wickersham, *Berossos and Manetho, Introduced and Translated: Native Traditions
    in Ancient Mesopotamia and Egypt* (Michigan: University of Michigan Press, 2001),
    pp. 13-34.

80 Alexander Heidel, *The Babylonian Genesis: The Story of the Creation*, 2nd edn.
    (Chicago: University of Chicago Press, 1951), pp. 1-3.

81 Shawn Malley, 'Austen Henry Layard and the Periodical Press: Middle Eastern
    Archaeology and the Evacuation of Cultural Identity in Mid-Nineteenth Century
    Britain', in *Victorian Review*, vol. 22, no. 2 (1996), pp. 152-70.

82 George Smith, *The Chaldean Account of Genesis. Containing the Description of*

the Creation, the Deluge, the Tower of Babel, the Destruction of Sodom, the Times of the Patriarchs, and Nimrod..., rev. A H Sayce (London: Sampson Low, Marston, Searle and Rivington, 1880). The close similarity that was perceived between the Mesopotamian and the Genesis stories is indicated by the subtitle of this book.

83   James John Garth Wilkinson, *Oannes According to Berosus: A Study in the Church of the Ancients* (London: James Speirs, 1888), p. 197.

84   See Swedenborg, *Arcana Caelestia*, vol. I, §40, pp. 21-2.

85   Oannes is now regarded as the Greek form of Uan, a name used for Adapa, who was the mythical first sage of humankind: see Stephanie Dalley, *Myths from Mesopotamia* (Oxford: Oxford University Press, 2000), pp. 182-3. In Wilkinson's time, Oannes was believed to be a derivative name for the Babylonian god Ea: see A H Sayce, *Lectures on the Origin and Growth of Religion, as Illustrated by the Religion of the Ancient Babylonians* (London: Williams and Norgate, 1887), p. 99 n.

86   J J G Wilkinson, *Oannes*, p. 125.

87   *The Poetic Edda*, tr. Carolyne Larrington (Oxford: Oxford University Press, 1996), pp. 3-4. It is likely that the *Voluspa* represents a much older oral tradition.

88   The *Poetic Edda* is a collection of Old Norse poems contained in the Codex Regius, which is now held in the Arnamagnaean Institute in Reykjavik: see *The Poetic Edda*, tr. Larrington, pp. x-xii. Another major source for Old Norse mythology is the so-called 'Prose Edda', a collection that was put together by Snorri Sturluson (1179-1241): see Snorri Sturluson, *Edda*, tr. Anthony Faulkes (London: Everyman, 1987).

89   Andrew Wawn, *The Vikings and the Victorians: Inventing the Old North in Nineteenth-Century Britain* (Cambridge: Brewer, 2000), p. 184. The information in this section is derived from Wawn's work, unless otherwise indicated.

90   Ibid., p. 183.

91   See Chapter 7.

92   Wawn, *Vikings*, p. 343.

93   Ibid., p. 351.

94   Ibid., p. 208. Jón Hjaltalin (1840-1908) had translated Swedenborg's *Divine Love and Wisdom* into Icelandic for the Swedenborg Society: see J J G Wilkinson, *The Book of Edda Called Voluspa*, pp. x-xi.

95   Jón Hjaltalin, letter to Florence Pertz, 19 August 1904, in Swedenborg Society Archive K/125 (43). Hjaltalin says that he had 'a great many letters' from Wilkinson, but unfortunately all but two of these were destroyed by fire.

96   Ibid.

[97] Carl Theophilus Odhner, 'James John Garth Wilkinson', in *New Church Life*, vol. XX, no. 2 (February 1900), pp. 57-63, no. 3 (March 1900), pp. 123-30, no. 4 (April 1900), pp. 199-206, no. 5 (May 1900), pp. 243-6, and no. 6 (June 1900), pp. 290-7 (quotation is on p. 205).

[98] J J G Wilkinson, *The Book of Edda Called Voluspa*, p. viii. Wilkinson wrote to Viktor Rydberg in 1890 that 'The Northern Mythology has to me a sacred character, and I have long seen that "Voluspa" is a tradition of holy things': J J G Wilkinson, letter to Viktor Rydberg, 1890, in Clement Wilkinson, *James John Garth Wilkinson*, p. 173.

[99] Andrew Wawn is very disparaging about Wilkinson's interpretation of the *Voluspa*, although the impact of his criticism is blunted somewhat by him referring to Wilkinson incorrectly as 'Sir J. J. Garth Wilkinson': Wawn, *Vikings*, pp. 208-9.

[100] J J G Wilkinson, *The Book of Edda Called Voluspa*, pp. 184-5.

[101] Sturluson, *Edda*, pp. 11-13. This account of the beginning of the world is cognate with the Sanskrit hymn Purusa-Sukta: see *The Rig Veda: An Anthology of One Hundred and Eight Hymns*, tr. Wendy Doniger O'Flaherty (London: Penguin, 1981), pp. 29-32. Garth Wilkinson noted that Viktor Rydberg, in his work *Teutonic Mythology* (1886), had remarked on the similarity between Northern and Sanskrit mythologies. The notion that the world was formed from a giant man resonates with Swedenborg's concept of the *Maximus Homo* as the archetype of creation.

[102] J J G Wilkinson, *The Book of Edda Called Voluspa*, p. 27. Wilkinson notes the similarity between this account and that given in Genesis of the formation of man from the dust of the earth.

[103] Ibid., p. 12.

[104] Ibid., p. 27.

[105] Ibid., p. 34.

[106] Ibid., p. 95. It is generally thought that the *Voluspa* includes a strong influence from Christianity that was emerging when the poem was recorded; the story of Ragnarok and the subsequent rebirth of a world populated only by the righteous is one such influence: Ursula Dronke, *The Poetic Edda. Volume II: Mythological Poems* (Oxford: Clarendon Press, 1997), pp. 93-104.

[107] J J G Wilkinson, 'Egypt in the Word and the Hieroglyphics', unpublished MS in Swedenborg Society Archive A/242.

[108] Ibid.

[109] Ibid.

[110] James John Garth Wilkinson, *Isis and Osiris in the Book of Respirations. Prophecy*

in the Churches. In the Word, God with us. The Revelation of Jesus Christ (London: James Speirs, 1899), p. 73.

Afterword

[1]   Ralph Waldo Emerson, 'Literature', in *English Traits* (Boston: Phillips, Sampson, and Company, 1856), pp. 232-59 (pp. 249-50).

[2]   J J G Wilkinson, letter to Ralph Waldo Emerson, 3 January 1874, in Swedenborg Society Archive K/125 (3).

[3]   Hanegraaff, *New Age Religion and Western Culture*, pp. 424-9, 437-8, 448-60. The influence of Swedenborg's theosophy on the 'New Thought' movement has been discussed by John S Haller, Jr, *The History of New Thought* (West Chester, PA: Swedenborg Foundation, 2012).

BIBLIOGRAPHY

BOOKS

Abernethy, John, *An Enquiry into the Probability and Rationality of Mr. Hunter's Theory of Life* (London: Longman, Hurst, Rees, Orme and Brown, 1814).

—— *Introductory Lectures, Exhibiting Some of Mr. Hunter's Opinions Respecting Life and Diseases* (London: Longman, Hurst, Rees, Orme and Brown, 1819).

Acton, Alfred, *Swedenborg's Preparation* (London: Swedenborg Society, 1951).

Adelman, Paul, *Gladstone, Disraeli and Later Victorian Politics* (London: Longman, 1970).

Ameriks, Karl (ed.), *The Cambridge Companion to German Idealism* (Cambridge: Cambridge University Press, 2000).

Antón-Pacheco, José Antonio, *The Swedish Prophet: Reflections on the Visionary Philosophy of Emanuel Swedenborg*, tr. Steven Skattebo (West Chester, PA: Swedenborg Foundation, 2012).

Arvidsson, Stefan, *Aryan Idols: Indo-European Mythology as Ideology and Science* (Chicago: University of Chicago Press, 2006).

Ashburner, John, *Notes and Studies in the Philosophy of Animal Magnetism and Spiritualism* (London: H Baillière, 1867).

Bacon, Francis, *New Atlantis. A Worke unfinished*, in his, *Sylva Sylvarum: or A Naturall Historie. In Ten Centuries* (London: William Lee, 1627).

Bailey, Cyril, *The Greek Atomists and Epicurus* (Oxford: Clarendon Press, 1928).

Baker, Alfred, *The Life of Sir Isaac Pitman* (London: Pitman & Sons, 1908).

Barczewski, Stephanie L, *Myth and National Identity in Nineteenth-Century Britain: The Legends of King Arthur and Robin Hood* (Oxford: Oxford University Press, 2000).

Barker, Margaret, *The Lost Prophet. The Book of Enoch and its influence on Christianity*

(London: SPCK, 1988).

Barrow, Logie, *Independent Spirits: Spiritualism and English Plebeians 1850-1910* (London: Routledge and Kegan Paul, 1986).

Barruel, Abbé, *Memoirs, Illustrating the History of Jacobinism*, tr. Robert Clifford, 4 vols. (New York: Cornelius Davis, 1799).

Beale, Lionel S, *Protoplasm; or, Life, Force, and Matter* (London: J Churchill, 1870).

Bebbington, David W, *William Ewart Gladstone: Faith and Politics in Victorian Britain* (Grand Rapids, MI: Eerdmans Publishing Co., 1993).

Beiser, Frederick C, *German Idealism* (Cambridge, MA: Harvard University Press, 2002).

Bellin, Harvey F and Darrell Ruhl (eds.), *Blake and Swedenborg: Opposition is True Friendship* (West Chester, PA: Swedenborg Foundation, 1985).

Beloff, John, *Parapsychology: A Concise History* (London: Athlone Press, 1993).

Bentham, Jeremy, *An Introduction to the Principles of Morals and Legislation*, 2 vols. (London: W Pickering, 1823).

Bentley, G E, *Blake Records* (Oxford: Clarendon Press, 1969).

—(ed.), *William Blake: The Critical Heritage* (London: Routledge & Kegan Paul, 1975).

—and Martin K Nurmi, *A Blake Bibliography: Annotated Lists of Works, Studies, and Blakeana* (Minneapolis: University of Minnesota Press, 1964).

Benz, Ernst, *Emanuel Swedenborg: Visionary Savant in the Age of Reason*, tr. Nicholas Goodrick-Clarke (West Chester, PA.: Swedenborg Foundation, 2002).

Bergquist, Lars, *Swedenborg's Dream Diary*, tr. Anders Hallengren (West Chester, PA.: Swedenborg Foundation, 2001).

—*Swedenborg's Secret* (London: Swedenborg Society, 2005).

Berkeley, George, *A Treatise Concerning the Principles of Human Knowledge. . . First Printed in the Year 1710* (London: Jacob Tonson, 1734).

Bernheim, Hippolyte, *Suggestive Therapeutics: A Treatise on the Nature and Uses of Hypnotism*, tr. Christian A Herter (Edinburgh and London: Pentland, 1890).

Bhagavad-Gita as it is, tr. A C Bhaktivedanta Swami Prabhupada, 2nd edn. (Watford: The Bhaktivedanta Book Trust, 2006)

Blake, William, *Blake Complete Writings*, ed. Geoffrey Keynes (Oxford: Oxford University Press, 1972).

—*Songs of Innocence and Experience. Shewing the Two Contrary States of the Human Soul*, ed. J J G Wilkinson (London: W Pickering and W Newbery, 1839).

Block, Marguerite Beck, *The New Church in the New World. A Study of Swedenborgianism in America* (New York: Henry Holt, 1932).

The Book of Enoch, tr. R H Charles (Mineola, NY: Dover, 2007).

Braid, James, *Braid on Hypnotism: Neurypnology*, ed. Arthur Edward Waite (London: George Redway, 1899).

——*The Discovery of Hypnosis. The Complete Writings of James Braid, the Father of Hypnotherapy*, ed. Donald Robertson ([n.p.]: National Council for Hypnotherapy, 2008).

——*Neurypnology; or, The Rationale of Nervous Sleep, Considered in Relation with Animal Magnetism. Illustrated by Numerous Cases of its Successful Application in the Relief and Cure of Disease* (London: John Churchill, 1843).

Brann, Noel L, *Trithemius and Magical Theology* (New York: SUNY Press, 1999).

Brent, Richard, *Liberal Anglican Politics: Whiggery, Religion, and Reform 1830-1841* (Oxford: Clarendon Press, 1987).

Brock, Erland J (ed.), *Swedenborg and His Influence* (Bryn Athyn, PA: Academy of the New Church, 1988).

Broomwell, Clyde W (ed.), *Divine Healing: The Origin and Cure of Disease As Taught in the Bible and Explained by Emanuel Swedenborg* (Boston: Geo. H Ellis, 1907).

Brown, J Macmillan, *The 'Sartor Restartus' of Carlyle. A Study* (Christchurch: Whitcombe and Tombs, n.d.).

Brown, Nicola, *Fairies in Nineteenth-Century Art and Literature* (Cambridge: Cambridge University Press, 2001).

Bryan, William, *A Testimony of the Spirit of Truth concerning Richard Brothers*... (London, 1795).

Buffon, Georges-Louis Leclerc, comte de, *Buffon's Natural History, abridged*, 2 vols. (London: C & G Kearsley, 1792).

Bulwer-Lytton, Edward, *Zanoni*, 2 vols. (Philadelphia: J B Lippincott & Co., 1862).

Bunge, Gustav von, *Text-Book of Physiological and Pathological Chemistry*, tr. Florence A Starling, ed. Ernest H Starling (Philadelphia: P Blakiston's Son & Co., 1902).

Buranelli, Vincent, *The Wizard from Vienna: Franz Anton Mesmer and the Origins of Hypnotism* (London: Peter Owen, 1975).

Burd, Van Akin (ed.), *Christmas Story: John Ruskin's Venetian Letters of 1876-1877* (Newark: University of Delaware Press, 1990).

Burn, W L, *The Age of Equipoise: A Study of the Mid-Victorian Generation* (New York: W W Norton, 1964).

Burnett, James Compton, *Fifty Reasons for Being a Homoeopath* (London: The Homoeopathic Publishing Co. 1888).

Bush, George, *Mesmer and Swedenborg; or, the Relation of the Developments of Mesmerism to the Doctrines and Disclosures of Swedenborg* (New York: Allen, 1847).

Bynum, William F and Roy Porter (eds.), *Companion Encyclopedia of the History of Medicine*, 2 vols. (London: Routledge, 1993).

—*Medical Fringe and Medical Orthodoxy* (London: Croom Helm, 1987).

Byrom, John, *A Catalogue of the Library of the late John Byrom* (London: privately published, 1848).

—*The Private Journal and Literary Remains of John Byrom*, ed. Richard Parkinson, 2 vols. (Manchester: Chetham Society, 1854-6).

Cannon, Garland, *The Life and Mind of Oriental Jones* (Cambridge: Cambridge University Press, 1990).

Capper, Charles, *Margaret Fuller: An American Romantic Life, Volume I: The Private Years* (New York: Oxford University Press, 1992).

Carlyle, Thomas, *Chartism* (London: James Fraser, 1840).

—*Sartor Resartus*, ed. Archibald MacMechan (Boston and London: Ginn and Company / The Athenaeum Press, 1902).

Carpenter, William B, *Nature and Man. Essays Scientific and Philosophical*, ed. J Estlin Carpenter (New York: D Appleton and Company, 1889).

—*Principles of Mental Physiology, with their applications to the training and discipline of the mind, and the study of its morbid conditions* (London: Henry S King, 1875).

Chambers, George F, *East Bourne Memories of the Victorian Period 1845 to 1901 and Some Other Things of Interest, Divers and Sundry* (Eastbourne: V T Sumfield, 1910).

Claridge, R T, *Hydropathy; or, The Cold Water Cure, as practised by Vincent Priessnitz*, 3rd edn. (London: James Madden and Co., 1842).

Clarke, M L, *George Grote: A Biography* (London: Athlone Press, 1962).

Clayton, Philip and Arthur Peacocke (eds.), *In Whom We Live and Move and Have Our Being: Panentheistic Reflections on God's Presence in a Scientific World* (Grand Rapids, MI: William B Eerdmans, 2004).

Clowes, John, *Letters on the Human Body* (London: Hodson & Son, 1862).

Cockburn, John, *Bourignianism Detected: or the Delusions and Errors of Antonia Bourignon and her Growing Sect* (London: Brome, 1698).

Cohn, Norman, *Warrant for Genocide: The Myth of a Jewish World-Conspiracy and the Protocols of the Elders of Zion* (London: Eyre & Spottiswoode, 1967).

Coleman, Benjamin, *Spiritualism in America* (London: F Pitman, 1861).

Coleman, William, *Biology in the Nineteenth Century* (Cambridge: Cambridge University Press, 1971).

Coleridge, S T, *Biographia Literaria* (London: J M Dent, 1930).

——*Collected Letters of Samuel Taylor Coleridge*, ed. Earl Leslie Griggs, 6 vols. (Oxford: Clarendon Press, 1956-9).

——*Marginalia*, ed. H J Jackson and George Whalley, 6 vols. (Princeton: Princeton University Press, 1980-2001).

Compton, Theodore, *The Life and Correspondence of the Reverend John Clowes M.A.* (London: Longmans, Green & Co., 1874).

Cooter, Roger, *The Cultural Meaning of Popular Science. Phrenology and the Organization of Consent in Nineteenth-Century Britain* (Cambridge: Cambridge University Press, 1984).

——(ed.), *Studies in the History of Alternative Medicine* (London: Macmillan Press, 1988).

Copenhaver, Brian P, *Hermetica: The Greek* Corpus Hermeticum *and the Latin* Asclepius *in a New English Translation, with Notes and Introduction* (Cambridge: Cambridge University Press, 1992).

Corbin, Henry, *Alone with the Alone. Creative Imagination in the Sūfism of Ibn 'Arabī*, tr. Ralph Manheim (New Jersey: Princeton University Press, 1997).

——*Swedenborg and Esoteric Islam*, tr. Leonard Fox (West Chester, PA: Swedenborg Foundation, 1995).

Crabtree, Adam, *From Mesmer to Freud: Magnetic Sleep and the Roots of Psychological Healing* (New Haven: Yale University Press, 1993).

Crookes, William, *Researches in the Phenomena of Spiritualism* (London: J Burns, 1874).

Crossland, Mrs Newton, *Light in the Valley. My Experiences of Spiritualism* (London: Routledge, 1857).

Csapo, Eric, *Theories of Mythology* (Oxford: Blackwell Publishing, 2005).

Cudworth, Ralph, *The True Intellectual System of the Universe*, 2 vols. (Andover and New York: Gould & Newman, 1837-8).

Cunningham, Allan, *Lives of the Most Eminent British Painters, Sculptors, and Architects*, 6 vols. (London: John Murray, 1829-33).

Cunningham, Andrew, and Roger French (eds.), *The Medical Enlightenment of the Eighteenth Century* (Cambridge: Cambridge University Press, 1990).

Curry, Patrick, *A Confusion of Prophets: Victorian and Edwardian Astrology* (London, Collins and Brown, 1992).

Dalley, Stephanie, *Myths from Mesopotamia* (Oxford: Oxford University Press, 2000).

Debus, Allen G, *The French Paracelsians* (Cambridge: Cambridge University Press, 1991).

——*Man and Nature in the Renaissance* (Cambridge: Cambridge University Press, 1978).

De Morgan, Sophia, (pseud. C. D.), *From Matter to Spirit. The Result of Ten Years' Experience in Spirit Manifestations. Intended as a Guide to Enquirers* (London: Longman, Green,

Longman, Roberts & Green, 1863).

Desmond, Adrian, *The Politics of Evolution: Morphology, Medicine, and Reform in Radical London* (Chicago and London: University of Chicago Press, 1992).

Dibb, Andrew M T, *Servetus, Swedenborg and the Nature of God* (Lanham, MD: University Press of America, 2005).

Dictionary of Gnosis and Western Esotericism (*DGWE*), ed. Wouter J Hanegraaff, Antoine Faivre, Roelof van den Broek et al. (Leiden: Brill, 2006).

Dobson, Austin, *At Prior Park and Other Papers* (London: Chatto & Windus, 1912).

Doyle, Arthur Conan, *The History of Spiritualism*, 2 vols. (London: Cassell, 1926).

Driesch, Hans, *The History and Theory of Vitalism*, tr. C K Ogden (London: Macmillan, 1914).

Dronke, Ursula, *The Poetic Edda. Volume II: Mythological Poems* (Oxford: Clarendon Press, 1997).

Dudgeon, R E, *Lectures on the Theory and Practice of Homoeopathy* (New Delhi: B Jain Publishers, 2007).

Dunbar, Pamela, *William Blake's Illustrations to the Poetry of Milton* (Oxford: Clarendon Press, 1980).

Du Potet de Sennevoy, Baron, *Magnetism and Magic*, tr. and ed. A H E Lee (London: George Allen & Unwin Ltd., 1927).

Durbach, Nadja, *Bodily Matters: The Anti-Vaccination Movement in England, 1835-1907* (Durham, NC: Duke University Press, 2005).

Eaves, Morris (ed.), *The Cambridge Companion to William Blake* (Cambridge: Cambridge University Press, 2003).

Eliade, Mircea, *Myths, Dreams and Mysteries*, tr. Philip Mairet (London: Harvill Press, 1960).

Ellenberger, Henri F, *The Discovery of the Unconscious: The History and Evolution of Dynamic Psychiatry* (London: Allen Lane, Penguin Press, 1970).

Elliotson, John, *Human Physiology* (London: Longman, Orme, Brown, Green & Longmans, 1840).

—*John Elliotson on Mesmerism*, ed. Fred Kaplan (New York: Da Capo Press, 1982).

Ellis, Havelock, *The Philosophy of Conflict and Other Essays* (London: Constable & Co., 1919).

Emerson, Ralph Waldo, *English Traits* (Boston: Phillips, Sampson, and Company, 1856).

—*The Letters of Ralph Waldo Emerson*, ed. Ralph L Rusk, 6 vols. (New York: Columbia University, 1939).

—*Nature and Selected Essays*, ed. Larzer Ziff (New York: Penguin, 2003).

—*Representative Men: Seven Lectures* (Boston: Ticknor and Fields, 1861).

—(ed.), *Parnassus* (Boston: James R Osgood and Company, 1875).

Ennemoser, Joseph, *The History of Magic*, tr. William Howitt, 2 vols. (London: Henry G Bohn, 1854).

Evans, Frederick H, *James John Garth Wilkinson: An Introduction* (Reprinted privately: Mrs Frank Claughton Mathews, 1936).

Evans, Warren Felt, *Esoteric Christianity and Mental Therapeutics* (Boston: H H Carter & Karrick, 1886).

Ewing, A C, *Idealism: A Critical Survey* (London: Methuen, 1934).

Faivre, Antoine, *Access to Western Esotericism* (Albany, NY: State University of New York, 1994).

——*Theosophy, Imagination, Tradition*, tr. Christine Rhone (Albany: State University of New York, 2000).

——and Wouter J Hanegraaff (eds.), *Western Esotericism and the Science of Religion* (Leuven: Peeters, 1998).

——and Jacob Needleman (eds.), *Modern Esoteric Spirituality* (London: SCM Press, 1993).

Fanger, Claire (ed.), *Conjuring Spirits: Texts and Traditions of Medieval Ritual Magic* (Pennsylvania: Pennsylvania State University Press, 1998).

Faulks, Philippa and Robert L D Cooper, *The Masonic Magician. The Life and Death of Count Cagliostro and his Egyptian Rite* (London: Watkins, 2008).

Fell-Smith, Charlotte, *John Dee (1527-1608)* (London: Constable, 1909).

Fernald, Woodbury M (ed.), *Memoirs and Reminiscences of the Late Prof. George Bush* (Boston: Otis Clapp, 1860).

Flew, Antony, *David Hume, Philosopher of Moral Science* (Oxford: Blackwell, 1986).

Frazer, James George, *The Golden Bough: A Study in Magic and Religion*, 3rd edn., Part I, *The Magic Art and the Evolution of Kings*, 2 vols. (London: MacMillan, 1920).

French, Richard D, *Antivivisection and Medical Science in Victorian Society* (Princeton: Princeton University Press, 1975).

Freud, Sigmund, *Collected Papers*, ed. J Riviere and J Strachey, 5 vols. (London: Hogarth Press and Institute of Psychoanalysis, 1950).

Fuller, Jean Overton, *Blavatsky and Her Teachers* (London: East-West Publications, 1988).

Gabay, Alfred J, *The Covert Enlightenment: Eighteenth-Century Counterculture and its Aftermath* (West Chester, PA: Swedenborg Foundation, 2005).

Garrett, Clarke, *Origins of the Shakers: From the Old World to the New World* (Baltimore: Johns Hopkins University Press, 1998).

——*Respectable Folly: Millenarians and the French Revolution in France and England* (Baltimore and London: John Hopkins University Press, 1975).

Gersh, Stephen, and Dermot Moran (eds.), *Eriugena, Berkeley, and the Idealist Tradition* (Notre Dame, IN: University of Notre Dame Press, 2006).

al-Ghazālī, *The Alchemy of Happiness*, tr. Claud Field (London: John Murray, 1910).

Gilbert, Robert A, and John Hamill (eds.), *The Rosicrucian Seer. Magical Writings of Frederick Hockley* (Wellingborough: Aquarian Press, 1986).

Gilchrist, Alexander, *The Life of William Blake*, 2 vols. (London: MacMillan, 1880).

Gill, Mary Louise, *Aristotle on Substance: The Paradox of Unity* (Princeton: Princeton University Press, 1989).

Gladstone, William E, *The Gladstone Diaries with Cabinet Minutes and Prime-Ministerial Correspondence*, ed. M R D Foot and H C G Matthew, 14 vols. (Oxford: Clarendon Press, 1968-94).

—*Studies on Homer and the Homeric Age*, 3 vols. (Oxford: Oxford University Press, 1858).

Godwin, Joscelyn, *The Theosophical Enlightenment* (Albany, NY: SUNY Press, 1994).

Godwin, Parke, *A Popular View of the Doctrines of Charles Fourier* (New York: J S Redfield, Clinton Hall, 1844).

Goodrick-Clarke, Nicholas, *The Western Esoteric Traditions. A Historical Introduction* (Oxford: Oxford University Press, 2008).

—(tr. and ed.), *Paracelsus: Essential Readings* (Berkeley, CA: North Atlantic Books, 1999).

Grant, Edward, *A History of Natural Philosophy: From the Ancient World to the Nineteenth Century* (Cambridge: Cambridge University Press, 2007).

Grayling, A C (ed.), *Philosophy: A Guide Through the Subject* (Oxford: Oxford University Press, 1995).

Greenhow, T M, *Cholera, as it Recently Appeared in the Towns of Newcastle and Gateshead* (Philadelphia: Carey & Lea, 1832).

Gregory, James, *Reformers, Patrons and Philanthropists. The Cowper-Temples and High Politics in Victorian England* (London and New York: Tauris Academic Studies, 2010).

Gregory, William, *Letters to a Candid Inquirer, on Animal Magnetism* (Philadelphia: Blanchard and Lee, 1851).

Griffith, Colin, *The New Materia Medica. Key Remedies for the Future of Homoeopathy* (London: Watkins Publishing, 2007).

Grote, George, *History of Greece*, 12 vols. (New York: Harper & Brothers, 1867).

Grote, Harriet, *The Personal Life of George Grote* (London: J Murray, 1873).

Guarneri, Carl J, *The Utopian Alternative: Fourierism in Nineteenth-Century America* (Ithaca: Cornell University Press, 1991).

Gura, Philip F, *American Transcendentalism: A History* (New York: Hill and Wang, 2007).

Habegger, Alfred, *The Father. A Life of Henry James, Sr* (Amherst: University of Massachusetts Press, 1994).

Hahnemann, Samuel, *Organon of Medicine*, tr. R E Dudgeon (London: W Headland, 1849).

Haley, Bruce, *The Healthy Body and Victorian Culture* (Cambridge, MA: Harvard University Press, 1978).

Haller, John S, Jr, *The History of American Homeopathy: The Academic Years, 1820-1935* (New York: Haworth Press, 2005).

—*The History of New Thought* (West Chester, PA: Swedenborg Foundation, 2012).

—*Swedenborg, Mesmer, and the Mind/Body Connection. The Roots of Complementary Medicine* (West Chester, PA: Swedenborg Foundation, 2010).

Hancox, Joy, *The Byrom Collection: and the Globe Theatre Mystery* (London: Jonathan Cape, 1997).

—*The Queen's Chamelion: The Life of John Byrom—A Study of Conflicting Loyalties* (London: Jonathan Cape, 1994).

Handley, Rima, *In Search of the Later Hahnemann* (Beaconsfield: Beaconsfield Publishers, 1997).

Hanegraaff, Wouter J, *New Age Religion and Western Culture* (Albany, NY: SUNY Press, 1998).

—*Swedenborg Oetinger Kant: Three Perspectives on the Secrets of Heaven* (West Chester, PA: Swedenborg Foundation, 2007).

Hankins, James, *Plato in the Italian Renaissance* (Leiden: Brill, 1990).

Harland, John, and T T Wilkinson, *Lancashire Folk-Lore: Illustrative of the Superstitious Beliefs and Practices, Local Customs and Usages of the People of the County Palatine* (London: John Heywood, 1882).

Harris, Thomas Lake, *A Lyric of the Golden Age* (New York: Partridge and Brittan, 1856).

Harrison, J F C, *Robert Owen and the Owenites in Britain and America: The Quest for the New Moral World* (London: Routledge and Kegan Paul, 1969).

—*The Second Coming. Popular Millenarianism 1780-1850* (London: Routledge & Kegan Paul, 1979).

Harvey, Graham, *Animism: Respecting the Living World* (London: C Hurst & Co., 2005).

Hawthorne, Julian, *Hawthorne and His Circle* (New York and London: Harper & Brothers, 1903).

—*Nathaniel Hawthorne and His Wife: A Biography*, 2 vols. (Boston and New York: Houghton Mifflin, 1884).

Haycock, David, *William Stukeley: Science, Religion and Archaeology in Eighteenth-Century England* (Woodbridge: Boydell Press, 2002).

Heidel, Alexander, *The Babylonian Genesis: The Story of the Creation*, 2nd edn. (Chicago: University of Chicago Press, 1951).

Heinberg, Richard, *Memories and Visions of Paradise: Exploring the Universal Myth of a Lost Golden Age* (Los Angeles: Tarcher, 1989).

Hempel, Charles Julius, *The True Organization of the New Church, as indicated in the Writings of Emanuel Swedenborg, and demonstrated by Charles Fourier* (New York: William Radde and London: H Ballière, 1848).

Hill, Howard, *Freedom to Roam. The Struggle for Access to Britain's Moors and Mountains* (Ashbourne: Moorland Publishing, 1980).

Hindmarsh, Robert, *Rise and Progress of the New Jerusalem Church, in England, America, and other Parts*, ed. Edward Madeley (London: Hodson & Son, 1861).

Hitchcock, Ethan Allen, *Swedenborg, a Hermetic Philosopher. Being a sequel to Remarks on Alchemy and the Alchemists. Showing that Emanuel Swedenborg was a Hermetic Philosopher and that his writings may be interpreted from the point of view of Hermetic Philosophy. With a Chapter comparing Swedenborg and Spinoza* (New York: D Appleton & Company, 1858).

Hoare, Philip, *England's Lost Eden: Adventures in a Victorian Utopia* (London: Harper Perennial, 2006).

Hobart, Nathaniel, *Life of Emanuel Swedenborg; with some account of his Writings* (Boston: Allen and Goddard, 1831).

Hobhouse, Stephen, *William Law and Eighteenth Century Quakerism* (London: George Allen & Unwin, 1927).

Hogg, James, *De Quincey and His Friends* (London: Sampson Low, Marston and Company, 1895).

Holcombe, William Henry, *How I became a Homoeopath* (New York: Boericke & Tafel, 1877).

——*The Truth about Homoeopathy. . . also a Sketch of the Life of Dr. Holcombe* (Philadelphia: Boericke and Tafel, 1894).

Hollander, Bernard, *In Search of the Soul and the Mechanism of Thought, Emotion, and Conduct*, 2 vols. (London: Kegan Paul, Trench, Trübner & Co., 1920).

Home, Daniel Dunglas, *Incidents in My Life* (New York: Carleton, 1863).

Home, Mme Dunglas, *D. D. Home. His Life and Mission*, ed. Arthur Conan Doyle (London: Kegan Paul, Trench, Trubner, 1921).

Horn, Friedemann, *Schelling and Swedenborg: Mysticism and German Idealism*, tr. George F Dole (West Chester, PA: Swedenborg Foundation, 1997).

Howe, Ellic, *The Magicians of the Golden Dawn. A Documentary History of a Magical Order 1887-1923* (London: Routledge & Kegan Paul, 1972).

Howitt, William, *The History of the Supernatural*, 2 vols. (London: Longman, Green, Longman, Roberts & Green, 1863).

Hume, George Haliburton, *The History of the Newcastle Infirmary* (Newcastle-upon-Tyne: Andrew Reid & Co., 1906).

Hunt, William Holman, *Pre-Raphaelitism and the Pre-Raphaelite Brotherhood*, 2 vols. (London: Macmillan, 1905).

Hutton, Ronald, *Blood and Mistletoe. The History of the Druids in Britain* (New Haven: Yale University Press, 2009).

Huxley, Thomas Henry, *On the Physical Basis of Life* (Yale College, New Haven, CT: The College Courant, 1869).

James, Henry, Jr, *The Letters of Henry James*, ed. Leon Edel, 4 vols. (Cambridge, MA: Belknap Press of Harvard University Press, 1974-84).

James, Henry, Sr, *Christianity the Logic of Creation* (London: William White, 1857).

—*Lectures and Miscellanies* (New York: Redfield, 1852).

—*Moralism and Christianity; or Man's Experience and Destiny. In Three Lectures* (New York: J S Redfield, 1850).

—*Society the Redeemed Form of Man, and the Earnest of God's Omnipotence in Human Nature: Affirmed in Letters to a Friend* (Boston: Houghton, Osgood and Company, 1879).

James, Norman G Brett, *The History of Mill Hill School, 1807-1907* (London: Melrose, [1909]).

James, William, *The Correspondence of William James*, ed. Ignas K Skrupskelis and Elizabeth M Berkeley, 12 vols. (Charlottesville and London: University Press of Virginia, 1992-2004).

—(ed.), *The Literary Remains of the Late Henry James* (Boston: James R Osgood and Co., 1885).

Jenkins, Roy, *Gladstone* (London: Papermac, 1996).

Johnson, P L, *Carl Bernhard Wadström: In Search of the New Jerusalem*, Swedenborg Society Transactions no. 9 (London: Swedenborg Society, 2013).

—*The Five Ages: Swedenborg's View of Spiritual History* (London: Swedenborg Society, 2008).

Johnson, Samuel, *The Rambler*, 3 vols. (Philadelphia: Abraham Small, 1831).

Jones, H S, *Victorian Political Thought* (Basingstoke: Macmillan, 2000).

Jones, Rufus M, *The Remnant* (London: Swarthmore Press, 1920).

Jonsson, Inge, *Visionary Scientist: The Effects of Science and Philosophy on Swedenborg's Cosmology* (West Chester, PA: Swedenborg Foundation, 1999).

Jung, C G, *Memories, Dreams, Reflections*, ed. Aniela Jaffé, tr. Richard and Clara Winston (London: Collins and Routledge & Kegan Paul, 1964).

Kant, Immanuel, *Kant on Swedenborg. Dreams of a Spirit-Seer and Other Writings*, ed. Gregory R Johnson, tr. Gregory R Johnson and Glenn Alexander Magee (West Chester, PA: Swedenborg Foundation, 2002).

Kent, James Tyler, *New Remedies, Clinical Cases, Lesser Writings, Aphorisms and Precepts* (Calcutta; Sett Dey, 1963).

Knox, Robert, *Great Artists and Great Anatomists; A Biographical and Philosophical Study* (London: John van Voorst, 1852; repr. New York: AMS, 1977).

Kopf, David, *British Orientalism and the Bengal Renaissance: The Dynamics of Indian Modernization 1773-1835* (Berkeley, CA: University of California Press, 1969).

La Mettrie, Julien Offray de, *Man a Machine and Man a Plant*, tr. Richard A Watson and Maya Rybalka (Indianapolis: Hackett, 1994).

Lamm, Martin, *Emanuel Swedenborg: the Development of his Thought*, tr. Thomas Spiers and Anders Hallengren (West Chester, PA: Swedenborg Foundation, 2000.

Larsen, Robin and Stephen Larsen, James F Lawrence and William Ross Woofenden (eds.), *Emanuel Swedenborg: A Continuing Vision* (New York: Swedenborg Foundation, 1988).

Lee, Amice, *Laurels and Rosemary. The Life of William and Mary Howitt* (London: Oxford University Press, 1955).

Leinster-Mackay, Donald, *The Rise of the English Prep School* (London and Philadelphia: The Falmer Press, 1984).

Levi, Eliphas, *Magic: A History of Its Rites, Rituals, and Mysteries*, tr. Arthur Edward Waite (Mineola, NY: Dover Publications, 2006).

Lewis, Frank A and Robert Bolton (eds.), *Form, Matter, and Mixture in Aristotle* (Oxford: Blackwell, 1996).

Liebig, Justus von, *Researches on the Motion of the Juices of the Animal Body*, tr. William Gregory (Philadelphia: T B Peterson, 1850).

Lines, Richard, *A History of the Swedenborg Society 1810-2010* (London: South Vale Press, 2012).

Luce, A A, *Berkeley and Malebranche: A Study in the Origins of Berkeley's Thought* (London: Oxford University Press, 1934).

Lukis, W C, *The Family Memoirs of the Rev. William Stukeley, M.D. and the Antiquarian and other Correspondence of William Stukeley, Roger & Samuel Gale, etc.* (London: Whittaker & Co., 1882).

Lynch, Hollis R, *Edward Wilmot Blyden, Pan-Negro Patriot 1832-1912* (London: Oxford University Press, 1967).

Mac Cormac, William, *An Address of Welcome Delivered on the Occasion of the Centenary Festival of the Royal College of Surgeons of England* (London: Ballantyne, Hanson & Co. 1900).

MacGregor, John M, *The Discovery of the Art of the Insane* (Princeton, NJ: Princeton University Press, 1989).

McGuckin, John Anthony (ed.), *The Book of Mystical Chapters: Meditations on the Soul's Ascent From the Desert Fathers and Other early Christian Contemplatives* (Boston: Shambhala, 2002).

McNeilly, Stephen (ed.), *In Search of the Absolute—Essays on Swedenborg and Literature* (London: Swedenborg Society, 2004).

——(ed.), *Philosophy, Literature, Mysticism: an anthology of essays on the thought and influence of Emanuel Swedenborg* (London: Swedenborg Society, 2013).

Mainauduc, John Benoit de, *The Lectures of J. B. de Mainauduc, M.D.* (London: Printed for the Executrix, 1798).

Martineau, Harriet, *A History of the Thirty Years' Peace, A.D. 1816-1846*, 4 vols. (London: George Bell, 1877).

Mattei, Count Cesare, *Electro-Homoeopathic Medicine: A New Medical System being a Popular and Domestic Guide Founded on Experience*, tr. R M Theobald, 2nd edn. (London: David Stott, 1891).

Mayr, Ernst, *The Growth of Biological Thought* (Cambridge, MA: Harvard University, 1981).

A Member of the Old Church, *An Inquiry into the Commission and Doctrine of the New Apostle, Emanuel Swedenborg* (Manchester: Thomson, 1794).

Mercer, L P (ed.), *The New Jerusalem in the World's Religious Congresses of 1893* (Chicago: Western New-Church Union, 1894).

Mill, John Stuart, *The Collected Works of John Stuart Mill*, ed. Francis E Mineka and Dwight N Lindley, 33 vols. (Toronto: University of Toronto Press, London: Routledge and Kegan Paul, 1972), vol. XV, *The Later Letters of John Stuart Mill 1849-1873 Part II*.

Monod, Paul Kléber, *Solomon's Secret Arts. The Occult in the Age of Enlightenment* (New Haven and London: Yale University Press, 2013).

Morell, J D, *An Historical and Critical View of the Speculative Philosophy of Europe in the Nineteenth Century* (New York: Carter and Brothers, 1853).

Müller, Max, *Chips from a German Workshop*, 2nd edn., 5 vols. (London: Longmans, Green & Co., 1867-75).

——*The Life and Letters of the Right Honourable Friedrich Max Müller*, ed. Georgina Adelaide Müller, 2 vols. (London: Longmans, Green & Co., 1902).

——*My Autobiography: A Fragment* (London: Longmans, Green & Co, 1901).

——*Three Introductory Lectures on the Science of Thought* (Chicago: Open Court Publishing, 1888).

Nasr, Seyyed Hossein, *The Need for a Sacred Science* (Albany: State University of New York Press, 1993).

Neff, Mary K (ed.), *Personal Memoirs of H. P. Blavatsky* (Wheaton, IL: Quest / Theosophical Publishing House, 1971).

Nelson, Geoffrey K, *Spiritualism and Society* (London: Routledge & Kegan Paul, 1969).

Nicholls, David, *Deity and Domination: Images of God and the State in the Nineteenth and Twentieth Centuries* (London and New York: Routledge, 1994).

Nicholls, Philip A, *Homoeopathy and the Medical Profession* (London: Croom Helm, 1988).

Noyes, John Humphrey, *History of American Socialisms* (Philadelphia: J B Lippincott & Co., 1870).

Odhner, Carl Theophilus, *Annals of the New Church with a chronological account of the life of Emanuel Swedenborg* (Bryn Athyn, PA: Academy of the New Church, 1904).

—*The Golden Age: The Story of the Most Ancient Church* (Bryn Athyn, PA: The Academy Book Room, 1913; repr. 1975).

—*Michael Servetus: His Life and Teachings* (Philadelphia: J B Lippincott, 1910).

—*Robert Hindmarsh: A Biography* (Philadelphia: Academy Book Room, 1895).

Odhner, Hugo Lj., *The Human Mind, its Faculties and Degrees: A Study of Swedenborg's Psychology* (Bryn Athyn, PA: Swedenborg Scientific Association, 1969).

—*Principles of the New Philosophy*, 2nd edn. (Bryn Athyn, PA: Swedenborg Scientific Association, 1986).

Oken, Lorenz, *Elements of Physiophilosophy*, tr. Alfred Tulk (London: The Ray Society, 1847).

Oppenheim, Janet, *The Other World: Spiritualism and Psychical Research in England, 1850-1914* (Cambridge: Cambridge University Press, 1985).

Owen, Alex, *The Darkened Room: Women, Power and Spiritualism in Late Nineteenth-Century England* (London: Virago Press, 1989).

—*The Place of Enchantment: British Occultism and the Culture of the Modern* (Chicago and London: Univesity of Chicago Press, 2004).

Owen, Robert, *The Life of Robert Owen. Written by Himself*, 2 vols. (London: Effingham Wilson, 1857-8).

Pagel, Walter, *Joan Baptista Van Helmont. Reformer of Science and Medicine* (Cambridge: Cambridge University Press, 1982).

—*Paracelsus. An Introduction to Philosophical Medicine in the Era of the Renaissance*, 2nd edn. (Basel; New York: Karger, 1982).

Pailin, David A, *Attitudes to Other Religions: Comparative Religion in Seventeenth- and Eighteenth-Century Britain* (Manchester: Manchester University Press, 1984).

Paracelsus, *The Diseases that Deprive Man of his Reason, such as St. Vitus' Dance, Falling Sickness, Melancholy, and Insanity, and their Correct Treatment*, tr. Gregory Zilboorg, in *Four Treatises of Theophrastus von Hohenheim called Paracelsus*, ed. Henry E Sigerist (Baltimore: The John Hopkins University Press, 1941), pp. 127-212,

—*Paracelsus: Selected Writings*, ed. Jolande Jacobi, tr. Norbert Guterman (Princeton, NJ: Princeton University Press, 1979).

Pasquin, Anthony, *Memoirs of the Royal Academicians* (London: H D Symonds, 1796).

Pater, Walter, *Greek Studies: A Series of Essays* (London: Macmillan, 1897).

—*Studies in the History of the Renaissance* (London: Macmillan, 1873).

Payne-Gaposchkin, Cecilia, *An Autobiography and Other Recollections*, ed. Katherine Haramundanis, 2nd edn. (Cambridge: Cambridge University Press, 1996).

Payson, Seth, *Proofs of the Real Existence, and Dangerous Tendency, of Illuminism* (Charlestown: The Author, 1802).

Peabody, Elizabeth Palmer, *Lectures in the Training Schools for Kindergartners* (Boston: D C Heath & Company, 1893).

Pearsall, Ronald, *The Table-Rappers: The Victorians and the Occult* (Stroud: Sutton Publishing, 2004).

Peebles, J M, *What is Spiritualism? Who are these Spiritualists? and What can Spiritualism do for the World?*, 5th edn. (Battle Creek, MI: Peebles Publishing, 1910).

Peltonen, Markku (ed.), *The Cambridge Companion to Bacon* (Cambridge: Cambridge University Press, 1996).

Perry, Ralph Barton, *The Thought and Character of William James*, 2 vols. (London: Oxford University Press, 1936).

Peterson, M Jeanne, *The Medical Profession in Mid-Victorian London* (Berkeley: University of California, 1978).

Piggott, Stuart, *William Stukeley: An Eighteenth-Century Antiquarian* (London: Thames and Hudson, 1985).

Pipes, Daniel, *Conspiracy: How the Paranoid Style Flourishes and Where It Comes From* (New York, Free Press, 1997).

Placido de Titi, *Astronomy and Elementary Philosophy, translated from the Latin of Placidus de Titus...the whole carefully revised by M. Sibly* (London: W Justins, 1789).

Plato, *Complete Works*, ed. John M Cooper (Indianapolis: Hackett Publishing, 1997).

Plotinus, *Enneads*, ed. A H Armstrong, 7 vols. (Cambridge, MA: Harvard University Press, 1966-88).

Podmore, Frank, *Modern Spiritualism: A History and a criticism*, 2 vols. (London: Methuen & Co., 1902).

—*Robert Owen A Biography*, 2 vols. (London: Hutchinson & Co., 1906).

The Poetic Edda, tr. Carolyne Larrington (Oxford: Oxford University Press, 1996).

Poovey, Mary, *Making a Social Body: British Cultural Formation 1830-1864* (Chicago: University of Chicage Press, 1995).

Popkin, Jeremy D, *A History of Modern France*, 3rd edn. (Upper Saddle River, NJ: Pearson Prentice Hall, 2005).

Porter, Roy (ed.), *Cambridge Illustrated History of Medicine* (Cambridge: Cambridge University Press, 1996).

Pratt, Mary, *A List of a Few Cures Performed by Mr and Mrs De Loutherbourg, of Hammersmith Terrace, Without Medicine* (London: The Author, 1789).

Raine, Kathleen, *Blake and the New Age* (London: George Allen and Unwin, 1979).

——*The Human Face of God: William Blake and the Book of Job* (London: Thames and Hudson, 1982).

Ramsay, Chevalier, *The Philosophical Principles of Natural and Revealed Religion. Unfolded in a Geometrical Order* (Glasgow: Robert Foulis, 1748).

Rehbock, Philip F, *The Philosophical Naturalists* (Madison, WI: University of Wisconsin, 1983).

Reichenbach, Baron Charles von, *Physico-Physiological Researches on the Dynamics of Magnetism, Electricity, Heat, Light, Crystallization, and Chemism, in their relations to Vital Force*, tr. John Ashburner (London: Hippolyte Baillière, 1850).

Reill, Peter Hanns, *Vitalizing Nature in the Enlightenment* (Berkeley: University of California Press, 2005).

Report on Spiritualism, of the Committee of the London Dialectical Society, together with the Evidence, Oral and Written, and a Selection from the Correspondence (London: Longmans, Green, Reader and Dyer, 1871).

Rich, Elihu, *Notes on Certain Forms of Spiritualism addressed to the Members of the "New Church", with remarks on a recent obituary* (London: William White, 1858).

Richardson, Robert D, *William James: In the Maelstrom of American Modernism* (New York: Houghton-Mifflin, 2006).

The Rig Veda: An Anthology of One Hundred and Eight Hymns, tr. Wendy Doniger O'Flaherty (London: Penguin, 1981).

Robinson, Henry Crabb, *Diary, Reminiscences, and Correspondence of Henry Crabb Robinson*, ed. Thomas Sadler, 2 vols. (London: Macmillan, 1872).

Robinson, John, *The Attwood Family, with Historic Notes and Pedigrees* (Sunderland: Published privately, 1903).

Robinson, Thomas, *A Remembrancer and Recorder of Facts and Documents illustrative of the Genius of the New Jerusalem Dispensation* (Manchester: Robinson, 1864).

Robison, John, *Proofs of a Conspiracy against All the Religions and Governments of Europe, Carried on in the Secret Meetings of the Free Masons, Illuminati, and Reading Societies* (Edinburgh: William Creech, 1797).

Rozemond, Marleen, *Descartes's Dualism* (Cambridge, MA: Harvard University Press, 1998).

Rutherford, Harry C, *The Religion of Logos and Sophia: From the Writings of Dimitrije Mitrinović* (Sausalito, CA: The Society for Comparative Philosophy, 1973).

Sargent, Epes, *Planchette; or, The Despair of Science* (Boston: Roberts Brothers, 1869).

Saumarez, Richard, *A New System of Physiology*, 2 vols. (London: T Cox, 1798).

Sayce, A H, *Lectures on the Origin and Growth of Religion, as Illustrated by the Religion of the Ancient Babylonians* (London: Williams and Norgate, 1887).

Scheffer, John, *The History of Lapland* (Oxford: George West and Amos Curtein, 1674).

Schelling, F W J, *The Ages of the World*, tr. Frederick de Wolfe Bolman, Jr (New York: Colombia University Press, 1942).

—*Clara, or, On Nature's Connection to the Spirit World*, tr. Fiona Steinkamp (New York: SUNY Press, 2002).

—*Historical-Critical Introduction to the Philosophy of Mythology*, tr. Mason Richey and Markus Zisselsberger (Albany: State University of New York Press, 2007).

Schuchard, Marsha Keith, *Why Mrs Blake Cried: William Blake and the Sexual Basis of Spiritual Wisdom* (London: Century, 2006).

Schuon, Frithjof, *The Transcendent Unity of Religions* (Wheaton, IL: Theosophical Publishing House, 1993).

Scruton, Roger, *Kant* (Oxford: Oxford University Press, 1992).

Servetus, Michael, *Michael Servetus: A Translation of His Geographical, Medical and Astrological Writings*, ed. Charles Donald O'Malley (Philadelphia: American Philosophical Society, 1953).

Shapiro, Arthur K, and Elaine Shapiro, *The Powerful Placebo. From Ancient Priest to Modern Physician* (Baltimore: Johns Hopkins University Press, 1997).

Shaw, Gregory, *Theurgy and the Soul. The Neoplatonism of Iamblicus* (University Park, PA: The Pennsylvania State University Press, 1995).

Sibly, Ebenezer, *A Key to Physic, and the Occult Sciences. Opening to mental view, The SYSTEM and ORDER of the Interior and Exterior HEAVENS; The analogy betwixt ANGELS, and SPIRITS of MEN. . .* (London: Champante and Whitrow, 1795).

—*A New and Complete Illustration of the Celestial Science of Astrology* (London: printed for the proprietor, and sold by W Nicoll, M Sibly, and E Sibly, 1784).

—*A New and Complete Illustration of the Occult Sciences: or, the Art of foretelling future*

Events and Contingencies...in Four Parts (London: printed for the author, 1790).

Sigstedt, Cyriel Odhner, *The Swedenborg Epic* (London: Swedenborg Society, 1981).

Silver, Harold, *The Concept of Popular Education; A Study of Ideas and Social Movements in the Early Nineteenth Century* (London: MacGibbon and Kee, 1965).

Smedley, Edward, and W Cooke Taylor, Henry Thompson and Elihu Rich, *The Occult Sciences: Sketches of the Traditions and Superstitions of Past Times, and the Marvels of the Present Day* (London and Glasgow: Richard Griffin and Company, 1855).

Smith, George, *The Chaldean Account of Genesis. Containing the Description of the Creation, the Deluge, the Tower of Babel, the Destruction of Sodom, the Times of the Patriarchs, and Nimrod...*, rev. A H Sayce (London: Sampson Low, Marston, Searle and Rivington, 1880).

Smith, W Anderson, *'Shepherd' Smith the Universalist: the Story of a Mind* (London: Sampson Low, Marston & Company, 1892).

Spence, William, *Essays in Divinity and Physic...with an exposition of animal magnetism and magic* (London: Robert Hindmarsh, 1792).

Spurgin, John, *Cure of the Sick: Not Homoeopathy, not Allopathy, but Judgment* (London: John Churchill, 1860).

Stewart, Dugald, *The Works of Dugald Stewart*, 7 vols. (Cambridge: Hilliard and Brown, 1829).

Stich, Stephen P and Ted A Warfield (eds.), *The Blackwell Guide to the Philosophy of Mind* (Oxford: Blackwell, 2003).

Sturluson, Snorri, *Edda*, tr. Anthony Faulkes (London: Everyman, 1987).

Swedenborg, Emanuel, *Angelic Wisdom Concerning the Divine Love and Wisdom*, tr. Clifford Harley and Doris H Harley (London: Swedenborg Society, 1987).

—*The Animal Kingdom*, tr. James John Garth Wilkinson, 2 vols. (London: W Newbery, 1843-4).

—*Apocalypse Explained*, tr. John C Ager, rev. John Whitehead, 6 vols. (West Chester, PA: Swedenborg Foundation, 1995-7).

—*Arcana Caelestia*, tr. John Elliott, 12 vols. (London: Swedenborg Society, 1983-99).

—*The Brain, Considered Anatomically, Physiologically and Philosophically*, tr. R L Tafel, 2 vols. (London: James Speirs, 1882-7; repr. Bryn Athyn, PA: Swedenborg Scientific Association, 2010).

—*A Compendium of the Theological and Spiritual Writings of Emanuel Swedenborg*, ed. W M Fernald (Boston: Crosby and Nichols, and Otis Clapp, 1854).

—*The Economy of the Animal Kingdom, Considered Anatomically, Physically, and Philosophically*, tr. Augustus Clissold, 2 vols. (New York: The New Church Press, 1919).

—*The Economy of the Animal Kingdom, Considered Anatomically, Physically, and Philosophically...Transaction III The Medullary Fibre of the brain and the Nerve Fibre of the Body. . .* , tr. Alfred Acton (Philadelphia: Swedenborg Scientific Association, 1918; repr. Bryn Athyn, PA: Swedenborg Scientific Association, 1976).

——*Heaven and Hell*, tr. J C Ager, rev. Doris H Harley (London: Swedenborg Society, 1989).

——*A Hieroglyphic Key to Natural and Spiritual Mysteries by Way of Representations and Correspondences*, tr. J J G Wilkinson (London: William Newbery, 1847).

——*On the Divine Love. On the Divine Wisdom*, tr. E C Mongredien (London: Swedenborg Society, 1986).

——*On the Sacred Scripture or the Word of the Lord from Experience*, tr. John Chadwick (London: Swedenborg Society, 1997).

——*Outlines of a Philosophical Argument on the Infinite, and the Final Cause of Creation; and on the Intercourse Between the Soul and the Body*, tr. James John Garth Wilkinson (London: William Newbery, 1847).

——*A Philosopher's Notebook*, tr. Alfred Acton (Pennsylvania: Swedenborg Scientific Association, 2009).

——*Posthumous Tracts*, tr. James John Garth Wilkinson (London: William Newbery, 1847).

——*The Principia; or, the First Principles of Natural Things*, tr. Augustus Clissold, 2 vols. (London: W Newbery, 1845-6).

——*Spiritual Diary*, tr. George Bush, John Smithson and James F Buss, 5 vols. (London: James Speirs, 1883-1902).

——*Swedenborg's Dream Diary*, tr. Anders Hallengren with commentary by Lars Bergquist (West Chester, PA.: Swedenborg Foundation, 2001).

——*Swedenborg's Journal of Dreams 1743-1744*, tr. J J G Wilkinson, ed. William Ross Woofenden, introd. Wilson Van Dusen, 2nd edn. (London: Swedenborg Society and Bryn Athyn, PA: Swedenborg Scientific Association, 1989).

——*A Theosophic Lucubration on the Nature of Influx*, tr. Thomas Hartley (London: M Lewis, 1770).

——*The True Christian Religion*, tr. John Chadwick, 2 vols. (London: Swedenborg Society, 1998).

——*The Universal Human and Soul-Body Interaction*, tr. and ed. George F Dole (New Jersey: Paulist Press, 1984).

——*The Worlds in Space*, tr. John Chadwick (London: Swedenborg Society, 1997).

Tafel, Rudolph Leonard, *Socialism and Reform in the Light of the New Church* (London: James Speirs, 1891).

Taylor, Anne, *Laurence Oliphant 1829-1888* (Oxford: Oxford University Press, 1982).

Theobald, F J, *More 'Forget-me-nots from God's Garden'* (London: Psychological Press Association, 1882).

Theobald, R M, *Passages from the Autobiography of a Shakespeare Student* (London: Robert Banks, 1912).

Thompson, Dorothy, *The Chartists* (London: Temple Smith, 1984).

Thompson, E P, *Witness Against the Beast* (Cambridge: Cambridge University Press, 1993).

Thomson, James, *Biographical and Critical Studies*, ed. Bertram Dobell (London: Reeves and Turner and Bertram Dobell, 1896).

——*The Speedy Extinction of Evil and Misery: Selected Prose of James Thomson*, ed. William David Schaefer (Berkeley: University of California Press, 1967).

Thomson, Thomas, *History of the Royal Society* (London: Robert Baldwin, 1812).

Thoreau, Henry David, *Walden*, ed. Jeffrey S Cramer (New Haven: Yale University, 2006).

Timbs, John, *English Eccentrics and Eccentricities*, 2 vols. (London: Richard Bentley, 1866).

Tulk, Charles Augustus, *Aphorisms on the Laws of Creation, as displayed in the Correspondencies that subsist between Mind and Matter* (London: William Newbery, 1843).

——*Spiritual Christianity. Collected from the Theological Works of Emanuel Swedenborg; with an Illustrative Commentary* (London: William Newbery, 1846).

Turner, Frank M, *Between Science and Religion: The Reaction to Scientific Naturalism in Late Victorian England* (New Haven and London: Yale University Press, 1974).

——*Contesting Cultural Authority: Essays in Victorian Intellectual Life* (Cambridge: Cambridge University Press, 1993).

——*The Greek Heritage in Victorian Britain* (New Haven: Yale University Press, 1981).

Tylor, Edward B, *Primitive Culture: Researches into the Development of Mythology, Philosophy, Religion, Art, and Custom*, 2 vols. (London: John Murray, 1871).

Ucko, Peter and Timothy Champion (eds.), *The Wisdom of Ancient Egypt: Changing Visions through the Ages* (London: UCL Press, 2003).

Velmans, Max, *Understanding Consciousness* (London: Routledge, 2000).

Verbrugghe, Gerald P, and John M Wickersham, *Berossos and Manetho, Introduced and Translated: Native Traditions in Ancient Mesopotamia and Egypt* (Michigan: University of Michigan Press, 2001).

Versluis, Arthur, *The Esoteric Origins of the American Renaissance* (New York: Oxford University Press, 2001).

Vlastos, Gregory (ed.), *Plato. A Selection of Critical Essays*, 2 vols. (New York: Doubleday, 1971).

Waddington, Keir, *Medical Education at St. Bartholomew's Hospital, 1123-1995* (Woodbridge, Suffolk: The Boydell Press, 2003).

Walker, D P, *The Ancient Theology* (London: Duckworth, 1972).

Walkowitz, Judith R, *Prostitution and Victorian Society. Women, Class, and the State* (Cambridge: Cambridge University Press, 1980).

Walton, Christopher, *Notes and Materials for an Adequate Biography of the Celebrated Divine and Theosopher William Law* (London: The Author, 1854).

Warnock, G J, *Berkeley* (Oxford: Blackwell, 1982).

Warren, Austin, *The Elder Henry James* (New York: Macmillan, 1934).

Watson, Robert I, *The Great Psychologists*, 3rd edn. (Philadelphia: J B Lippincott, 1963).

Wawn, Andrew, *The Vikings and the Victorians: Inventing the Old North in Nineteenth-Century Britain* (Cambridge: Brewer, 2000).

Webster, Charles, *Paracelsus: Medicine, Magic and Mission at the End of Time* (New Haven: Yale University Press, 2008).

Weeks, Andrew, *Paracelsus: Speculative Theory and the Crisis of the Early Reformation* (Albany, NY: State University of New York Press, 1997).

White, William, *Emanuel Swedenborg: His Life and Writings*, 2 vols. (London: Simpkin, Marshall & Co., 1867).

——*The Story of a Great Delusion* (London: E W Allen, 1885).

Wilkinson, Clement John, *James John Garth Wilkinson; A Memoir of his Life, with a Selection from his Letters* (London: Kegan Paul, Trench, Trübner & Co., 1911).

Wilkinson, James John Garth, *The Affections of Armed Powers: a Plea for a School of Little Nations* (London: James Speirs, 1897).

——*The African and the True Christian Religion, his Magna Charta. A Study in the Writings of Emanuel Swedenborg* (London: James Speirs, 1892).

——*The Book of Edda Called Voluspa: A Study in Its Scriptural and Spiritual Correspondences* (London: James Speirs, 1897).

——*The Combats and Victories of Jesus Christ* (London: James Speirs, 1895).

——*Emanuel Swedenborg: A Biography* (London: William Newbery, 1849).

——*Epidemic Man and His Visitations* (London: James Speirs, 1893).

——*The Forcible Introspection of Women for the Army and Navy by the Oligarchy, Considered Physically* (London: F Pitman, 1870).

——*The Greater Origins and Issues of Life and Death* (London: James Speirs, 1885).

——*The Grouping of Animals: A Paper read before the Veterinary Medical Association, Thursday, May 16, 1845* (London: Compton and Ritchie, 1845).

——*The Homoeopathic Principle Applied to Insanity. A Proposal to Treat Lunacy by Spiritualism* (Boston: Otis Clapp, 1857).

——*The Human Body and its Connection with Man* (Philadelphia: Lippincott, Grambo and

Co., 1851).

—*Improvisations from the Spirit* (London: William White, 1857).

—*The Infectious Nature of the Vaccine Disease, and the necessity of excluding the vaccinated and re-vaccinated, during that disease, from intercourse with healthy persons* (London: The Mothers' Anti-Compulsory Vaccination League, 1877).

—*Isis and Osiris in the Book of Respirations. Prophecy in the Churches. In the Word, God with us. The Revelation of Jesus Christ* (London: James Speirs, 1899).

—*The New Jerusalem and the Old Jerusalem. The Place and Service of the Jewish Church among the Aeons of Revelation with other essays* (London: James Speirs, 1894).

—*Oannes According to Berosus: A Study in the Church of the Ancients* (London: James Speirs, 1888).

—*On Human Science, Good and Evil, and its Works; and on Divine Revelation and its Works and Sciences* (London: James Speirs, 1876).

—*Our Social Health. A Discourse delivered before the London "Ladies' Sanitary Association," February 28, 1865* (Boston: S Welles Cone, 1865).

—*Remarks on Swedenborg's Economy of the Animal Kingdom* (London: Walton and Mitchell, 1846).

—*Revelation, Mythology, Correspondences* (London: James Speirs, 1887).

—*A Safe and Easy Way in which Poor and Rich alike can Isolate Themselves, and Treat Themselves, if they take the Smallpox* (London: William Young, 1878), in Swedenborg Society Archive L/452.

—*Small-Pox and Vaccination* (London: F Pitman, 1871).

—*The Soul is Form and doth the Body make: The Heart and the Lungs, the Will and the Understanding. Chapters in Psychology* (London: James Speirs, 1890).

—*Swedenborg Among the Doctors. A Letter to Robert T. Cooper. M.D.* (London: James Speirs, 1895).

—*Swedenborg's Doctrines and the Translation of his Works* (London: James Speirs, 1882).

—*Unlicensed Medicine; with a Plan for Extending Homoeopathy* (London: R Theobald and Manchester: H Turner, 1855).

—*Vaccination as a Source of Small-Pox* (London: London Society for the Abolition of Compulsory Vaccination, 1884).

—*War, Cholera, and the Ministry of Health. An Appeal to Sir Benjamin Hall and the British People* (Boston: Otis Clapp, and Crosby, Nichols, & Co., 1855).

—(pseud. John Lone), *Painting with Both Hands; or, the Adoption of the Principle of the Stereoscope in Art, as a Means to Binocular Pictures* (London: Chapman and Hall, 1856).

——and William Young (eds.), *Vaccination Tracts* (Providence: Snow & Farnham, 1892).

Wilkinson, William M, *The Cases of the Welsh Fasting Girl and her Father. On the Possibility of Long-Continued Abstinence from Food; with Supplementary Remarks by J.J. Garth Wilkinson*, 3rd edn. (London: J Burns, 1870).

——*Spirit Drawings: A Personal Narrative* (London: Chapman & Hall, 1858).

Williams, Elizabeth A, *A Cultural History of Medical Vitalism in Enlightenment Montpellier* (Aldershot: Ashgate, 2003).

Wilson, Bryan R, *Magic and the Millennium. A Sociological Study of Religious Movements of Protest among Tribal and Third-World Peoples* (London: Heinemann, 1973).

Winkler, Kenneth P, *Berkeley: An Interpretation* (Oxford: Clarendon Press, 1989).

Winter, Alison, *Mesmerized: Powers of Mind in Victorian Britain* (Chicago and London: University of Chicago Press, 1998).

Wood, Matthew, *The Magical Staff: The Vitalist Tradition in Western Medicine* (Berkeley, CA: North Atlantic Books, 1992).

Wozniak, Robert H, *Classics in Psychology 1855-1914: Historical Essays* (Bristol: Thoemmes Press, 1999).

Wright, John, *A Revealed Knowledge of Some Things That Will Be Speedily Fulfilled in the World. . .for the Good of All Men* (London, 1794).

Wyld, George, *Notes of My Life* (London: Kegan, Paul, Trench, Trubner & Co., 1903).

Yates, Frances A, *The Rosicrucian Enlightenment* (London: Routledge and Kegan Paul, 1972).

Young, Frederic Harold, *The Philosophy of Henry James, Sr.* (New York: Bookman Associates, 1951).

ARTICLES, ESSAYS AND THESES

Abell, T, 'The Phrenology of Swedenborg', in *Boston Medical and Surgical Journal*, vol. IX, no. 18 (11 December 1833), pp. 277-80.

Adler, Hermann, 'The Baal Shem of London', in *Transactions of the Jewish Historical Society of England*, vol. 5 (1902-5), pp. 148-73.

Akert, Konrad, and Michael P Hammond, 'Emanuel Swedenborg (1688-1772) and his contributions to neurology', in *Medical History*, vol. 6 (July 1962), pp. 254-62.

Ameriks, Karl, 'Idealism from Kant to Berkeley', in Gersh and Moran (eds.), *Eriugena*, pp. 244-68.

App, Urs, 'William Jones's Ancient Theology', in *Sino-Platonic Papers*, no. 191 (July 2009), pp. 1-125.

Aspiz, Harold, 'Whitman's "Poem of the Road" ', in *Walt Whitman Quarterly Review*, vol. 12, no. 3 (Winter 1995), pp. 170-85.

Barrow, Logie, 'An Imponderable Liberator: J.J. Garth Wilkinson', in *Society for the Social History of Medicine Bulletin*, no. 36 (June 1985), pp. 29-31.

——'Socialism in Eternity: The Ideology of Plebeian Spiritualists, 1853-1913', in *History Workshop Journal*, no. 9 (Spring 1980), pp. 37-69.

Bergé, Christine, 'Illuminism', in *DGWE*, pp. 600-6.

Bestor, Arthur E, Jr, 'The Evolution of the Socialist Vocabulary', in *Journal of the History of Ideas*, vol. 9, no. 8 (June 1948), pp. 259-302.

Bos, Abraham P, 'Aristotle on Soul and Soul-"Parts" in Semen (*GA* 2.1, 735a4-22)', in *Mnemosyne*, vol. 62, no. 3 (2009), pp. 378-400.

Breidbach, Olaf, and Michael T Ghiselin, 'Lorenz Oken and *Naturphilosophie* in Jena, Paris and London', in *History and Philosophy of the Life Sciences*, vol. 24, no. 2 (2002), pp. 219-47.

Broadie, Sarah, 'Soul and Body in Plato and Descartes', in *Proceedings of the Aristotelian Society*, vol. 101 (2001), pp. 295-308.

Brock, William Hall, 'The Swedenborgianized Fourierism of Henry James: A Study in Pathology', at <http://leavesofgrass.org/billbrock/fch06.htm>.

Butler, Alison, 'Beyond Attribution: The Importance of Barrett's Magus', in *Journal for the Academic Study of Magic*, no. 1 (2003), pp. 7-32.

Carpenter, William B, 'On the Influence of Suggestion in Modifying and directing Muscular Movement, independently of Volition', in *Proceedings of the Royal Institution of Great Britain*, vol. 1 (12 March 1852), pp. 147-53.

——'On the Mutual Relations of the Vital and Physical Forces', in *Philosophical Transactions of the Royal Society of London*, vol. 140 (1850), pp. 727-57.

Chalmers, David J, 'Consciousness and its Place in Nature', in Stephen P Stich and Ted A Warfield (eds.), *The Blackwell Guide to the Philosophy of Mind* (Oxford: Blackwell, 2003), pp. 102-42.

Chenevix, Richard, 'Experiments and Observations on Mesmerism', in *The London Medical and Physical Journal*, vol. 62 (1829), pp. 315-24.

Christison, Grant, 'African Jerusalem: The Vision of Robert Grendon', Ph.D. Thesis (University of KwaZulu-Natal, 2007), at <https://www.yumpu.com/en/document/view/19304820/african-jerusalem-the-vision-of-robert-grendon-researchspace->.

Cockle, John, 'A Supplementary Address on Psychological Physiology', in *British Medical Journal*, vol. 2, no. 984 (8 November 1879), pp. 723-4.

Cook, Harold J, 'Boerhaave and the Flight from Reason in Medicine', in *Bulletin of the History of Medicine*, vol. 74, no. 2 (2000), pp. 221-40.

Cooter, Roger, 'Alternative Medicine, Alternative Cosmology', in Cooter (ed.), *Studies in the History of Alternative Medicine*, pp. 63-78.

Couzens, Timothy J, 'Robert Grendon: Irish Traders, Cricket Scores and Paul Kruger's Dreams', in *English in Africa*, vol. 15, no. 2 (October 1988).

Crandon, Edwin S, 'Swedenborg and Masonry', in *Morning Light*, vol. 31 (1908), pp. 458-9, 469-70, 478-9.

Cunningham, Andrew, 'Medicine to Calm the Mind: Boerhaave's Medical System and Why It Was Adopted in Edinburgh', in Andrew Cunningham and Roger French (eds.), *The Medical Enlightenment of the Eighteenth Century* (Cambridge: Cambridge University Press, 1990), pp. 40-66.

Dakeyne, James, 'Samuel Dawson', in *The New Church Magazine* (London), vol. IX, no. 103 (July 1890), pp. 316-25.

Danilewicz, M L , ' "The King of the New Israel": Thaddeus Grabianka (1740-1807)', in *Oxford Slavonic Papers*, new series, vol. 1 (1968), pp. 49-73.

Davies, Owen, 'Cunning-Folk in England and Wales during the Eighteenth and Nineteenth Centuries', in *Rural History*, vol. 8 (April 1997), pp. 91-107.

Dawson, Gowan, 'X-Club not X-Files: Walter Pater, Spiritualism and Victorian Scientific Naturalism', in Julie Scanlon and Amy Waste (eds.), *Crossing Boundaries: Thinking Through Literature* (Sheffield: Sheffield Academic Press, 2001), pp. 56-71.

Debus, Allen G, 'Scientific Truth and Occult Tradition: The Medical World of Ebenezer Sibly (1751-1799)', in *Medical History*, vol. 26, no. 3 (July 1982), pp. 259-78.

DeCharms, Richard, 'Have the Principles of Homoeopathy an Affinity with the Doctrines of the New Church?', in *New Church Repository*, vol. 3, no. 11 (November 1850), pp. 501-8.

Deck, Raymond H, Jr, 'Blake's *Poetical Sketches* finally arrive in America', in *The Review of English Studies*, New Series, vol. XXXI, no. 122 (May 1980), pp. 183-92.

——'New Light on C. A. Tulk, Blake's Nineteenth-Century Patron', in *Studies in Romanticism*, vol. 16, no. 2 (1977), pp. 217-36.

——'The "Vastation" of Henry James, Sr.: New Light on James's Theological Career', in *Bulletin of Research in the Humanities*, vol. 83, no. 2 (Summer 1980), pp. 216-47.

De Ridder, Dirk, and Jan Verplaetse and Sven Vanneste, 'The predictive brain and the "free will" illusion', in *Frontiers in Psychology*, vol. 4 (April 2013), p. 131.

Drysdale, John James, 'A Few Remarks on Animal Poisons as Remedies', in *The British Journal of Homoeopathy*, vol. XII (1854), pp. 260-6.

Elliotson, John, 'Animal Magnetism. Experiments of Baron Dupotet', in *The Lancet*, vol. II (2 September 1837), pp. 836-40.

——'Cure of a true Cancer of the Female Breast with Mesmerism', in *The Zoist*, vol. VI, no. XXIII (October 1848), pp. 213-37.

——'Utility of Mesmerism in various Diseases treated by different Gentlemen', in *The Zoist: A Journal of Cerebral Physiology & Mesmerism*, vol. II, no. VII (October 1844), pp. 376-88.

Engelhardt, Dietrich von, 'Natural Science in the Age of Romanticism', in *Modern Esoteric Spirituality*, ed. Antoine Faivre and Jacob Needleman (London: SCM Press, 1993), pp. 101-31.

Erdman, David, 'Blake's Early Swedenborgianism: A Twentieth-Century Legend', in *Comparative Literature*, vol. 5, no. 3 (Summer 1953), pp. 247-57.

Faivre, Antoine, 'Egyptomany', in *DGWE*, pp. 328-30.

——'Naturphilosophie', in *DGWE*, pp. 822-6

Fitzpatrick, Martin, 'Latitudinarianism at the Parting of the Ways: A Suggestion', in *The Church of England c. 1689-1833: From Toleration to Tractarianism*, ed. John Walsh, Colin Haydon and Stephen Taylor (Cambridge: Cambridge University Press, 1993), pp. 209-27.

Fulford, Tim, 'Conducting the Vital Fluid: The Politics and Poetics of Mesmerism in the 1790s', in *Studies in Romanticism*, vol. 43, no. 1 (2004), pp. 57-78.

Gabay, Alfred, 'The Reverend Jacob Duché and the Advent of the New Church in England', in *The New Philosophy*, vol. 109 (July-December, 2006), pp. 381-94.

Gansten, Martin, 'Placidean teachings in early nineteenth-century Britain: John Worsdale and Thomas Oxley', in *Astrologies: Plurality and Diversity. Proceedings of the Eighth Annual Sophia Centre Conference 2010*, ed. Nicholas Campion and Liz Greene (Lampeter: Sophia Centre Press, 2011).

Garrett, Clarke, 'Swedenborg and the Mystical Enlightenment in Late Eighteenth-Century England', in *Journal of the History of Ideas*, vol. 45, no. 1 (1984), pp. 67-81.

Giglioni, Guido, 'What Ever Happened to Francis Glisson? Albrecht Haller and the Fate of Eighteenth-Century Irritability', in *Science in Context*, vol. 21, no. 4 (2008), pp. 465-93.

Gilbert, Robert A, 'Barrett, Francis', in *DGWE*, pp. 163-4.

Godwin, Joscelyn, 'Bulwer-Lytton, Edward George', in *DGWE*, pp. 213-17.

Grant, Alice E, 'A New Church Work on Mythology', in *New Church Life*, vol. XLVII, no. 10 (October 1927), pp. 604-5.

Green, Rayna, 'The Tribe Called Wannabee: Playing Indian in America and Europe', in *Folklore*, vol. 99, no. 1 (1988), pp. 30-55.

Greenough, George Bellas, 'Remarks on the Theory of the Elevation of Mountains', in *Edinburgh New Philosophical Journal*, vol. 17 (1834), pp. 205-27.

Greiner, Frank, 'Flamel, Nicholas', in *DGWE*, pp. 370-1.

Guthrie, W K C, 'Plato's Views on the Nature of the Soul', in Gregory Vlastos (ed.), *Plato. A Selection of Critical Essays*, 2 vols. (New York: Doubleday, 1971), vol. II, pp. 230-43.

Haigh, Elizabeth L, 'The Vital Principle of Paul Joseph Barthez: The Clash Between Monism and Dualism', in *Medical History*, vol. 21 (1977), pp. 1-14.

Hall, Vance M D, 'The contribution of the physiologist, William Benjamin Carpenter (1813-1885), to the development of the principles of the correlation of forces and the conservation of energy', in *Medical History*, vol. 23, no. 2 (April 1979), pp. 129-55.

Hancock, David Boyd, 'Ancient Egypt in 17th and 18th Century England', in Peter Ucko and Timothy Champion (eds.), *The Wisdom of Ancient Egypt: Changing Visions through the Ages* (London: UCL Press, 2003), pp. 133-60.

Harrison, J F C, 'Early Victorian Radicals and the Medical Fringe', in W F Bynum and Roy Porter (eds.), *Medical Fringe and Medical Orthodoxy* (London: Croom Helm, 1987), pp. 198-215.

Harrold, Charles Frederick, 'The Mystical Element in Carlyle (1827-34)', in *Modern Philology*, vol. 29, no. 4 (May 1932), pp. 459-75.

Haycock, David Boyd, 'Ancient Egypt in 17th and 18th Century England', in *The Wisdom of Egypt: Changing Visions through the Ages*, ed. Peter Ucko and Timothy Champion (London: UCL Press, 2003), pp. 133-60.

Hayek, F A, 'Scientism and the Study of Society', in *Economica*, New Series, vol. 9, no. 35 (August 1942), pp. 267-91.

Hills, Gordon P G, 'Notes on Some Contemporary References to Dr. Falk, the Baal Shem of London, in the Rainsford MSS. at the British Museum', in *Transactions of the Jewish Historical Society of England*, vol. 8 (1915-17), pp. 122-8.

——'Notes on some Masonic Personalities at the end of the Eighteenth Century', in *Ars Quatuor Coronatorum*, vol. 25 (1912), pp. 141-64.

——'Notes on the Rainsford Papers in the British Museum', in *Ars Quatuor Coronatorum*, vol. 26 (1913), pp. 93-129.

Hindmarsh, Robert, 'Observations on Astrology, the Science of Palmistry, and the Transmigration of Souls', in *The Intellectual Repository for the New Church* (London), vol. V, no. XXXIX (January-March 1819), pp. 305-14.

Holcombe, William H, 'Hekla-lava', in *Transactions of the Twenty-Third Session of the American Institute of Homoeopathy*, New Series (Chicago: Lakeside Press, 1871), pp. 441-4.

——'Homoeopathy and Its New Church Affinities', in *New Church Repository*, vol. 3, no. 12 (December 1850), pp. 540-5.

Hoover, Suzanne R, 'William Blake in the Wilderness. A Closer Look at his Reputation, 1827-1863', in *William Blake. Essays in honour of Sir Geoffrey Keynes*, ed. Morton D Paley and Michael Phillips (Oxford: Clarendon Press, 1973), pp. 310-48.

Hotson, Clarence Paul, 'Emerson's Biographical Sources for "Swedenborg"', in *Studies in Philology*, vol. 26, no. 1 (January 1929), pp. 23-46.

Howitt, Mary, 'Appendix', in Joseph Ennemoser, *The History of Magic*, tr. William Howitt, 2 vols. (London: Henry G Bohn, 1854), vol. II, pp. 341-518.

Hyde, James, 'Benedict Chastanier and the Illuminati of Avignon', in *The New-Church Review* (Boston), vol. 14, no. 2 (April 1907), pp. 181-205.

Jackson, H J, ' "Swedenborg's *Meaning* is the truth": Coleridge, Tulk, and Swedenborg', in *In Search of the Absolute—Essays on Swedenborg and Literature*, ed. Stephen McNeilly (London: Swedenborg Society, 2004), pp. 1-13.

Jacyna, L S, 'Immanence or Transcendence: Theories of Life and Organization in Britain, 1790-1835', in *Isis*, vol. 74, no. 3 (September 1983), pp. 310-29.

Kaufman, Matthew H, 'William Gregory (1803-58): Professor of Chemistry at the University of Edinburgh and Enthusiast for Phrenology and Mesmerism', in *Journal of Medical Biography*, vol. 16, no. 3 (2008), pp. 128-33.

Keynes, Geoffrey, 'Blake, Tulk, and Garth Wilkinson', in *Library* 4th Series, vol. 26 (1945), pp. 190-2.

Kissane, James, 'Victorian Mythology', in *Victorian Studies*, vol. 6 (September 1962), pp. 5-28.

Lamberton, Robert, 'Language, Text and Truth in Ancient Polytheistic Exegesis', in Jon Whitman (ed.), *Interpretation and Allegory: Antiquity to the Modern Period* (Boston: Brill Academic Publishers, 2003), pp. 73-88.

Latham, Jackie, 'The Political and the Personal: the radicalism of Sophia Chichester and Georgiana Fletcher Welch', in *Women's History Review*, vol. 8, no. 3 (1999), pp. 469-87.

Leclercq, Jean, *The Love of Learning and the Desire for God: A Study of Monastic Culture*, tr. Catharine Misrahi, 3rd edn. (New York: Fordham University Press, 2003).

Lineham, Peter James, 'The English Swedenborgians 1770-1840: A Study in the Social Dimensions of Religious Sectarianism', Ph.D. Thesis (University of Sussex, 1978).

Lines, Richard, 'Charles Augustus Tulk—Swedenborgian Extraordinary', in *Arcana*, vol. 3, no. 4 (1997).

Lipman, Timothy O, 'Vitalism and Reductionism in Liebig's Physiological Thought', in *Isis*, vol. 58, no. 2 (Summer 1967), pp. 167-85.

McCully, R, 'Benedict Chastanier: An Early New Church Worthy', in *The New Church Magazine*, vol. IX, no. 107 (November 1890), pp. 527-35.

——'Mr. Tulk on the Divine Humanity', in *The New Church Magazine*, vol. IX, no. 101 (May 1890), pp. 202-8.

McFarland, Thomas, 'Coleridge and the Charge of Political Apostasy', in *Coleridge's Biographia Literaria: Text and Meaning*, ed. Frederick Burwick (Columbus: Ohio State University Press, 1989).

McLean, Adam, 'Bacstrom's Rosicrucian society', in *Hermetic Journal*, no. 6 (1979), reprinted at <http://www.levity.com/alchemy/bacstrm1.html>.

——'General Rainsford. An Alchemical and Rosicrucian Enthusiast', in *Hermetic Journal*, vol. 13 (1990).

Male, Roy R, Jr, 'The Background of Coleridge's Theory of Life', in *The University of Texas Studies in English*, vol. 33 (1954), pp. 60-8.

Malherbe, Michel, 'Bacon's Method of Science', in *The Cambridge Companion to Bacon*, ed. Markku Peltonen (Cambridge: Cambridge University Press, 1996), pp. 75-98.

Malley, Shawn, 'Austen Henry Layard and the Periodical Press: Middle Eastern Archaeology and the Evacuation of Cultural Identity in Mid-Nineteenth Century Britain', in *Victorian Review*, vol. 22, no. 2 (1996), pp. 152-70.

Mander, W J, 'Hegel and British Idealism', in Lisa Herzog (ed.), *Hegel's Thought in Europe: Currents, Crosscurrents and Countercurrents* (Basingstoke: Palgrave Macmillan, 2013), pp. 165-76.

Maudsley, Henry, 'Emanuel Swedenborg', in his *Body and Mind: An Inquiry into their Connection and Mutual Influence, Specially in Reference to Mental Disorders: An Enlarged and Revised Edition* (New York: D Appleton, 1890), pp. 163-217.

Mayer, Jean-François, 'Swedenborgian Traditions', in *DGWE*, pp. 1105-10.

Mee, Jon, 'Blake's Politics in History', in *The Cambridge Companion to William Blake*, ed. Morris Eaves (Cambridge: Cambridge University Press, 2003), pp. 133-49.

Morrell, Peter, 'Triumph of the light—isopathy and the rise of transcendental homeopathy, 1830-1920', in *Medical Humanities*, vol. 29, no. 1 (2003), pp. 22-32.

Müller, Max, 'Comparative Mythology' (1856), in *Chips from a German Workshop*, 2nd edn., 5 vols. (London: Longmans, Green & Co., 1867-75), vol. II, pp. 1-146.

Murdoch, William M, 'Homoeopathy Again', in *The New Church Messenger* (Cincinnati), vol. II, no. VII (1 June 1854), p. 112.

Myers, Charles S, 'Vitalism: A Brief Historical and Critical Review', in *Mind*, New Series, vol. 9, no. 34 (April 1900), pp. 218-33, and no. 35 (July 1900), pp. 319-31.

Neuburger, Max, 'An Historical Survey of the Concept of Nature from a Medical Viewpoint', in *Isis*, vol. 35, no. 1 (Winter 1944), pp. 16-28.

Odhner, Carl Theophilus, 'An Autobiography', in *New Church Life*, vol. XL, no. 6 (June 1920), pp. 343-8.

——'James John Garth Wilkinson', in *New Church Life*, vol. XX, no. 2 (February 1900), pp. 57-63, no. 3 (March 1900), pp. 123-30, no. 4 (April 1900), pp. 199-206, no. 5 (May 1900), pp. 243-6, and no. 6 (June 1900), pp. 290-7.

Osorio, Ivan, and Mark G Frei, Didier Sornette, John Milton and Ying-Cheng Lai, 'Epileptic Seizures: Quakes of the Brain?', in *Physical Review E*, vol. 82, no. 2 (20 August 2010), article no. 21919.

Pagel, Walter, 'Giordano Bruno: the Philosophy of Circles and the Circular Movement of the Blood', in *Journal of the History of Medicine and Allied Sciences*, vol. 6 (Winter 1951), pp. 116-24.

——'William Harvey: Some Neglected Aspects of Medical History', in *Journal of the Warburg and Courtauld Institutes*, vol. 7 (1944), pp. 144-53.

Paley, Morton D, ' "A New Heaven is Begun": Blake and Swedenborgianism', in *Blake and Swedenborg: Opposition is True Friendship*, ed. Harvey F Bellin and Darrell Ruhl (West Chester, PA: Swedenborg Foundation, 1985), pp. 15-34.

Payne, William E, 'Homoeopathy. Or the Science of Medicine considered in its Relation to the Doctrines of the Church', in *The Newchurchman*, vol. 2, no. 6 (April 1844), pp. 509-64.

Pearson, Joanne E, 'Neopaganism', in *DGWE*, pp. 828-34.

Pépin, Jean, 'Saint Augustine and the Indwelling of the Ideas of God', in Gersh and Moran (eds.), *Eriugena*, pp. 105-22.

Pickstone, John V, 'Establishment and Dissent in Nineteenth-Century Medicine: An Exploration of some Correspondence and Connections between Religious and Medical Belief-Systems in Early Industrial England', in W J Shiels (ed.), *The Church and Healing* (Oxford: Blackwell, 1982), pp. 165-89.

Politis, Vasilis, 'Non-Subjective Idealism in Plato (*Sophist* 248e-249d)', in Gersh and Moran (eds.), *Eriugena*, pp. 14-38.

Power, Henry, 'Physiology in 1800', in *The British Medical Journal*, vol. 2, no. 2087 (29 December 1900), pp. 1841-5.

Preece, Rod, 'Darwinism, Christianity, and the Great Vivisection Debate', in *Journal of the History of Ideas*, vol. 64, no. 3 (July 2003), pp. 399-419.

Raine, Kathleen, 'The Human Face of God', in *Blake and Swedenborg*, ed. Bellin and Ruhl, pp. 87-101.

Rehbock, Philip F, 'Transcendental Anatomy', in *Romanticism and the Sciences*, ed. Andrew Cunningham and Nicholas Jardine (Cambridge: Cambridge University Press, 1990), pp. 144-60.

Ridgway, Elizabeth S, 'John Elliotson (1791-1868): a bitter enemy of legitimate medicine? Part I: Earlier years and the introduction to mesmerism', in *Journal of Medical Biography*, vol. 1 (1993), pp. 191-8.

Rix, Robert W, 'Healing the Spirit: William Blake and Magnetic Religion', in *Romanticism on the Net* (online journal), no. 25 (February 2002), at <http://www.erudit.org/revue/ron/2002/v/n25/006011ar.html>.

——'William Blake and the Radical Swedenborgians', in *Esoterica*, vol. V (2003) pp. 95-137, at <http://www.esoteric.msu.edu/VolumeV/Blake.htm>.

Roberts, Eric J, 'Plato's View of the Soul', in *Mind*, vol. 14, no. 55 (July 1905), pp. 371-89.

Robertson, C Lockhart, 'The Homoeopathic Principle applied to Insanity: a Proposal to treat Lunacy by Spiritualism: By JAMES JOHN GARTH WILKINSON, M.D.', in *The Asylum Journal of Mental Science*, vol. IV, no. 25 (April 1858), pp. 360-96.

Robertson, Donald, 'James Braid's Life & Work', in James Braid, *The Discovery of Hypnosis. The Complete Writings of James Braid, the Father of Hypnotherapy*, ed. Donald Robertson ([n.p.]: National Council for Hypnotherapy, 2008), pp. 8-16.

Sargent, Rose-Mary, 'Bacon as an Advocate for Cooperative Scientific Research', in *The Cambridge Companion to Bacon*, pp. 146-71.

Schuchard, Marsha Keith, 'Blake's "Mr. Femality": Freemasonry, Espionage, and the Double-Sexed', in *Studies in Eighteenth-Century Culture*, vol. 22 (1993), pp. 51-71.

——'Dr. Samuel Jacob Falk: A Sabbatian Adventurer in the Masonic Underground', in *Millenarianism and Messianism in Early Modern European Culture: Jewish Messianism in the Early Modern World*, ed. M D Goldish and R H Popkin (Dordrecht: Kluwer Press, 2001), pp. 203-26.

——'Jacobite and Visionary: the Masonic Journey of Emanuel Swedenborg (1688-1772)', in *Ars Quatuor Coronatorum*, vol. 115 (2003), pp. 33-72.

——'The Secret Masonic History of Blake's Swedenborg Society', in *Blake, an Illustrated Quarterly*, vol. 26, no. 2 (Fall 1992), pp. 40-8.

——'Swedenborg, Jacobitism, and Freemasonry', in *Swedenborg and His Influence*, ed. Erland J Brock (Bryn Athyn, PA: Academy of the New Church, 1988), pp. 359-79.

Segal, Robert A, 'Myth and Science: Their Varying Relationships', in *Religion Compass*, vol. 3, no. 2 (March 2009), pp. 337-58.

Shapin, Steven, 'Descartes the Doctor: Rationalism and its Therapies', in *The British Journal for the History of Science*, vol. 33, no. 2 (June 2000), pp. 131-54.

Shariff, Azim F, and Jonathan Schooler and Kathleen D Vohs, 'The Hazards of Claiming to Have Solved the Hard Problem of Free Will', in John Baer, James C Kaufman and Roy Baumeister (eds.), *Are we Free? Psychology and Free Will* (New York: Oxford University Press, 2008), pp. 181-204.

Shiah, Yung-Jong, and Wai-Cheong Carl Tam, 'Do Human Fingers "See"?—"Finger-Reading" Studies in the East and West', in *European Journal of Parapsychology*, vol. 20, no. 2 (2005), pp. 117-34.

Skinner, Alice B, 'Poets with Swedenborgian Connections', in *Emanuel Swedenborg: A*

Continuing Vision, ed. Robin Larsen, Stephen Larsen, James F Lawrence and William Ross Woofenden (New York: Swedenborg Foundation, 1988), pp. 53-60.

Snoek, Jan A M, 'Illuminés d'Avignon', in *DGWE*, pp. 597-600.

——'Pernety, Antoine-Joseph', in *DGWE*, pp. 940-2.

Solmsen, Friedrich, 'Epicurus on Void, Matter and Genesis: Some Historical Observations', in *Phronesis*, vol. 22 (1977), pp. 263-81.

Sorabji, Richard, 'Body and Soul in Aristotle', in *Philosophy*, vol. 49, no. 187 (January 1974), pp. 63-89.

Spector, Sheila A, 'Blake, William', in *DGWE*, pp. 173-7.

Spilling, James, 'Dr. Wilkinson's Reminiscences of Carlyle', in *The New Church Magazine*, vol. VII, no. 75 (March 1888), pp. 107-12.

——'Emerson and Dr. Wilkinson', in *The New Church Magazine*, vol. VI, no. 71 (November 1887), pp. 529-33.

Stock, Armin, and Claudia Stock, 'A short history of ideo-motor action', in *Psychological Research*, vol. 68 (April 2004), pp. 176-88.

Stocking, George W, 'Animism in Theory and Practice: E.B. Tylor's Unpublished "Notes on Spiritualism"', in *Man*, vol. 6 no. 1 (March 1971), pp. 88-104.

Syme, James, 'The Address in Surgery', in *British Medical Journal*, vol. 2, no. 241 (12 August 1865), pp. 142-9.

Tafel, R L, 'Swedenborg and Freemasonry', in *New Jerusalem Messenger* (New York), vol. XVII, no. 17, 27 October 1869, pp. 266-7.

Temkin, Owsei, 'Albrecht von Haller, "A Dissertation on the Sensible and Irritable Parts of Animals"', in *Bulletin of the Institute of the History of Medicine*, vol. IV, no. 8 (October 1936), pp. 651-99.

——'The Classical Roots of Glisson's Doctrine of Irritation', in *Bulletin of the History of Medicine*, vol. 38 (1964), pp. 297-328.

Thomé, Marquis de, 'Remarks by the Marquis de Thomé, On an Assertion of the Commissioners appointed by the King [of France] for the Examination of Animal Magnetism', in *The Intellectual Repository*, vol. 2, no. XII (October-December 1814), pp. 191-7.

Treuherz, Francis, 'The Origins of Kent's Homeopathy', in *Journal of the American Institute of Homeopathy*, vol. 77, no. 4 (1984), pp. 130-49.

Tulk, Charles Augustus, 'The inventions of William Blake, painter and poet', in *London University Magazine*, vol. 2 (March 1830), pp. 318-23; repr. in Bentley (ed.), *William Blake: The Critical Heritage*, pp. 199-205.

——'Remarks Respecting Double Consciousness, &c.' (dated 8 October 1845), in *The Intellectual*

Repository, vol. VI, no. 71 (November 1845), pp. 418-21.

——'To the Editors of the New Jerusalem Magazine', in *The New Jerusalem Magazine and Theological Inspector* (London: Thomas Goyder), no. 6 (June 1828), pp. 188-9

Tyson, Donald, 'On the *Occult Philosophy*', in Henry Cornelius Agrippa of Nettesheim, *Three Books of Occult Philosophy*, tr. James Freake, ed. Donald Tyson (Woodbury, MN: Llewellyn, 1993), pp. xxxix-xliii.

van den Doel, Marieke J E, and Wouter J Hanegraaff, 'Imagination', in *DGWE*, pp. 606-16.

Versluis, Arthur, 'Western Esotericism and the Harmony Society', at <http://www.esoteric.msu.edu/Versluis.html>.

Voegelin, Eric, 'The Origins of Scientism', in *Social Research*, vol. 15, no. 4 (December 1948), pp. 462-94.

Waite, Arthur Edward, 'Biographical Introduction', in James Braid, *Braid on Hypnotism: Neurypnology*, ed. Arthur Edward Waite (London: George Redway, 1899), pp. 1-66.

Wakley, Thomas, 'Animal Magnetism', in *The Lancet*, vol. II (1838), pp. 282-8, 377-83, 400-3, 441-6, 516-9, 546-9, 585-90, 615-20.

——Editorials, in *The Lancet*, vol. II (8 September 1838), pp. 834-6 and vol. II (15 September 1838), pp. 873-7.

——'Expulsion of Elizabeth O'Key–Resignation of Dr. Elliotson.–Meeting of Students', in *The Lancet*, vol. I (5 January 1839), pp. 561-2.

——'Rejection of a farewell letter from ex-Professor Elliotson', in *The Lancet*, vol. I (9 March 1839), p. 888.

Wallen, Jeffrey, 'Physiology, Mesmerism and Walter Pater's "Susceptibilities to Influence"', in *Walter Pater: Transparencies of Desire*, ed. Laurel Brake, Leslie Higgins and Carolyn Williams (Greensboro, NC: ELT Press, 2002), pp. 73-93.

Ward, Aileen, 'William Blake and his Circle', in *The Cambridge Companion to William Blake*, ed. Morris Eaves (Cambridge: Cambridge University Press, 2003), pp. 19-36.

Webster, Charles, 'The Nineteenth-Century Afterlife of Paracelsus', in *Studies in the History of Alternative Medicine*, ed. Roger Cooter (London: Macmillan Press, 1988), pp. 79-88.

Wilkinson, James John Garth, 'Correspondence', in *Aesthetic Papers*, ed. Elizabeth Palmer Peabody (Boston: The Editor, 1849), pp. 112-45.

—— 'From our London Correspondent' (letter dated 3 March 1847), in *The New Jerusalem Magazine* (Boston), vol. XX, no. CCXXXVI (April 1847), pp. 331-3.

——'From our London Correspondent' (letter dated 3 April 1847), in *The New Jerusalem Magazine* (Boston), vol. XX, no. CCXXXVII (May 1847), pp. 377-9.

——'From our London Correspondent' (letter dated 3 May 1847), in *The New Jerusalem*

Magazine (Boston), vol. XX, no. CCXXXVIII (June 1847), pp. 412-15.

——'From our London Correspondent' (letter dated 3 July 1847), in *The New Jerusalem Magazine* (Boston), vol. XX, no. CCXL (August 1847), pp. 541-5.

——'From our London Correspondent' (letter dated 2 October 1847), in *The New Jerusalem Magazine* (Boston), vol. XXI, no. CCXLII (November 1847), pp. 80-1.

——'Introductory Remarks by the Translator', in Emanuel Swedenborg, *The Animal Kingdom*, tr. James John Garth Wilkinson, 2 vols. (London: W Newbery, 1843-4), vol. I, pp. xv-lxiv.

——'Introductory Remarks by the Translator', in Emanuel Swedenborg, *Outlines of a Philosophical Argument on the Infinite, and the Final Cause of Creation; and on the Intercourse Between the Soul and the Body*, tr. James John Garth Wilkinson (London: William Newbery, 1847), pp. ix-xxx.

——'Magic'. Undated notebook, in Swedenborg Society Archive A/245.

——'Medical Specialism', in *The Homoeopathic World*, vol. 24 (September 1889).

——'Mesmerism', in *The Monthly Magazine*, vol. IV (1840), pp. 443-58.

——'Preface' to William Blake, *Songs of Innocence and Experience. Shewing the Two Contrary States of the Human Soul* (London: W Pickering and W Newbery, 1839), pp. iii-xxiii.

——'Preface and Supplement', in J J G Wilkinson and William Young (eds.), *Vaccination Tracts* (Providence: Snow & Farnham, 1892), pp. 3-31.

——'Sleep II. Mesmerism and Hypnotism', handwritten lecture notes, in Swedenborg Society Archive A/56 (i).

——'Some Deductions from the Principle involved in Vaccination. A Paper read before the Hahnemann Medical Society, Feb. 7, 1854', in *The British Journal of Homoeopathy*, vol. XII (1854), pp. 250-60.

——'Swedenborg on Trance', in *The Zoist*, vol. V, no. XX (January 1848), pp. 345-7.

——(pseud. A Realist), 'Passages from the Oeconomia Regni Animalis, and de Cultu et Amore Dei, of Swedenborg, with original comments thereon, by the late Samuel Taylor Coleridge', in *The Monthly Magazine*, 5 (1841), pp. 607-20.

Williams-Hogan, Jane, 'The Place of Emanuel Swedenborg in Modern Western Esotericism', in Antoine Faivre and Wouter J Hanegraaff (eds.), *Western Esotericism and the Science of Religion* (Leuven: Peeters, 1998), pp. 201-52.

Wilson, James, 'Swedenborg, Paracelsus, and the Dilute Traces: A Lyrical and Critical Reflection on Mysticism, Reform, and the Nature of Influence', in *The New Philosophy*, vol. CXIV, nos. 3-4 (July-December 2011), pp. 175-206.

Wilson, John B, 'Emerson and the "Rochester Rappings"', in *The New England Quarterly*, vol. 41, no. 2 (June 1968), pp. 248-58.

Zuber, Devin P, 'Spiritualized science and the celestial artist: Nathaniel Hawthorne and Swedenborgian aesthetics', in *Philosophy, Literature, Mysticism: an anthology of essays on the thought and influence of Emanuel Swedenborg*, ed. Stephen McNeilly (London: Swedenborg Society, 2013), pp. 175-216.

MANUSCRIPT

Swedenborg Society Archive, file nos. A/8, A/9, A/56, A/149, A/150, A/151, A/153, A/183, A/242, A/245, K/4, K/75, K/89, K/123, K/124, K/125, K/126, K/143, L/67, L/403, M.

Wilkinson, James John Garth, 1812-1899, 38 letters to Henry James, Sr. William James papers, 1803-1941 (inclusive) 1862-1910 (bulk). MS Am 1092.9 (4049-4086). Houghton Library, Harvard University, Cambridge, Mass.

——5 A.L.s.to William James. Letters to William James from various correspondents and photograph album, 1865-1929. MS Am 1092 (1170-1174). Houghton Library, Harvard University, Cambridge, Mass.

——Travel Diary: manuscript, 1869 Aug. 20 - 1869 Sept. 25. MS Eng 1302. Houghton Library, Harvard University, Cambridge, Mass.

Thomas Carlyle, *The Carlyle Letters Online*, at <http://carlyleletters.dukejournals.org>.

INDEX

Abernethy, John (1764-1831), 79, 156-7; *An Enquiry into the Probability and Rationality of Mr. Hunter's Theory of Life*, 157
abolitionism, *see* antislavery
aboriginal (people), 241
absolute idealism, 70, 78, 211, 249
Académie de Médicine (Paris), 98
activism, xvi, xx, 18, 96, 209-35
Acton Street (Gray's Inn Lane, London), 1
Adam, 75
Adamic, 254; (Church), 248, 255; (Golden Age), 254; (language), 240
Aesir, 258
Africa, 23, 37, 44; African, 23
Age of Magic, 241-2, 245
Age of Religion, 241
Age of Science, 241
Agrippa von Nettesheim, Heinrich Cornelius (1486-1535), 30, 48, 102
alchemy, 39-40, 42, 46-8, 58, 194, 246; alchemist, 30, 38-9, 47
Alexander the Great (356-323 BC), 174

allopathy, 184, 186, 190-1
Alpine Club (London), 19
alternative (medicine *or* therapy), viii, 96, 151-2, 154, 179, 189, 266
Althing (Iceland), 257
American Indian, 132
anatomy, 4, 6, 9-10, 12, 56, 63, 78-81, 121, 164, 166-70, 195, 229-30
Ancient Church, 249, 254, 260
Andreae, Johannes Valentinus (1586-1654), 30
angels, 35, 43-4, 46-7, 54, 65, 67-9, 106, 110-11, 115, 127, 131-2, 144, 147, 156, 168, 175, 216, 254, 265; angelic, 14, 33, 167, 181, 248
Anglican(ism), 5-6, 9, 28-9, 33, 41, 95, 211, 231; *see also* Church of England
Anglo-Saxon, 246
animal(s), animal kingdom *or* world, 9-11, 65-9, 73, 78-81, 103, 107, 109, 135, 157, 159-61, 164-7, 169, 172, 183, 189-90, 196-7, 223, 229-30, 247, 253
animal magnetism, 38-9, 41, 43-4, 56,

423

73-5, 82, 84, 145, 234; childhood and schooling, xvii, 1-3, 5-6, 63, 239; and Contagious Diseases Act, 225, 227, 230-5; and deregulation of medicine, xv, 201, 212, 223-5; and Emerson, R W, viii, xv, xxi, 11-12, 16, 22, 62, 73-4, 79, 82, 89, 145, 221, 264; and empiricism, 70-6; and environmentalism, 222-3, 266; and Fourierism, xvii, xx, 140-2, 175, 215-21, 264; and Harris, Thomas Lake, 142-4; and homoeopathy, xv-xix, 4, 6, 17, 22, 59, 89, 96, 115, 121, 136, 138, 148, 151-206, 224-5, 257, 264-5; and idealism, 63, 70-8; and James, Henry, Sr, viii, xv-xvii, 8, 10-13, 16-19, 22, 73-5, 83-91, 93, 104, 127, 129, 139, 142, 145, 185-6, 191, 196, 219-21, 239; marriage and family, 3, 5-6, 16-21, 64, 84, 127-8, 134, 147-8, 191; and medical practice, viii, xv, xvii, xix, 3, 5-6, 10-11, 16-18, 21, 63, 97, 101, 105, 117-18, 148, 151-206, 212-13, 223-5, 232-3, 239, 264; and mesmerism, viii, xv, xvii-xix, 16, 59, 76, 91, 93-122, 126, 129-31, 140, 152, 179, 185, 195, 264-6; and mythology, viii, xvii-xviii, xx, 18, 21, 23, 239-60; and *Naturphilosophie*, 77-81, 163; and Paris uprising of 1848, xvii, xx, 140, 214-15; as a poet, viii-ix, 3, 14-16, 20, 136, 195, 198; and psychological physiology, 169-76; and psychology, xix, 103, 112, 117-22, 139, 193, 264; and spiritualism, xv-xix, 16, 18, 59, 89, 91, 112, 119, 123-48, 195-6, 198-9, 205, 240, 257, 263-6; and Swedenborg Society, 7-10, 14, 26, 135, 143-4; and translation, viii, xv, 7-10, 14, 16, 59, 72, 74, 109, 120, 164-5, 258; travels, (to America), 17-19, 87-8,

90, 191; (to Iceland), 18, 196, 257; (to Norway), 18, 20, 238; (to Paris), xvii, xx, 140, 214-15; and Tulk, Charles Augustus, ix, xvi-xviii, 14, 54-5, 57, 70-3, 75, 77-8, 80-1, 86-7, 90-1, 99, 103, 169, 175, 220, 239; and vitalism, xix, 91, 151-3, 157-64, 185; and women's rights, xx, 212, 225, 227, 230-5, 267
Wilkinson, Mary James, *see* Mathews, Mary Claughton
Wilkinson, Mary Ridley (sister of JJGW) (1817-62), 1
Wilkinson, William Martin (brother of JJGW) (1814-97), 1-2, 5, 81, 133, 135, 143-4, 214-15
Williams-Hogan, Jane, 162, 164
Wilson, Bryan, 140
Winter, Alison, 110
witchcraft, 77, 159
women's rights, xx, 131, 212, 217, 227, 232-4, 267; *see also* feminist(s)
Wordsworth, William (1770-1850), 16
World's Parliament of Religions (Chicago, 1893), 23
Wornum, Ralph Nicholson (1812-77), 9
Woulfe, Peter (1727-1803), 38
Wyld, George (1821-1906), 23

Yorkshire, 5, 131
Yorkshire Spiritual Telegraph, 131

Zinzendorf, Count Nikolaus Ludwig von (1700-60), 30
The Zoist, 94, 104, 109